QUIET REVOLUTIONARIES

This book tells the previously untold story of the Married Women's Association. Unlike more conventional histories of family law, which focus on legal actors, it highlights the little-known yet indispensable work of a dedicated group of life-long activists.

Formed in 1938, the Married Women's Association took reform of family property law as its chief focus. The name is deceptively innocuous, suggesting tea parties and charity fundraisers, but in fact the MWA was often involved in dramatic confrontations with politicians, civil servants, and Law Commissioners. The Association boasted powerful public figures, including MP Edith Summerskill, authors Vera Brittain and Dora Russell, and barrister Helena Normanton. They campaigned on matters that are still being debated in family law today.

Quiet Revolutionaries sheds new light upon legal reform then and now by challenging longstanding assumptions, showing that piecemeal legislation can be an effective stepping stone to comprehensive reform and highlighting how unsuccessful bills, though often now forgotten, can still be important triggers for change. Drawing upon interviews with members' friends and family, and thousands of archival documents, the book is compulsory reading for lawyers, legal historians, and anyone who wishes to explore histories of law reform from the ground up.

Quiet Revolutionaries

The Married Women's Association and Family Law

Sharon Thompson

•HART•

OXFORD • LONDON • NEW YORK • NEW DELHI • SYDNEY

HART PUBLISHING

Bloomsbury Publishing Plc

Kemp House, Chawley Park, Cumnor Hill, Oxford, OX2 9PH, UK

1385 Broadway, New York, NY 10018, USA

29 Earlsfort Terrace, Dublin 2, Ireland

HART PUBLISHING, the Hart/Stag logo, BLOOMSBURY and the Diana logo are
trademarks of Bloomsbury Publishing Plc

First published in Great Britain 2022

Copyright © Sharon Thompson, 2022

Sharon Thompson has asserted her right under the Copyright, Designs and
Patents Act 1988 to be identified as Author of this work.

A catalogue record for this book is available from the British Library.

A catalogue record for this book is available from the Library of Congress.

Library of Congress Control Number: 2022936728

ISBN:	HB:	978-1-50992-941-2
	ePDF:	978-1-50992-943-6
	ePub:	978-1-50992-942-9

Typeset by Compuscript Ltd, Shannon

To find out more about our authors and books visit www.hartpublishing.co.uk.
Here you will find extracts, author information, details of forthcoming events
and the option to sign up for our newsletters.

For Marion, Peggy and Pat. Their strength is a constant source of inspiration.

Foreword

'The cock bird can feather his nest precisely because he is not required to spend most of his time sitting on it'.

THUS DECLARED SIR Jocelyn Simon in his 1964 Holdsworth Club Presidential Address at the University of Birmingham, entitled 'With All my Wordly Goods'. He was voicing the notion that the hen bird's work in sitting on the nest made a genuine economic contribution to the family's wealth. This was a radical idea and that he should be voicing it was all the more powerful because he was then President of the Probate, Divorce and Admiralty Division of the High Court, the top Family Law judge in England and Wales. His words struck a chord with other judges and were cited by Lord Hodson in the House of Lords case of *Pettitt v Pettitt* dealing with matrimonial property,[1] who in turn was cited by Lord Denning in the Court of Appeal case of *Wachtel v Wachtel*, dealing with sharing out property on divorce.[2] His view became an orthodox view among law reformers in the 1960s and 1970s. I well remember the meeting convened by the Law Commission in Manchester University (which crops up in chapter nine) to discuss options for the reform of matrimonial property law on just this assumption.

But where had Sir Jocelyn got such a radical notion from? After all, the conventional stance of the law was that a woman's work in the home was not 'money or money's worth', that is, not economically valuable. Indeed, despite Lord Hodson's citation, *Pettitt v Pettitt* had endorsed the rule that it was not an economic contribution to the acquisition of the family home, such as to entitle her to a share in its ownership. There were a few academics, such as Otto Kahn-Freund and Olive Stone, arguing for a change in the law, but it is far more likely that Sir Jocelyn was seriously influenced by the quiet campaigning of the Married Women's Association. The Association was born in 1938 of the realisation that husbands and wives led different lives and that the wives did the lion's share of the domestic and caring work. Married women had acquired the right to own property and to keep their own earnings in the nineteenth century, but this did not produce true equality for the great majority of wives, who worked hard in the home, bringing up their children and looking after their families, including their husbands. Their work was not valued or remunerated and so they might have nothing or very little both during and after the marriage.

---

[1] [1970] AC 777, 811.
[2] [1973] Fam 72, 92.

The Married Women's Association aimed to put this right by providing that marriage should be a genuinely equal partnership. Money earned and property acquired during the marriage by either spouse should be equally owned, not only at the end of the marriage, but while it was a going concern. Each should have the right to know the other's income and assets. The Association considered but soon rejected the alternative idea of 'wages for housework'. This would turn the wife into a household servant rather than a genuinely equal partner in the relationship. They produced several drafts of an equal partnership Bill but none of them became law. However, they did achieve some successes: the attachment of earnings to enforce maintenance payments in 1958; the equal sharing of any savings a wife made from a housekeeping allowance from her husband in 1964; and right of a non-owning spouse (usually the wife) to stay in the matrimonial home and protect it against disposal to third parties, such as purchasers or mortgagees, in 1967.

But their major success came with the passage of the Divorce Reform Act 1969 – which Edith Summerskill, first President of the Association, famously dubbed a 'Casanova's Charter' because it meant that a wife could be divorced against her will despite have done nothing to break up the marriage. While the Bill was going through Parliament, the Association persuaded Edward Bishop MP to introduce a Matrimonial Property Bill which, whatever its defects, gained considerable support. Although this Bill was eventually withdrawn, the implementation of the Divorce Reform Act was delayed until the Law Commission had produced their recommendations on the financial consequences of divorce. The result was the Matrimonial Proceedings and Property Act 1970 which came into force at the same time as the Divorce Reform Act. Although it only dealt with property and finance on divorce, and not during the marriage, it did introduce radical new powers to share out property and income which are still with us today and it required the court to take into account the parties' contributions to the welfare of the family including 'any contribution by looking after the home or caring for the family'. And in *White v White*, the courts did eventually get round to establishing that the starting point should be the equal sharing of matrimonial property.[3] But the idea of equal sharing during the marriage seems as far away as ever, as indeed does the idea that spouses should have the right to know about one another's financial affairs. Yet the lack of any such right makes operating the present law on divorce, which depends upon full disclosure, much more difficult and expensive than it would be if there were such a right. Perhaps someone should dust off the Association's Bill providing for this.

Of course, the leaders of the Association were feminists. But there are at least two types of feminist. Both believe in the equality of the sexes. But on one view, here dubbed the 'old' feminism, this means treating them the same

---

[3] [2001] 1 AC 596.

and, more to the point, taking no special account of the different lives which many women lead from the lives led by many men. This may have been the old style of feminism but it is also increasingly popular today. On another view, here dubbed the 'new' feminism, many women do lead very different lives from the lives led by many men. This is largely because of the different roles they undertake within the family. The law should take account of those differences. The Married Women's Association espoused this 'new' feminism. It happens to be the view that I also take – for a whole host of reasons, women lead different lives from men, and the experience of leading women's lives should be just as important in shaping the law as is the experience of leading men's lives. But this does not mean that men and women should be treated differently. Househusbands who make savings from the housekeeping allowances made to them by their breadwinning wives should also share those savings equally. It is the roles, rather than who plays them, which should make the difference.

The influence and importance of the Married Women's Association and its visionary leading lights – not only Edith Summerskill, but Vera Brittain, Dora Russell, Helena Normanton, its founder Juanita Frances and many more – ought to be much better known, not only among family lawyers, but among everyone who is interested in the movement for women's equality. Sharon Thompson has enriched our knowledge and understanding by shining a light upon these quiet revolutionaries.

Brenda Hale

Contents

Timeline

1882
The Married Women's Property Act 1882 (MWPA 1882) introduced the doctrine of separate property, enabling married women to own and control property independently of their husbands.

1921
The Six Point Group (SPG) was established.

1937
Dorothy Evans created an SPG sub-committee to promote the legal status of housewives. It became the Married Women's Association (MWA) and Juanita Frances was brought in as Chairman.

1938
The MWA separated from the SPG and became an independent organisation. Edith Summerskill became the MWA's first President shortly thereafter.

1943
The Court of Appeal held in *Blackwell v Blackwell* [1943] 2 All ER 579 that a wife's savings derived from housekeeping allowance were owned by the husband because he had provided that allowance. The MWA funded the wife's (ultimately unsuccessful) case, using it to launch a reform campaign lasting 21 years.

1951
Edith Summerskill brought the Women's Disabilities Bill to the House of Commons. Though unsuccessful, the Bill's provisions relating to maintenance and housekeeping savings foreshadowed later reform. In the same year, Edith Summerskill resigned as President of the MWA but continued to work closely with the Association.

1952
The MWA split following a disagreement over evidence submitted to the Royal Commission on Marriage and Divorce. Several Executive Committee members (including then President Helena Normanton) formed the breakaway group the Council of Married Women (CMW).

1956
The Royal Commission on Marriage and Divorce published its report. It endorsed the concept of equal partnership in marriage (the MWA's objective) but did not recommend substantial reform to achieve it.

1958
The Maintenance Orders Act 1958 enabled maintenance to be deducted from the defaulting spouse's pay packet. This was prompted by an MWA campaign and a Bill drafted by MWA members.

1964
The *Blackwell* campaign culminated in the Married Women's Property Act 1964 (MWPA 1964); a Private Member's Bill introduced by Edith Summerskill. The Act provided that where a husband makes a housekeeping allowance to his wife, money derived from the allowance and property bought with that money belong to the husband and wife in equal shares.

1967
The Matrimonial Homes Act 1967, introduced into Parliament by Edith Summerskill, gave spouses a right to occupy the matrimonial home.

1969
Edward Bishop MP's Matrimonial Property Bill, which was inspired by an MWA Bill of the same name, received a Second Reading in the House of Commons. It was subsequently withdrawn after an agreement with the government that the introduction of the Divorce Reform Act 1969 would be delayed so the financial consequences of divorce could be reformed too.

1970
The Matrimonial Proceedings and Property Act 1970 was passed following pressure to reform the financial consequences of divorce alongside changes to divorce procedure. Both the 1970 Act and the Divorce Reform Act 1969 were later consolidated in the Matrimonial Causes Act 1973.

1980
The Matrimonial Homes (Co-Ownership) Bill, which provided for statutory co-ownership of the matrimonial home, was introduced into the House of Lords by Lord Simon. After being withdrawn and redrafted following the decision in *Williams & Glyn's Bank Ltd v Boland* [1980] UKHL 4, it was ultimately blocked by the Campaign for Justice in Divorce.

1981
The MWA's rough minute book noted there would be no further meetings, but archival evidence suggests MWA activities continued into the late 1980s and beyond.

1985
The Family Law (Scotland) Act 1985 (ss 25 and 26) repealed the MWPA 1964 in Scotland and replaced it with a presumption for household goods and housekeeping allowance to be owned in equal shares.

1988
The Law Commission proposed a Matrimonial Property Bill which was never introduced. It sought to replace the MWPA 1964 with rules facilitating joint ownership of property when property was transferred between spouses or used for the benefit of both spouses.

Abbreviations

CMW	Council of Married Women
MWA	Married Women's Association
MWPA	Married Women's Property Act
NUSEC	National Union of Societies for Equal Citizenship
SPG	Six Point Group
TNA	The National Archives
TWL	The Women's Library
WSPU	Women's Social and Political Union

A note on the text: Leadership positions within the Married Women's Association are referred to as they were by members at the time, eg, 'Chairman'.

Prologue

THE 1935 GENERAL election was imminent, and Juanita Frances still didn't know who to vote for. She asked her husband, banker Gerard Schlesinger.

> I said: 'Who should I vote for?' because I didn't know much about politics, and he said 'The Conservatives'. Well I wasn't going to swallow that, I wanted to know why. 'Oh', he said, 'they've got the best economic system'.[1]

Frances needed a better reason than that. In the end, she said: 'I didn't vote at all because my husband was unconvincing, and he couldn't explain anything'.[2] So, Frances began to educate herself in politics. She joined the Fawcett library[3] and read everything she could on the suffrage movement 'and that rather pointed the way'.[4] As Frances recalls, she was inspired by the attitude of getting the vote 'at all costs'. She could see this was 'the stepping-stone to all other reform'.[5] But as a self-proclaimed 'novice' in her thirties she felt keenly a need to learn more about how to use her recently acquired right to vote.[6]

Thirty-one years later in 1966, Juanita Frances' picture is featured in the Associated Press above the headline 'Women Seek Equal Rights'.[7] She has found her place in the political world and is now one of the 'outstanding feminist campaigners of her day'.[8] Lobbying outside the Houses of Parliament in London, the photo shows Frances clutching a stack of papers and staring into the distance. 'Britain's small but dedicated Married Women's Association

---

[1] Michael Summerskill interview with Juanita Frances, SUMMERSKILL/1/46, TWL.
[2] ibid.
[3] Then located in Marsham Street, Westminster, London.
[4] Above n 1.
[5] ibid.
[6] Universal suffrage was not introduced until the enactment of the Representation of the People Act 1928.
[7] MK Myers, 'Women Seek Equal Rights' *Associated Press* (21 August 1966).
[8] M Stott, 'Caring and Sharing, Obituary: Juanita Frances' *Guardian* (2 December 1992) 27.

(MWA) has fought for 23 years to bring economic equality between man and wife', the report says:

> It's had a good many setbacks and a few successes. But its chairman and founder, Juanita Frances, thinks the day is not far off when the British housewife will be part owner of husband's pay check.[9]

This book tells the stories of how these setbacks and successes have influenced family law.

---

[9] Myers, above n 7.

1

Quiet Revolutionaries

'The Married Women's Association has been described as the "quiet but persistent organisation". This sums up the efforts we make on behalf of women'.[1]

While some revolutions are violent and bloody, dominating the headlines and crashing on the world stage, other revolutions are slower, unseen but often more enduring. As the historian Brian Harrison once argued: 'Feminist ambitions for social change are revolutionary' and militancy is not necessary for intense commitment.[2] Quiet revolutions often affect the lives of as many people as those dramatic and combative battles and can have a long-term legacy. Behind twentieth-century reforms which helped form the legal landscape of English family law was a small, non-party political pressure group of overlooked agitators: the Married Women's Association (MWA). Founded in 1938 by former suffragettes, the MWA had one overriding ambition: equal partnership in marriage. Its leading members included Labour MP and socialist doctor Edith Summerskill; writers Vera Brittain and Dora Russell; the BBC's first female Executive Doreen Gorsky;[3] and, Helena Normanton QC, the first woman to practise as a barrister. Their campaigns represent a turning point in the history of marital property and family law, yet their story has never been told.

'[W]e of the MWA are very chicken-hearted in our efforts compared with those of the very courageous pioneer suffragettes'.[4]

Their strategy of working behind the scenes might account for why the MWA's work has been curiously overlooked. While the arrests, hunger strikes and civil disobedience of the suffragettes is part of mainstream feminist history, the quieter work of feminist groups established in the aftermath of these campaigns has largely been consigned to oblivion.[5] In other words, we know so much less about what the suffragettes did *next*. And what about the younger generation, too young to campaign for suffrage, yet still facing grave legal injustices of their own?

---

[1] MWA Annual General Report 1970–72, 5SPG/M10, TWL.
[2] B Harrison, *Prudent Revolutionaries: Portraits of British Feminists Between the Wars* (Oxford University Press 1987) 1.
[3] Who used her maiden name 'Stephens' at the BBC.
[4] *Wife and Citizen*, April 1951, 7TBG/1/32, TWL.
[5] B Caine, *English Feminism 1780–1980* (Oxford University Press 1997) 173.

That the MWA described itself as 'quiet but persistent',[6] is as interesting as it is revealing. The group worked quietly, not employing the newsworthy strategies of the militant suffragettes,[7] and it persisted campaigning from the interwar years into the late 1980s and beyond.[8] As Barbara Caine has noted, the 'persistent yet always polite lobbying of MPs' helped make the work of the MWA and other similar groups 'much less visible' than their predecessors.[9] Militant methods had been abandoned because, once enfranchised, women felt they could not spurn parliamentary methods, and pursued a path of political pragmatism instead.[10] The MWA was also ideologically distinct from other women's rights groups;[11] instead of sidelining married women's interests in favour of unmarried women's rights to employment and education, it focused on the married woman as an individual who needed economic independence. It was therefore revolutionary by being the first group of the twentieth century to demand, as its core focus, legal and economic equality for spouses by emphasising the language of partnership. As the MWA's Bulletin declared: 'We cannot understand why men and women in their thousands do not join the MWA. The justice of our cause is so obvious, so blatant and demonstrable'.[12]

The MWA might have been understated, but it had its own dramatic confrontations. It delved into the problems of marriage, normally hidden from the public sphere, and brought them into the light. And it demanded legal recognition and compensation for married women for their work in the home through reform of family property law. Though unremarkable today, this idea seemed ludicrous in the early years of the MWA. As the Association's first President Edith Summerskill asserted in 1939 when addressing the House of Commons as a Labour MP:

> The time must come – I believe it will come in my lifetime – when this House will listen without laughter and the principle will be established that the married woman

---

[6] MWA Annual General Report 1970–72, above n 1.

[7] However, the MWA was clearly inspired by the suffragettes' work. As MWA Vice President Teresa Billington-Greig once put it: 'I am going to ask you to recognise that the MWA is in the direct line of descent from the suffragette militant movement, marked by the same sort of determination, persistence and courage, and showing the same consistency in direct approach to this goal'. Handwritten notes (undated), 7TBG/1/32, TWL.

[8] It is unclear when the MWA wound up. Archival records cease in 1989, but the Association is mentioned in Hansard in 1996: see HL Deb 29 February 1996, vol 569, col 1625 (MWA President Baroness Gardner, in relation to the need for reform of pension sharing on divorce).

[9] Caine, above n 5, 174.

[10] Harrison, above, n 2.

[11] Other groups, such as the Women's Cooperative Guild, advocated the extension of state welfare and an increase in family allowances (typically controlled by the male breadwinner), which did little to alleviate married women's economic dependence upon their husbands: see R Probert, 'Family Law Reform and the Women's Movement in England and Wales' in S Meder and C Mecke (eds), *Family Law in Early Women's Rights Debates: Western Europe and the United States in the Nineteenth and Early Twentieth Centuries* (Bohlau Verlag 2013).

[12] MWA Bulletin June–July 1981, 5MWA/8/1, TWL.

is earning her livelihood and is making a useful contribution to society inside her home, and is in fact helping to earn the worker's wage just as much as he is outside the home.[13]

*

The name 'Married Women's Association' may imply an organisation that is rather benign; even conservative. Given that marriage historically made women financially dependent and subservient, and the separate, purportedly private domain of the marital home has been the site of deep inequalities (and sometimes violence),[14] one would expect a group of feminists to oppose the institution, not to promote and reform it. The MWA did not reject existing legal structures. Nor did it seek an alternative to marriage. *Nor* did it seek to redefine the gendered roles of housewife and breadwinner within it. In spite of this, the seemingly quaint guise of the MWA masked a membership with varied and often radical ideas about law reform.

The idea to establish the MWA came from Dorothy Evans, a former suffragette who was lesbian and was in fact personally opposed to marriage. However, she saw reforming marriage as part of a wider feminist cause. As the historian Nancy Cott argued, marriage was seen as 'the vehicle through which the apparatus of state can shape the gender order'.[15] In the mid-twentieth century, marriage was of such central importance that practically no other status for women was acceptable.[16] Thus the law's failure to value married women's unpaid caregiving and domestic work was arguably detrimental to the lives and status of *all* women. As we shall see, these inequalities helped justify women being paid less than men. Many of the lowest paid jobs were traditionally women's jobs. Meanwhile the so-called 'family wage' was a larger pay packet that was paid to men with the expectation that they were the heads of a household – the patriarchs. Yet if these men married, their wives had no right whatsoever to this 'family wage', and in many cases did not even know what their husbands earned. In failing to count the value of married women's work, the experiences of married women – a significant portion of society – were not accounted for in the way law and policy was being designed. They were invisible. And the MWA sought to rectify this with a 'new marriage law'.

This book posits two questions: how did the MWA influence family law? And, what can be learned from the MWA's strategies as law reformers? Like many women's organisations of the mid-twentieth century, the MWA did not attract widespread public support for its campaigns, nor did it bring

---

[13] HC Deb 24 October 1939, vol 352, cols 1260–61.

[14] R Auchmuty, 'Law and the power of feminism: How marriage lost its power to oppress women' (2012) 20 *Feminist Legal Studies* 71, 74.

[15] N Cott, *Public Vows: A History Of Marriage And The Nation* (Harvard University Press 2002) 3.

[16] Auchmuty, above n 14, 72.

about major reform. However, this book argues that the subtle, *subterranean* influence of the MWA was an important yet overlooked part of changes to family property law from the 1960s onwards.

I. CHAPTER OUTLINE

Each chapter of this book explores a different aspect of the MWA's influence upon family law and strategies for reform. Chapter two examines the legal and socio-political context of married women when the MWA was formed. In the aftermath of the Second World War, married women were legally inferior to their husbands. As Martin Pugh has pointed out, a wife's financial stake in her marriage was 'scarcely recognised' at all.[17] Not only was the matrimonial home rarely in the wife's name, if she did work, she would not be paid as much as her husband. This chapter explores the roots of these inequalities, outlining why and how marriage oppressed women, and what the MWA – as part of a broader network within the women's rights movement – sought to do about it. As the latter half of chapter two explains, the MWA was influenced ideologically by the development of 'new feminism', an approach that drew attention to the fact that society's structures placed men and women in gendered roles that were unequal. Proponents of new feminism argued that treating men and women the same when they were not only served to reinforce inequalities further. As Eleanor Rathbone, whose views helped shape new feminism, explained:

> [A]t last we have done with the boring business of measuring everything that women want or is offered to them, by male standards, to see if it is exactly up to sample ... We can demand what we want for women, not because it is what men have got, but because it is what women want.[18]

In the 1940s and 1950s advocates of new feminism brought the language of equality to the private sphere, arguing for women's unpaid work to be valued economically on a par with men's. And the core tenets of this approach were translated into the MWA's draft legislation to reform marriage.

This background provides important context for chapter three, which outlines the structure, activities and membership of the MWA. Chapter three is an example of group biography, an approach which examines the individual lives of a collective. As we shall see, the MWA's committee was run by mostly middle-class, highly educated women and men and was often centred around a close-knit group of London lawyers, politicians and associated intelligentsia. But the demographic of the MWA *branches* was different, often comprised of

[17] M Pugh, *Women and the Women's Movement in Britain since 1914*, 3rd edn (Palgrave 2015) 185.
[18] E Rathbone, 'The Old Feminism and the New', Presidential Address at the Annual Meeting of NUSEC (11 March 1925) in E Rathbone (ed), *Milestones* (Liverpool 1929) 29.

mainly working-class members. Looking at the individual lives and personalities of MWA members helps explain tensions within the Association, and decisions over its strategy, policy and direction.

In chapter four, we see how these decisions are translated into draft law, as the development of the MWA's Bill for equal partnership in marriage is explored over the course of four decades. This Bill in its different iterations sought to reform property ownership *during* marriage instead of on relationship break-down. It provided for spousal income and the marital home to be shared, as the MWA viewed this as being one way in which unpaid care and housework could be valued by law. When pursuing this reform, MWA members relied on non-confrontational methods of campaigning: working behind the scenes, sending deputations to Attorneys General and Lord Chancellors, and cultivating contacts with establishment figures. As the historian Catherine Blackford observed, this was seen by MWA members as an 'effective political strategy for winning reform'.[19]

Chapter five focuses on the case of Dorothy Blackwell, which became another important element of MWA strategy. After Dorothy Blackwell's husband took her to county court and successfully claimed her savings, the MWA funded her appeal and held a watching brief over the case. This chapter explores how her case – more than any other the MWA assisted in – strengthened the cause for reform of family property during marriage. Press coverage of this case provoked outrage over the legal status of married women. And, *Blackwell v Blackwell*[20] arguably became the Association's best propaganda tool.

By contrast, chapter six explores a low point for the Association, when it split apart. In 1952, Helena Normanton QC submitted evidence to the Royal Commission on Marriage and Divorce on the MWA's behalf, which went against the Association's policy and was submitted without consultation with the Executive Committee of the Association. In the words of an MWA member, an 'enormous row'[21] broke out and several leading members left the group to form the breakaway Council of Married Women. This dramatic split attracted substantial press attention and was a major setback for the MWA. But as chapter seven explores, following its fragmentation, the MWA was still able to make some progress in terms of legislative success as it entered its third decade.

Chapter seven also addresses a long-standing debate in law: the effectiveness of piecemeal reform. The Association had previously rejected an incremental approach, preferring to pursue holistic change. However, changing tack in its

---

[19] C Blackford, 'Ideas, Structures and Practices of Feminism 1939–64' (PhD thesis, University of East London 1996) 54.
[20] [1943] 2 All ER 579.
[21] Letter from Joyce Nottage to Mary Stott (undated), 5MWA/5/2, TWL.

third decade helped the group play a key role in pushing through piecemeal changes to the law on maintenance and ownership of housekeeping savings.[22]

Development of the Association's reform strategy is investigated further in chapter eight. By resisting divorce reform, and helping to slow the passage of the Divorce Reform Act 1969, the MWA helped trigger debate about reform of women's property rights on divorce. Significantly, this included recognition of the value of spouses' unpaid caring and domestic contributions to the welfare of the family. But as chapter nine shows, these advances were swiftly followed by a backlash at the start of the 1980s. As the Law Commission was finally giving serious consideration to the notion of joint ownership of the family home during marriage,[23] the Campaign for Justice in Divorce – arguing that the financial consequences of divorce now oppressed men, *not* women – was gaining traction. Support for further reform of married women's property rights was snuffed out.[24]

The final chapter takes stock of the MWA's efforts to reform family law, while exploring the relevance of the Association's story to family law reform today. It sets out five findings about the feminist pursuit of law reform (concerning the iconic case, the 'omnibus Bill', resisting reform, the problem with maintenance, and repetition) based upon the experiences of the MWA.

In addition to the 10 substantive chapters in this book, there are four short interludes between chapters. The purpose of these interludes is to interrupt the MWA's story to provide snapshots of discussions, debates or supplementary context that provide further insight into the work and personalities of MWA members. Each chapter is also prefaced with extracts from letters written by married women about their experiences of marriage. This ensures the voices of the women let down by the law are brought to the fore, which is sometimes difficult when following the relatively privileged lives of MWA leaders. These letters also serve as a reminder of who the MWA represented, and why they sought to reform the law.

When exploring the personalities, decisions and experiences of MWA members as family law reformers over the course of this book, there is much to be learned from the advantages and pitfalls of their strategies, of the bills they drafted and redrafted over the course of 50 years. While the MWA has been largely ignored by legal academics, it was important. It shifted expectations, norms and mores. It exposed inequalities and applied indirect but nonetheless significant pressure. And in spite of their ostensible setbacks, this book will

---

[22] Pursuant to the Maintenance Orders Act 1958 and the Married Women's Property Act 1964 respectively.

[23] Law Commission, *Third Report on Family Property: The Matrimonial Home* (Law Com No 86, 1978); Law Commission, *Property Law: The Implications of Williams & Glyn's Bank Ltd v Boland* (Law Com No 115, 1982).

[24] The Matrimonial Homes (Co-Ownership) Bill was thwarted by MPs lobbying for the Campaign for Justice in Divorce.

argue that MWA members left their mark, both on British society and family law reform.

II. THROUGH A FEMINIST LENS

All history depends upon the perspective of the writer. When describing the process of history writing, EH Carr famously compared researching the past to exploring 'a vast and sometimes inaccessible ocean; and what the historian catches will depend, partly on chance, but mainly on what part of the ocean he chooses to fish in'.[25] Everyone's perspective of the past is influenced by their theoretical approach; it influences the sources used, the questions asked, the analysis reached. Carr's analogy is therefore a useful way to explain both the feminist approach in this book, and the fact that even dominant textbook-based histories of family law are neither complete nor immutable, because their focus has defined parameters. This is explored in the rest of this chapter. First, the historiography of this book is outlined: explaining why it is an example of feminist legal history, what this means and how this affects the sources and methods informing the study. A feminist lens influences not only the research undertaken in this book, but is also at the core of its analysis of processes of legal reform. This theoretical approach is explained in the last part of this chapter, outlining the significance of a feminist mode of analysis and how this impacts upon understandings of family law and its history. Put simply, the sections that follow argue this book is an example of feminist legal history because of the sources it uses, the approach it adopts and the challenges it presents to legal orthodoxy.

A. Sources

Though the MWA campaigned during the era of the Women's Liberation Movement, it was also active throughout the 1940s and 1950s; a time when traditionally, as Joyce Freeguard has noted, it was assumed women had little interest in feminist politics.[26] Historians have revisited and revised this negative picture; however, the dominant *legal* history within which the MWA is situated still neglects the importance of women's legal activism at this time. This might be because, as Rosemary Auchmuty and Erika Rackley have argued:

> The need to locate the law and legal actors in their historical setting, in all its 'social, economic and political dimensions', and to undertake in depth research into secondary sources written by historians as well as non-legal records, runs counter to

---

[25] EH Carr, What is History? (Kompf 1962) 23, as discussed in A Stephanson, 'The Lessons of *What is History?*' in M Cox (ed), *EH Carr: A Critical Appraisal* (Palgrave Macmillan 2000) 285–86.
[26] J Freeguard, 'It's Time for Women of the 1950s to Stand Up and Be Counted' (PhD thesis, University of Sussex 2004) i.

the training of many legal scholars, who are not only not familiar with this material, but have been trained to disregard it – to rely only on strictly legal sources.[27]

Learning about the MWA thus requires researchers to depart from 'strictly legal sources' to instead access a diverse range of sources that are 'non-legal'.

This book relies chiefly upon archival material, nearly all of which is housed in the Women's Library at the London School of Economics in London. The documents in these archives include, for example, correspondence, files in relation to MWA campaigns, newsletters, pamphlets, conference flyers, reports, handwritten notes, speeches, newspaper clippings and minutes of meetings. As well as the records of the MWA, this book also draws upon the records of Teresa Billington-Greig, Helena Normanton, Edith Summerskill, the Six Point Group and the Council of Married Women. Other primary sources drawn upon from the Women's Library include Brian Harrison's oral evidence on the suffragette and suffragist movements[28] and Michael Summerskill's interview transcripts,[29] both of which include interviews with MWA members and individuals connected with the Association. In addition to the Women's Library Archives, correspondence relating to the MWA was obtained from The National Archives in London, mostly from the files of the Lord Chancellor's office and the Law Commission of England and Wales.

There are inevitably gaps in the material generated by the MWA, which posed challenges when uncovering the story of the Association and its members.[30] Interesting insights scrawled on scrap pieces of paper are undated, and sometimes their context is unclear. Action points are noted in meetings, to follow up on a case, or to announce that an as yet unnamed MP will support the MWA's draft Bill, but incomplete records mean it is often not possible to find out what happened next. Membership records are virtually non-existent, so it is difficult to get a sense of the size of the Association beyond members' own non-specific accounts. It is also important to bear in mind the subjective nature of these sources, as they could be exaggerated or one-sided. As a result, this material is substantiated by new interview data and secondary sources, both of which help provide a more complete picture of the MWA.

The seven new interviews on which this book is based were undertaken between 2018 and 2020 with friends and family of MWA members. These revealed new information on MWA members that could not be gleaned from the archives, as well as members' private papers and an unpublished memoir written by Doreen Gorsky, the former MWA Chairman.[31] This adds to the published

---

[27] R Auchmuty and E Rackley, 'Feminist Legal Biography: A Model for All Legal Life Stories' (2020) 41 *Journal of Legal History* 186, 193.

[28] 8SUF, TWL.

[29] SUMMERSKILL/1/46, TWL.

[30] eg, two minute books were removed by the MWA in 1988 and have not as yet been returned.

[31] Further detail on methodology and ethics considerations is outlined in ch 3.

autobiographies of MWA members Edith Summerskill,[32] Dora Russell[33] and Vera Brittain.[34] These primary sources have been crucial to research for this book. As June Purvis argues, 'where possible, finding women's own words on the past is a critical aspect of "feminist" research'.[35] The MWA's own words are used throughout this book when telling the group's story of family law reform.

A number of key secondary texts have also been drawn upon in this book. As noted above, feminist histories of the 1940s and 1950s – in other words, the first 20 years of the MWA's existence – are relatively scarce. This period has often been characterised as a period of unabated decline for the women's movement.[36] The historian Sheila Rowbotham, who grew up in the 1950s, describes women then as 'creatures sunk' into 'very deadening circumstances from which I was determined to escape. Most older women seemed like this to me'.[37] To Rowbotham it seemed there was a 'political feminist hiatus'. The book relies upon a number of noteworthy texts that challenge this view of the women's movement. Dale Spender,[38] Barbara Caine,[39] Caitríona Beaumont,[40] the Birmingham Feminist History Group,[41] Elizabeth Wilson,[42] Martin Pugh[43] and Brian Harrison[44] have all brought attention to women's activism after the Second World War and before the emergence of the Women's Liberation Movement in the 1960s. Still, the MWA is mostly absent from these accounts. The only materials to provide substantive accounts of the MWA and their activities are the PhD theses of Blackford and Freeguard. Both theses uncover the MWA's rich social history and the organisation's place within the women's movement, with Blackford's work including interview data from several MWA members while they were still alive. Therefore, these secondary materials provide an invaluable resource for this book.

---

[32] E Summerskill, *A Woman's World* (Heinemann 1967).

[33] See, eg, D Russell, *The Tamarisk Tree* (Virago 1977).

[34] See, eg, V Brittain, *Testament of Youth* (Victor Gollancz 1933).

[35] J Purvis, 'Doing Feminist Women's History: Researching the Lives of Women in the Suffragette Movement in Edwardian England' in M Maynard and J Purvis (eds), *Researching Women's Lives From A Feminist Perspective* (Routledge 1994) 167.

[36] C Beaumont, 'The Women's Movement, Politics and Citizenship 1918–1950s' in I Zweiniger-Bargielowska, *Women in Twentieth-Century Britain* (Routledge 2001) 273–74.

[37] S Rowbotham, *Woman's Consciousness, Man's World* (Pelican 1973) 3, as cited in J Liddington, *The Road to Greenham Common: Feminism and Anti-militarism in Britain Since 1820* (Syracuse University Press 1991) 173.

[38] D Spender, *There's Always Been a Women's Movement This Century* (Harper Collins 1983).

[39] Caine, above n 5.

[40] C Beaumont, 'What *Do* Women Want? Housewives' Associations, Activism and Changing Representations of Women in the 1950s' (2017) 26 *Women's History Review* 147.

[41] Birmingham Feminist History Group, 'Feminism as femininity in the nineteen-fifties?' (1979) 3(1) *Feminist Review* 48.

[42] E Wilson, *Only Halfway to Paradise: Women in Postwar Britain 1945–1968* (Tavistock 1980).

[43] Pugh, above n 17.

[44] Harrison, above n 2.

This book builds upon and is distinctive from this literature for four reasons. First, in Blackford and Freeguard's theses, the MWA is not the sole focus and is just one of several women's organisations examined. Second, this book covers a broader time period and follows the MWA's activities until 1984, while Freeguard's thesis focuses on the MWA's work in the 1950s, and Blackford's does not go beyond 1964. Including the MWA's work throughout the 1970s and 1980s is important when considering family law history as it incorporates the MWA's views on and interventions in key legal moments such as the Matrimonial Homes Act 1967, the Divorce Reform Act 1969, the Matrimonial Proceedings and Property Act 1970 (consolidated in the Matrimonial Causes Act 1973), the Matrimonial Homes (Co-ownership Bill) 1980 and the Matrimonial and Family Proceedings Act 1984. In short, the influence of the MWA upon law cannot be properly understood without exploring members' work after 1964. Third, as explained above, this book includes new materials from interviews with the families of MWA members about whom there is little existing information, and previously unexplored material from private records. Finally, existing accounts of the MWA tend to focus on the group's impact upon feminism and society, but do not take the broader legal context into account. As the approach in this book is socio-legal as well as feminist, it posits different questions, and looks at how family law has been shaped by the MWA's campaigns and in turn, how legal processes shaped the MWA's campaigns. The only other *legal* texts to include the MWA are Dorothy Stetson's book *A Woman's Issue*, which examines the politics of family law reform in England from 1850 to 1970[45] and Stephen Cretney's tome *Family Law in the Twentieth Century*.[46] Both are invaluable sources for understanding family law reform but neither have the space nor scope to present a detailed assessment of the MWA's work. So far, this is the only book to do so.

B. Approach

This book is an example of feminist legal history not just because of the sources on which it is based, but because of its perspective on the MWA and family law. There are numerous studies of the nexus between feminism and family law.[47] However, defining precisely what this feminist lens looks like is difficult for a variety of reasons. Even a cursory glance at MWA members and their

---

[45] D Stetson, *A Woman's Issue: The Politics of Family Law Reform in England* (Oxford University Press 1982).
[46] S Cretney, *Family Law in the Twentieth Century* (Oxford University Press 2003).
[47] Notable examples include: C Smart, *Feminism and the Power of Law* (Routledge 1989); A Diduck and K O'Donovan, *Feminist Perspectives on Family Law* (Routledge-Cavendish 2007); J Somerville, *Feminism and the Family: Politics and Society in the UK and USA* (Palgrave Macmillan 2000); J Wallbank, S Choudhry and J Herring (eds), *Rights, Gender and Family Law* (Routledge 2010).

broader network of women's activist groups reveals a plurality of feminisms.[48] Indeed, many of these activists did not necessarily identify as 'feminist'. Yet as Blackford argues, it is sometimes necessary for historians of women's politics to adopt broader terms of reference when defining feminism, and include within feminist history organisations and individuals who might not have been explicitly feminist but who 'shared ideas similar to those of women who did'.[49] The feminist perspective of this book is therefore not driven solely by the individuals explored within it, but rather is part of the broader methodological approach of feminist legal history. In doing so, it seeks to transform our understanding of the past by writing the story of the MWA back into legal history, while confronting the question of why it has been excluded from accounts of family law reform for so long.

The term 'family law' also requires clarification. It might appear strange at first to describe MWA members as 'family law' reformers. The Association was established in 1938, but the discipline of family law was not taught as an academic subject until the 1950s,[50] and the first textbook on the subject was not published until 1957.[51] However, Rebecca Probert has pointed out that the term 'family law' was in use before the 1950s and is older than one might assume.[52] For as Martha Minow has argued, family law sits 'underneath' other areas of the law in that the obligations and commitments between women and men, children and parents, and families and strangers also underpin the histories of other areas such as property law.[53] Reference to MWA members' attempts to reform family law relates mostly to the financial consequences of marriage and divorce, which includes the development of property law too. However, reform of wider legal issues affecting the family that are not necessarily included within the scope of 'family law', such as tax, labour law and social security were of some concern to the MWA, but are not the central focus of this book. It should also be noted that unlike books dedicated to the meaning of family law and what the law considers 'family',[54] this book focuses instead on how the MWA navigated processes of family law *reform*.

[48] R Delmar, 'What is Feminism?' in J Mitchell and A Oakley (eds), *What is Feminism?* (Blackwell 1986).
[49] C Blackford, 'Wives and Citizens and Watchdogs of Equality: Post-War British Feminists' in J Fyrth (ed) *Labour's Promised Land: Culture and Society in Labour Britain 1945–51* (Lawrence & Wishart 1995).
[50] R Probert, 'The History of 20th-Century Family Law' (2005) 25 *Oxford Journal of Legal Studies* 169, 175.
[51] P Bromley, *Family Law* (Butterworths 1957).
[52] Probert, 'The History of 20th-Century Family Law', above n 50, 175.
[53] M Minow, 'Forming Underneath Everything That Grows: Toward a History of Family Law' (1985) 4 *Wisconsin Law Review* 819, 819.
[54] See, eg, A Brown, What is the Family of Law? The Influence of the Nuclear Family (Hart Publishing 2019).

Exploring Processes of Law Reform

As this book is concerned with the MWA's campaigns to reform family law, these waters are ostensibly ripe for feminist analysis given the gendered power entrenched within legal questions about intimate relationships. Moreover, a feminist focus on family law reform provides important commentary *beyond* the family too, on how law is reformed more generally. Feminist analyses can usefully break down the boundaries between public and private, showing that far from being confined to the family unit, the MWA's campaigns could have broader policy implications for women's legal rights and responsibilities.

Yet family law history is far from synonymous with feminist and gendered approaches. Though many commentators acknowledge family law's inextricable links with feminism, it is perhaps more accurate to describe feminism and family law as being mutually antagonistic, because as Carl Degler once put it: 'The equality of women and the institution of the family have long been at odds with each other'.[55] Traditional descriptions of family law history tend to be based on the notion of family law as having evolved steadily, from being rooted in patriarchal structures towards a system which aims to protect the autonomy and equality of family members.[56] Such dominant accounts of twentieth-century legal developments are often blinkered as those producing these accounts have focused mostly (or even solely) on the work of institutions: commissions (most notably the Law Commission of England and Wales); the courtroom; Parliament. Understanding the processes of such institutions in reforming law has obvious importance. But in a world of law-making that has historically been led by men,[57] women – and the grass roots pressure groups led by women – are obliterated from the story of reform. Whether we choose to recognise it or not, gender is never absent from a discussion about the fundamental underlying values in law. This is especially true when examining the wider context of social relations. The conversation of course changes depending on whether we choose to emphasise or ignore gender. And so, a feminist approach uncovers important tools that help bring gender inequalities to the fore. Feminism, then, is especially useful when thinking about power, because it directs critical fire at how social and legal structures create and reinforce power imbalances. By choosing explicitly to recognise this, issues of power are placed at the core of reform discussions rather than on the margins.

Employing a feminist perspective also means acknowledging the privileged position of the MWA leadership in terms of class, ethnicity and privilege. As a single-issue pressure group, it did not seek to unite all women, because

---

[55] C Degler, *At Odds: Women and the Family in America from the Revolution to the Present* (Oxford University Press 1980) vi. Though he was writing about America, Degler's assertion is equally applicable to the British context.

[56] As observed by G Douglas, *Obligation and Commitment in Family Law* (Hart Publishing 2018); and Minow, above n 53, 819.

[57] S Fredman, *Women and the Law* (Oxford University Press 1998) 2.

it was focused on equal partnership in marriage. Yet the Association did view reform of the financial and legal consequences of marriage as transformative for *married* women. Of course, married women's experience was not universal. As Laura Lee Downs has pointed out, male dominance in the home was 'not always the most problematic [form] of discrimination and inequality that marked' the lives of women of colour and of poor women.[58] There are glimpses of this being acknowledged by MWA members. For example, at the MWA's Annual General Meeting in 1955, Vera Brittain addressed the accusation that the MWA was 'only a middle class organisation'.[59] In Brittain's words: 'Women's movements had a middle class origin because … women from these classes had leisure and money', working-class women did not. In spite of this, she argued, the work of the MWA 'would mostly benefit the working class housewife'.[60] Unfortunately, there is not enough evidence to ascertain whether this was also the case for women of colour.[61]

C. Challenges

In this book, examining processes of law reform through a feminist lens presents two clear challenges to legal orthodoxy; first, that the law is not a neutral arbiter and second, that institutions are not solely responsible for legal change.

Challenge 1: Law is not a Neutral Arbiter

Feminist critique of law challenges the neutrality of law itself, and examines the gendered power dimensions of its production. Such gendered readings can change the narratives of legal history, and this in turn questions assumptions about who brought cases to court, where legal change over time can be located and how legal doctrine has developed.[62] This alternative reading leads to a richer understanding of how women have participated in law-making processes. These women include those in the MWA who pursued reform, the early women lawyers funded by the MWA to litigate cases concerning married

---

[58] L Downs, *Writing Gender History* (Bloomsbury 2010) 23. See also P Corfield, J Purvis and A Weatherill, 'History and the Challenge of Gender History' in S Morgan (ed), *The Feminist History Reader* 128.

[59] Minutes of MWA Annual General Meeting 1955, 7TBG/1/32, TWL.

[60] ibid.

[61] However, there is evidence of some reflexivity in the MWA's networks. At a conference called 'The Feminine Point of View' (in which several MWA members participated) it was noted that 'the views expressed are those of a small body of educated British women and that they relate mainly to conditions in this and other Western nations. How far our diagnosis and recommendations would be approved by other groups, and other countries, it is not possible for us to say': O Campbell, *The Feminine Point of View* (Williams & Norgate Ltd 1952) 5.

[62] F Batlan, 'Engendering Legal History' (2005) 30 *Law & Social Inquiry* 823, 842.

women's property rights, the women represented by these lawyers, and the women writing to the MWA who were affected adversely by the laws the Association sought to reform. All of these stories are baked into the history of family law, but an assumption that the law is and has been a neutral arbiter of family justice has helped render them invisible. Instead, texts that ignore the gendered aspects of this history ultimately give little credit to female lawyers and women's rights advocates for the revolutionary change initiated by their networks and organisations.[63] Of course, the notion of law's neutrality is a powerful force which helps maintain public confidence in the legal system[64] and reinforces the assumption that the law will be applied equally to everyone. Importantly, however, gender neutrality and gender equality are not the same.[65] The former – gender neutrality – seeks to quell feminism into dormancy[66] by claiming injustice and inequality has already been removed and replaced by neutrality. The latter – gender equality – recognises the need to pursue gender equality as a goal, thus highlighting existing problems of injustice. By challenging the premise of neutrality therefore, one can, as Minow has observed, 'look underneath'[67] and discover the attitudes and experiences of women, who 'neither crafted nor debated' law's formal rules and were historically given less status than men by the legal system.[68]

While a feminist approach provides the theoretical framework for this book, the compatibility of feminism and law in practice needs to be assessed if the failures of the MWA are to be properly understood. In *Feminism and the Power of Law*, Carol Smart argues that resorting to law raises a dilemma for feminism since law is 'structured on patriarchal precedents ... [and so] women risk invoking a power that will work against them rather than for them'.[69] Therefore, when one talks about the various gendered power imbalances that feminism pays critical attention to, it is crucial to also recognise that law (particularly common law) is in part responsible for these imbalances since it is based on gendered norms and assumptions. Put simply, if law is part of the problem, how can feminism operate *within* law to produce solutions? Perhaps the greatest challenge for a feminist approach to law is for it to be consistent with, and transformative of, mechanisms of law in practice.

The MWA took on this challenge, and the obstacles members experienced indicate how difficult it was to introduce reform driven by an agenda centred on women's concerns. Clashes between feminist ideology and legal practice were

---

[63] ibid, 834.
[64] See discussion of neutrality in R Blakey, 'The Conceptualisation of Family Mediation: Access to Justice after LASPO' (PhD thesis, Cardiff University 2021) ch 3.
[65] N Lacey, 'Feminist Legal Theory Beyond Neutrality' (1995) 48 *Current Legal Problems* 1, 12.
[66] Freeguard, above n 26, 3.
[67] Minow, above n 53, 821.
[68] ibid.
[69] Smart, above n 47, 138.

constant. As the MWA learned, it was a struggle to reform the law in line with feminist aims when the law was so frequently detached from these aims. Yet the MWA was not prepared to conclude that the law was unable to recognise feminist concerns and clearly viewed legislation as a vehicle for improving the legal rights of married women. As we shall see, pursuing this strategy often required compromise, and reform often did not turn out as MWA members had hoped. MWA members repeatedly found themselves working within legal frameworks and systems that were not neutral and with individuals who were not always prepared to accept claims of gender inequality, especially if this challenged the notion of law's inherent neutrality.

Yet far from being impotent, making feminist and gendered dimensions both visible and explicit in law and questioning its neutrality, particularly as it is navigated by the MWA, is a valuable exercise. At the same time, it is important to be sensitive to the constraints and limitations of law, and to not be dismissive of Smart's 'warning to feminism to avoid the siren call of law'.[70] Heeding this warning and looking past assumptions of neutrality in law also challenges the textbook account of how legal change happens – in other words, that institutions are mostly or solely responsible for reform.

Challenge 2: Institutions are not Solely Responsible for Legal Change

Once one lifts the lid on law's neutrality, assumptions about how legal change has happened historically can be questioned too. MWA President Edith Summerskill was mindful of this when she said in a House of Commons speech that institutions such as 'the Church of England, the Methodist Church ... and the Law Reform Committee ... are organisations composed almost entirely of men'. Summerskill added that, women and women's organisations 'are not represented in this House in great numbers'.[71] Men have been the insiders in these institutional reform bodies and parliamentary structures. With women on the periphery, pushing for reform using strategies such as those employed by the MWA, it is unsurprising that its members faced so many setbacks.

Certainly, the fact that institutions have the power to decentre women's issues is clear. Yet by applying a feminist perspective to the history of law reform, the role of *institutions* can be decentred instead, to make space for the omitted stories of the MWA and how the married women they sought to help were affected by law. This also enables the idea of MWA successes to be questioned, and to be framed differently. While recognising the patriarchal constraints the MWA faced when navigating legal reform, it is, in Lori Williamson's words 'counterproductive, not to mention tedious and inaccurate' to present their story simply in terms of what they were *not* able to achieve because of male

[70] ibid, 160.
[71] HL Deb 10 July 1969, vol 303, col 1295.

dominated institutions, 'rather than what they *did* achieve in spite of them'.[72] If success is measured by the number of MWA bills that became statutes, it could be argued in *institutional* terms that their success was limited. But when the MWA's work is assessed through an alternative feminist lens, a different conclusion can be reached. By instead looking to how social and legal patterns can be influenced by feminist campaigns, this approach can also highlight the importance of grass-roots pressure for change, or even *resistance* to change, and helps one make sense of the relationship between women and men in law. Perhaps Lena Jeger MP (who was affiliated to the MWA) explained this best when she said:

> Certainly it is true in the history of women's rights in Great Britain that progress has not been automatic, that if women (and a few good men) had not organized, campaigned, and exhorted to the point, sometimes of boredom, about the vote or equal pay or wifely rights in the marital home, these things would not have descended upon us as the gentle dew from heaven.[73]

Yet unless we *know* about these campaigners, their roles in reform of family law are all too easily forgotten. As we shall see, the history of feminism and of family law in England and Wales is incomplete without inclusion of the MWA. Processes of law reform cannot be fully understood without examining failed attempts at reform, failed attempts at opposing reform, piecemeal legislation and backroom conversations in the Houses of Parliament. This book seeks to show that the MWA encapsulates all of this and much more.

[72] L Williamson, 'Women's History and Biography' (1999) 11 *Gender & History* 379, 381.
[73] L Jeger, 'Power in Our Hands' in H Huskins-Hallinan (ed), *In Her Own Right* (Harrap 1968) 148.

2

Housewives: 'That Vast Army of the Great Unpaid'[1]

The MWA aims at the enforcement of justice. You must admit that under existing man-made, archaic law, a married woman, even in these enlightened days, is still more or less regarded as her husband's chattel.

Mary Anderton, St Annes-on-Sea[2]

INTRODUCTION

SOMETIMES, IT IS the forgotten moments in law that can reveal the most.

The Second World War was ongoing, and in Trafalgar Square women stood on one side, men on the other, displaying injuries with bandages, slings, splints and eye patches. Their slogan was BOMBS SHOW NO SEX BIAS.[3]

This is because if a married woman were permanently disabled in an air raid, she would not be entitled to compensation. But her husband *could* claim enough to hire someone else to undertake her domestic labour. And so under law, women's work within marriage was not work unless the husband needed to replace it. He would be compensated for his incapacity to work outside the home *and* he would be compensated for *her* incapacity to work inside the home. She would get nothing. The message was clear: she would work for free.

These were the implications of emergency wartime legislation when it was first introduced.[4] The Personal Injuries (Civilians) Schemes of 1939 and 1940 compensated injuries such as those sustained during air raid strikes, but only if the claimant was 'gainfully employed' – and this excluded housewives.[5]

To Juanita Frances, this was 'nonsense'.[6] She had formed the Married Women's Association (MWA) only a year earlier and like other women's

---

[1] HC Deb 24 October 1939, vol 352, col 1254.
[2] *Wife and Citizen*, November 1948, 5MWA/8/2, TWL.
[3] Sybil Morrison interview with Hazel Huskins Hallinan, 5SPG/M10, TWL. A report in *Time* magazine suggests this took place in September 1941: Anon, 'Great Britain: Women's Rights' *Time* (New York, 29 September 1941).
[4] The Personal Injuries (Civilians) Scheme 1941 was first foreshadowed in 1939, with the 1941 scheme replacing earlier schemes from 1939 and 1940. The enabling Act was the Personal Injuries (Emergency Provisions) Act 1939.
[5] Pursuant to s 1(1) of the Personal Injuries (Emergency Provisions) Act 1939.
[6] Brian Harrison interview with Juanita Frances, 14 November 1974, 8SUF/B/022, TWL.

organisations, the group was appalled by the Scheme.[7] 'Everyone was to be compensated if injured', she said, 'but not the housewife. But if she lost a leg or an arm or an eye, her husband could have an allowance to get a housekeeper. Which you see was such an outrage!'

The Personal Injuries Schemes are not normally considered relevant to family law reform. Yet they are symptomatic of an issue deeply rooted in family law history: the undervaluing of women's domestic labour in the home. When MPs Dr Edith Summerskill (the MWA's first President) and Jennie Adamson sought to have the Personal Injuries Schemes annulled in the House of Commons,[8] they were defending, in their words, 'that vast army of the great unpaid' – housewives. They were pointing out the fact that when a woman married, she was not a worker, but a servant to her husband. 'The Scheme', Summerskill argued,

> which is really nineteenth century in its attitude towards this question, could not be drawn up by the Government and their advisers if the principle is established that the married woman is engaged in gainful occupation as a wife because she is doing work in the household.[9]

The Scheme was subsequently amended to compensate war injury to housewives; albeit at a lower rate than men.[10] Morris Finer wrote at the time that the discriminatory aspects of the Scheme were highlighted 'thanks to the energetic activities of the women MPs'[11] and that 'the framers of the original Scheme seem to have been *unaware* that in the average household the housewife earns her living by the work she does, which is work of high national importance'.[12] This apparent lack of awareness showed more broadly just how entrenched women's subservience in law was. And, that their work was invisible.

The question of how to value housework in law is at the heart of this book. Specifically, this chapter explores how the debate over proper recognition of housewives' work became a concern for feminists from the 1920s to the 1950s. While there are some notable accounts of the history of the women's movement during this time (particularly throughout the 1940s and 1950s),[13] there is a dearth of information on the connections during this period between feminist

---

[7] According to the MWA, it pressurised the Ministry of Pensions from July 1940, eventually gaining 14s compensation for the housewife (while her husband could be compensated 21s). MWA Chairman's Report, 8 March 1940, 7TBG/1/32, TWL.

[8] HC Deb 24 October 1939, vol 352, col 1253. The Prayer for annulment was lost by 137 votes to 113. Though the statute was not annulled, it was amended as part of the Personal Injuries (Civilians) Scheme 1941. This change can in part be attributed to the collective feminist resistance against this legislation.

[9] HC Deb 24 October 1939, vol 352, col 1261.

[10] Pursuant to the Personal Injuries (Civilians) Scheme 1941.

[11] M Finer, 'The Personal Injuries (Civilians) Scheme 1941' (1942) 5 *MLR* 224, 233.

[12] ibid (emphasis added).

[13] B Caine, *English Feminism 1780–1980* (Oxford University Press 1997); C Beaumont, *Housewives and Citizens: Domesticity and the Women's Movement in England 1928–64* (Manchester University Press 2015).

organisations and the broader framework of married women's status in law.[14] But this did not mean feminist organisation was not happening, or that there was no need for it. Indeed, the aftermath of women's suffrage, changing economic conditions, the Second World War, and the creation of the welfare state combined to form the backdrop to evolving feminist ideas about women's role in the home.

*

This chapter sets out the broader legal and social context of housewives to explain why the MWA emerged and who it sought to represent. Section I explores the legal status of married women at the time of the MWA's emergence, making it clear why a group reforming the legal position of the housewife was needed urgently. This section examines the doctrine of legal unity of husband and wife, known as coverture, and how even when it was eroded by the Married Women's Property Acts in 1870 and 1882, its after-effects continued to oppress women. Antiquated aspects of spousal unity into the 1950s and beyond became issues that the MWA would grapple with throughout its history. Yet as this section will also explain, the doctrine of separate property was not a panacea for married women's economic subjugation either. While it counteracted some of the most oppressive aspects of coverture, it barely touched the women who had no way of independently owning property.

The reality for these women is investigated in section II. With a significant long-term rise in marriage rates beginning in the 1930s alongside the emerging 'cult of domesticity',[15] women's freedom was tied up in lowering expectations of housework, which filled housewives' working days.[16] Yet instead of recognising this labour, the law was stacked against married women, and especially the housewife. The original provisions in the Personal Injuries (Civilians) Schemes give us a snapshot that demonstrates how the law failed to protect women or recognise the value of their domestic labour. But as this chapter will show, there was a litany of other ways in which this inequality manifested. It was this hardship being experienced by housewives that motivated the founders of the MWA, who were convinced that women's emancipation outside the home and their participation as equal citizens hinged upon them first being treated as legal equals *inside* the home.

Though the women's movement is often considered to have declined and fragmented following campaigns for women's suffrage,[17] section III explores

---

[14] E Wilson, *Only Halfway to Paradise: Women in Postwar Britain 1945–1968* (Tavistock 1980) 186; C Blackford, 'Ideas, Structures and Practices of Feminism 1939–64' (PhD thesis, University of East London 1996) 79.

[15] M Pugh, *Women and the Women's Movement in Britain since 1914*, 3rd edn (Palgrave 2015) 172.

[16] ibid.

[17] See, eg, C Beaumont, 'The Women's Movement, Politics and Citizenship 1918–1950s' in I Zweiniger-Bargielowska, *Women in Twentieth-Century Britain* (Routledge 2001) 273.

the strand of 'new feminism' that emerged at this time, which is often over-looked as a result of the frequently used terminology of first and second wave feminism.[18] Instead of associating equality with sameness of treatment, new feminism sought to highlight work typically undertaken by women as being different yet equally valuable to work typically done by men. Finally, section IV examines how within this context of new feminism the MWA was, in Catherine Blackford's words, established as 'a modern face of feminism' distinctive to the 1940s and 1950s.[19] And so, by considering this broader context, it is possible to explain more fully the nexus of law reform, society, housewives and the MWA in the chapters that follow.

I. THE ROOT OF THE PROBLEM: LEGAL UNITY OF WIFE AND HUSBAND

Twentieth-century debates over married women's legal status and reform of matrimonial property law cannot be understood properly without going back to the Married Women's Property Acts (MWPAs) of the nineteenth century. When the first of these Acts was passed in 1870, Otto Kahn-Freund argued that at this time 'nobody in this country considered as yet the problem of the effect of marriage on property in its entirety'.[20] But feminist legal historians know this is not quite true. The problem of who should own what in marriage might not have been of prior concern to legislators, judges and policymakers, but it had been an issue for feminists for decades.[21] Coverture was a common law doctrine that removed women's separate legal status upon marriage, making wives their husbands' de facto chattels.[22] Women ceased being *feme sole*, single women and on marriage became *feme covert*, in Henry de Bracton's words, 'a single person [that person being the husband], one flesh and one blood'.[23] This did not only represent what was, in effect, a civil death for the wife; it gave the husband immense power and control over her. Though he had a legal obligation to support his wife, the husband took over ownership of all her property and income. He could dispose of any money his wife earned before or during the

---

[18] ibid, 274.

[19] Blackford, 'Ideas, Structures and Practices of Feminism 1939–64', above n 14, 79.

[20] O Kahn-Freund, 'Recent Legislation on Matrimonial Property' (1970) 33 *MLR* 601, 601.

[21] eg, in the 1850s the Langham Place Circle was established – a pressure group awakened to the injustices of the coverture doctrine by Barbara Lee Smith Bodichon's publication of *A Brief Summary, in Plain Language, of the Most Important Laws Concerning Women: Together With A Few Observations Thereon*.

[22] The complexity of the meaning of coverture is explored in G Seabourne, *Women in the Medieval Common Law* (Routledge 2021) 35.

[23] H Bracton, *On the Laws and Customs of England* (Belknap Press of Harvard University 1968–77) book 4, 287, cited in S Butler, 'Discourse on the Nature of Coverture in the Later Medieval Courtroom' in T Stretton and K Kesselrin, *Married Women and the Law: Coverture in England and the Common Law World* (McGill-Queen's University Press 2013) 25.

marriage as he wished.[24] Moreover, wives had no economic independence or responsibility.[25]

Campaigners seeking to dismantle this doctrine would not accept assertions that the impediments wrought by coverture were beneficial for married women by placing them under the protection or 'cover' of their husbands.[26] On the contrary, the Victorian women's movement sought to show that men could exploit their wives when they had unfettered access to all of their property. High-profile cases helped bring attention to the injustice of coverture, such as writer Caroline Norton and actress Sarah Siddons having their earnings seized by their husbands. Then, there were the everyday examples revealed in parliamentary debates of 'drunken husbands deserting wives and returning to seize their earnings'.[27] Aside from the cruelty and hardship women experienced because of coverture, there were also the absurdities of its practical legal effects. Suffragist and leading figure of the Married Women's Property Committee Millicent Fawcett is said to have been motivated to campaign for reform of married women's property law following an incident at Waterloo station in London when her purse was stolen. When the thief was caught and she pressed charges, she discovered he was to be charged with 'stealing from the person of Millicent Fawcett a purse containing £1 18s 6d, the property of Henry Fawcett' – her husband.[28]

Tackling these oppressive consequences of coverture was therefore inextricably linked to furthering women's emancipation. Marriage tied women up in a form of 'legal bondage',[29] as their husbands had almost complete control over their property and person. And as Sandra Fredman notes, coverture challenged the ideal that all individuals were equal before the law, because the law 'unabashedly excluded married women from the category "individuals"'.[30] The MWPAs were therefore important legal landmarks for women. First, the narrowly constrained 1870 Act permitted married women to hold a limited range of property for their separate use. Then, the much broader 1882 Act provided for

---

[24] However, the husband did need the wife's consent to sell her land, though he was still entitled to any rent and profits made from the land during the marriage.

[25] The only way of escaping the impediments of coverture was to divorce. Secular divorce was not introduced until the Divorce and Matrimonial Causes Act 1857 was introduced, and even then, divorce was not an option for most women, who unlike their husbands, needed to prove *aggravated* adultery (ie, adultery aggravated by factors such as bigamy, incest, desertion or cruelty). The grounds for divorce were not equalised until the Matrimonial Causes Act 1923.

[26] William Blackstone said coverture was 'intended for her protection and benefit': W Blackstone, *Commentaries on the Laws of England*, 21st edn (Sweet, Maxwell, Stevens and Norton 1844) book 1, 444. As late as 1947, Glanville Williams described the doctrine as an instance of humanitarianism: G Williams, 'The Legal Unity of Husband and Wife' (1947) 10 *MLR* 16, 31.

[27] A Hayward, 'Married Women's Property Act 1882' in E Rackley and R Auchmuty (eds), *Women's Legal Landmarks: Celebrating the History of Women and Law in the UK and Ireland* (Hart Publishing 2019) 73.

[28] L Holcombe, *Wives and Property* (University of Toronto Press 1983) 3.

[29] S Fredman, *Women and the Law* (Oxford University Press 1998) 40.

[30] ibid.

separate property, enabling married women to own and dispose of property as if they were single. For married women in employment or with property, this ability under law to legally control earnings and/or property could have meant 'the difference between independence and subservience, comfort and penury, even life and death'.[31]

As will become clear, the consequences of these Acts underpinned much of the MWA's story, even though the Association was not formed until almost 60 years later. The constant desire not to undermine the MWPAs – which members viewed as a feminist achievement – eventually led to irreparable fragmentation within the MWA. Furthermore, addressing the lingering effects of coverture and the new hardships produced by strict separation of property shaped the MWA's reform agenda.

A. An Extant Doctrine?

Even after the momentous 1882 Act, the idea of wives as 'perpetual legal minors'[32] was difficult to erase entirely. The Victorian feminists had wanted a 'clean sweep of the old fiction of our common law that a woman on marrying became merged in the personality of her husband and ceased to be a fully qualified and separate human person'.[33] Whether the MWPAs succeeded in doing so was a different question.[34] In some ways, the 1882 Act 'expressly reaffirmed' the spirit of coverture, in spite of the separate property doctrine it introduced. This was because any inequalities stemming from the idea that wives were dependants under the control of their husbands remained built into the law in numerous ways.[35] And the reach of coverture's concept of unity – that husband and wife became 'one flesh' – extended beyond property.[36] If a woman was married, she would have no domicile of her own but must take that of her husband. Legal judgments were not enforceable against married women in the same way as they were against men and until 1935 women were not personally responsible for their own torts; their husbands were liable instead.[37] The patriarchal idea of

---

[31] R Auchmuty, 'Unfair Shares for Women: The Rhetoric of Equality and the Reality of Inequality' in A Bottomley and H Lim (eds), *Feminist Perspectives on Land Law* (Glass House Press 2007).

[32] Fredman, above n 29, 40.

[33] O Kahn-Freund, 'Inconsistencies and Injustices in the Law of Husband and Wife' (1952) 15 *MLR* 133, 134.

[34] ibid.

[35] It was not until 1991 that a husband could be convicted for raping his wife: *R v R* [1991] UKHL 12.

[36] S Cretney, *Family Law in the Twentieth Century* (Oxford University Press 2003) 91.

[37] This was not reformed until the Law Reform (Married Women and Tortfeasors) Act 1935 furnished married women with the same contractual rights and obligations as men. The equitable device of Restraint On Anticipation meant married women could not touch their capital under a settlement until reform in 1949: see R Auchmuty, 'Married Women (Restraint Upon Anticipation) Act 1949' in E Rackley and R Auchmuty (eds), *Women's Legal Landmarks: Celebrating the History of Women and Law in the UK and Ireland* (Hart Publishing 2019).

the husband as head of the household and possessor of his wife was therefore reflected in every corner of property law affecting married women. The tenacity of this idea was evident, for instance, in Lord Sumner's assertion in the House of Lords in 1925 that the unity doctrine between husband and wife applied unless it was specifically excluded.[38] It was not until the 1980s that it could be claimed with confidence that husband and wife could acquire and control property, enter contracts and be responsible for debts and legal wrongs on equal terms.[39]

Not only were there inherent injustices in the survival of the antiquated notion of unity; this concept justified discriminations built into law which had *not* existed for centuries, and served to depress married women's status as workers too. For instance, the Naturalisation Act 1870 provided that a British woman lost her nationality upon marriage to a foreign man.[40] This was at the very time resistance *against* the oppressive consequences of coverture and women's loss of legal identity on marriage was intensifying. It was not until the British Nationality Act 1948 was introduced that a woman would no longer lose her British nationality on marriage[41] – something feminist groups[42] had campaigned against for years. An issue that took much longer to reform was the taxation of married women. As chapter four explains further, a married woman was not taxed separately from her husband until 1990. Instead, her income was deemed to be that of her husband.[43] This meant she was required to disclose her income to her husband, but he could conceal his from her if he wished to do so. This originated from before the MWPAs, when, in fact, the income of the wife *did* belong to her husband and was controlled by him. By combining the incomes of husband and wife for the purposes of income tax, and calling them his, the message persisted that he had the financial information and therefore power in the marriage, not her.

Then, there was the marriage bar,[44] which required women, with a few exceptions, to resign from occupations such as banking and the Civil Service on marriage.[45] Women's marital status also affected their ability to claim

---

[38] *Edwards v Porter* [1925] AC 1 (HL); see Fredman, above n 29, 46.

[39] Cretney above n 36, 91, referring to the statement by Lord Denning MR in *Midland Bank Trust Co Ltd v Green (No 3)* [1982] Ch 529, 538.

[40] Naturalisation Act 1870, s 10(1).

[41] British Nationality Act 1948, s 14.

[42] This included the MWA, as well as the Six Point Group, the National Union of Societies for Equal Citizenship (NUSEC), the National Council of Women and the Women's Freedom League. For more information on the importance of this feminist activism as part of the British Nationality Act 1948, see M Baldwin, 'Subject to Empire: Married Women and the British Nationality and Status of Aliens Act' (2001) 40 *Journal of British Studies* 522.

[43] Pursuant to the Income Tax Act 1842.

[44] This existed in spite of the Sex Disqualification Act 1919, which provided explicitly in s 1 that any person would not be disqualified by reason of marriage from any public function, civil profession or vocation.

[45] H Samuels, 'Education Act 1944' in E Rackley and R Auchmuty (eds), *Women's Legal Landmarks: Celebrating the History of Women and Law in the UK and Ireland* (Hart Publishing 2019) 219. According to Helen Glew, it was common practice for women working for local authorities to be dismissed when they married: H Glew, *Gender, Rhetoric and Regulation: Women's Work*

unemployment insurance.[46] If married, the 1931 Anomalies Regulations required women to satisfy more onerous conditions than men or single women before they could qualify for any benefits, and in certain cases married women had to pay additional contributions.[47] These regulations resulted in excluding married women from benefitting in hundreds of thousands of cases.[48]

Not only were married women legally pressed into a state of dependence on others in terms of taxation, insurance,[49] unemployment benefit,[50] nationality and right to work, but in spite of the MWPA 1882, their economic rights within marriage were barely recognised in law.[51] The marital home was normally purchased in the husband's name. As chapter five explores in detail, wives' money made from taking in lodgers, dividends at the Co-op or savings out of house-keeping money was ultimately deemed to be their husbands' property.[52] And so, even though the MWPA was undoubtedly significant in giving married women the ability to deal with earnings and property as men and single women could, the *reality* for most housewives in the decades that followed was that this reform did very little to alleviate their position if they had no property or earnings.[53] They were financially dependent upon their husbands. And the economic power of the breadwinner husband over the homemaker wife remained virtually the same. That the MWPAs had not given married women equal property rights in law was clear.

B. Separate Property

Lingering aspects of the unity doctrine were not the only source of problems for married women when it came to economic and legal equality in marriage. If the housewife's work did not entitle her to any property, she did not benefit from the doctrine of separate property. Therefore, the concept of separate property enshrined in the MWPA 1882, though 'couched in the language of change or progression'[54] did not equate to equality for most married women. It would only give women economic power on a par with their husbands if their socio-economic situation was the same. Treating married women and men as two

---

in the Civil Service and the London County Council, 1900–55 (Manchester University Press 2016) 16. Some women even married in secret to avoid losing their jobs: H McCarthy, *Double Lives: A History of Working Motherhood* (Bloomsbury 2020) 151.

[46] Pursuant to the Unemployment Insurance (Anomalies Regulations) Act 1931.

[47] See Ministry of Labour, *Report on the Operation of the Anomalies Regulations, 3rd October 1931 to 29th April 1933* (Cmd 4346, 1933).

[48] D Benjamin and L Kochin, 'Searching for an Explanation of Unemployment in Interwar Britain' (1979) 87 *Journal of Political Economy* 441, 461–62.

[49] Fredman, above n 29, 169.

[50] J Sonrab, 'Women and Social Security' (1994) 1 *Journal of Social Welfare & Family Law* 5.

[51] Pugh, above n 15, 185.

[52] *Blackwell v Blackwell* [1943] 2 All ER 579.

[53] M Glendon, 'Is There a Future for Separate Property?' (1974) 8 *Family Law Quarterly* 315, 316.

[54] Hayward, above n 27, 74.

economically independent individuals in marriage, when this was mostly not the case, proved that women's achievement of *full* equality was not inextricably linked to the separate property doctrine.[55]

As a result, the MWPAs made it a possibility for married women to be financially independent by enabling them to legally own property in their own right. But the *reality* for most married women throughout much of the twentieth century prevented this possibility from being realised.[56] This became more of a problem in the twentieth century than it had been in the nineteenth, as trends in property ownership changed. In the 1800s, the majority of society had no savings and lived on their earnings.[57] This meant that most married women were much less likely to have issues with matrimonial property. Where there were issues for wives' provision, they were – as Kahn-Freund put it – 'crudely and inadequately' resolved by maintenance and later by social security. This also helps explain the focus of the MWPA 1870 upon income, which principally aimed to protect the wife from having current cash income being seized by her husband. By the 1930s, however, maintenance was no longer sufficient to protect housewives who were not gainfully employed outside the home, as families owned capital assets in a way that was different from earlier generations.[58] But the law did not adapt to these changing social trends. This influenced conveyancing practices too, as even in the 1950s and 1960s, building societies would not lend money to married women, and husbands *not wives* tended to have sole ownership or tenancy rights in the family home 'almost automatically'.[59]

Separate property was not only a problem because of married women's lack of opportunity to earn and own property. It also resulted in 'grave injustices and no less grave inconsistences',[60] from the gap between how married couples managed property together according to law and how they actually managed property in reality. In other words, it seemed anomalous for the law to treat spouses' property as strictly demarcated, when in marriage, spouses merged many of their possessions and the line between his and hers was much murkier than the law supposed.

II. THE HOMEMAKER/BREADWINNER DICHOTOMY

By the mid-twentieth century, most women still gave up paid employment on marriage, and those who did work tended to occupy low-paid jobs. These material inequalities were in many ways reinforced because of the sexual division of

---

[55] Fredman, above n 29, 48.

[56] Parts of this discussion appear in S Thompson, 'Married Women's Property Act 1964' in E Rackley and R Auchmuty (eds), *Women's Legal Landmarks: Celebrating the History of Women and Law in the UK and Ireland* (Hart Publishing 2019).

[57] Kahn-Freund, 'Recent Legislation of Matrimonial Property', above n 20, 606.

[58] ibid.

[59] C Smart, *The Ties That Bind* (Routledge 1984) 29.

[60] Kahn-Freund, 'Inconsistencies and Injustices in the Law of Husband and Wife', above n 33, 136.

labour within the family. Work in the home was almost exclusively the wife's domain and was unpaid. Unless she did this work, the husband was not free to earn a living for the family in the public sphere. However, this indirect contribution to the production of household earnings was not recognised in law. The principle of separate property meant that only the husband could have a legal interest in the money and property he earned. Though money earned by a wife would also belong to her outright, the little money she could earn was generally spent on food, clothing and other consumables for the family. This also left married women economically vulnerable on divorce, as before the 1970s they would be dependent on maintenance from their ex-husbands, and this was not always paid. In short, married women had no claim to property directly earned by their husbands and had little opportunity to accumulate property in their own right.

This section examines these socio-economic inequalities further by briefly outlining the position of the housewife in the 1930s, 1940s and 1950s. Much has been written about how the legal consequences of marriage reproduce and reinforce sex-segregated spheres of public and private. Yet it is too simplistic to place the blame for this entirely at coverture's door, and to suggest that the law set out earlier in this chapter is solely responsible for the marginalisation of women in the history of law reform. It is therefore important to look beyond legal texts to non-legal sources, in order to identify how patterns and structures such as the division of labour in the home are conceptualised not just legally, but socially and politically too.

A. The Cult of Domesticity

Alongside the image of the domestic goddess, the notion that management of the household was a prestigious job for women[61] was popularised in the 1920s and 1930s, and persisted into the 1950s. The 1930s song 'Keep Young and Beautiful' helps epitomise what was expected of women culturally and socially: 'it's your duty to be beautiful, keep young and beautiful, if you want to be loved'.[62]

When the MWA was starting out in the late 1930s, members' efforts to raise women's consciousness about their legal status were hindered by propaganda designed to persuade working and middle-class women of the necessity of managing their households in a *professional* fashion.[63] This propaganda was fuelled by a massive rise in the popularity of women's magazines in the 1920s and 1930s, which have proven to be an important source in providing context

---

[61] Pugh, above n 15, 69.

[62] Written by Al Dubin (music by Harry Warren). The version popularised in the 1930s was performed by Eddie Cantor. Also referenced in ibid.

[63] Pugh, above n 15, 68.

for the kinds of pervasive pressures faced by women from day to day.[64] By 1940, five out of six women in Britain read at least one woman's magazine every week.[65] The influence of such magazines is immeasurable, but their message was ubiquitous: marriage and domesticity were aspirational ideals for women of the period.

One of the most popular magazines of the period was *Good Housekeeping*, which was first published in 1922. In the first issue, the editors wrote: 'We are on the threshold of a great feminine awakening';[66] an awakening that Martin Pugh argues was not a new phenomenon of homemaking but was instead an 'improved competence in the performance of the traditional female functions'.[67] Either way, that housekeeping would go on to attain a prestige and aspirational sheen across the social spectrum *did* seem new to many women in the 1930s, simply because the seemingly 'ideal home' was more attainable than it had been previously.[68] Housing standards had improved, and with four million new houses built between the World Wars, new semi-detached houses could be purchased in some parts of Britain for as little as £200 to £300, with a deposit of £25 and an interest rate of 4.5 per cent on the mortgage. This interwar housing was built to a higher standard, with larger and brighter rooms thanks to the 1918 Tudor Walters Report on desirable housing, which influenced standards imposed by the state.[69]

However, this did not improve housewives' everyday life. Middle-class homes were more likely to have access to electrical appliances such as washing machines and vacuum cleaners (though Pugh notes the spread of such goods was slow).[70] But the expense of these goods meant they were not an option for many working-class homes, where the most common item was a sewing machine.[71] Indeed, working-class women had been barely touched by the women's movement, and as Blackford has pointed out, 'unemployment and the domestic poverty which accompanied it raised a host of women's issues relating to the welfare of working-class mothers and wives'.[72] This highlights the importance of noting that in analysing the inequalities affecting married women, their experiences were not uniform throughout different classes.[73] But the consequences for housewives resulting from such inequalities were still detrimental across class boundaries, albeit for different reasons. Even in the middle-class homes with washing machines, cookers and/or vacuum cleaners, housework was still

---

[64] ibid, 172.
[65] ibid.
[66] *Good Housekeeping*, March 1922, cited in ibid, 68.
[67] Pugh, above n 15, 69.
[68] ibid, 180.
[69] ibid, 181.
[70] ibid.
[71] ibid, 182.
[72] Blackford, 'Ideas, Structures and Practices of Feminism 1939–64', above n 14, 84.
[73] Fredman, above n 29, 44.

heavy and time-consuming work,[74] expanding, as Betty Friedan put it, to fill the time available.[75]

Thus, the 'happy housewife' depicted in women's magazines limited the complexity of women's lives.[76] Despite increasingly glamourised notions of housework and femininity, the reality for many women working inside the home was that greater prestige often meant more pressure to meet *higher* standards of cleanliness and domesticity. This became an issue for middle-class women, who often no longer had the domestic help their parents had been able to access.[77] The problem for groups like the MWA was that the creeping 'home sweet home' ideal positioned the housewife as her own boss. When seen as a boss, it became more difficult to expose the somewhat less sanguine reality for many wives as subordinates within marriage, who were in urgent need of better legal rights and protections. In contrast to the campaigns for domesticity in magazines such as *Woman's Own*,[78] the notion of the housewife as the goddess of her private domain was challenged by the MWA in its magazine *Wife and Citizen* in 1951:

> MOTHER WORKS 12-HOUR DAY
>
> Such is the average day of working class housewives according to a survey on three LCC housing estates by Mr CA Moser of the London School of Economics. General housework, cooking and care of children take up most working hours, with very little time spent on laundry or mending. About two hours goes on work outside the home. Practically all leisure is of the home type and nearly half of it comes after supper.[79]

The glamour of housework in magazines was a reality of domestic drudgery. And the portrayal of housewives as managers of their homes was somewhat misleading. As Carole Pateman put it, the boss – at least when he returned home from work – was the husband. The demands of *his* work would largely determine how the housewife organised her time.[80]

B. The 'Private' Sphere

These problems for married women were stuffed into a closet, away from the attention of lawyers and judges. In the private domestic sphere, the unequal relationship between housewife and breadwinner was 'natural' and did not 'detract from the universality of the public world'.[81] But as Susan Atkins and

---

[74] Blackford, 'Ideas, Structures and Practices of Feminism 1939–64', above n 14, 85.

[75] B Friedan, *The Feminine Mystique* (WW Norton 1963).

[76] C Beaumont 'What *Do* Women Want? Housewives' Associations, Activism and Changing Representations of Women in the 1950s' (2017) 26 *Women's History Review* 147, 148.

[77] A Oakley, *Housewife* (Allen Lane 1974) 52.

[78] See Pugh, above n 15, 174.

[79] *Wife and Citizen*, January 1951, 5MWA/8/2, TWL.

[80] C Pateman, *The Sexual Contract* (Polity 1988) 130.

[81] ibid, 117.

Brenda Hale have noted, 'we do not have to believe that the existing gender order is inevitable in order to recognise that it exists'.[82] Dismantling, subverting and exposing the fallacy of the public and private has historically been a central part of feminist activism. As Pateman affirmed, 'the dichotomy between the public and the private ... is, ultimately, what the feminist movement is all about'.[83] Because the housewife's work is privatised, her position – where she is oppressed because she works for free and has little property of her own – is maintained.

For married women, the consequence of their legal subordination into the private sphere was that the family was outside the public, political arena, and outside state intervention.[84] Pateman has argued that women's consent to subservience was implied by their entry into marriage.[85] The marriage contract carved out the domestic sphere as being women's domain, but this space was presided over by patriarch husbands. When the state is kept out of the family home, the gendered power disparities within the family and especially between housewife and breadwinner are intensified. A clear example of these gendered imbalances was the control and ownership of family finances. Although housewives were often placed in charge of the economics of the household, the housekeeping money they were given did not belong to them.[86] The breadwinning husband retained control of his earnings, while wielding discretion over how much money to allocate to the wife for housekeeping expenses.[87] The considerable economic vulnerability resulting from this was a private matter, and therefore not something the state would become involved with. The state's decision to stay away from family issues occurring behind closed doors in the private sphere, feminists argued, *facilitated* the exercise of gendered power and violence. Lack of intervention could, therefore, be viewed as a political choice and a form of state regulation in itself.[88] As Susan Okin has put it, 'the very notion that the state can choose whether or not to intervene in family life makes no sense'.[89] From this perspective, the private/public dichotomy is a misleading construct, as it obscures cyclical patterns of inequality between women and men.[90] Power, Okin explains, 'which has always been understood as paradigmatically political' is also of central importance to the family. Indeed, the family is 'undeniably political' as 'it is the place where we *become* our gendered selves'.[91] As a result,

---

[82] S Atkins and B Hale, *Women and the Law* (Institute of Advanced Legal Studies 2018) 2.

[83] C Pateman, 'Feminist Critiques of the Public/Private Dichotomy' in S Benn and G Gaus (eds), *Private and Public in Social Life* (Croon Helm 1983) 281.

[84] Fredman, above n 29, 42.

[85] Pateman, *The Sexual Contract*, above n 80, 156.

[86] This was not reformed until the introduction of the Married Women's Property Act 1964 (see chs 5 and 7).

[87] S Appleton, 'How feminism remade American family law (and how it did not)' in R West and C Bowman, *Research Handbook on Feminist Jurisprudence* (Elgar 2019) 428.

[88] ibid.

[89] SM Okin, *Justice, Gender, and the Family* (Basic Books 1989) 111.

[90] ibid.

[91] ibid.

a non-interventionist approach in law and policy could be seen as equating to a decision to allow these gendered power dynamics to take hold. And, as we shall see throughout this book, this non-interventionist approach is used repeatedly to undermine and withhold support from the MWA's attempts to reform family law. Moreover, when the family is divided into the structured, gendered roles of housewife and breadwinner, practical and psychological barriers are raised against women in *all* other facets of life, married or not.[92]

*

The story of the private, family sphere of the 'domestic' goddess – a domain for women, not men – helped justify and entrench the very policies that *contributed* to their inequality. One important example of this was the family wage. The family wage was an inflated income paid to men, not women, to support a family. If women received allowances directly in support of their children, feminists argued, the family wage could no longer be justifiably paid to men.[93] But instead of paying women workers more, married women were pushed further into the ideal of the housewife, even though many women undertook paid work (and had always done so). The family wage meant that women's financial needs were seen as being less than men's, and so working women were only in need of 'pin money'.[94] Hilary Land has argued that the family wage was part of women being actively *excluded* from the labour market so that men could benefit from the leverage that came with needing to support a family, without having women undercutting them.[95] This argument is especially interesting given that Land also notes that the idea of an individual male bread-winner earning a wage to keep a wife and children was not a familiar one in the nineteenth century.[96] Yet by the twentieth century, economic and social change alongside structural commercial changes cemented the male-headed household and the ideal bourgeois family form of a dependent wife and children.[97] The cult of domesticity, combined with the promotion of marriage as the ultimate goal for women, provided a rationale for women's lower salaries and fewer opportunities in the 'public' sphere.[98] Among lower income families this was especially disastrous for women on relationship breakdown. A husband's salary was not sufficient to support financially his divorced wife and her children as well as a new wife and family if he remarried. And as Lena Jeger argued, paying a family wage to men and not women 'may be all right until a woman is deserted or widowed and suddenly finds that her wage is the family income and that it is

---

[92] ibid.
[93] Fredman, above n 29, 91.
[94] ibid, 74.
[95] H Land, 'The Family Wage' (1980) 6(1) *Feminist Review* 55, 62.
[96] ibid.
[97] ibid.
[98] L Adkins and M Dever, 'Housework, Wages and Money' (2014) 29 *Australian Feminist Studies* 50, 52.

not enough'.[99] Women could do little legally, because no earnings meant no property rights for women on divorce.[100] This was not ameliorated until 1970.[101]

In short, the homemaker/breadwinner dichotomy permeated the law. It also became a fundamental challenge for the MWA, becoming pervasive legally, politically and economically at the very time the Association was being established in the late 1930s. Addressing this entrenched ideal presented a different challenge for feminists who had campaigned for separate property rights and equal suffrage. For some feminists, the strategies of these old campaigns were not working when it came to reforming family law. As Dorothy Stetson has contended:

> The equal rights that married women had achieved over their own property and earnings had little value for those married women who raised children and kept a home and were dependent on their husbands. In other words, family law based on separate-but-equal sex roles in marriage led to economic and financial dependency for most married women who pursued the duties expected of them as wives and mothers.[102]

As the next section explores, some feminists recognised this problem with strict equality, believing that treating men and women the same under law without recognising women's structural oppression would only oppress women further. And so, a different approach was developed, which would become influential to the direction of MWA ideology: 'new feminism'.

III. NEW FEMINISM

Faced with the weight of social expectations, while isolated from the public sphere legally and politically, housewives were exposed to discrimination from all sides. By the 1920s, it was becoming clear to feminists that the legal and social disabilities imposed upon women by marriage served to oppress *all* women. This section traces how these concerns shaped and stimulated new feminist debates, and how this created a 'new' feminism which laid the foundations for MWA policy and direction. Exploring the broader context of feminist debate at this time is crucial, for understanding the MWA's ideas and their place within the women's movement is intrinsic to discovering not just how they sought to reform family law, but *why*.

[99] L Jeger, 'Power in Our Hands' in H Huskins-Hallinan (ed), *In Her Own Right* (Harrap 1968) 154.
[100] D Stetson, *A Woman's Issue: The Politics of Family Law Reform in England* (Oxford University Press 1982) 157.
[101] Matrimonial Proceedings and Property Act 1970, consolidated in the Matrimonial Causes Act 1973.
[102] Stetson, above n 100, 157.

A. The Birth of 'New' Feminism

By 1928, the vote had been won.[103] But for those women who continued to organise, an important decision needed to be made: what next for women's activism in the Western world? MWA member Hazel Huskins-Hallinan argued:

> The revolutionary nature of giving women the vote and the reforms that sprang from it, coupled with the magnitude of the effort expended to win it, contrived to make the success of the project seem, for a while at least, that emancipation itself had been won. But that was not the case. The vote was the beginning.[104]

It seemed there was an assumption that once women had the vote, they could effectively use the ballot box to radically transform women's place in society. This did not happen. It could have been that many pioneers of suffrage were no longer young or able to pursue the militant strategies they had previously relied upon. Some of them did continue in their campaigns, but an organised movement for women's rights was more difficult, as unemployment spread[105] and new, younger leaders with the popular appeal of the suffragettes did not emerge. It was against this backdrop of dwindling women's rights campaigns that ideas of 'new' feminism emerged.

Differences between feminist groups had become more marked by the mid-1920s. These differences were frequently described by historians as being a clash between 'old equal rights' and 'new' feminism.[106] The 'old' strategy was associated with breaking down barriers; reforming laws that said women could not vote like men, that women could not be solicitors or be awarded university degrees like men. 'New' feminism contended when women were treated the same as men in law, the work that women typically did – housework and care work – continued to be undervalued and unrecognised, *because men did not do this work*. New feminism drew attention to this, arguing that women's roles were different yet were of equal value. And by focusing on the family, this new feminist approach unsurprisingly directed more attention to reform of family law.

The figurehead of new feminism was Eleanor Rathbone. Along with the National Union of Societies for Equal Citizenship (NUSEC), of which she was President, her strategies were less centred on eradicating inequalities between men and women, and instead focused on securing 'improvements in the status of wives and mothers'.[107] Rathbone's definition of feminism was different from those advocating equal rights. Instead, her book *The Disinherited Family*[108]

---

[103] Pursuant to the Equal Franchise Act 1928.

[104] H Huskins-Hallinan, 'A Revolution Unfinished' in H Huskins-Hallinan (ed), *In Her Own Right* (Harrap 1968) 12.

[105] See Benjamin and Kochin, above n 48.

[106] Caine, above n 13, 188.

[107] ibid, 187.

[108] E Rathbone, *The Disinherited Family* (Falling Wall Press 1924).

became the starting point for a redefined feminism emphasising the value and support of women in fulfilling their 'peculiar and primary function' as wives and mothers.[109] Where feminists had previously fought to attain legal, political and economic privileges denied to them because of their sex, this new definition instead sought recognition for the work women did as mothers and homemakers. As Barbara Caine saw it, rather than a 'negative clearing way' this was a 'positive demand for fulfilment'.[110]

A 'new' approach to feminist activism was central to Rathbone and her networks. While she did not oppose the push for women's equality with men in terms of pay and the franchise, she believed that focusing purely on equal rights meant 'looking at all our problems through men's eyes and discussing them in men's phraseology'.[111] She articulated these views in a momentous address to NUSEC in 1926, promoting the value of an alternative feminist approach that celebrated women's differences instead of fighting for their sameness with men:

> Hitherto we have contended ourselves with demanding that in the economic sphere women shall be free to attempt the same tasks as men and shall be paid at the same rates *when they are doing men's work*. But under what conditions are they to labour and at what rates are they to be paid when they are doing work which only women can do or for which they have a special fitness?[112]

Rathbone was not a member of the MWA and died in 1946. But the MWA was influenced intellectually by Rathbone. Her comments were important in framing the Association's new direction – how to value the work men did not tend to do, that is, the unpaid work carried out by women in the home. If women were to be equal, Rathbone argued, the work of most women of the 1920s and 1930s needed to be valued in economic terms. 'I want women to build up their *own* status', Rathbone argued.[113] Women entering the legal or medical professions, or a political career, or being awarded university degrees, tended to be middle-class women. But most women did not do these things and were typically economically dependent wives and mothers.[114] Put simply, the removal of legal barriers for women to become doctors and lawyers and to work alongside men did not do much to raise the status of housewives. 'New' feminism was needed for the essential value of housework and care work to be recognised.

In legal terms, Rathbone's tour de force was the Family Allowances Act 1945, passed one year before she died. It was the first time in English law that

---

[109] Caine, above n 13, 187.

[110] ibid, 188.

[111] E Rathbone, 'The Old Feminism and the New', Presidential Address at the Annual Meeting of NUSEC (11 March 1925) in E Rathbone, *Milestones* (Liverpool 1929).

[112] ibid.

[113] The Woman's Leader, 9 March 1923, 44, Women's Rights Collection, LSE Digital Library (emphasis added).

[114] Stetson, above n 100, 112.

welfare was provided to women for the support of children.[115] As well as being a milestone within family law and married women's rights, the rationale of this legislation and the differing opinions surrounding it provides important context for dissentions within the later history of the MWA.

Rathbone began campaigning for family allowances in 1917.[116] In her view, family allowances sent a message that housework and childcare were occupations of social significance and value.[117] Providing benefits in recognition of this work would force the state to acknowledge that women should not have to be like men to qualify for social assistance. Rathbone also argued persuasively that family allowances were an effective form of poverty reduction.[118] Yet she faced staunch resistance, as the Family Allowances Act was not passed until 28 years later.[119] Trade unionists were concerned that the policy would drive down men's wages.[120] And some feminists were opposed too. Millicent Fawcett, who had founded NUSEC (formerly known as the National Union of Women's Suffrage Societies), resigned from the organisation in 1926 because she disagreed with Rathbone's views. For many women of the 'old guard' who had campaigned for the vote, equality was of primary importance, and to them the policy of family allowances overshadowed issues like equal pay and women's right to work.[121] Here, we can see the roots of a debate that continues to challenge questions of reform today: how can we recognise the legal and social importance of caregivers without reinforcing gendered roles and women's exclusion from the public domain?

B. Valuing Women's Work in Law

Many of the issues from the first half of the twentieth century are still being debated.[122] While the specific term 'new feminism' may not be a familiar concept within family law literature, debates about women's equality with, and difference from men have long been discussed. Such debates also uncover an important tension. As we saw in the second part of this chapter, gendered roles in intimate adult relationships have served to exacerbate and reinforce women's

---

[115] For an overview of the feminist significance of this Act, see L Vickers, 'Family Allowances Act 1945' in E Rackley and R Auchmuty (eds), *Women's Legal Landmarks: Celebrating the History of Women and Law in the UK and Ireland* (Hart Publishing 2019).

[116] Fredman, above n 29, 91.

[117] Stetson, above n 100, 113.

[118] A contributing factor to the inclusion of a system of family allowances within the Beveridge Report's package of social reforms published in 1942: Vickers, above n 115, 228.

[119] R Cross, 'The Family Allowances Act, 1945' (1946) 9 *MLR* 284, 284.

[120] Vickers, above n 115, 228.

[121] Stetson, above n 100, 113.

[122] Vickers, above n 115, 231. For a comprehensive discussion of how such debates play out today, see G Douglas, *Obligation and Commitment in Family Law* (Hart Publishing 2018).

subordination both economically and under law. However, recognising women's equality while highlighting their difference from men through the payment of family allowances to mothers was not what triggered the epoch of the 'domestic goddess'. It was how the idea of family allowances was subsequently interpreted by policymakers and legislators.

A notable example of this is the Beveridge report.[123] It recommended family allowances while pointedly marking the private domestic sphere as the domain of married women. It is one thing to demand financial support for homemakers, as the new feminists did. But it is quite another to claim that the stay-at-home wife is the ideal. In effect, Beveridge's recommendations excluded married women from paid work on the same terms of men, and as Anne Barlow notes, cast married women 'in law as dependants of breadwinning men'.[124]

Furthermore, family allowances were originally to be paid to men, not women, and this was only amended following vehement opposition from Rathbone and her networks.[125] The MWA appear to have been influential in this amendment,[126] as Beveridge wrote to the Association stating: 'Until we saw you we had still been talking of benefits to the man with allowances to his wife as a dependant person'.[127] Ultimately, family allowances were not paid directly to fathers, but despite this, the Beveridge report and subsequent welfare reforms are still seen as responsible for raising the status of the housewife in a way that was not necessarily helpful to women's participation in the public sphere, because women were encouraged to stay at home and procreate.[128]

This was disappointing for those feminists who saw recognition of women's unpaid work as a means of challenging the family wage. And it was not what Rathbone and the 'new' feminists had sought. Instead, their campaign for family allowances had been part of a broader feminist agenda to provide married women with financial control.[129] For as we have seen, just as the unity of husband and wife continued to influence the legal status of married women, strict separation of property following the MWPA 1882 meant wives had no

---

[123] W Beveridge et al, *Social Insurance and Allied Services* (The Beveridge Report) (Cmd 6404, 1942).

[124] A Barlow, 'Configuration(s) of Unpaid Caregiving within Current Legal Discourse In and Around the Family' (2007) 58 *Northern Ireland Legal Quarterly* 251, 251.

[125] Vickers, above n 115, 230.

[126] The MWA held mass meetings with other organisations and made deputations to the House of Commons. 5MWA/2/1, TWL.

[127] MWA Annual Report 1942–1943, 7TBG/1/32, TWL. The report also states: 'The contribution of the Married Women's Association to my [Beveridge's] report is from para 107, p49'.

[128] As Blackford notes, procreation was also a concern of the Royal Commission on Population: C Blackford, 'Wives and Citizens and Watchdogs of Equality: Post-War British Feminists' in J Fyrth (ed), *Labour's Promised Land: Culture and Society in Labour Britain 1945–51* (Lawrence & Wishart 1995) 61. Worse still, when family allowances were introduced after Rathbone's 28-year campaign it was not, according to Fredman, motivated so much by 'the recognition of the importance of economic independence for women working in the home, but a desire to keep down male wage demands, and therefore to stem inflation'. Fredman, above n 29, 92.

[129] Vickers, above n 115, 227.

legal right to their husband's property. And so aside from any individual income they might have earned in addition to their domestic labour, they depended upon their husbands for access to funds. Family allowances, according to Rathbone and her proponents, could provide women with a greater degree of financial independence than they would otherwise have had. Recognising women's work in the home was not, as Vickers put it, 'part of a return to hearth and home rhetoric'[130] but was instead based on Rathbone's first-hand knowledge of the harsh realities of life for most working-class women. It was this thinking that influenced the MWA.

IV. THE MARRIED WOMEN'S ASSOCIATION: A SUB-COMMITTEE OF THE SIX POINT GROUP

The story of the MWA began with the Six Point Group (SPG). The SPG met for the first time on 17 September 1921 as a pressure group to work on six points that could be achieved by women with the vote at that time.[131] If, after a hard-fought campaign, one of the Group's six points was achieved, another issue replaced it, and so collectively the Group chipped away at barriers that obstructed women's equality.[132] One of these barriers was the legal and financial oppression of the housewife. In later years these objectives became broader in scope, with the Group aiming for 'equality in economic, legal, moral, social occupational as well as the political spheres of life'.[133]

It was SPG leader Dorothy Evans' idea to create the MWA. Evans was a former militant suffragette with strongly held feminist views. She had been imprisoned a number of times,[134] took part in hunger and thirst strikes and suffered force feeding.[135] Evans also co-organised the aforementioned BOMBS SHOW NO SEX BIAS protest in Trafalgar Square. Though not a lawyer, she had a profound understanding of the law[136] and was a driving force behind the creation of the MWA as a legal pressure group to reform married women's property rights.

---

[130] ibid, 229.

[131] Pursuant to the Representation of the People Act 1918, women with the vote at this time were over 30 with the necessary property qualifications.

[132] The first six points were: equal pay for teachers; equal pay in the civil service; satisfactory legislation on child assault; satisfactory legislation for the widowed mother; satisfactory legislation for the unmarried mother and her child; and equal guardianship of children. 5SPG/M10, TWL.

[133] ibid.

[134] Including for a foiled attempt to bomb Lisburn castle in the north of Ireland in 1913.

[135] C Blackford, 'Dorothy Evans (1888–1944)' in *Oxford Dictionary of National Biography* (Oxford University Press 2004), available at: https://doi.org/10.1093/ref:odnb/63844.

[136] According to lawyer Michael Summerskill, Unpublished Biography of Edith Summerskill, SUMMERSKILL/7, TWL.

The connection between Evans and the MWA, with its focus on housewives and the domestic sphere, might appear surprising at first. This is because Evans was personally opposed to marriage.[137] She had been in a long-term relationship with Fabian Society treasurer Emil Davies and had a child with him, but they never married and she subsequently formed a long-term lesbian relationship with feminist and fellow SPG member Sybil Morrison.[138]

Nevertheless, Evans was convinced that feminists needed to focus on the legal position of married women to further the emancipation of all women. And so, as Blackford put it: 'through her concern for the welfare of married women and housewives, [she believed] that feminist groups should shift their focus of concern to married women's position in the home'.[139] By the mid-1930s, SPG meetings had become increasingly turbulent[140] with members' anger triggered by the status of women and their lack of legal rights. And as their meeting records show, the rights of married women became an important point of discussion.[141]

In a report of an SPG meeting dated 15 February 1937 it was noted that 'Miss Evans is in touch with Mrs Littlejohn and they are collaborating in the formation of a report on the "Housewife" for the League of Nations'.[142] At this time Mrs Littlejohn – Linda Littlejohn – was President of a group called Equal Rights International which had been founded by SPG members to pressurise the League of Nations into passing an Equal Rights Treaty.[143] Two months later Dorothy Evans and Linda Littlejohn reported that the sub-committee on rights of the housewife had agreed the following:

> That a wife who manages the family home ought to have a legal claim on half her husband's income, collectible from the source of that income, ie his employer, etc where necessary. That both husband and wife should be jointly liable for the domestic expenses and that for this purpose any income earned or possessed by the wife should be regarded as part of the domestic fund.[144]

These two sentences encapsulate the direction of legal reform promulgated by the MWA. A wife working in and managing the home should have such work

---

[137] M Whately, 'Dorothy Evans: The Story of a Militant' in C Madden (ed), *Dorothy Evans and the Six Point Group* (Published by Claire Madden for the Six Point Group 1945). Whately, who was a friend and colleague of Evans, also noted that it was 'typical' of Evans to devote the last years of her life to support for the housewife in spite of her views on marriage.

[138] Blackford, 'Wives and Citizens and Watchdogs of Equality', above n 128.

[139] ibid.

[140] R Gorb, 'Wives' Unequal Battle' *Hampstead and Highgate Express* (11 July 1986).

[141] SPG Executive Minutes, 19 April 1937, 5SPG/A10/18, TWL.

[142] SPG Executive Minutes, 15 February 1937, 5SPG/A10/18, TWL.

[143] Founded in 1930, Equal Rights International was established as women's activism in the West moved from suffrage to campaigning more broadly for equality with men. In addition to Linda Littlejohn, the group, which was based in Geneva, included Vera Brittain and other prominent feminist figures of the day. 5ERI, TWL.

[144] SPG Executive Minutes, 15 February 1937, above, n 142.

recognised in financial terms, through rights over half of the income, and joint control over expenses. This related directly to the emergence of new feminism at that time as it demanded recognition of women's work in the home – work men did not do.

A. New Feminism, the SPG and the MWA

Given Evans' and Littlejohn's demands for housewives, it may seem surprising that the SPG is typically associated with 'old' feminism.[145] But the boundaries between old and new feminist ideas were often unclear. In outlining the differences between old and new feminism, typically associated with the well-trodden debates about equality and difference feminism, it is therefore important not to oversimplify the extent to which such viewpoints are opposed. Certainly, 'old' and 'new' feminist demands for legal reform came from disparate ideological starting points, with, on the one hand, the 'old' aim to *remove* disabilities in law so women's rights could be equal to men's, versus the 'new' aim to *augment* wives' legal status in recognition of their value *separate from* men. But these different aims could lead to the same demands in legal terms.[146]

No group complicated and blurred these divisions better than the MWA, which blended old with new by virtue of both its membership and ideas. This is in part because of the influence of Dorothy Evans. As Blackford has argued, Evans was one of the 'few feminists able to bridge the generation gap between older women, like herself, who had been involved in the suffrage struggle, and younger women who had come into politics during the 1930s and 1940s'.[147] As later chapters will show, she was also the mastermind of the first draft of the MWA's Bill for equal partnership in marriage; the group's most ambitious and revolutionary programme of family law reform. As a result, looking closer at MWA politics challenges assumptions that divisions between old and new feminism were clearly drawn, suggesting instead that as Beaumont and others have also argued, such divisions might previously have been overstated.[148]

This is not to say the tensions between old and new were insignificant. In fact, they were arguably responsible for the public altercation and fragmentation of the MWA in 1952, which later chapters will explore further. And these differences might also be why the MWA was never again amalgamated with the

---

[145] C Beaumont, 'Citizens not feminists: the boundary negotiated between citizenship and feminism by mainstream women's organisations in England, 1928–39' (2000) 9 *Women's History Review* 411, 413.

[146] One example of this is the activism surrounding the Married Women (Restraint Upon Anticipation) Act 1949, which Auchmuty credits both Lady Rhondda (SPG founder and a leader of 'old' equal rights feminism) and Rathbone's 'new' feminist NUSEC as having driven forward. Auchmuty, 'Married Women (Restraint Upon Anticipation) Act 1949', above n 37, 244.

[147] Blackford, 'Wives and Citizens and Watchdogs of Equality', above n 128.

[148] Beaumont, 'Citizens not feminists', above n 145; see also Caine, above n 13.

SPG after it became independent from it, in spite of the efforts of some of its members.[149] When understanding how the MWA sought to translate its feminist ambitions into law, it is important to interrogate both how the MWA brought these old and new feminist aims together, and how its unsuccessful attempts to reconcile these same aims tore it apart.

CONCLUSION

Given the history of coverture and its after-effects, it is not an exaggeration to conclude that law is responsible – at least in part – for creating a married woman's dependence upon her husband.[150] Indeed, coverture provides a back-drop for many legal inequalities the MWA sought to eradicate. When husbands' control of wives' property was replaced by strict separation of property that was blind to the socio-economic experiences of housewives, women's subservience in marriage was reinforced once again. Even when driven out with a pitchfork, to borrow Kahn-Freund's expression,[151] injustice on gendered lines can come back. Feminists of the 1920s and 1930s realised that recognising the plight of housewives required a *new* language of equality, that did not insist on women and men's sameness.

For some men, the pendulum had swung too far in favour of women's rights.[152] And so there was a perception that with suffrage and separate property rights, the need for feminism had disappeared. Yet the reality for most married women was very different from this portrayal of women's privilege over men. Just as suffrage only represented the beginning of political and civic emancipation for women, the 1882 Act had not made wives legal and economic equals of their husbands.

Even after the MWPAs, married women still faced the pernicious effects of the concept of spousal unity for some time. In addition to this, the harsh edges of separate property made things worse, as the law purported to treat women and men as economic equals when the reality for married women was very different. As we will see, addressing these issues through legal reform later led to problems for the MWA. Those in the MWA who identified with 'old' feminism and who believed in women being treated *the same* as men tended to define equality differently from those 'new' feminists of the Association who believed equality lay in acknowledging the differences between the sexes. These ideological differences had practical consequences for the direction of MWA policy. Recognising the need for married women to own property independently from their husbands, while calling for the law to mitigate the injustice that could

---

[149] Ch 3 outlines Teresa Billington-Greig's attempts to amalgamate the MWA and the SPG.
[150] F Batlan, 'Engendering Legal History' (2005) 30 *Law & Social Inquiry* 823, 833.
[151] Kahn-Freund, 'Inconsistencies and Injustices in the Law of Husband and Wife', above n 33, 136.
[152] Smart, above n 59, 29.

result from a stringent application of separate property, became a complicated and divisive problem.

Yet as this chapter has argued, the experiences of housewives indicated an urgent need for reform. Dorothy Evans founded what became the MWA to address this; to lift the veil on the private sphere and to begin to politicise the relationship between husband and wife.[153] When exploring the foundations of this SPG sub-committee (and by extension the MWA) it is clear it was not based simply upon the idea of a group of married women representing married women. It was part of a broader initiative to recognise and combat injustice for *all* women by advocating recognition of the financial value of domestic and reproductive labour. For as Stetson has argued, under English custom 'all women [were] wives, potential wives or former wives'.[154] Thus, laws defining the status of married women would affect opportunities for all women, albeit in different ways, and depending on class, race and personal circumstance. To Evans, this was clear. Though she never married, Evans saw that the law had failed married women, and that something needed to be done. As the SPG was concerned with a broad range of concerns for women outside marriage, it was decided that someone else was needed to chair the new SPG sub-group for the housewife. Luckily, Evans had spotted the organisational potential of someone she deemed ideal for the role – Juanita Frances.

[153] Blackford, 'Ideas, Structures and Practices of Feminism 1939–64', above n 14, 63.
[154] Stetson, above n 100, 3.

Interlude: Juanita Frances

J UANITA FRANCES WAS a young, outgoing, married woman when she was recruited by Dorothy Evans to lead the Married Women's Association (MWA), taking forward the Six Point Group (SPG) policy to promote the status of the housewife.[1] Known by her maiden name 'Frances' or 'Miss Frances' to her friends and feminist networks (but never by her married name Mrs Schlesinger), the political climate affecting married women is woven into Juanita Frances' story. Her professional career began first as a nurse in Australia, and she then moved to London in the late 1920s. In London, Frances had jobs as a nurse, a burlesque dancer[2] and a conjuror's assistant[3] before having to give up work to get married in 1934.[4] Now Frances could vote, her husband Gerald Schlesinger – a banker working opposite the Stock Exchange – advised her to choose the Conservative Party because he viewed it as being good for business.[5] Frustrated with her husband's advice on how to vote and keen to learn more about politics, Frances was desperate for any and all opportunities for a political education. Although she would later describe her political views as socialist,[6] she accepted an invitation from a friend to attend a meeting of fascists near London's Rutland Gate,[7] which she concealed from her Jewish husband: 'I didn't want to upset him', she said.[8] Yet it was her decision to 'skip down there to watch … all the young of Chelsea … have a punch-up'[9] that led to her introduction to prominent suffragette Flora Drummond.[10]

Frances was told that Drummond was looking for people like her to assist with the Women's Guild of Empire and to run a branch for impoverished women in the economically deprived area of North Kensington. But Frances had not

---

[1] C Blackford, 'Ideas, Structures and Practices of Feminism 1939–64' (PhD thesis, University of East London 1996) 89.

[2] In the back row of the chorus in a show produced by Jack Hulbert: R Gorb, 'Wives' Unequal Battle' *Hampstead and Highgate Express* (11 July 1986).

[3] Specifically, a decorative assistant to a telepathy act at the Coliseum, ibid.

[4] C Blackford, 'Juanita Frances (1901–1992)' in *Oxford Dictionary of National Biography* (Oxford University Press 2004), available at: https://doi.org/10.1093/ref:odnb/63847.

[5] Michael Summerskill interview with Juanita Frances, SUMMERSKILL/1/46, TWL.

[6] Gorb, above n 2.

[7] It is not clear from Juanita Frances' account which group this was.

[8] Summerskill interview with Juanita Frances, above n 5.

[9] ibid.

[10] Drummond had formerly been an organiser of the Women's Social and Political Union, and as part of her fight for women's suffrage she was imprisoned nine times, enduring hunger strikes and force feeding.

found a political home with the Women's Guild of Empire[11] either, for she was concerned that it was right-wing and 'anti-Labour party'.[12] Drummond asked Frances to resign when she refused to join her platform. Yet only days before this conversation, Frances had a path-changing experience.

It happened when she was sent by Drummond to represent the Women's Guild of Empire at the British Commonwealth League[13] (an international feminist organisation). Frances recalled sitting 'with my mouth open'[14] at the event, thinking: 'Hell … how have I missed this all my life? I came bang into the feminist movement and it amazed me'.[15] She watched as the speakers 'agitat[ed] against men' while deploring 'how men treat women'. It was here that Frances met 'a very vivacious woman' named Linda Littlejohn – the very same who had, with Dorothy Evans, just established an SPG sub-group focusing on the rights of married women. Frances credits Littlejohn with bringing her 'into the feminist world'. 'She was quite an inspiration', Frances said.[16]

Frances felt the need to introduce herself to Littlejohn: 'Hello, I'm an Australian also'.[17] Frances recounts them walking together and that by the time they reached Littlejohn's flat, 'she'd asked me could I be one of her secretaries to the Equal Rights International' (ERI) 'and I said "I've never been secretary of anything"'.[18] Littlejohn told Frances: 'I'll train you'. In the early stages of her involvement in feminist activism, Frances worked with ERI in Geneva to advocate equal treatment for women and to get League of Nations members to adopt an Equal Rights treaty that would address laws discriminating against women internationally, including equal pay.[19]

On one of these trips to Geneva for an International Labour Organisation meeting, Frances met Dorothy Evans and SPG colleague Monica Whately. This meeting was a turning point for Frances. She was invited to join the Executive Committee of the SPG and to lead their group for housewives, which became the MWA. This development was made official in the SPG minutes of 15 November 1937, where it was noted that Frances would become 'Chairman' – a term historically applied to both women and men – 'so as to bring in some new workers'.[20]

---

[11] An organisation that sought to oppose strikes and Communism: M Pugh, *Women and the Women's Movement in Britain since 1914*, 3rd edn (Palgrave 2015) 47.

[12] Summerskill interview with Juanita Frances, above n 5. Frances was dedicated to cross-party politics but was personally more affiliated to the Labour Party: Blackford, 'Juanita Frances (1901–1992)', above n 4.

[13] Now known as the Commonwealth Countries League.

[14] Summerskill interview with Juanita Frances, above n 5.

[15] Gorb, above n 2.

[16] Summerskill interview with Juanita Frances, above n 5. Littlejohn died shortly after the Second World War.

[17] ibid.

[18] ibid.

[19] Throughout most of the 1930s, this lobbying produced little success and appears to have been wound up some time around 1940. See 5ERI, TWL.

[20] 5SPG/A10/18, TWL.

By the time this had become Frances' occupation, the Second World War was imminent and she had two children to care for, but she went from strength to strength in her new leadership role. As for her husband, they divorced in 1948: 'He was old-fashioned and conservative, and I was too much for him. Now, in my dotage, I'm sorry for him; I think I ill-treated him intellectually'.[21]

Frances did not like being under the control of the SPG. This was, in part, because of a clash of personalities between Frances and Whately, who was described by Frances as 'a flamboyant person', often wearing a flowing black cloak.[22] Her dominant influence over Frances' work caused friction, to the point that Frances made a decision: 'I thought, well that won't do ... So, I made an appointment to see Dorothy Evans and said: "I've drawn up a constitution and I think I would like a separate organisation"'.[23] The SPG Committee, less surprised than Frances expected them to be, accepted the plans.[24] Only one month after its inception, the MWA separated from the SPG.[25] 'What a cheek', Frances said, when explaining her actions years later in an interview. 'Here I am, a complete novice, and these experienced feminists, I've taken it completely out of their hands'.[26]

But this move by Frances was what marked the beginning of the MWA as a separate autonomous organisation with a distinctive ideology and a new plan to reform the law of marriage. She might have considered herself to be a novice, but her dogged personality was clear in this push for independence. Though Frances explained her decision as being due to tensions with Monica Whately, historians such as Catherine Blackford considered her motivations to be pragmatic.[27] Dorothy Evans could see the importance of reforming structures that could improve the welfare of married women, but Blackford notes that many *other* prominent SPG members were much less enthusiastic about this cause. In an interview with Gillian Elinor, Frances recalled that before the MWA became independent these SPG members made comments in meetings about 'women who were stupid enough to get married'.[28] And so, the MWA would only be able to effectively develop and expand its work among married women if it maintained a distance from these predominantly equal rights feminists, who did not necessarily agree with the ideas of 'new feminism' beginning to gain prominence.[29] The Association needed a membership that would not be hostile to marriage, seeking instead to reform its unequal structures through law.

---

[21] Gorb, above n 2.

[22] Summerskill interview with Juanita Frances, above n 5.

[23] ibid.

[24] ibid.

[25] G Elinor, An Outline of the Early Years of the MWA 1938–1950, October 1988, 5MWA/9/1, TWL.

[26] Above n 5.

[27] C Blackford, 'Wives and Citizens and Watchdogs of Equality: Post-War British Feminists' in J Fyrth (ed), *Labour's Promised Land: Culture and Society in Labour Britain 1945–51* (Lawrence & Wishart, 1995) 60.

[28] Blackford, 'Ideas, Structures and Practices of Feminism 1939–64', above n 1, 88.

[29] Blackford, 'Wives and Citizens and Watchdogs of Equality', above n 27, 60.

3

A Composite Portrait

I am very interested to see in the newspapers that the Married Women's Association is demanding amendments to the law to give a fair share to wives. I agree with your statement that it will end a very great injustice to women. Alone, women are helpless. We must all join the MWA!

S Henderson South Devon[1]

I do so wish I could be more active for the Association, and would be if it were in my power, but at present I find all my time and energy taken up by looking after my house, two small children, a big garden etc single-handed … I find that I work almost until bedtime on most days and even so, it is difficult to find time enough for gardening, cleaning of windows, etc. Although I would love to have more children … I cannot face the utter drudgery and complete giving up of one's personal interests and recreation that having more than two children would mean … It would be almost too good to be true to have one or two afternoons a week free in which to do work for the Association or pursue one's personal hobbies … All this is not meant as a grumble, merely an explanation.

I N-J Northants.[2]

The Married Women's Association Meeting At Bloomsbury In London, 29 April 1939 (Credit: ANL/Shutterstock)

[1] *Wife and Citizen*, August 1947, 7TBG/1/32, TWL.
[2] MWA Newsletter (undated), 7TBG/1/32, TWL.

INTRODUCTION

S EVERAL MEMBERS OF the Married Women's Association (MWA) were prominent figures in their day and have left pieces of their stories for historians to find. There are autobiographies, notes for speeches and reams of papers now secured in the archives. These documents provide important insights into MWA members' personalities and beliefs. We know, for example, that MWA founder and Chairman Juanita Frances credits *The Cause* by suffragette Ray Strachey[3] for helping educate her about the women's movement.[4] In it, Strachey tells of valiant individuals leading a series of successful campaigns to forge the path to women's suffrage and emancipation. The women in *The Cause* are united, and the story, as historian Rosalind Delmar has put it, 'is one of trials, vicissitudes, but eventual success'.[5] Yet while Strachey's book inspired Frances and is still considered to be a major work of the women's movement,[6] it is important that this book does not fall into the same trap of *The Cause*'s 'heroine narrative'.[7] Stories of anti-climax and defeat rectify misleading, evolutionary narratives of progress.[8] Indeed, as this chapter will argue, an accurate, feminist biography of the MWA must not simply focus on its achievements or most famous members. Unless we explore the MWA's ideological tensions and practical struggles, we cannot understand the MWA. It is unavoidable that we know more about the members who left the most paperwork behind, with family members willing to preserve these records after their death. Thus, there are glaring holes in what we know about most MWA members. The members we know best were not necessarily the people most deeply involved in the MWA, nor were they always the longest serving members. While these gaps are not filled by this book, being mindful of them has shaped the study on which this book is based.

This chapter presents a composite portrait of women and men involved in the MWA using a combination of archival sources and new interview material, which has helped glean new information about the personalities of members we only get glimpses of in the archives. For as Rebecca Probert has argued, the personalities of reformers 'may also be as important as principles in ensuring reform, from the high-profile advocates of reform to the less well-known members of committees and those toiling backstage'.[9] A closer look at the

---

[3] R Strachey, *The Cause: A Short History of the Women's Movement in Great Britain* (Bell 1928).

[4] Brian Harrison interview with Juanita Frances, 14 November 1974, 8SUF/B/022, TWL.

[5] R Delmar, 'What is Feminism?' in J Mitchell and A Oakley (eds), *What is Feminism?* (Blackwell 1986) 23.

[6] However, as Barbara Caine put it, Strachey's approach to the women's movement is 'no longer accepted as appropriate by historians of feminism': B Caine, 'Feminist biography and feminist history' (1994) 3 *Women's History Review* 247, 249.

[7] E Rackley and R Auchmuty, 'The case for feminist legal history' (2020) 40 *Oxford Journal of Legal Studies* 878, 897.

[8] Delmar, above n 5.

[9] R Probert, 'The History of 20th-Century Family Law' (2005) 25 *Oxford Journal of Legal Studies* 169, 177.

MWA's membership reveals a group comprised of members that could be obstinate and overbearing, and others who were reserved, yet radical in their beliefs. This portrait also reveals more about how these women and men decided to become family law reformers, and how they were influenced both by the 'old' feminism of the Six Point Group (SPG) and the 'new' feminism of Eleanor Rathbone and others, as we saw in the previous chapter.

I. A NOTE ABOUT BIOGRAPHY

While this book aims throughout to use feminist legal history and the story of the MWA to revise and challenge dominant historical narratives of family law, this chapter in particular emphasises the importance of uncovering the lives of MWA members as part of this book's biographical approach.[10] A variety of different and interconnected approaches and terminologies can be employed when writing the biography of an organisation, and in this chapter, relevant approaches include 'collective biography', 'group biography' and feminist perspectives on biography.

A. Collective Biography

Collective biography presents the life stories of individuals within one publication.[11] It is an ostensibly useful approach when exploring the work of the MWA, as investigating the lived experiences and subjective perceptions of a collective group of individuals can provide a fresh outlook on historical developments.[12] In using this approach, however, it is important to be specific about its scope. According to Krista Cowman, there is imprecision surrounding the definition of collective biography, and so constructing and explaining the methodology of the term here arguably presents some challenges.[13] It is more than just the study of a collection of individuals and is conceptually distinct from prosopography, which investigates the common characteristics of a group of individuals by studying their lives collectively. Rather, Cowman's explanation suggests that a collective biographical approach requires a more subjective assessment of the *individual* lives within that group, their personalities and how their backgrounds affected the work they did.

---

[10] See R Auchmuty, 'Recovering Lost Lives: Researching Women in Legal History (2015) 42 *Journal of Law and Society* 34.

[11] See GDH Cole, *Chartist Portraits* (Macmillan 1941) and B Harrison, *Prudent Revolutionaries: Portraits of British Feminists Between the Wars* (Oxford University Press 1987) for examples of historians who have employed this method.

[12] K Cowman, 'Collective Biography' in S Gunn and L Faire, *Research Methods for History*, 2nd edn (Edinburgh University Press 2016) 86.

[13] ibid, 86.

B. Group Biography

The method employed in this chapter is best described as 'group biography', which is a subset of collective biography in that the individuals studied all belong to the same collective. This method can be used to highlight the inter-actions between the leading personalities of a group and so can provide a rich and subjective analysis of MWA membership, especially when compared with other methods. For instance, Barbara Caine has suggested that prosopography is not in any way aimed at creating a 'better understanding of *individuals* and their motives or their life experiences'.[14] Yet when exploring the MWA's role in family law reform, more information is needed not just about the aims and activities of the group, but about *who* was in the Association too, if its relationship with law is to be better understood. The insight gleaned from this chapter therefore informs the rest of this book, which is focused more on the MWA as a collective of family law reformers, but still requires insight into the people *within* the MWA – especially if the group dynamic, decision-making and conflicts are to make sense.

C. Feminist Perspectives on Group Biography

Group biography is also consistent with the feminist perspectives threaded throughout this book. As we saw in chapter one, following a feminist approach requires widening the scope through which law has traditionally been seen to be reformed, while considering who was demanding change and why. A group biography approach would seem to facilitate this. The approach is also feminist because of the sources it relies upon. As Felice Batlan has argued, looking beyond traditional legal sources allows us to discover new legal actors and to locate how some women 'sought to transform law as part of a broader and potentially radical agenda for social change'.[15] This is especially important in telling the story of the MWA, as they are obscured from traditional legal sources such as parliamentary debates and court judgments almost entirely, even if they had played an important role in drafting the Bill being debated, or the case being decided.[16]

But even archival documents, secondary sources and newspaper articles can only tell us so much about the MWA members. As noted at the start of this book, relying upon the papers generated by the MWA to uncover its story has

---

[14] Cowman, above n 12, 87, citing B Caine, *Biography and History* (Palgrave Macmillan 2010) 58 (emphasis added).

[15] F Batlan, 'Engendering Legal History' (2005) 30 *Law & Social Inquiry* 823, 847.

[16] See also C Smith, 'The Disruptive Power of Legal Biography: The Life of Lord Phillimore – Churchman and Judge' (2020) 41 *Journal of Legal History* 164.

pitfalls; the records are incomplete, and the materials produced for the group's campaigns often appeared to present a one-sided, sometimes misleading view. And so, further details are gleaned from a study of seven interviews with the family and friends of MWA members[17] who were able to provide insights into the lives of those in the Association.[18] This interview data, alongside secondary analysis of interview data produced by Brian Harrison and Michael Summerskill, is brought to the fore in this chapter.[19]

Locating interviewees was not straightforward; most MWA members have died, and their relatives often have different surnames.[20] Hence, even within a small pressure group the number of living relatives that could be located was even smaller. As a result, the new interview data drawn upon here does not purport to provide a representation of all MWA members. But it *has* revealed additional information about members who did not have papers stored in the archives. Interviewees uncovered private papers, an unpublished memoir and short biographies written by relatives.

Finding out more about the women and men of the MWA is worthwhile from a social history point of view, exploring questions such as what it was like to be in a pressure group such as the MWA at that time. But it is important not only for social historians; it matters for feminist legal historians too. As Rosemary Auchmuty argues, asking the right questions of these sources is important, going further than the facts of 'birth, death and a few achievements in between'.[21] Susan Bartie asserts that instead of asking how an individual overcame obstacles, when writing feminist legal history 'the better questions are simply "who was she?" and "what did she do?"'[22] These are the sorts of queries that are important in this book, especially when addressing its central questions, which ask how MWA members influenced family law, and what is to be learned from their strategies. Although interview data and archival details about the Association's members are threaded throughout, this chapter explores

---

[17] Seven interviews with MWA family and friends were carried out from June 2018 to June 2020. I am also indebted to Joey Freeman and Stephen Holden for providing me with access to Doreen Gorsky's private papers, and to Geoff Tann and Kate Steane who provided further additional biographical information about their relatives Nora Bodley, May Carroll and Nina Steane, as well as a letter Carroll wrote about the MWA from her private papers.

[18] Ethics approval and appropriate informed consent was obtained from all interviewees. All interviews were carried out in person except for one interview on Zoom (interviewee was in Australia) and one interview by phone (because of Covid-19 restrictions).

[19] Catherine Blackford also carried out interviews for her PhD thesis. Secondary analysis of this interview data has not been possible, but quotations from these interviews helped me compile the group biography for this chapter. C Blackford, 'Ideas, Structures and Practices of Feminism 1939–64' (PhD thesis, University of East London 1996).

[20] As well as actively contacting interviewees, some interviewees contacted me after encountering the project online. The website www.marriedwomensassociation.co.uk advertised the project on which this book is based.

[21] Auchmuty, above n 10, 42.

[22] S Bartie, 'Studying women legal scholars: the challenges' (2018) 25 *International Journal of the Legal Profession* 279, 284.

in particular how a collection of relatively outgoing, strong and often obstinate personalities came together for a common cause and strategised to achieve it.

II. RADICAL BELIEFS, CONSERVATIVE METHODS?

As we saw in chapter two, the early years of the MWA in the 1940s also saw a shift more generally in feminist politics. This 'new' strand of feminism taken forward by the MWA emphasised the ways in which women were equal to but different from men. It represented the belief that, in Catherine Blackford's words, it was 'no longer necessary for women to use men as yardsticks'.[23] Policies such as the introduction of family allowances underscored the value of childcare work for the first time. This belief in the value of work typically done by women influenced the MWA's calls for equal partnership in marriage, and equal value of the contributions made to the family inside and outside the family household. And these demands made the MWA distinct from other groups of the day as family law reformers.

Yet other historians such as Jill Liddington have sometimes misrepresented demands along these lines as being merely 'within the confines of the domestic sphere, rather than expanding their terrain to include the public sphere'.[24] This narrowly constrained view of new feminism and of MWA policy underplays the significance of the Association's claims. When assessing MWA activity, Blackford debunked the notion that the MWA was simply 'an organisation committed to the promotion and idealisation of marriage and family'.[25] Though she acknowledges that the Association did not challenge the primacy of marriage or the family in women's lives, Blackford's work uncovers precisely why the MWA made an important contribution to feminist debate and broke new ground in this arena. First, by bringing power imbalances to the fore within marriage, the group was politicising the relationship between men and women in the family. In other words, it was politicising the private sphere. When viewed in this way, MWA policy reveals a previously overlooked connection with the later Women's Liberation Movement of the 1960s and 1970s – that the personal is the political. Second, MWA campaigns to elevate married women's status in law were of more relevance to working-class women and/or women without property than the earlier feminist campaigns for married women's property rights. For as chapter two explained, the Married Women's Property Act (MWPA) 1882 dealt an important blow to the oppressive effects of coverture but barely touched women with neither the means nor opportunity to own property independently of their husbands. Put simply, by locating the family as a major site of women's

---

[23] Blackford, 'Ideas, Structures and Practices of Feminism 1939–64', above n 19, 80.

[24] J Liddington, *The Road to Greenham Common: Feminism and Anti-militarism in Britain since 1820* (Syracuse University Press 1991) 173.

[25] Blackford, 'Ideas, Structures and Practices of Feminism 1939–64', above n 19, 63.

oppression, the MWA 'clearly foreshadowed the concerns of post-1960s feminists' typically associated with the 'second wave'.[26]

There is some indication that MWA members viewed their own demands as ground-breaking. The Association's first President Edith Summerskill said if 'married women were afraid to identify themselves with the crusade for family allowances for fear of offending their husbands then there must be millions who would shrink from joining the Married Women's Association'.[27] After all, establishing the legal right of the housewife by giving her a share in the family income during marriage *was* controversial. It departed significantly from the financial consequences of marriage then and now. However, while the MWA's aims for law reform may have been radical, at first glance, its structure and methods were not.

A. Structure and Organisation

The MWA operated in a similar way to older generations of feminists such as the SPG.[28] The Association's structure was based upon a committee system, with a London-based Executive Committee and local branches across England. It grew rapidly from three branches in 1938 to 42 by the 1940s.[29] The MWA even established a branch in New Zealand in 1942.[30] It was non-sectarian, non-party political and encouraged membership across the political spectrum. Membership was open to both women and men, unlike many similar women's organisations and pressure groups at that time.[31] When it was first established as a sub-committee of the SPG it had only three female members but Frances soon drew in membership from outside the SPG, with two men – solicitor Ambrose Appelbe and journalist Joseph Sault – joining and remaining with the Association for many years.[32]

It was a self-financing organisation, relying on money from membership fees, donations and fundraisers. During Executive Committee meetings, reports on the group's activities were read out and resolutions were made regarding policy. A typical resolution denoting general MWA policy was: 'This House resolves that, in order to create and preserve an equal marriage

---

[26] ibid.

[27] *Wife and Citizen*, January 1945, 7TBG/1/32, TWL.

[28] J Freeguard, 'It's Time for Women of the 1950s to Stand Up and Be Counted' (PhD thesis, University of Sussex 2004) 32.

[29] This is based upon Gillian Elinor's outline, which was produced based upon consultation with Nora Bodley in the 1980s. G Elinor, 'An Outline of the Early Years of the MWA 1938–1950', October 1988, 5MWA/9/1, TWL. With gaps in records, this is difficult to verify.

[30] Founded by Dr Mary Morgan. This wound up in 1981: MWA Bulletin April–May 1981, 5MWA/8/1, TWL.

[31] Freeguard, above n 28, 32.

[32] Elinor, 'An Outline of the Early Years of the MWA 1938–1950', above n 29.

partnership, it is necessary to amend the Married Women's Property Act and bring it into line with equal partnership'.[33]

To plan the shape reform would take and to promote legislation drafted by the MWA, regular conferences took place in venues such as Caxton Hall, which had previously hosted suffrage meetings of the Women's Social and Political Union (WSPU) and other historically significant feminist events.[34] Titles of these MWA conferences included: 'A Married Women's Charter',[35] 'The Wife of the Industrial Worker'[36] and 'Wanted: A New World for Wives'.[37] Flyers in the MWA's records indicate the Association continued to hold conferences and debates into the 1960s and 1970s but Frances' account to Brian Harrison suggests these events only happened occasionally after the MWA's first decade:

> In 1948 we stopped having conferences because people just didn't come. You see during the war you would have crowded meetings because there wasn't anything else to go to but then husbands came back from the wars and people started taking up their old life … so they're not in so much need.

Presidents were invited to take up the position by the Association's Committee members, but officials on the Executive Committee were elected by the wider MWA membership. The role of MWA Vice Presidents varied. Some, such as Teresa Billington-Greig, were closely involved in MWA policy, but others appear to have been invited as figureheads and nothing more. As Frances remarked:

> Some Vice Presidents were inaccessible. You see, we would court MPs to put them on our note paper to influence other MPs to look into the status of the married woman. It has a little bit of a snowballing effect.[38]

This strategy had some pitfalls. There were instances of married women contacting MPs listed as MWA Vice Presidents for help, and later complaining that these MPs had failed to mention the MWA, or the help and support the Association could have provided.[39]

Sub-committees were formed. The MWA's first committee was set up for 'propaganda', aiming to help members gain confidence in communicating

---

[33] Letter from Juanita Frances to Teresa Billington-Greig, 9 October 1954, 7TBG/1/32, TWL.

[34] See M Mayall '"No surrender!": the militancy of Mary Leigh, a working-class suffragette' in J Purvis and M Joannou, *The Women's Suffrage Movement: New Feminist Perspectives* (Manchester University Press 1998) 180.

[35] Eleanor Rathbone spoke at this event: Conference programme, 21 March 1942, 5MWA/6/1, TWL.

[36] MWA Annual Report 1953–1954, 7TBG/1/32, TWL.

[37] Several MWA members also took part in a conference on the Feminine Point of View in 1951. A book outlining their discussions and findings was published: O Campbell, *The Feminine Point of View: The Report of a Conference* (Williams & Norgate Ltd 1952).

[38] Harrison interview with Juanita Frances, above n 4.

[39] See, eg, MWA Executive Committee Minutes, April 1965, 5MWA/3/1, TWL, where it was reported that a deserted wife with a daughter suffering from polio wrote to the MPs on the Association's notepaper, and they did not inform her of the existence of the MWA.

MWA policy to the public. A political committee was subsequently established in 1940 aiming to educate women to demand better rights.[40] Then in 1942, a legal committee was formed. It worked with the Executive Committee on draft legislation and advised on the 'numerous unpublished cases' where the MWA gave help.[41]

The Association communicated directly with its members through its own feminist magazines.[42] *Wife and Citizen* – viewed by members as the 'organ of the Association'[43] – was launched in 1945, edited by Frances and sold through WH Smith & Son.[44] This was succeeded by the MWA Newsletter, and later the MWA Bulletin in the 1960s, 1970s and 1980s, which were published more sporadically as membership and resources dwindled. These publications gave the MWA an opportunity to disseminate information to members while ascertaining members' views, whose letters were published in the magazines.

With the aim of marriage law reform, the MWA sought both to pressurise lawmakers and to awaken public opinion to the need for such reform too. Their activities indicated an awareness that pressure was needed from the bottom up if their demands were to be taken seriously. And so in earlier years, when their membership numbers had peaked, the MWA used a range of strategies to mobilise and strengthen support at a grass-roots level. The Association held public meetings, arranged debates and social activities and cooperated with other organisations locally and nationally. It was affiliated to the National Council of Women, Status of Women Committee and British Commonwealth League, which helped strengthen the Association's power base.[45] At the upper echelons, the MWA sent deputations to ministries and lobbied MPs. Luncheons were held at the House of Commons so that politicians and policymakers could participate in discussions about law reform.

Overall, information on MWA membership across all levels is both limited and fragmented[46] but as Blackford has noted, there does appear to have been a noticeable difference in social class between women in local groups, and those working within the MWA as executive members at a national level.[47] This has also created a stumbling block for historians. Studying the lives of the famous and noteworthy personalities of politicians and professionals recruited to the Executive Committee is significantly easier than learning about the working and lower middle-class women involved in the MWA's local branches. Therefore, in

---

[40] Elinor, 'An Outline of the Early Years of the MWA 1938–1950', above n 29.

[41] As Teresa Billington-Greig put it in her personal notes. 7TBG/1/31, TWL.

[42] First, the Hampstead Branch started a 'Journal' in 1940, which became the Journal of the MWA in 1942. Elinor, An Outline of the Early Years of the MWA 1938–1950, above n 29.

[43] *Wife and Citizen*, November 1948, 5MWA/8/2, TWL.

[44] Its first issue noted that MWA membership was two thousand, and subscriptions to *Wife and Citizen* was six thousand. Elinor, 'An Outline of the Early Years of the MWA 1938–1950', above n 29.

[45] Freeguard, above n 28, 32.

[46] As noted by Blackford, 'Ideas, Structures and Practices of Feminism 1939–64', above n 19, 96.

[47] ibid.

the sections that follow there is more focus upon members at the executive level than the local level. Yet finding biographical information for even the leading members of the MWA is still extremely difficult.

III. PORTRAITS OF INDIVIDUAL MEMBERS

Having members of the Executive Committee who were also in positions of power was useful to the MWA when organising and lobbying for reform and orchestrating the group's public relations. The Committee was organised mostly by middle-class, highly educated women and men. As well as Juanita Frances, whom we have already encountered, members also included authors Vera Brittain and Dora Russell, Labour MP Edith Summerskill, barrister Helena Normanton and former suffragette Teresa Billington-Greig. Other members of the MWA leadership who appear regularly in the archives include Doreen Gorsky, Lady Helen Nutting and Ambrose Appelbe. Women such as Nora Bodley were integral to running local branches of the Association. And, when it came to law reform, barrister Roxane Arnold formed an integral part of the MWA's legal sub-committee.

A. Political Connections and Founding Members

In the summer of 1938, Dr Edith Summerskill attended the MWA's first public meeting. Afterwards, Frances wrote to Summerskill asking if she could help the newly formed MWA. Summerskill's son Michael later emphasised the bond between Frances and his mother:

> Over the years I saw the friendship develop, as they constantly consulted each other about meetings, delegations to Ministers, proposals for new laws to protect married women and garden parties to raise funds. They addressed each other by surnames, the relationship seeming rather formal to an outsider. I would see 'Dear Frances' and 'Dear Summerskill' at the beginning of their letters, and at home Edith would talk of seeing 'Frances', never Juanita, and certainly not Mrs Schlesinger. I called her Miss Frances.[48]

Summerskill was an ideal choice for the MWA's first President in 1941. She was a politician and doctor, married to another doctor, Jeffrey Samuels. Summerskill had been elected in a by-election earlier that year as Labour MP for Fulham West[49] – previously a Tory stronghold that had been won with the support of

---

[48] Unpublished Biography of Edith Summerskill, SUMMERSKILL/7, TWL.
[49] When the Fulham West constituency was abolished for the 1955 general election, Summerskill was returned to the House of Commons as MP for Warrington. She became one of the earliest female life peers in 1961, when she joined the House of Lords.

working-class women.[50] She took the seat in her own name (not her husband's) with some controversy, as she was the first to do so. Her background was not working-class, but she had deep empathy for the plight of others. Her experiences as a doctor and as a doctor's daughter meant she had witnessed such suffering first hand, and she was a founder of the Socialist Medical Association, and a driving force behind the establishment of the National Health Service. In a speech titled 'Why I Am a Socialist' broadcast on radio in 1948 Summerskill told a story about the moment her political views were cemented, when working as a doctor she treated a young mother starving and living in squalor, with her wedding ring tied to her finger with thread to stop it slipping from her shrunken hands.[51] This early speech typified the focus of her work throughout her career, where she was influenced strongly by the experiences of women as she saw them. Summerskill's socialism was inextricably linked to her work in improving the lives of women too.

Summerskill had a record of fighting for women's rights throughout her life. As chapter seven will explore further, she spearheaded the Married Women's Property Act 1964, which gave wives a one-half share of housekeeping savings[52] and the Matrimonial Homes Act 1967, which gave deserted wives the right to occupy the matrimonial home. Like Frances, her activism was underpinned by a belief that the institution of marriage could be strengthened by improving the economic and legal status of married women. They worked together in the early years of the MWA to build links with the labour movement. In London, joint meetings were held with women's sections of the Labour Party, and from the late 1930s Summerskill was closely involved in the preparation of MWA bills and a Housewife's Charter for the Labour Party. And, as Blackford notes, Summerskill was not only able to arrange women's deputations to government ministries, but could give MWA views 'a voice in parliament and consequently a higher public profile'.[53] Getting the Association's issues inside the House of Commons was undeniably essential, for the MWA knew this was where justice happened, and where the structures that oppressed married women could be changed. She was able to do this both by raising issues in the Commons and by sponsoring MWA bills. As a result, to the MWA, Summerskill was 'our god'.[54]

Summerskill's feminism was often dismissed in Parliament by non-feminists. Former Labour Minister of Health Kenneth Robinson saw Summerskill as 'pushing at a door that's already open' and the inequality she spoke of as

---

[50] In the view of SPG member Sybil Morrison, Edith Summerskill was helped enormously by Dorothy Evans, who 'worked *very* hard for Edith' during this election. Morrison told Brian Harrison that Summerskill 'got into Parliament by Dorothy's efforts': Brian Harrison interview with Sybil Morrison, 3 April 1975, 8SUF/B/038, TWL.

[51] E Summerskill, 'Party Political Broadcast: Why I am a Socialist' *The Listener* (8 April 1948) 582.

[52] Summerskill had fought for this reform since the 1940s and put forward provisions to reform the issue of housekeeping savings in the Women's Disabilities Bill 1952.

[53] Blackford, 'Ideas, Structures and Practices of Feminism 1939–64', above n 19, 91.

[54] Gillian Elinor interview with Juanita Frances, August 1989, as cited in Blackford, ibid, 54.

being 'grossly exaggerated'.[55] This reaction might seem unsurprising given that throughout Summerskill's time as an MP, Parliament was, as Paula Bartley put it, 'a male privileged institution dominated by men'.[56] Yet Summerskill's female parliamentary peers often disagreed with her too, believing that her focus on women's issues could perpetuate a stereotype of female politicians that made it more difficult for women to occupy men's territory in Parliament.[57] Labour MP Barbara Castle said she was not her sort of feminist, and that she was 'conscious of her as a very sort of dominating feminist'.[58] Indeed, Castle thought Summerskill's decision not to take her husband's name and for her children to be called Summerskill was 'going too far'.[59] In Summerskill's son's interviews with other politicians and contemporaries of hers, she is described as unwavering yet pragmatic, with a touch of arrogance and shyness,[60] all of which appeared to set her apart from other members of the House. As Castle saw it, she was 'a bit of a loner'.[61]

Some of Summerskill's causes unrelated to women's issues were the subject of satire, such as her campaign for butter to be replaced by margarine as Minister of Food in the 1940s and her later condemnation of the sport of boxing. But she was not a loner in the MWA, and shared personality traits in common with other MWA members; an unwillingness to compromise, stubbornness verging on obstinance, and a strong belief in what was right even in the face of widespread dissent. Her grandson Ben Summerskill described her as follows:

> [S]he tended to just be very single-minded, and see things in quite a binary way. And while that sometimes comes over as confrontational or non-consensual, both in her personal life and publicly, of course sometimes it also helps you get where you need to be, because you have to paint things in quite monochrome colour – you know, if you get too nuanced and apologetic, you don't actually drive forward the political argument you want to prosecute.[62]

*

Summerskill and others had seen that oppression can be invisible to those untouched by it, and that in the minds of many, women had already achieved equality with men. The MWA aimed to change this view that issues relating to women were of concern only to women, and instead promoted the idea that gender discrimination is a problem for everyone.[63] With this in mind,

---

[55] Michael Summerskill interview with Kenneth Robinson, SUMMERSKILL/1/46, TWL.

[56] P Bartley, *Labour Women in Power: Cabinet Ministers in the Twentieth Century* (Palgrave 2019) 7.

[57] M Phillips, *The Divided House: Women at Westminster* (Sidgwick & Jackson 1980) 156.

[58] Michael Summerskill interview with Barbara Castle, SUMMERSKILL/1/46, TWL.

[59] ibid.

[60] Michael Summerskill interview with Michael Stewart, Lord Denning and Suzanne Knowles, SUMMERSKILL/1/46, TWL.

[61] Summerskill interview with Barbara Castle, above n 58.

[62] Author interview with Ben Summerskill, 20 June 2018.

[63] MWA Annual Report 1944, TBG/1/32, TWL.

membership was open to everyone – married, single, divorced and men – because the Association saw the issue of equality in marriage as being of urgent importance for all of society – not just married women. As more men took an interest in their work, the MWA noted it was 'interesting to see how far we have moved on from the days when it was a brave man indeed who raised his voice on behalf of the feminist cause'.[64] Helping to spread this message was founding member and male solicitor Ambrose Appelbe. Divorced from Britain's first female solicitor Carrie Morrison, with whom he continued to run a law firm, Appelbe was committed to elevating the status of women in law. He later told the *Hampstead and Highgate Express* that he joined the MWA because of his experiences working in the East End of London, where he was 'overwhelmed by a sense of injustice': 'Sad tragic stories, such as the woman who came to me in despair because her husband had pawned the baby's cot; she couldn't get it back because it was her husband's property by law'.[65]

According to Appelbe's son Felix, his father 'felt very strongly about people's lack of rights' because 'being a lawyer acting for what I call "really poor people", he could see their plight every day'.[66] Ambrose Appelbe was the son of a missionary and was born in Botswana (at that time, Bechuanaland). He boarded at a 'missionary's school' in Bath and ran away at age 15 to fight in the First World War:

> He didn't know it was near the end of the war, and he said the conditions in the trenches were terrible. One night he had to go over the top … and all hell was let loose. The entire sky was lit up with bullets, and bombs, and god knows what. And he dived down into a cesspit and hung around till dawn just saving his life, basically, until an old Sergeant Major stumbled over him and said, 'What are you doing down there, son?' And … he said that was the end of the war. Two of his friends were killed and one had his fingers shot off – and my father was very lucky.[67]

After this experience, Appelbe became a pacifist, and went on to provide legal representation for prominent conscientious objectors such as Bertrand Russell, who had been married to another leading MWA member and pacifist – Dora Russell. He briefly pursued a political career, standing unsuccessfully as a Labour candidate for Frinton-on-Sea; 'the most conservative place you've ever met' according to his son.[68] Appelbe started his own law practice in London in 1923.[69] 'He had no money and he would do anything, any [area of] law', his son said.[70] Appelbe also lived and worked at the charitable

---

[64] MWA Newsletter, December 1959, TBG/1/33, TWL.

[65] R Gorb, 'Wives' Unequal Battle' *Hampstead and Highgate Express* (11 July 1986).

[66] Author interview with Felix Appelbe, 13 February 2019.

[67] ibid.

[68] ibid.

[69] Before this, Appelbe's first job as a solicitor 'was pretty boring and upsetting' according to his son, because he represented banks in cases where people had defaulted on their mortgages and 'his job was to kick people out of their homes'. ibid.

[70] ibid.

institution Toynbee Hall in London's East End, as part of the institution's Poor Man's Lawyer Service. The Prince of Wales shadowed Appelbe working at Toynbee Hall for three weeks because he wanted 'to hear what was being said by ordinary people'.[71]

Appelbe did not always conform to the Establishment and some of his causes were viewed as 'eccentric'.[72] For instance, he founded the Smell Society along with George Bernard Shaw[73] and HG Wells which sought to eliminate foul odours, while aiming to create new words to describe smells such as roast turkey, mimosa and tar. Appelbe was a sartorial man with an idiosyncratic style, wearing flamboyant bow ties and floral buttonholes plucked from his garden.[74] As a solicitor, his clients included Casablanca actress Ingrid Bergman and Mandy Rice-Davies, whom he guided through the infamous Profumo affair. But he also gave legal advice to poverty stricken MWA members who could not otherwise afford legal advice to navigate their limited legal rights. As his son put it: 'I think he felt deeply that women needed a better lot'.[75]

In this sense, being 'up against the Establishment',[76] often meant representing women who could not afford his local rates, and Appelbe needed to 'think outside the box'[77] in order to assist as many women as possible. His son recalled that Appelbe 'acted for a lot of women in divorces' and could do so cheaply and simply by having divorce petitions pre-printed with blank spaces left for the clients' personal details. When one of these pre-printed petitions was produced in court, the judge 'looked down his nose and said, "I want to see the solicitor who's done this! It's appalling! ... It's ruining the sanctity of marriage!"' On recounting this story about his father, Felix Appelbe, who also became a lawyer, reflected upon legal procedure today: 'How funny that I mention the pre-printed divorce petition ... What [my father is] asking for is something that people view as being important and the norm now, but back then it absolutely was not'.[78] In his son's words, he was 'a maverick'.[79]

This innovative thinking is also evident in Appelbe's work within the MWA. As well as drafting its constitution,[80] he founded and chaired the MWA's Legal Committee,[81] which provided legal advice and updated the Association on legal

---

[71] ibid.

[72] 'Obituary: Ambrose Appelbe' *Daily Telegraph* (20 March 1999).

[73] According to Appelbe's son Felix, he met Bernard Shaw at a summer school and wrote to him asking if he would become President of the Smell Society. Bernard Shaw wrote his reply on the back of Appelbe's letter: 'Delighted to become the President of Stink Society'. Author interview with Felix Appelbe, above n 66.

[74] 'Obituary: Ambrose Appelbe', above n 72.

[75] Author interview with Felix Appelbe, above n 66.

[76] ibid.

[77] ibid.

[78] ibid.

[79] ibid.

[80] ibid. Harrison interview with Juanita Frances, above n 4.

[81] Appelbe was also Vice-Chairman of MWA, taking over briefly as Chairman in 1952 (replaced by Elizabeth Pomeroy only weeks later).

developments, such as recent cases. This opened up the need for more legal expertise within the Association.

B. Other Lawyers in the MWA

Appelbe was not the only leading member of the MWA with legal expertise. In later years, the MWA was to have as its Presidents barristers Helena Normanton and Betty Knightly. Normanton is better known than Knightly. She was the second woman called to the Bar and the first to practise as a barrister. Her papers in the archives record a colourful life of activism and legal work, while her biographer Judith Bourne has published a detailed and revealing portrait of her life.[82] Like Summerskill, after marriage Normanton insisted upon keeping the name she was born with, and was the first married woman to hold a passport in her own name.[83] She joined the MWA in later life, having taken over as MWA President following her retirement in 1951. Though she was not President of the Association for long,[84] she made a significant impact, reversing major MWA policies and railing against long-standing views held by the group. Normanton's niece Elsie Cannon described 'life near her' as on occasion 'like having a volcano as a neighbour'.[85] As chapter six explores in greater detail, her resignation in 1952 was followed by the dramatic departure of the MWA's leading Executive Committee officers, which received substantial media attention. As we shall see, however, she was not the only obstinate personality who ran the Association in an apparently undemocratic manner.

In contrast to Normanton, finding biographical evidence about barrister Betty Knightly is extremely difficult.[86] She was one of nine children, married twice and had four children of her own.[87] In addition to her legal career special-ising in family law, she ran unsuccessfully as a Conservative Party candidate.[88]

Knightly was featured as MWA President several times in national newspa-pers throughout the late 1960s and 1970s. In the *Daily Mail*, she was described

[82] J Bourne, *Helena Normanton and the Opening of the Bar to Women* (Waterside Press 2016).

[83] ibid, 164.

[84] The date when Normanton officially joined the MWA does not appear to be in the Association's files, but in an MWA meeting in 1952 following Normanton's departure, Dora Russell claims Normanton had only been a member for 'three months': Report of MWA special meeting, 1 April 1952, 5MWA/3/1, TWL. Note, however, that Normanton is pictured second from left in the above photo of a 1939 MWA meeting.

[85] J Workman, 'Normanton, Helena Florence (1882–1957)' in *Oxford Dictionary of National Biography* (Oxford University Press 2004), available at: https://doi-org.abc.cardiff.ac.uk/10.1093/ref:odnb/39091.

[86] Betty Knightly was called to the Bar in 1951 and was a member of Gray's Inn.

[87] C Thomson, 'Interview with Betty Knightly, Conservative Parliamentary Candidate, *Sunday Telegraph* (20 August 1978), reprinted in MWA Bulletin 1978, 5MWA/8/1, TWL.

[88] ibid.

in sexist terms:[89] 'Mrs Knightly is a tall, slim woman of 49 – "I don't mind who knows it" – with a lot of charm, excellent legs and the kind of figure dress designers dream of'.[90] The reporter added: 'to put it at its lowest she doesn't look like the stereotype feminist'. Descriptions in the *Sunday Telegraph* were not much better, where she is described as 'tall, angular in the style of Virginia Woolf, she wears bright lipstick and whirls through the Temple and the law courts like a begowned, benevolent dervish'.[91] There is no information about the length of Knightly's MWA presidency in these reports. However, like Helena Normanton Knightly also appeared to contradict MWA policy. In 1973, she was described in the *Daily Express* as being 'against maintenance [on divorce] (except for the mothers of young children)', believing it was 'degrading'.[92] The Association's long-standing view was that the need for maintenance would be eliminated only once their ambitions for equal partnership in marriage were realised. Until then, maintenance was one way in which the housewife could be compensated for her work in the home during marriage.

*

Another barrister who became one of the MWA's main legal advisers was Roxane Arnold. Arnold was not married and only became an adviser when SPG leader Dorothy Evans, who had instigated the MWA in the first place, persuaded her to help. When interviewed in 1992, Arnold confessed to having been much more interested in 'issues such as pay and taxation'.[93] Understanding Arnold's background as a single woman who was not focused upon the plight of married women is important because of her role in drafting MWA legislation. According to Helen Xanthaki, a level of detachment can be beneficial for the drafter, as it allows them to place themselves in the position of the lay user and to make the message of the legislation accessible to those who do not share the views of the Bill's proponents.[94] Arnold produced numerous drafts of the MWA's Bill for equal partnership in marriage,[95] and assisted with deputations to ministers and policymakers that the Association used to disseminate its reform objectives. Arnold was also director of the National Council for the Single Woman and her Dependants, and argued in the national press that single women should

---

[89] In 1938, the *Daily Mail* described Juanita Frances in sexist terms too, calling her a 'fragile, blue-eyed little woman'. P Bewsher, Romance With C.O.D.' *Daily Mail* (10 September 1938) 7.

[90] J Innes, 'Battling Betty starts her new fight today' *Daily Mail* (17 April 1969) 10.

[91] Thomson, 'Interview with Betty Knightly, above n 87.

[92] ibid. In an article in the *Daily Express*, Knightly expressed similar views: I Ramsay, 'What an insult, by the 10p wife' *Daily Mirror* (28 February 1973) 3.

[93] Blackford, 'Ideas, Structures and Practices of Feminism 1939–64', above n 19, 121.

[94] H Xanthaki, 'Gender inclusive legislative drafting in English: A drafter's response to Emily Grabham' (2020) 10(2) Feminists@Law, available at: https://doi.org/10.22024/UniKent/03/fal.952.

[95] It was especially important that the MWA could rely upon Arnold to do this, as this was not Appelbe's forte according to his son: 'I've never thought of him as a draftsman of legislation': Author interview with Felix Appelbe, above n 66.

be compensated for their care of elderly parents.[96] This suggests Arnold may have been involved closely with the MWA's legal objectives out of a broader concern that unpaid care work should be valued in financial terms; work that was often – though not always – undertaken by married women.

The involvement of prominent lawyers within the MWA also helped the Association foster useful legal connections outside its membership. Family law judge Roger Ormrod and legal academic Olive Stone both helped to produce drafts of legislation promoted by the MWA.[97] Solicitor Alan Nabarro[98] also attended MWA meetings and provided legal advice and representation to married women seeking help from the organisation. Nabarro, Arnold and Appelbe gave speeches on the law at MWA conferences and published articles on married women's legal status in the MWA's publication *Wife and Citizen* and in later years, the MWA Newsletter.

These publications provided another outlet for married women to seek help from the Association. A column in *Wife and Citizen* titled 'Legal Queries: The Solicitor Replies' included brief answers to married women's legal problems, which sometimes did more to expose the shortcomings of the law than it did to address the woman's query constructively. Take, for example, the one-word answer to a question from LUP of Rochester in 1947:

> My husband and I are purchasing the house in which we live through a Building Society and, of course, the repayments are made out of my husband's earnings as I am fully occupied looking after it and our children. Should our marriage break, have I any claim to my share of the house?
>
> *None.*[99]

There are only glimpses of the women from the cases in which the MWA gave help in the archives. 'Mrs E', a member of the MWA, is one example. She was left destitute after a London county court decided that her husband was the owner of the family's home and furniture which, she claimed, was bought partly from £3 a week housekeeping allowance and partly from her own earnings.[100] She was also denied her claim to maintenance for herself and for two of her three children by a police court as she refused to live at another address offered by the husband. There is no information available about what happened to Mrs E, other than the MWA's stated intention to take her case to the Court of Appeal.[101]

---

[96] See: By Our Social Services Correspondent, 'Pay single daughters as home helps' *Times* (14 May 1975) 3; R Gilchrist, 'The lone women who are evicted' *Daily Mail* (1 May 1972) 11.

[97] MWA Annual Report 1953–1954, 7TBG/1/32, TWL.

[98] Who, incidentally, was one of the first people in the UK to be prescribed insulin for diabetes in 1923.

[99] *Wife and Citizen*, May 1947, 7TBG/1/32, TWL.

[100] There are no law reports that can be connected to this case, and so the facts draw upon the MWA's account.

[101] A Appelbe, MWA Legal Department Report, November 1944, 7TBG/1/31, TWL.

The MWA also reported cases where their help came too late. Mrs Shields worked in a cotton mill and a laundry in Lancashire for the best part of 22 years of marriage. She left her job while pregnant, but continued earning by minding neighbours' children and doing domestic work, earning about £1 per week. As Ambrose Appelbe recounted: 'She worked hard, early and late. For periods of months at a time, when the husband was on part-time or on sick leave, Mrs Shield's earnings proved to be the mainstay of the family'.[102] He goes on to evidence this by describing Mrs Shields' typical day:

> After working 10 ½ hours a day as a tenter-rover in the mill, she would do the family washing until about 8 o'clock, then cook a meal for 7, followed by preparation of next day's dinner, housework and mending for the family. The husband gave her £2 housekeeping for the family of seven (later in Court it was revealed that he had been earning £6.4s.0d. a week). She paid his 1/6d. insurance and bought some of his clothes and cigarettes.

Shortly before the beginning of the Second World War, Mrs Shields began to save in a banking account in her husband's name. Her sons gave her a portion of their earnings to save in this account too, and in return she gave them pocket money and bought their clothes. When the savings account reached £208, the husband deserted the family, and took the savings with him.

Had the savings been comprised of Mrs Shields' housekeeping allowance, she would have had no legal right over the money. However, on Mrs Shields' account, this was not the case as she and her sons had contributed to the fund. It appears that this was not made clear in court as her claim for a half share of the £208 was not granted. Mrs Shields had no money to appeal the decision. And by the time she had sought the help of the MWA, it was too late for an appeal to be brought on her behalf.

Mrs E and Mrs Shields provide insights into the types of cases the MWA assisted with. By taking MWA members' cases to the Court of Appeal, the Association claimed it could expose the 'gross contravention' of the MWPA 1882 in the courts. Such cases occurred 'continually' according to Appelbe, with 'judgment being given usually in favour of the husband'.[103] And as we shall see in chapter five, a case similar to Mrs Shields' ultimately became the MWA's best source of propaganda.

*

It is noteworthy that the MWA's legal limb included early women lawyers. This is not because the Association broke new ground in its struggle to reform law; after all, women had been campaigning for legal reform for decades by the time the MWA was established. But what *was* new was that women could now be on

---

[102] ibid.
[103] ibid.

the inside of law-making processes. Before the Sex Disqualification (Removal) Act 1919, women protesting the harsh effects of law did so as outsiders of courts and Parliament. Women's entry to the legal profession was an important turning point, as women lawyers could use this new access to try and erode from the inside further injustices towards women embedded in law. In reality, however, this was not straightforward in institutions still dominated by men. In Parliament and in the courtroom, male politicians and judges did not always agree that there were laws disadvantaging or discriminating against women. Lord Denning contended in 1950 that it was yet to be seen whether 'the fact' of equality between men and women was 'good or bad'.[104]

Yet for some early female lawyers such as Normanton, Arnold, or Carrie Morrison (who provided legal representation as a solicitor for some of the women the MWA helped), their relatively recent entry to the profession was only the beginning of a battle for further reform. As a result, examining the individual members of the MWA provides insight into women's often overlooked engagement with law and its reform, while showing how many changes for women in law and society would not have happened without the work of female lawyers.

*

The function of the legal arm of the MWA could be seen as both practical and reformist. The legal expertise within the MWA was essential when it came to deconstructing the essence of what was wrong with marriage law, and what needed to be fixed. Put simply, this part of the membership was crucial when it came to translating MWA policy into clear legal demands. This, too, is what arguably set the Association apart from other organisations influenced by the 'new feminist' ideas considered in the previous chapter. Legal expertise enabled a concentrated focus on law. And, by combining feminism with demands to reform family law, the MWA could transform the conversation from women's *needs* in the domestic sphere to women's acquisition of equal *legal* rights.[105]

C. Stalwarts of the Women's Movement

As well as legal and political connections, the MWA leadership also benefited from women who had been feminist campaigners for a long time. Teresa Billington-Greig (or 'Mrs B-G' as she was often known) is arguably the best example of this. The MWA called her an 'old fighter',[106] having been a suffragette, founding member of the Women's Freedom League and prominent

---

[104] Anon, 'Cost Of Sex Equality' *Times* (13 May 1950) 3.
[105] Blackford, 'Ideas, Structures and Practices of Feminism 1939–64', above n 19, 104.
[106] MWA Newsletter, January 1956, 5/MWA/4/2, TWL.

member of the WSPU (though she resigned from the latter as she believed the Pankhurst leadership to be too autocratic).[107] Juanita Frances described her as being: 'Tall, middle aged thickness, she was fairly motherly. Almost affectionate. On the other side she could be very nasty, I knew that. The way she'd speak about some people, their lack of intelligence and ability. Her brown eyes flashing'.[108] Frances first recalls Billington-Greig joining the MWA around 1939 when Frances was speaking at 'a suffragettes' club' in London.[109] She remained a MWA member until her death in 1964.

The Association clearly benefited from Billington-Greig's expertise in the women's movement. Her archives hold multiple examples of letters from Frances asking for advice. When interviewed by Brian Harrison, Frances confirmed: 'Anything I would decide to do I would let her know, possibly with pride that we are doing her job and in respect of her being the Vice President'.[110] Frances 'admired her very much', noting that she 'wasn't humorous' but 'made up for' this in another way: 'She was precise and earnest and an emotional speaker. She felt that this was the right thing to do and therefore it should be done'.[111] MWA member and SPG leader Hazel Huskins-Hallinan described her in similar terms: 'She was a very determined person. She wasn't afraid of God or the devil'.[112]

Yet her style could be abrasive too. Take, for instance, Frances' description of her behaviour at one MWA Executive Committee meeting:

> A woman had some plan. So a special meeting was called and B-G was there. She was furious. She stood up and she went for this woman. She said 'you've wasted all our time and we've all given up our evening and look what you've done, nothing but a lot of rubbish!' Something like that she said. And we were all thinking that. But to have the courage to say it![113]

This assertiveness and belief in what was right sometimes created tension within the Association because of her tendency to take charge. SPG member Sybil Morrison said 'I admired her enormously, but I didn't like her – or at least I didn't like her methods'.[114] One of Billington-Greig's more controversial moves within the MWA was her attempt to merge it with the SPG. Huskins-Hallinan said it was 'a terrible time' even though it was 'an obvious marriage' because 'we had all the money and the Married Women's Association had all the numbers'.[115] She recalls the amalgamation did not go ahead as Billington-Greig could not agree on organisational matters: 'Where did the power lie and who would direct

---

[107] Harrison, *Prudent Revolutionaries*, above n 11, 49–50.
[108] Harrison interview with Juanita Frances, above n 4.
[109] The Minerva Club, Brunswick.
[110] Harrison interview with Juanita Frances, above n 4.
[111] ibid.
[112] Brian Harrison interview with Hazel Huskins-Hallinan, 8 February 1975, 8SUF/B/032, TWL.
[113] Harrison interview with Juanita Frances, above n 4.
[114] Transcribed conversation between Hazel Huskins-Hallinan and Sybil Morrison, SPG/M10, TWL.
[115] Harrison interview with Hazel Huskins-Hallinan, above n 112.

the parliamentary action'. This suggests Billington-Greig could be inflexible to a fault, with Huskins-Hallinan describing her as being 'Just like the rock of Gibraltar. She knew she was right ... if there ever was a warrior (laughs) it was Mrs B-G'.[116]

*

Vera Brittain was one of the MWA's most high-profile Presidents.[117] This is turn boosted the MWA's reputation, and in the Association's Newsletter of June 1958, Brittain reported that her position as President 'provoked a great deal of interest' and she 'was always careful to stress it at Press interviews'.[118] Best known as an author[119] and pacifist, much is known about Brittain's life outside the MWA.[120] However, archival sources provide only snippets of her work as President mostly from speeches and articles published in *Wife and Citizen*. This suggests the possibility she might have been a figurehead for the Association; an eminent figure who would draw attention and prestige. Huskins-Hallinan talks of the MWA getting people 'to take the window dressing'.[121] Yet any suggestion that this was the case for Brittain belies her work for the Association. She participated in conferences and events, and displayed clear interest in the Association's reform agenda, as shown by her letters of support to Edith Summerskill when Summerskill brought MWA issues to Parliament for debate or sponsored MWA bills.[122] An MWA Annual Report noted that she spoke at meetings 'with an ease of style' and 'combined the feminine with the feminist point of view most admirably'.[123]

*

Vera Brittain was not the only literary heavyweight in the MWA. Political and philosophical writer Dora Russell was also a 'stalwart of the Association',[124] being a Chairman before becoming MWA President in 1952. Like several other leading MWA members, Russell was divorced, having been married to mathematician and philosopher Bertrand Russell. Her involvement in the MWA is ostensibly surprising given she 'disapproved of marriage' and had only agreed to marry Bertrand Russell because she wanted her son to be a legitimate heir to

---

[116] ibid.

[117] Brittain became MWA President in 1954 as announced in MWA Newsletter, March 1954, 7TBG/1/32, TWL.

[118] MWA Newsletter, June 1958, 7TBG/2/J/08, TWL.

[119] Books include the memoirs *Testament of Youth* (1933), *Testament of Friendship* (1940) and *Lady Into Woman* (1953).

[120] See, eg, M Bostridge, *Vera Brittain and the First World War: The Story of Testament of Youth* (Bloomsbury 2015); M Bostridge and P Berry, *Vera Britain: A Life* (Virago 2016).

[121] Harrison interview with Hazel Huskins-Hallinan, above n 112.

[122] MWA Annual General Meeting Minutes, 25 June 1966, 5MWA/3/1, TWL.

[123] MWA Annual Report 1953–1954, above, n 36.

[124] Gorb, above n 65.

Bertrand's hereditary earlship.[125] But her experiences demonstrate a keen awareness of gendered inequality in marriage, which might explain her devotion to the
MWA's cause. Historian Anne Baker described some of the difficulties Russell
faced in being married to a 'much older, famous man'.[126] Bertrand Russell
believed women's intelligence was inferior to men's, and their 'main function
was to be wives and mothers'. His friends patronised her, 'assuming that any
ideas she might express came from him'.[127]

Dora Russell's political involvement enabled her to carve out an identity
independent from her husband. She claimed that 'no one knows the importance
of being a person in one's own right better than I do', having lived 'in the shadow
of [Bertrand Russell's] reputation'.[128] She ran unsuccessfully as a Labour
candidate for Chelsea in 1924. Russell also helped establish the Workers' Birth
Control Group, campaigning for women's access to advice about birth control
(an issue Edith Summerskill was also committed to). According to Baker, she
loved campaigning and public speaking, chain smoked, was 'small, red-haired,
and untidy'.[129] In her memoirs, Russell declared she was one of the first women
in England to wear shorts, when in the 1920s she would 'buy a roomy pair of
men's grey longs and cut them off short'.[130]

Her causes were sometimes controversial. She ran a 'progressive and much-
maligned school'[131] for 16 years until 1943 and she supported the Soviet Union.
After a paper she wrote for closed down in 1950,[132] Russell decided to dedicate her time to feminist activism and the women's peace movement, joining
both the MWA and SPG. She argued strongly in letters to *The Times* for the
MWA's policy of equal economic partnership in marriage as the law had 'not yet
abandoned the conception of a married couple as one person and that person
the husband'.[133] So, Russell was an effective spokesperson for the MWA. In
another letter published by *The Times*, she warned of the dangers of focusing
on reform of divorce and not marriage: 'the Married Women's Association is
right in its contention that economic questions play a very large part in marital
dissentions'.[134]

---

[125] Russell's marriage was not conventional and permitted affairs. However, it broke down after she
became pregnant with another man. Following her divorce from Bertrand Russell, she was married
again to Gordon (Pat) Grace, a working-class Irish communist: AP Baker, 'Russell, Dora Winifred
[née Black] (1894–1986)' in *Oxford Dictionary of National Biography* (Oxford University Press
2004), available at: https://doi.org/10.1093/ref:odnb/40676.
[126] ibid.
[127] ibid.
[128] J Turner, 'The woman who refused to live in the shadow of Bertrand Russell' *Times* (2 October
1974) 16.
[129] Baker, above n 125.
[130] D Russell, *The Tamarisk Tree* (Virago 1977) 181.
[131] Turner, above n 128.
[132] *British Ally*, a weekly paper published by the British government in Moscow.
[133] D Russell, 'Equal Partnership In Marriage' *Times* (16 May 1950) 5.
[134] D Russell, 'Divorce Law Reform' *Times* (14 July 1950) 7.

D. The Breakaways

Both Doreen Gorsky and Helen Nutting were formidable forces within the MWA and devoted years to campaigning for reform of marriage law. But as we shall see in later chapters, while they supported the MWA's aim of equal partnership in marriage, they disagreed with the Association's methods of achieving it. This disagreement reached breaking point in 1952 when the MWA had the opportunity to present evidence to the Royal Commission on Marriage and Divorce. Gorsky and Nutting resigned over the matter and went onto become executive members of the MWA breakaway group, the Council of Married Women.

*

There is little information available about Doreen Gorsky (known professionally as Doreen Stephens)[135] in the archives and public domain. As a result, interviews with three of her family members, who also permitted access to her unpublished autobiography titled *No One Special*, provided invaluable primary material about who she was.

Gorsky's grandson remembers her as 'unconventional'.[136] She loved to smoke cigars and was 'down to earth', he said. While Edith Summerskill had strong views about married women's property rights and reproductive rights in part because of the women she encountered as a doctor and politician, Gorsky had experience of the law in these areas first hand. By the time she joined the MWA, she had divorced, experienced life as a single mother of two children and had in her own words 'visited a backstreet abortionist'.[137] Gorsky's daughter considered her views about women's rights were in part influenced by her own experiences.[138] This was supported by John Butler, who wrote Gorsky's obituary and was her friend and relative:

> I think she was living at a time when people realised things had to change. And she was able to articulate what was needed in change. That came partly from her own personal experience of divorce, and having to bring up children as a single parent ... And that was not an easy thing to do, in the late 1930s, 1940s. It must have made her very aware of where things were very severely lacking.[139]

Gorsky was a member of the Liberal Party and ran unsuccessfully for Parliament four times. But she is best known for her role in television. After years of work with the MWA and then the breakaway Council of Married Women,[140] she left

---

[135] She used Gorsky in the MWA. Gorsky was the surname of her second husband, a doctor named Jack.

[136] Author interview with Stephen Holden, 1 August 2018.

[137] D Gorsky, *No One Special*, Private Papers of Jocelyn Freeman.

[138] Author interview with Jocelyn Freeman, 20 July 2018.

[139] Author interview with John Butler, 21 June 2018.

[140] She was also President of the Women's Liberal Foundation: J Butler 'Doreen Stephens Obituary' *Guardian* (24 April 2001), available at: http://www.guardian.co.uk/media/2001/apr/24/guardianobituaries.obituaries.

to become the first woman to hold an executive position at the BBC.[141] Still, she is 'almost entirely absent' from histories of early television.[142] On her forty-first birthday, she joined the BBC as editor of women's programmes, later becoming head of family programmes on television.

Gorsky's family members describe her as being a 'incredibly pragmatic',[143] but not an ideologue. When asked individually, none of them believed she would have called herself a feminist.[144] However, her advocacy for women's rights influenced her subsequent career at the BBC:

> I've done my stint in Trafalgar Square flanked by the lions at the base of Nelson's Column, adding my voice to women's demands for fair and equal treatment not privilege both inside and outside the home. I can see no anomaly in my position as Editor of women's programmes in television.[145]

Depictions of Gorsky's personality by family members suggests she was an invaluable member of the MWA leadership. She was 'very, very aware of the difficulties women encountered', 'tough' and was able to 'put up with criticism and opposition'.[146] She was also a 'massive organiser'.[147] As Vice Chairman and subsequently Chairman of the MWA in the late 1940s and early 1950s, Gorsky would have been part of the everyday management of the Association. She also spoke at MWA debates and conferences and contributed articles to *Wife and Citizen*. Her skills as an orator were emphasised by Butler: 'she wasn't dictatorial or domineering; she listened to people, but she could quickly sum up situations and she was a very thoughtful speaker. It wasn't just off the cuff'.[148]

Despite Gorsky's high-profile resignation from the MWA in 1952 she does not appear to have been as headstrong as other leading MWA members: 'I don't think she was that rigid in her outlook. She would modify if she saw reason to', her daughter said.[149]

*

Lady Helen Nutting[150] worked alongside Gorsky in both the MWA and the breakaway Council of Married Women. Her outlook differed politically from the MWA members examined so far. According to Juanita Frances she was a

---

[141] She left the Council of Married Women to take up this position.

[142] M Irwin, 'What Women Want On Television: Doreen Stephens and BBC Television Programmes For Women, 1953–64' (2011) 8(3) *Westminster Papers in Communication & Culture* 99, 99.

[143] Author interview with Stephen Holden, above n 136.

[144] But see Irwin, above n 142, 122, who referred to 'Stephens' explicitly 'feminist' outlook'.

[145] D Stephens, 'What Women Want on Television' *The Star* (13 December 1954) 7.

[146] Author interview with John Butler, above n 139.

[147] Author interview with Jocelyn Freeman, above n 138.

[148] Author interview with John Butler, above n 139.

[149] Author interview with Jocelyn Freeman, above n 138.

[150] Nutting was descended from nobility. She was the daughter of the sixth Earl of Airlie: 7LHN, TWL.

'typical Tory',[151] though there is not enough biographical information available about Nutting to confirm her support of the Conservative Party. Like Gorsky, Frances, Russell and Knightly, Nutting was divorced. Blackford has speculated that this personal experience influenced her interest in married women's legal and economic equality.[152]

Nutting created and filled the role of Public Relations Officer shortly after joining the MWA in 1944. She sought to expand the MWA's contacts and to establish links with other women's organisations.[153] She also visited MWA branches outside London and forged closer relationships with local branch members. Many of these members went on to vote for Nutting as Chairman of the Association in 1948. Before Nutting took over, Frances had chaired the MWA since she helped found it in 1938, but after pressure from local branches the MWA revised its constitution so that the position of Chairman had a three-year tenure.

Nutting supported the MWA's primary aim of legal and economic equality in marriage. But she placed considerable emphasis on other concerns too, such as the promotion and preservation of marriage.[154] This diverted attention away from legal reform and temporarily shifted the focus of the Association towards the social aim of promoting the institution of marriage. To be clear, the MWA had always sought to strengthen marriage through the promotion of equal partnership, but this was secondary to *legal* reform of women's rights in marriage. Unsurprisingly, this shift in focus away from law reform led to tensions within the group, as we shall see later in this chapter.

E. Lesser-Known Leaders

Finding out information about long-standing members within the MWA who had not been publicly renowned is more difficult. Other available sources on prominent figures like Summerskill, Brittain, Russell[155] and some of the professional men within the organisation allow us to construct more rounded lives for them. But many of the other members are hidden from history,[156] with little information in archival materials aside from details of the work they did for the Association. For example, personal information about Nora Bodley – who appears to have been one of the longest serving MWA members[157] – can only

---

[151] Gillian Elinor interview with Juanita Frances, August 1989, as cited in Blackford, 'Ideas, Structures and Practices of Feminism 1939–64', above n 19, 95.

[152] Blackford, 'Ideas, Structures and Practices of Feminism 1939–64', above n 19, 99.

[153] ibid, 98.

[154] ibid, 99.

[155] See, eg, Russell, *The Tamarisk Tree*, above n 130; E Summerskill, *A Woman's World* (Heinemann 1967).

[156] A phrase made famous by S Rowbotham, *Hidden from History* (Pluto Press 1973).

[157] Bodley joined in 1945 and was still a very active member in the 1980s: Letter from R Pugh to N Bodley, 19 February 1981, 5MWA/5/2, TWL.

be included in this book because her family members generously contacted me. Bodley was in charge of the Hornsey branch of the MWA[158] and organised luncheons in the House of Commons, which proved an effective lobbying tactic for the Association. Her sister May Carroll was the MWA's Press Secretary[159] and her niece Nina Steane was also a member. The position of Press Secretary was one of significant responsibility, requiring Carroll to navigate a complex relationship with journalists, who may have been suspicious of feminist aims, yet were crucial to have on-side when promoting MWA campaigns. As Teresa Billington-Greig explained: 'Naturally, the press at first was critical, amused and superior, even condemnatory – as with the suffragettes. But it gave publicity – essential to all causes seeking changes in legislation'.[160]

Carroll's son John recalls both his mother and Bodley as having 'very strong personalities'. For instance, they refused to evacuate London during the blitz of the Second World War. And in later life when May Carroll's husband died, she retrained as a chef, obtained a cordon bleu certificate and set up her own cooking business.[161] Like other MWA members, John said that Bodley and Carroll were concerned about women's access to birth control, and advocated for it to be freely distributed. Analysis of the MWA's records, however, indicates that Bodley's work was focused mostly on married women's legal and economic status, as shown by her articles in the MWA's Newsletter, lobbying of MPs[162] and letters published in national newspapers.[163]

For other members who did not have organisational roles at the top of the Association, accessing information is very difficult indeed. There are no comprehensive membership records in the archives: most MWA members are long deceased, and many did not keep their own names after marriage. This makes the task for historians in tracing these women's lives near impossible. Yet glimpses of the membership are possible in other ways. As the following section explores, letters from housewives, and articles in the MWA publication *Wife and Citizen* document some of the ideas and activities of the membership and of different branches.

IV. TENSIONS WITHIN THE MWA

Examining individuals within the MWA leadership can paint an overall picture of the MWA as being comprised mostly of members concerned with law reform.

---

[158] MWA Newsletter, June 1958, 7TBG/2/J/08, TWL.
[159] The dates of her membership are unclear, but records list Carroll as Press Secretary in 1975 on MWA notepaper: 5MWA/5/2, TWL.
[160] Handwritten notes (undated), 7TBG/1/32, TWL.
[161] John Carroll recalled she cooked for EH Shepard, the illustrator of AA Milne's books: Author interview with John Carroll, 16 June 2020.
[162] See, eg, Letter from N Bodley to H Rossi MP, 10 May 1982, 5MWA/2/2/1, TWL.
[163] See, eg, N Bodley, 'Mailbox' *Daily Mail* (14 March 1970) 3.

But this picture is overly simplistic, and there were sometimes tensions between the concerns of local branch members and those running the Association in London at an executive level. In the 1940s, the MWA experienced a surge in membership, though it remained a relatively small organisation, with 2,000 members at its peak.[164] This rapid expansion was in part boosted by press coverage of the Association's role in the case of Mrs Blackwell, which is explored more fully in chapter five. Blackford has argued that the MWA was attracting younger women at this time, who tended to be working-class wives and mothers. This contrasted with some of the older feminist groups of the period such as the SPG, whose membership 'was overwhelmingly composed of women in their fifties, sixties and seventies'.[165]

A. A Feminist Identity?

Several leading MWA members, such as Edith Summerskill, Vera Brittain and Juanita Frances openly identified as feminist. And as chapter one explained, the ideology of the MWA aligned with activities historians would classify as 'feminist' too.[166] But this did not mean that *all* MWA members considered themselves to be ideologically feminist, Doreen Gorsky being one notable example. With the cult of domesticity taking hold in the 1940s, there was little explicit support for the terminology of feminism and the MWA appeared to be conscious of this. At an Executive Committee meeting in February 1940, it was resolved that the word 'feminism' should be eliminated from MWA propaganda 'as it seemed to antagonise some people'.[167] The Association appeared to be concerned with avoiding the marginalisation of members who would support the Association's aims to further women's rights, but would be alienated by specific labels. According to Blackford, Frances believed this would give the MWA a better chance of attracting the support of 'young women, many of whom had not previously been politically active'.[168]

The MWA still remained implicitly feminist in its outlook. By the 1960s and 1970s, when the MWA's membership was smaller and support for feminism was growing significantly, the MWA Newsletter displayed the group's feminism more overtly. But in the 1940s, it appears some branches of the Association were more political than others, and the work of the local MWA branches was mixed.

---

[164] Still, Blackford notes that this expansion was 'significant' as 'few other feminist organisations had branches during this period or were recruiting members'. Blackford, 'Ideas, Structures and Practices of Feminism 1939–64', above n 19, 94–95.

[165] ibid, 96.

[166] Delmar, above n 5, 9.

[167] MWA Executive Committee Minutes, 27 February 1940, 7TBG/1/32, TWL.

[168] C Blackford, 'Frances, Juanita [née Juanita Frances Lemont; married name Juanita Frances Schlesinger] (1901–1992)' in *Oxford Dictionary of National Biography* (Oxford University Press 2004), available at: https://doi.org/10.1093/ref:odnb/63847.

Some branches, such as Walney Island, operated very differently from the hub of executive members in London and members appeared to be more preoccupied with social activities than with reform of law and policy.[169] However, in her interviews with relatives of MWA members Blackford found evidence that other branch members did *not* necessarily join the Association as a social outlet, but rather were discontented with their economic status in marriage, and the diminished value of their work in the home. As the daughter of MWA member Dorothy Wilson said of her mother: 'she had this strand of understanding of how valuable women's contribution is in areas where they've not been recognised … as housewives and particularly as mothers'.[170]

The letter at the start of this chapter gives an example of the correspondence received by the MWA from women who wanted to be involved in the Association but had neither the resources nor the time. Vera Brittain identified this as a 'historical' reason why 'women's movements had a middle-class origin'; middle-class women had time and money to dedicate to MWA activities that poorer women did not.[171]

Membership in local branches differed from other women's organisations such as the Women's Institute because of its reformist aims and focus. Frances was keen to make this distinction when interviewed by Brian Harrison. She recalled speaking to the Women's Institute about the legal and political work of the MWA:

> I get one or two questions and it's over. And I think that's simply amazing. It affects all of them [Women's Institute members], and yet they're so anxious to get on to the group that was doing the choir, or the one that was doing the lampshades … what *we* are doing is to change the law. And after that it will be to educate people about the process of changing the law to educate people that women are just as important as the people who bring home the pay packet.[172]

Frances did not appear to view MWA branch members in the same way as these members of the Women's Institute. Still, there were notable tensions between MWA branches which differed in their concerns about law. For example, Blackford notes that the Walney Island branch was criticised by the neighbouring Barrow branch for neglecting the aims and campaigns of the MWA.[173] Moreover, while local branches *were* political in their activities, these activities were often disconnected from the Association's core focus of legal equal partnership in marriage. The campaigns reported in *Wife and Citizen* within local branches included sex education in schools, the extension of school dinner services, and analgesia in childbirth. This gave rise to tensions with the leading MWA members in London, who were under pressure from branch members

---

[169] Blackford, 'Ideas, Structures and Practices of Feminism 1939–64', above n 19, 97.
[170] ibid.
[171] MWA Annual General Meeting Minutes, 30 April 1955, 7TBG/1/32, TWL.
[172] Harrison interview with Juanita Frances, above n 4.
[173] Blackford, 'Ideas, Structures and Practices of Feminism 1939–64', above n 19, 95.

to widen the scope of the Association beyond legal reform of marriage. And resolving this issue also brought dissention within the leadership to the fore, with Helen Nutting stating: 'We should be far from fulfilling our mission if we embraced nothing more fundamental than the dry bones of the law.'[174]

As we have seen already, Nutting successfully engaged with local branches in a way that other MWA leaders did not. When she became Chairman she stated that as 'first servant' of the MWA, her 'first function' was to 'coordinate all the varying and conflicting views' of its members.[175] Yet this democratic approach sometimes meant departing from the MWA's long-standing message of reforming marriage law, which only exacerbated tensions between other members of the Executive Committee.

B. 'Difficult' Personalities

Blackford has observed that: 'In a small organisation, it is possible for individuals to have considerable influence over direction and development of policy'.[176] This is clear when the MWA is compared with the work and organisation of larger women's organisations such as the Women's Institute. On the one hand, this must have been beneficial for the MWA when drafting and reacting to law reform, as the agreement of fewer people was needed on such matters. And for a relatively small group, the MWA arguably needed strong personalities within its leadership to make any impact upon married women's property rights. As Vera Brittain asserted, the MWA should not 'be depressed by its smallness', as 'small groups were often the most efficient at getting the work done'.[177] But cracks are more visible in a smaller group. And personality clashes can be very damaging indeed. One example of this was the ongoing disagreement between 'terrier like'[178] Juanita Frances and Helen Nutting, whose politics appears to have been more right-wing than Frances. There are various examples of Frances attempting to frustrate Nutting's work as MWA Chairman in the late 1940s, because Frances disagreed with the direction in which Nutting was taking the Association. Under Frances' leadership, the MWA had a clear focus as a pressure group concerned with legal reform to ameliorate women's economic dependence in marriage. But when Nutting took over, the emphasis shifted away from law to a broader focus on the strengthening and promotion of marriage as an institution.

Frances became disruptive. She directed the Legal Committee without reference to the Executive Committee and issued statements to the press without

---

[174] Letter to MWA members from Helen Nutting as new Chairman (undated) 7TBG/1/32, TWL.
[175] ibid.
[176] Blackford, 'Ideas, Structures and Practices of Feminism 1939–64', above n 19, 87.
[177] MWA AGM Minutes, 30 April 1955, above n 171.
[178] As characterised by Billington-Greig in MWA Newsletter, June 1958, 7TBG/2/J/08, TWL.

consultation.[179] Frances also faced criticism from executive members for her editorship of *Wife and Citizen*, because she rejected appeals to include recipes and knitting patterns in the publication. Instead, Frances believed *Wife and Citizen* should be 'a forum for feminist debate'.[180] In Blackford's view, publishing the only feminist journal of the period was 'an achievement against the odds' for the MWA, particularly given the narrowly constrained focus on domestic life of other women's publications at this time.[181]

But these smaller disagreements underpinned a more fundamental split between Nutting's desire to broaden the scope of the MWA and encourage a more diverse membership, and Frances' narrower focus on law reform. It could be argued that Frances got her way in the end. Nutting left the Association in 1952, and as Hazel Huskins-Hallinan put it 'Juanita has been at the helm pretty much the entire time'.[182] That Frances ultimately regained control suggests it was not always the most blustering of personalities that had the most clout in the MWA. Edith Summerskill's son's observation of Frances is particularly interesting in this respect:

> Juanita's style was deceptive, as I saw, even as a small boy. She talked so quietly that you had to lean towards her, and so pay attention. It is a classic way of controlling people. She was utterly determined, her diffident and tentative manner concealing a strong will. She fluttered and she charmed.[183]

Another instance of tensions among members relates to Summerskill's resignation as MWA President in 1951.[184] Officially, this was because of Summerskill's time constraints,[185] but there may have been other motivating factors. Conflict with Dora Russell is one possibility. According to Huskins-Hallinan, there was a dispute over a pamphlet on peace and women written by Russell and issued as an SPG publication in 1950.[186] It argued against the Korean War that had broken out that year, and because Summerskill was President of the SPG as well as the MWA at the time, her name appeared at the top, even though she claimed to have had nothing to do with it. Huskins-Hallinan recalled:

> [The pamphlet] was sent to every MP and it landed on [Clement] Atlee's desk when he was PM [Prime Minister] ... and there was part of his Government – Edith Summerskill – being against the avowed Government policy to support the Korean War.[187]

---

[179] Blackford, 'Ideas, Structures and Practices of Feminism 1939–64', above n 19, 100.
[180] ibid.
[181] ibid, 101.
[182] Harrison interview with Hazel Huskins-Hallinan, above n 112.
[183] SUMMERSKILL/1/7, TWL.
[184] Retiring Address of Edith Summerskill, *Wife and Citizen*, May/June 1951, 7TBG/1/32, TWL.
[185] In Summerskill's words, it was time for her to retire 'and allow somebody who has more free time to be appointed', ibid.
[186] Transcribed conversation between Hazel Huskins-Hallinan and Sybil Morrison, above n 114.
[187] ibid.

Summerskill was Minister of National Insurance at the time. Atlee reportedly called her and reprimanded her for being allied with an organisation publicly opposing the war. 'She had to disavow the whole thing' according to Huskins-Hallinan,[188] and she resigned from the SPG, writing in her resignation letter that she believed the group to have been 'duped by Communists'.[189] But as we have seen, Dora Russell, a known communist sympathiser, was a leading figure of the MWA too, and so Summerskill's resignation as MWA President shortly thereafter may not have been coincidental.[190]

A final glimpse into the views of MWA members is provided by one of the individuals interviewed for this book. Maryly Lafollette, a family lawyer and the daughter-in-law of Edith Summerskill was asked to speak at an MWA meeting in 1988. She was reported in the Association's Bulletin as 'emphasising her opinion that married women must be financially independent and not have children without certain guarantees'.[191] LaFollette confirmed the reports, and said MWA members plainly did not agree with her, and the meeting went sour. 'I was practically dismissed from the room', LaFollette recalls:

> There was almost total silence, there was a little bit of polite sort of [slowly claps], nobody came up and talked to me afterwards, it was just – it was a very hostile atmosphere. And, I mean, I obviously just went too far [laughs] … I'm not quite sure why they got so angry, but they did. I mean it was palpable.[192]

CONCLUSION

As the composite portrait presented in this chapter shows, the MWA was an organisation full of contradictions. Though it was a non-party group, it told its members that it was 'imperative that women should think politically'.[193] Some members wanted to maintain the group's narrow focus on family law reform, while lamenting its small numbers and lack of resources. Others argued that boosting membership required broadening the group's focus beyond reform of marriage law. Sometimes, the MWA operated as a committee; other times it was a community-based organisation. Mostly, it was a mixture between the two. Membership boosted funds, and created what the Association defined as a 'trade union' whereby members could seek legal help. Yet the archives suggest decisions on law and policy were made by those in charge of the organisation,

---

[188] ibid.

[189] Blackford, 'Ideas, Structures and Practices of Feminism 1939–64', above n 19, 97.

[190] In Russell's autobiography, she recalls an MWA garden party while Summerskill was still President, where Summerskill threatened to leave unless a World Council for Peace petition was removed from the event: Russell, *The Tamarisk Tree* above n 130, 122–23.

[191] MWA Bulletin No 1, 1989, SUMMERSKILL/1/7, TWL.

[192] Author interview with Maryly LaFollette, 26 July 2018.

[193] MWA Hampstead Group Monthly Journal, 1 April 1940, 7TBG/1/32, TWL.

on whom this chapter has focused. As we have seen, this apparent top-down structure could cause friction between members. But despite this, the MWA was still able to develop a distinctive ideology and identity regarding the need for equal partnership in marriage.

However, the MWA's methods for achieving reform were not new. Members looked upon the methods of those involved in the campaigns of the Women's Liberation Movement with suspicion, viewing them as disorganised.[194] But the group's reliance on committees and democratic methods clearly derived from their feminist foremothers, who had had successful campaigns culminating in the passage of the MWPA 1882 and the Matrimonial Causes Act 1923 (which enabled women to petition for divorce on the same grounds as men).[195] MWA members looked upon the struggles and successes of the nineteenth and early twentieth-century women's movement with veneration. Many had read suffragette Ray Strachey's book *The Cause*.[196] Some, like Teresa Billington-Greig, had played important roles in the suffrage campaigns themselves. But the MWA's struggle was a new one, requiring a *different* understanding of equality that was not based on sameness (as the suffragettes had argued). Therefore, it is perhaps surprising that the MWA's structural methods did not evolve with its ideology.

On the other hand, the MWA's strategies arguably make sense when the personalities of the Executive Committee members are looked at more closely. While many of these women and men were outliers and pioneers in society, they were also united by pragmatism; hopeful in terms of persuading lawmakers to introduce reform, yet aware this would take time. But tensions within the Association, particularly among its leading members, also indicate obstinance and disunity. This shows that just because a group of reformers is small does not mean it is harmonious. Indeed, as we shall see in chapter six, dissention *inside* the MWA could be as important an obstacle to reform as the legal and political institutions outside it. As historian Brian Harrison has noted, infighting was a common problem in the MWA and other similar women's organisations.[197]

By 1948, tensions between members had already been building. As the first decade since the MWA's formation was ending, the frustration among some leading members was palpable in *Wife and Citizen*: 'In retrospect we have accomplished little' the magazine said, 'in spite of a great deal of hard work. So much more remains to be done before we can hope for new legislation'.[198] But what did the MWA mean by new legislation? Understanding this requires closer inspection of the new marriage law the Association sought.

---

[194] Harrison interview with Juanita Frances, above n 4.

[195] D Stetson, *A Woman's Issue: The Politics of Family Law Reform in England* (Oxford University Press 1982) 229.

[196] Strachey, above n 3.

[197] Harrison interview with Sybil Morrison, above n 50.

[198] 'New Year's Greetings', *Wife and Citizen*, January 1948, 7TBG/1/32, TWL.

4

A New Marriage Law

May I wish you success in your efforts to obtain a legal financial partnership in marriage? The cause is a just and right one. Both my mother and myself have suffered because we both had husbands who were extremely selfish whilst we were diligent and faithful housewives, putting the interests of home and family before anything.[1]

E Paul, Manchester

INTRODUCTION

WHEN THE MWA's first Chairman, Juanita Frances, decided to make the Married Women's Association (MWA) independent from the Six Point Group (SPG) in 1938, the Association had an opportunity to shape its own brand of feminism that was distinctive from the ideology shared by SPG members. And so, in the midst of ideological debates about old and new feminism, the MWA summarised their own take on equality:

We must discard the old idea that equality of status lies along the road of sameness ... the time has now come when we must realise that we have a contribution to human welfare which cannot be made by men.[2]

Addressing the question of how housewives' work should be properly valued in law, the MWA had a clear solution: equal partnership in marriage. Equal partnership did not mean equality on strict and exact terms because the MWA knew most married women's experiences were different from men's and pretending otherwise would be pointless. For the MWA, asserting formal equality between husbands and wives without proper regard for the gendered divisions of power in the household would ignore the structural inequalities relegating most married women to the private sphere.[3] Equality and independence for men and women on the statute books without accounting for the domestic labour that was done by women, and *not* by men, meant housewives could not utilise political and legal rights on the same par as men.

---

[1] *Wife and Citizen*, August 1947, 7TBG/1/32, TWL.
[2] *Wife and Citizen*, December 1948, 7TBG/1/32, TWL.
[3] S Atkins and B Hale, *Women and the Law* (Institute of Advanced Legal Studies 2018) 4.

However, while the MWA's criticism of women's economic oppression in marriage alongside campaigns to promote the idea of equal partnership in marriage were important, the Association went beyond this to push actively for reform. It drew upon its legal expertise and connections inside and outside the Association to propose a new marriage law. Building upon themes from the previous chapters, such as married women's unequal legal status, the separate and unequal gendered marital roles of housewife and breadwinner, and the tensions within the MWA, it becomes clear that assuming this group was only committed to the idealisation and promotion of marriage and the family would be a mistake.[4] Yet while the MWA believed change was important to stabilise and promote marriage as an institution, it did not challenge the dominance of marriage within women's identity.[5] To this end, it relied upon the tactics found by historian Dorothy Stetson to have been most effective in influencing family law reform in the twentieth century:

> When feminists define family law reform as affecting the goals of equality for women, rather than sex roles in marriage, they use pressure-group tactics to transfer the conflict from the legal administration to the legislature where they can have influence.[6]

The MWA could do little about the state of the common law, but they could potentially influence statute using their political connections. In this chapter, these efforts to achieve equal partnership through legislation represent (at least on the face of it) examples of feminist efforts *not* bearing fruit. However, as this chapter argues this does not stop these efforts from being worthy of consideration, for these failures can bring about change in their own underappreciated way.

This chapter follows MWA members as they craft a manifesto for equal partnership in marriage. It explores how they developed their ideology into a plan for family law reform and how, in practical terms, they went about this. Section I explores the MWA's developing ideology as to how women's work in the home should be valued in the pursuit of equal partnership in marriage. It tracks the evolution of MWA ideas, from the demand for direct payment to housewives by husbands in return for their work in the home, to the demand for joint ownership of income and the home during marriage. Indeed, understanding why the MWA settled upon the idea of joint partnership in marriage instead of wages for wives is key to explaining and justifying the complexities of valuing housewives' work in the home in economic terms.

---

[4] C Blackford, 'Wives and Citizens and Watchdogs of Equality: Post-War British Feminists' in J Fyrth (ed), *Labour's Promised Land: Culture and Society in Labour Britain 1945–51* (Lawrence & Wishart 1995) 63.

[5] ibid.

[6] D Stetson, *A Woman's Issue: The Politics of Family Law Reform in England* (Oxford University Press 1982) 230.

The second and third sections of this chapter investigate how the MWA translated this ideology into a new marriage law. As chapter two explained, the root of the problem was what OR McGregor called the 'unintentionally institutionalised inequality' that the Married Women's Property Acts of 1870 and 1882 had created between spouses.[7] To uproot this institutionalised inequality, the MWA believed the solution was legislative reform.

Ultimately, the MWA's efforts to achieve equal partnership through draft bills reveals important information about how the group developed its ideology, and its practical view of reform. It also reveals much about the MWA's view of and relationship with law; how members took strategy into account when drafting legislation, and their awareness of the opposition they would face. And most importantly, it emphasises why the ideal of a new marriage law is radical per se. With hindsight, we know that the financial consequences of relationship breakdown have been reformed over the years. But reform facilitating the legal sharing of assets during marriage, as the MWA was proposing, was (and still is) the reform which never happened.[8]

I. FROM WAGES FOR WIVES TO JOINT OWNERSHIP

As the MWA split away from the SPG and created its own new Executive Committee, it also adopted different legislative policy considerations and ambitions. This was most notable in the Association's efforts to address the constant conundrum of how best to value women's work in the home in legal terms. Initially, it was 'wages for wives'; a policy inherited from the SPG. The press identified the MWA with this moniker,[9] and some MWA members indeed believed in it. But as this section will show, the slogan later caused some confusion as the Association sought to abandon it as a concept. The MWA increasingly eschewed the idea that husbands should pay their wives a wage and preferred the idea that spouses should own property jointly. Examining and evaluating this shift from 'wages for wives' to the arguably less catchy concept of 'joint ownership' is important for a number of reasons. It foreshadows the divisions that later led to the Association's fragmentation as well as showing how the MWA developed its own model of reform distinct from the 'old' and 'new' feminism explored in chapter two.

The MWA, in its focus on equal partnership in marriage, was developing new feminist ideas that built upon both old and new feminism. Catherine

---

[7] In a debate on the Law Commission's proposals for co-ownership of the matrimonial home: HL Deb 18 July 1979, vol 401, col 1437, cited in S Cretney, *Family Law in the Twentieth Century* (Oxford University Press 2003) 115.

[8] Stephen Cretney has described proposals for a law governing property ownership during marriage in this way: ibid, 136.

[9] Brian Harrison interview with Juanita Frances, 14 November 1974, 8SUF/B/022, TWL.

Blackford has pointed out that the MWA did this by going beyond the arguments of the 'new' feminists. For example, while the MWA supported family allowances, such payments represented financial assistance to women in their role as housewives but did not go far enough in addressing wives' dependence on their husbands.[10] Instead, the MWA aimed to bring the economic status of married women into line with that of women in paid employment outside the home by asserting her right as an individual worker.[11] There were two possible ways of doing this: as this section explains, the MWA considered both a 'wages for housework' model, whereby the wife is paid by her husband for her work; and a 'joint ownership model', whereby both spouses have equal agency and rights of ownership over property accumulated during marriage.

A. The Wages-for-Housework Model

After a few MWA meetings, when it was still annexed to the SPG and operated as the Committee of the Association of Married Women, a document outlining the group's vision for reform was distributed arguing for the economic position of married women to be legally recognised in the following ways:

> In marriage a wife should be entitled, legally to a proportion of her husband's income, for the maintenance of the home and for her own needs, as if she were a housekeeper or working in a trade or a profession. The proportion should be arranged amicably, by mutual consent, preferably before marriage and should bear a fair relation to the husband's income and standard of living, but when a marriage breaks down, or a wife is not satisfied with the proportion allotted to her, she should be able to apply to the courts to grant her a larger proportion of her husband's income. In the same way, the husband having recourse against his wife should she misappropriate the allowance made for the maintenance of the home. When a woman has money of her own or is a wage earner, the law should require her to contribute to the maintenance of the home on a basis of equality, excepting during pregnancy or lactation.[12]

This model values a housewife's labour literally: she is paid a wage by her husband. It transforms the sexual division of labour into contractual terms, where the wife can negotiate payment for her domestic and caregiving labour. Instead of a husband providing his wife with a housekeeping allowance to cover household outgoings such as groceries, which the wife had no proprietary right in, she would instead receive money as a worker.

Theoretically, this could have strengthened the economic power of housewives. After all, for most housewives of the 1940s and 1950s, housework took up

---

[10] C Blackford, 'Ideas, Structures and Practices of Feminism 1939–64' (PhD thesis, University of East London 1996) 110.

[11] J Freeguard, 'It's Time for Women of the 1950s to Stand Up and Be Counted' (PhD thesis, University of Sussex 2004) 162.

[12] Report on The Association of Married Women, undated, 5SPG/I/08, TWL.

most of their time and was unpaid. Women had no way of acquiring property for themselves because the work they did was historically seen as 'unskilled, naturally feminine, and therefore women's duty'.[13] For working-class women who also worked outside the home, their subordination was maintained by a combination of limited options in a low-waged service economy alongside the relegation of their work in the home to the private sphere, outside economic and political discourses. As a result, the MWA's early claims for a housewife's wage were subversive and arguably disruptive, because they pulled back the curtain on the private sphere of the family home and demanded recognition of the housewife like any other worker. If housework were recognised as work that was valuable and skilled, it was possible that housewives would have greater strength and bargaining power in marriage.

Strategically, the policy benefited from its simplicity and clarity. It was an eye-catching idea, had radical implications and was later picked up by feminists of the 'second wave'. In the 1970s, the concept of wages for housework re-emerged as a key demand of the Women's Liberation Movement. As Joyce Freeguard notes, this was considered 'new and revolutionary' at the time even though it had been campaigned for by the MWA in the early 1940s,[14] and later (as chapter six shows) by a group of defecting MWA members who formed the Council of Married Women. However, Freeguard does not distinguish the feminist theory underpinning the MWA and the 1970s 'Wages for Housework' campaigns. The activism of the 1970s was driven by Marxist feminist analysis of housework as reproductive labour.[15] This view posited housework as sustaining capitalism, because although it was not part of the *direct* production of labour power,[16] the additional labour or 'reproduction' to maintain and restore the energy of the worker[17] included all the cooking, cleaning and caring done by the housewife. Based on this Marxist critique, Wages for Housework campaigns emphasised the reliance of capitalism upon the domestic sphere and adopted an anti-work stance, suggesting those responsible for reproductive labour – housewives – could and should exercise power in refusing to do this work.[18]

The early MWA policy of wages for wives did not share this view. Unlike the feminists of the political Left who connected patriarchy and class, the early MWA policy was based on classlessness. Wages for wives was a long-standing

---

[13] A Gotby, 'They Call It Love: Wages For Housework And Emotional Reproduction' (PhD thesis, University of West London 2019) 9.

[14] Freeguard, above n 11, 170.

[15] As Gotby, above n 13, notes, the theorists most commonly associated with Wages For Housework are Mariarosa Dalla Costa, Silvia Federici, Leopoldina Fortunati and Selma James, active in the Italian, American and British branches of the network. Allies of the Wages for Housework campaign and its demands included Wages Due Lesbians and Power of Women Collective: Stetson, above n 6, 251.

[16] However, see G Rubin, *The Traffic in Women* (Duke University Press 2011) 162 who notes that some argue housework can be viewed as productive labour.

[17] ibid.

[18] Gotby, above n 13, 22.

feminist aspiration, or what Stetson called a 'recurring dream',[19] for housewives to receive direct payment in return for their work. But it was not a radical demand for women to abandon housework and to undermine the sexual division of labour. As the aforementioned MWA document indicated, once a wage was agreed between spouses, the Association proposed that the wife should be required by law to exercise her duties like any other worker, providing the husband with legal recourse in the event his wife went on strike from her wifely duties. This stance appears to be framed to make the proposal attractive to men. After all, as MWA members pointed out, their support was needed if legal reform were to happen:

> A carefully drafted Bill for a Statute law may do a lot to win male sympathy to our side, if we make it quite clear that we are against the irresponsible woman as well as the irresponsible man.[20]

*

In keeping with the concept of wages for housework, the MWA argued that the housewife should have 'employment rights and protection in her "domestic workshop"'.[21] So, in an effort to promote women's work inside the home as being of equal value to work outside it, the MWA encouraged the view of the housewife not as an invisible and unemployed citizen, but as a member of the working population deserving of recognition by the labour movement. To this end, the MWA began calling itself the Housewives' Union[22] and unsuccessfully attempted to formally obtain trade union (TUC) recognition several times. According to Blackford, the MWA's claim for TUC affiliation and support was based on the view that women's work in the home was highly skilled, arduous and had social value, even though this labour was unpaid. By representing these unpaid workers, the MWA argued it should be afforded the same recognition as other unions representing paid workers.

On a practical level, the MWA's positioning of itself as the Housewives' Trade Union made sense.[23] As a union (albeit an unofficial one), housewives in a legally precarious position with potentially insufficient funds to meet the needs of the family could connect with others in a similar position requiring

---

[19] Stetson, above n 6, 251.

[20] Report on The Association of Married Women, above n 12.

[21] Blackford, 'Ideas, Structures and Practices of Feminism 1939–64', above n 10, 92.

[22] This account draws on Blackford, ibid, 90–93.

[23] The MWA was not the only group to raise awareness of the economic dependency of the unpaid housewife. For co-operative movements such as the Women's Co-operative Guild (with which Juanita Frances had briefly been involved) the financial status of housewives was a primary concern between 1914 and 1920. However, the Co-operative Guilds' solutions to this problem were different from those put forward by the MWA. The MWA demanded an independent income for women, while the Co-operative Guilds encouraged support for trade union efforts to raise male wages and to finance maternity and child welfare services (See Blackford, 'Ideas, Structures and Practices of Feminism 1939–64', above n 10, ch 3).

help and support. Constance Colwill, an academic lawyer[24] who was one of the first female barristers[25] and was a legal adviser to the MWA in court, saw the Housewives' Trade Union as a way of bolstering the legal recognition of housewives. The MWA 'have it in their hands', Colwill said, to 'lead the way' and encourage women before marrying to understand what their standard of living will be and how much their husbands will allocate to the household budget.[26] Housewives within this union should view themselves as joint treasurers and equal partners of the family income and could provide 'help-your-neighbour' schemes to support housewives struggling to 'make reduced family incomes go further'. As a union, the MWA could provide women with legal advice or could help women to bring their cases to court when they did not have the means to do so themselves.

But the MWA's branding as the Housewives' Trade Union was also confusing and contradictory on an ideological level. After all, the MWA stood for *equal* partnership in marriage, while the purpose of trade unions was (and is) to regulate the inherently *unequal* relationship of employer and employee. If housewives were to be viewed as workers, like any other paid individual in gainful employment, did this make them employees too? It was one thing for the MWA to draw attention to power imbalances between husband and wife, and quite another to entrench this inequality by equating married women to employees. This was what happened when the concept was considered in the courtroom.

In *re Kendrew*,[27] Augusta Kendrew left her house, furniture and personal effects to her housekeeper Mary Clark (subject to a life interest to her husband George Kendrew), provided Clark continued to provide services to herself and her husband. Mrs Kendrew died, and Mary Clark married the husband of the deceased. Before marrying, they entered a prenuptial deed whereby George Kendrew would continue to employ Clark as his housekeeper throughout their marriage, paying her £52 a year. When he died, the residuary legatees challenged the legacy bequeathed to Mary Clark, arguing that the prenuptial deed contracting her to continue working as a housekeeper was invalided by their marriage. This is because, the residuary legatees argued, a normal wife is *expected* to perform housekeeping duties, as this role is 'ascribable to her status as a wife ... and not the subject of a special contract'.[28] In other words, housekeeping duties after the marriage could not be performed by a servant when

---

[24] Colwill had been a part-time lecturer before the Second World War. When she applied to join the Society of Public Teachers of Law in 1938, she was rejected for not being, as stipulated in the Society's constitution, a gentleman. P Polden, 'Portia's progress: women at the Bar in England, 1919–1939' (2005) 12 *International Journal of the Legal Profession* 293, 316.

[25] According to Patrick Polden, Colwill was the daughter of a barrister's clerk. She entered Gray's Inn in 1923 and was called to the Bar in 1925: ibid, 313.

[26] C Colwill, 'Advantages of Housewives Trade Union' MWA Newsletter, November 1942, 7TBG/1/32, TWL.

[27] *In re Kendrew Hird v Kendrew and Others* [1952] K 374 (CA) 1 Ch, 291.

[28] ibid, 294 (Jenkins LJ) who noted that counsel referred to *Thomas v Thomas* [1948] 2 KB 294; 64 TLR and *Wanbon v Wanbon* [1946] 2 All ER 366.

this work was part of the married woman's role. To be effective, the contract of service had to relate to duties a wife would not normally perform. As a result, the condition under the will for Mary Clark to continue providing housekeeping services to receive the legacy was not met.[29]

This argument was not accepted by the Court of Appeal. Instead, it held that it was 'possible to have the relationship of a master and servant between husband and wife'.[30] Clark met the condition under the will. Providing the leading judgment, Jenkins LJ considered: 'If a wife is injured, her husband may bring an action for loss of her services. Is it not possible to double the functions of a paid housekeeper and a wife?' By considering that a wife could be paid for her housework subject to a premarital contract, Jenkins LJ could be seen as upholding a 'wages for wives' type structure. In doing so, the 'patriarchal template' of the marriage contract is subverted,[31] whereby housework is not necessarily the moral and expected duty of the wife but can be valued instead in 'solid cash'.[32]

However, there is an important problem with this approach. For Mary Clark to win her case in *re Kendrew*, the Court had to deem her to be in a 'dual relationship' with her husband 'as wife and as servant'.[33] Her work had economic value instead of being treated as an unpaid moral obligation, but for this to be so, she was not in an equal legal partnership with her husband: he was her master.

Yet some members could still see the benefits of wages for housework, and remained convinced that money paid to the wife for housekeeping services was the best route to her independence. For others, like Teresa Billington-Greig, paying wives a wage created an undesirable master/servant dynamic[34] but her personal notes suggest she still saw it as having some important advantages:[35]

> Wages for wives was the first slogan [of the MWA], coined or publicised by the Press and much disliked by an increasing number of [MWA] supporters. Personally, I think it did more good than harm! It emphasised that in a world full of wage-workers there was one enormous section of workers who got no wages at all – the taken for granted habit became a matter for question.[36]

Nevertheless, while the idea might have stimulated debate about women's unpaid work, there appeared to be a consensus that permitting men to behave as employers behaved further entrenched women's subservience both inside

---

[29] *Kendrew*, ibid, 294.

[30] ibid.

[31] A Barlow, 'Configuration(s) of Unpaid Caregiving within Current Legal Discourse In and Around the Family' (2007) 58 *Northern Ireland Legal Quarterly* 251, 251–52.

[32] As Virginia Woolf put it in *Three Guineas* (Hogarth Press 1938) 54, of which the MWA published extracts with Woolf's permission, 5CMW/B/12, TWL.

[33] *Kendrew*, above n 27, 295.

[34] Draft of Teresa Billington-Greig speech, 1958, 7TBG/1/31, TWL.

[35] Teresa Billington-Greig handwritten notes, undated, 7TBG/2/J/08, TWL.

[36] ibid.

and outside the home. For the MWA, moving towards a joint ownership model instead was one way of undermining women's subservience, because it embodied the concept of equality between husbands and wives, albeit in their separate, gendered marital roles.

B. The Joint Ownership Model

In promoting equal partnership in marriage, the MWA needed to address the power imbalances between husband and wife. It soon became clear to them that valuing women's work in the home through payment of a wage from husband to wife was not the way to do this and propositions for reform based on wages for housework were abandoned. As Juanita Frances later pointed out, it was not compatible with the MWA's central aim of equal partnership in marriage: 'It's nothing to do with Wages for Housework; *we think we're part of the management.* A good marriage is one of agreement on money matters between husband and wife – a partnership marriage'.[37] Yet the MWA continued to maintain that it was a Housewives' Trade Union, thereby simultaneously emphasising the housewife as a worker while ditching the idea of wages for housework.

Meanwhile, the MWA needed a new strategy for equal partnership. The Association could see that working towards this meant that legal reform had to challenge the root of the problem – married women's lack of property ownership. Instead of being owned and controlled by the family, the 'family wage' in reality belonged to the male breadwinner.[38] Women's economic vulnerability in marriage was built into social structures and into the law. Because the husband controlled the finances, he owned the household furniture and could determine how much money was set aside for housekeeping expenses, thereby controlling the quality of the family's food, shelter and clothing.[39] If the marriage broke down, this lack of property rights was exacerbated by the enforcement problems associated with maintenance. For instance, though a wife could claim maintenance for herself and her children in a police court, she had limited recourse when the husband failed to pay it.

For the MWA, the solution to these problems was joint ownership, whereby equal partnership meant equal ownership of the family finances throughout marriage. The Association therefore took the view that the husband's sole ownership of the family wage was not justified simply because he earned it directly. Members argued that the wife should have a right to this wage too in recognition of her work in the home. In short, the MWA's joint ownership model started out as a demand for a married woman's right to half of her husband's income.

[37] R Gorb, 'Wives' Unequal Battle' *Hampstead and Highgate Express* (11 July 1986).
[38] Blackford, 'Ideas, Structures and Practices of Feminism 1939–64', above n 10, 110.
[39] J Frances, 'Wages for Wives India Broadcast', 14 July 1944, 7TBG/1/32, TWL.

As time went on, the MWA calls for joint ownership extended beyond a right to share in capital, to rights in property too. This was because the Association recognised the effect of the evolving economic landscape after the Second World War. With the acute housing shortages during and after the War, it became difficult for many wives to leave their husbands and find somewhere else to live. Strict rent controls discouraged property owners from letting houses, less accommodation was available to rent, and according to Cretney there was a 'shift in preference to buying rather than renting' which 'combining with the scarcity caused by the lack of new building, no doubt contributed to the inflation in owner occupied house prices'.[40] As Lord Wilberforce later noted,[41] this shift since 1945 meant that while maintenance payments might previously have enabled a wife to rehouse herself on separation, this was no longer possible:[42]

> To a woman, whose husband has left her, especially if she has children, it is of little use to receive periodical payments for her maintenance (even if these are in fact punctually made) if she is left without a home.[43]

The MWA recognised this and expanded its principle of equal sharing to encompass joint ownership of income *and* the marital home.

Underpinning the concept of joint ownership was the belief that work undertaken inside the home was as valuable to the family as the work done outside it. Put in the context of the 1940s, the Association was radical in seeking solutions for equality by focusing on the economic roots of women's oppression. After all, it was not until the turn of the twenty-first century that the courts in England and Wales upheld the principle that spouses' homemaking and breadwinning contributions are equally valuable in marriage, therefore justifying equal sharing on divorce.[44] The MWA had put forward this idea in the 1940s, in a Bill which was redrafted throughout the course of the Association's history and shaped its policy over the years. The Bill also encapsulated what the MWA meant by equal partnership and gave the spokespeople of the group a clear answer when asked what their goals for reform were. As Juanita Frances summarised in a 1944 radio broadcast:

> The [MWA] plan ... expresses women's discontent with her present position, but in the proposed new relationship, husband and wife are equal, neither employs the other, but each share their earnings and income by adding them together. From this pool is paid the maintenance of home and care of the children, and the remainder then shared equally ... The mother's economic status is basically a legal question. It must be defined in a new Act of Parliament on a basis of equality, giving her equal obligations ... The presentation of such a Bill would set a pattern of social behaviour

---

[40] Cretney, above n 7, 118.
[41] *National Provincial Bank v Ainsworth* [1965] UKHL 1.
[42] A point also made by Cretney, above n 7, 118.
[43] *Ainsworth*, above n 41, 15.
[44] Pursuant to *White v White* [2000] UKHL 54.

and would automatically lead a front-line attack on the lethargy of custom which permits this grave injustice to our mothers to continue.[45]

Clearly then, legislation was at the centre of the MWA's plan. Drafting legislation that captured these demands for joint ownership became one of the primary occupations of the MWA throughout its history. The Bill for equal partnership in marriage provides important insight into the MWA's strategies for law reform and how the Establishment responded to its demands. Examining this Bill in detail also reveals more about what the MWA meant by joint ownership as a regime regulating property ownership in marriage, and whether this could have resolved issues for married women if it had been taken more seriously.

II. A BILL FOR EQUAL PARTNERSHIP IN MARRIAGE

The MWA believed it could achieve its aims best by changing legislative structures. Its Bill for equal partnership in marriage was both the MWA's greatest achievement, and its greatest failure. As later chapters will show, this Bill helped the MWA influence a patchwork of reforms. But the Bill itself was never passed. This section explores the response to different iterations of this Bill, as its evolution over a series of different drafts provides a unique insight into how the MWA's specific vision for legal reform developed over time.

Though it was redrafted several times, the preamble of the MWA's 1975 draft sets out the Bill's consistent aim, which was to

> provide for greater equality of rights and status between husband and wife; for the mutual provision by them for the outgoings of their household and for the mutual division of their income; for their mutual rights in the matrimonial home and contents; and for matters ancillary thereto.[46]

The MWA's core economic principles can be distilled into seven key points:

1. The income of both spouses was to be regarded as the income of the partnership and disposed of by mutual agreement.
2. Spouses should mutually decide as to the family's standard of living, so that an appropriate periodic sum for housekeeping and maintenance of the family could be agreed to maintain this standard.
3. Housekeeping savings (and any surplus once housekeeping expenses were met) was to be joint property.
4. There should be mutual disclosure of all income, financial liabilities and debts incurred by either party during marriage, or before marriage if outstanding at the date of the marriage.

---

[45] Frances, 'Wages for Wives India Broadcast', above n 39. Perhaps confusingly, this broadcast was titled 'Wages for Wives'.

[46] Equal Partnership Bill 1975, 5MWA/1/2/2/2, TWL.

5.   The matrimonial home should be jointly owned. However, all other capital assets owned by the partners at the time of the marriage would remain their individual property.
6.   In the event of divorce or judicial separation, the court should have discretion to redistribute the matrimonial home and other assets as it thinks fit, having particular regard to the interests of any children of the marriage.
7.   These principles should apply to all marriages unless the spouses prior to marriage enter into a special marriage contract by deed.[47]

Those familiar with the financial consequences of divorce today might not see these seven points as controversial. While there is no marital property regime triggered by marriage in England and Wales, on divorce the court has broad discretionary powers[48] to divide property according to the circumstances, needs and sacrifices generated by the marriage.[49] Like the sixth point, the court now gives first consideration to the welfare of any children of the marriage.[50] Assets such as the marital home and income acquired during marriage are subject to the equal sharing principle, while assets in existence before the marriage (referred to in the fifth point) are less susceptible to division on divorce.[51] However, under current law marriage is still underpinned by the doctrine of separate property. This means the court does not normally intervene in questions of property ownership until the marriage has broken down. The MWA's Bill provided for the pooling of respective incomes, sharing of any surplus income and savings and full financial disclosure of all assets not on divorce, but *during marriage*. Even though the MWA did not use the language of community of property, point one could be interpreted as such. In property law terms, such restrictions over expenditure mean in effect that neither spouse would have complete legal and beneficial ownership of their income during marriage. However, the MWA was at pains to explain how its proposed reform differed from a community of property regime. Understanding this distinction first requires some insight into what community of property entails, how the MWA Bill shares some similarities with this regime, and how it is also distinctive from it.

A. Similarities to Community of Property

The MWA's proposals for pooling income and certain types of property look like community of property, as community of property similarly provides for the

---

[47] Paraphrased from the MWA's Evidence for the Royal Commission on Marriage and Divorce, 1952, 5SPG/I/08, TWL. These principles were incorporated into multiple drafts of the MWA Equal Partnership Bill throughout the 1940s and 1950s.
[48] Conferred by s 23, Matrimonial Causes Act 1973.
[49] As enshrined in a list of factors the court can consider under s 25, Matrimonial Causes Act 1973.
[50] s 25(1), Matrimonial Causes Act 1973.
[51] See, eg, *Jones v Jones* [2011] EWCA Civ 41.

systematic sharing of property, automatically triggered by relationship statuses such as marriage. This could be perceived as meaning spouses own and manage communal property jointly, and depending on the system of rules, communal property could range from property acquired only after the marriage, to all property held by both spouses.[52] This joint ownership approach to community of property is based on a very different premise from the concept of unity explored in chapter two. Instead, as Elizabeth Cooke, Anne Barlow and Thérèse Callus have pointed out, it is 'compatible with the need for equality between the spouses', as it entitles 'the non-earning spouse to some property by virtue of the marriage union'.[53]

For this reason, the MWA expressed strong interest in the Swedish Marriage Code of 1920, where deferred community was adopted after women were given the right to vote. This differed from Sweden's previous system of immediate community of property, because while the latter regime pooled *all* spouses' assets, the deferred system only applied to marital assets, meaning inherited, gifted and premarital assets remained separate property over which the other spouse would have no claim. Keen to learn more, the MWA sent a delegation of three members to Scandinavia, which was reported in *Wife and Citizen*. They interviewed 'married women in all walks of life' and concluded that 'the operation of the laws has worked itself into the social pattern of the community and no husband or wife thinks it strange to share equally and that the wife should know – and she certainly does – her husband's income'.[54] At an SPG conference with a session devoted to Equal Partnership, the MWA reported on Swedish law as it had been explained to them by Swedish Ambassador Bengt Akerren.[55] The Association noted in particular that the Marriage Code 'specifically sets forth the principle of equality in marriage', that 'each spouse has special marriage rights in the property of the other spouse' and that 'each spouse manages his or her own property but must observe special rules safeguarding it' so that nothing must be done to the property to the detriment of the other spouse.[56] Finally, the MWA described spouses' obligation to disclose information about income and assets to their partner to determine how much property should be designated for common use.

Several aspects of these MWA reports on Swedish law are echoed in the Association's legislation. This is perhaps unsurprising given the MWA's aims, for as Cooke et al have noted, within the Swedish regime:

---

[52] E Cooke, A Barlow and T Callus, *Community of Property: A Regime for England and Wales?* (Nuffield Foundation 2006) 4.

[53] ibid.

[54] Delegation of Married Women's Association to the Scandinavian Countries, *Wife and Citizen*, August 1950, 7TBG/1/32, TWL.

[55] Report on Weekend Conference of the Six Point Group, MWA Newsletter, December 1958, 7TBG/2/J/08, TWL.

[56] ibid.

[T]he equality of the sexes is promoted through the recognition that in the traditional division of roles within a marriage, there may be one breadwinner and one homemaker, but that both activities are of equal value to the marriage union and consequently any property of the union must be held in community for the benefit of both spouses.[57]

Sweden's codification of the requirement for spouses to disclose their own property interests was also important to the MWA. The Association repeatedly emphasised the importance of this. It included a clause requiring disclosure in each version of its Bill for equal partnership in marriage and also drafted a separate Bill solely on this issue titled the Married Persons Income Disclosure Bill.[58] In its Newsletter, the MWA illustrated the problem of non-disclosure through anecdotes such as this:

Recently a woman applying for a home help to look after her and her family during a confinement filled in the application form from the local council stating her husband's wages as £6.10. a week. The organiser in that particular department knew that the mother was starving herself to keep the children clothed and fed, but when the form was checked with the husband's employer it was disclosed that the husband, with overtime, was earning £16.17.0. The organiser had to keep that news to herself because it was confidential. The wife got the home help free – she thought, but the husband unbeknown to her, paid the full rate of 3/- per hour.[59]

The other issue with disclosure of income related to tax, which Ambrose Appelbe publicly condemned as being one of the 'appalling anomalies which are an insult to women'.[60] As he explained:

[W]hen a married couple's income is assessed jointly, a man can keep his income secret but a woman has to reveal hers because it is added to his for tax purposes. If a couple are assessed separately, the husband still gets the tax form addressed to him.[61]

This clearly placed the power in the husband's hands. His ability to keep information about his own finances to himself – a privilege not afforded to his wife – created an imbalance of both financial knowledge and control. This was not ameliorated until 6 April 1990[62] when independent taxation was introduced for all individuals.[63] For other parts of the British Isles, this reform took even longer. Independent taxation for married and civilly partnered women in Jersey was not introduced until 2022.[64]

---

[57] Cooke et al, above n 52, 4.

[58] Dated 1975. 5MWA/1/2/2/2, TWL.

[59] J Frances, Chairman's Address, MWA Newsletter, undated, 7TBG/1/32, TWL.

[60] Gorb, above n 37.

[61] ibid.

[62] Announced in Budget statement in 1988: HC Deb 15 March 1988, vol 129, cols 997–98.

[63] See A Seely, 'Income tax allowances for married couples', House of Commons Library Research Briefing, 9 September 2019, available at: https://commonslibrary.parliament.uk/research-briefings/sn00870/.

[64] 'Separate assessments for married couples and civil partnerships', *Information and public services for the Island of Jersey*, available at: https://www.gov.je/TaxesMoney/IncomeTax/Technical/Guidelines/pages/separateassessments.aspx.

Taking these different elements of the Bill and the Swedish inspiration behind it into account, the MWA's Bill for equal partnership in marriage looks rather like a proposal for a system of deferred community of property in all but name. This was not the case.

B. Distinctive from Community of Property

In spite of the similarities between the MWA's Bill and community of property, the Bill was distinctive in three respects. First, under a system of community of property, communal assets are automatically divided in half when the regime is dissolved on divorce.[65] The MWA did not favour 50/50 division and instead preferred property distribution on divorce to be based on judicial discretion. Second, the doctrine of separate property is maintained. The draft bills only dealt with the sharing of income, with amendments in later years to include joint ownership of the matrimonial home, but all other property would remain separate. The third key distinction was that the MWA proposed for joint ownership during marriage to be legally enforceable. Yet under a deferred community of property regime in practice, equal division of assets does not happen until the dissolution of the regime on divorce. This falls short of what the MWA was looking for: married women's legally enforceable property rights to ensure equal partnership *during* marriage.

Furthermore, although the MWA clearly admired aspects of the Swedish system, even referring to it as part of the 'vanguard of modern matrimonial practice',[66] it was still hesitant about the concept of community of property. Opinion among MWA members was divided on the subject and meetings were held to discuss the relative merits of Equal Partnership and Community of Property.[67] Conceptually, the distinction seemed important in the context of the Married Women's Property Act 1882. One of the reasons separate property was a significant achievement for feminists was that it contradicted the idea of marriage as 'one flesh', and instead carved out a separate and independent identity for women within marriage. Maintaining this independence was important for MWA members, several of whom were especially concerned that the Bill for equal partnership in marriage would undermine this.[68] Therefore, the MWA believed that under their proposals, separate ownership of property and capital by each spouse once an agreed division of matrimonial assets had occurred was distinctive from any blanket idea of community. And by making this distinction,

---

[65] Immediate community divides assets from the start of the marriage and deferred community divides assets acquired during the marriage.

[66] Report on Weekend Conference of the Six Point Group, above n 55.

[67] One example of such a meeting took place on 10 November 1965 at the Ivanhoe Hotel, with legal adviser Dennis Walker speaking on community of property and Roxane Arnold speaking on Equal Partnership: MWA Bulletin, September 1965, 5MWA/3/1, TWL.

[68] Such as Doreen Gorsky and Helen Nutting.

the MWA saw married women as maintaining an individual but equal identity within the marital partnership.

As well as *conceptual* issues with community of property, the MWA sought to distinguish its Bill from community regimes practically too. Sharing half of all property and debt might still leave some women in a financially precarious position. For instance, if the sole asset was the matrimonial home, half of the proceeds of its sale might not leave the wife with enough capital to rehouse herself in the event of divorce. The MWA's idea of discretionary provision would give a judge power to make property adjustment on divorce to prevent this from happening, a prescient proposal given that this has been the direction of travel family law has since followed. In short, the Bill for equal partnership in marriage provided for equal control and ownership of marital assets during the marriage, but unlike a community regime, this did not translate into strict equal division on divorce.

However, even though the MWA's Equal Partnership idea was not tantamount to community of property, it was quite radical when appreciated within the broader context of family law history. There is still no law governing the ownership of income or property during marriage and spouses today have complete autonomy to arrange their financial matters as they see fit. Legal intervention continues to focus on questions of property ownership only when the marriage ends.

The idea of joint ownership was also arguably radical as it had socialist leanings.[69] Just as the wages for housework model foreshadowed ideas that would later emerge from the Marxist feminists of the Women's Liberation Movement (albeit with very different ideological underpinnings, as we have seen), it could also be suggested that the joint ownership model foreshadowed ideas that emerged much later in the writings of feminist theorists. The MWA proposal that the wife shares in the husband's pay cheque mirrors an idea later put forward by Susan Moller Okin in her 1989 'treatise for greater gender justice and equality in the family',[70] *Justice Gender, and the Family*.[71] Here, Okin suggested that when labour is divided according to the 'traditional' housemaker/breadwinner pattern, the breadwinner's employer should pay half of the breadwinner's salary to the homemaker. This proposal, which prioritises the question of who owns what during marriage is closer to the MWA's Bill for equal partnership in marriage than a community of property regime. Okin's justification for this also echoes MWA reasoning; housewives are given equal economic power to their husbands, thereby undermining a key tenet of women's inequality: power and control over finances. Like the MWA, Okin is clear that the husband should not pay the wife a wage. And criticism of Okin's

---

[69] Though it is important to note that the MWA was a cross-party organisation.

[70] NJ Hirschmann, 'The Sexual Division of Labor and the Split Paycheck' (2016) 31 *Hypatia* 651, 651.

[71] SM Okin, *Justice, Gender, and the Family* (Basic Books 1989).

proposal could be equally levied against the MWA Bill. As Nancy Hirshmann has argued, this proposal undermines 'the root of the problem of gender equality: the unequal sexual division of labour'.[72] Her description of the intrigue provoked by this proposal also encapsulated the complexity of what the MWA stood for:

> [T]he idea is so fundamentally radical while being lodged in a liberal or even conservative framework: it combines corporate involvement with familial relations with indirect state involvement, vis-à-vis enforcing corporate behavior to permit a 'traditional' form of life.[73]

The Bill for equal partnership in marriage is similarly oxymoronic. It is radical, because of its ideas of property sharing, equality and economic entitlement based on domestic work. And yet it is also conservative, as it reinforced the traditional dichotomy of the housewife and husband as breadwinner. The Bill marked a shift in thinking from the feminist attitudes in previous decades towards married women's legal status. The economic roots of women's oppression were not properly understood until a younger generation of feminists went beyond the ideas of the 'new' feminists like Eleanor Rathbone to identify with socialism and the labour movement. 'At this point', Blackford noted, 'a distinctive labour women's perspective which prioritised women's social and economic needs within marriage began to emerge'.[74]

C. Drafting Strategy

Once the MWA had agreed upon the core tenets of its reform, the next step was to translate these principles into a Bill that could be put before Parliament. For Billington-Greig, getting the wording right was of crucial importance:

> Once this Bill is publicised nothing *we say* will compare with *what the Bill says*. The impression it makes on the Parliamentarian and the Press will depend very largely on what we do in the drafting: *not* on our arguments or speeches. Hence my emphasis on making the Bill as simple, as clear, and as explanatory as possible – so that the supporters in getting it passed are assisted and the opponents are deprived of arguments against it.[75]

This letter reveals how the MWA's strategy as a small pressure group turned towards working within legal institutions to effect change. In the view of Billington-Greig and other members, their Bill mattered more than the Association's public statements, as they believed their best chance of having

---

[72] Hirschmann, above n 70, 654.
[73] ibid.
[74] Blackford, 'Ideas, Structures and Practices of Feminism 1939–64', above n 10, 111.
[75] Letter from Teresa Billington-Greig to Juanita Frances, 28 August 1958, 7TBG/2/J/08, TWL (emphasis in original).

their specific proposals taken forward was for a member of the Commons or the Lords successful in the Private Member's Bill ballot to agree to introduce the Bill in Parliament.

The MWA's strategy when drafting shows the importance of its legal connections. Barrister and long-term MWA and SPG member Roxane Arnold took on most of this work, though other noteworthy lawyers were also involved.[76] Legal academic Dr Olive Stone assisted the Association with drafts and explanatory notes in the 1960s and 1970s. And family lawyers might be surprised to learn that Roger Ormrod, who is best known for his work as an English Lord Justice of Appeal, proffered his services when working as a barrister in the 1950s. But the MWA Executive Committee was critical of the draft he produced. Juanita Frances disclosed privately: 'Unexpectedly Mrs Ormrod has sent a draft Bill put together by herself and her husband. There are some good points in it, but it is not equal partnership as we understand it and agree'.[77] Why this was the case is unclear.

*

Taking the 1975 draft as an example, the Bill spans 10 pages and includes 14 clauses, comprehensively covering the principles considered above.[78] First, spouses would retain separate property but must pool their income[79] (unless it is subject to a trust, charge, or settlement).[80] Once this happened, husband and wife would be expected to decide mutually what part of that common income was to be used for household expenses, for their children or other dependants and for their own requirements and necessities. Then, any money left over, or any property purchased out of this common income, could be divided at mutually agreed intervals. This is an important distinction from community of property, as the division of property occurs periodically and without the need for separation to trigger such division.[81] Once each spouse had their share, this would be classified as separate property and they would be free to manage it independently of their partner.[82]

Under the 1975 draft, spouses also could not dispose of their capital income in a way that would frustrate the effect of the Bill[83] and if this happened, the other spouse could apply to an 'Equal Partnership Tribunal' to have such a disposition set aside and/or give consequential directions on payments or

---

[76] Solicitor Dennis Walker played a significant role in the 1975 draft of the Equal Partnership in Marriage Bill.

[77] Letter from Juanita Frances to Teresa Billington-Greig dated 3 September (no year), 7TBG/2/J/08, TWL.

[78] Equal Partnership Bill 1975, above n 46.

[79] Clause 1.

[80] Clause 9.

[81] Clause 2.

[82] Clause 3.

[83] Clause 3(2).

property dispositions.[84] Earlier drafts of the Bill stipulated that either spouse would 'have the right to apply to court at any time if he is dissatisfied with the management of the family income.[85] This is open to criticism, for it could be argued that this tribunal would do nothing to help the spouse unprepared to seek official adjudication. The Bill also stipulated that disclosures of income tax must be signed by both spouses to ensure full disclosure of income,[86] and a spouse would have the right to request copies of their partner's income tax returns either from the date of the marriage or for a period within the last six years.[87] The matrimonial home and its contents were designated common property under the Bill.[88]

Once drafts of the Bill were produced, members of the MWA Executive Committee provided feedback. Billington-Greig's papers include several drafts she had obviously scrutinised,[89] which are covered in her handwritten comments. Other members' notes are more scarce among the archival documents. Billington-Greig's papers reveal that after the legal provisions of the Bill were drafted satisfactorily, the next stage in drafting strategy could be engaged – identifying and addressing opposition. She wrote to Roxane Arnold with her thoughts:

> I send on my comments and expectations. The draft – so far as I am judge – promises to become quite admirable as a *legal* document. I am now more concerned with the psychological problem of how to minimise opposition ... We would be badly off without your skilled guidance.[90]

Billington-Greig's concern to minimise opposition implies that the MWA was having difficulty doing exactly that. Presenting the proposed legislation to the world, unfiltered, without strategically dealing with potential opposition, would in her view make the Bill destined to fail. So Billington-Greig suggested in her comments on the draft Bill that while it was 'really bad policy' to assume 'immediate opposition', the Bill should anticipate the need for 'explanation and guidance' to 'minimise opposition and irritation and family discomfort.[91] Put simply, 'the strategic angle' according to Billington-Greig was 'not only what we are to claim?' but how the MWA was 'to give all those affected the easiest way to understand how it will affect their lives'.[92]

The content of these letters helps explain the time and effort put into the drafting of the guidance notes as well as the Bill itself. The 1975 Bill, for

---

[84] ibid.
[85] Married Persons (Equal Partnership) Bill 1958 Bill, 5MWA/1/2/2/2, TWL.
[86] Clause 4.
[87] Clause 5.
[88] Clause 6.
[89] As she died in 1964, she did not peruse the 1975 draft outlined above.
[90] Letter from Teresa Billington-Greig to Roxane Arnold, 21 August 1958, 7TBG/2/J/08, TWL.
[91] Teresa Billington-Greig's comments on draft of Equal Partnership Bill, July 1958, 7TBG/2/J/08, TWL.
[92] Letter from Teresa Billington-Greig to Juanita Frances, above n 75.

instance, includes a clause providing that on giving notice of the marriage, couples would be provided with statements giving guidance on the effect of the Equal Partnership legislation.[93] By explaining its purpose, the MWA strategy was to minimise the

> personal objections from both sides – husbands resenting the reduced dominance of the 'master of the house' and the wife shirking conflict and/or unwilling to have to deal with financial matters with which she does not wish to be burdened. Or she may object through fear of finding out more than she wants to know.[94]

Though Billington-Greig believed these obstacles could not be removed, she was keen to reassure those who potentially would be uncomfortable with shaking the status quo of the patriarchal household.

III. THREE FAILED ATTEMPTS

The rest of this chapter outlines the MWA's failed efforts to pass the Bill for equal partnership in marriage during 1943 to 1944, 1958 and 1975 to 1981. The focus on these three periods should not create the misleading impression that in other years the Association was not promoting this draft legislation. Indeed, as chapter six shows, its efforts to influence the Royal Commission on Marriage and Divorce during the first half of the 1950s was a turning point for the MWA and its legal ambitions. As a result, the snapshots provided in this chapter instead reveal some of the strategies implemented by the Association, and how their Bill provoked a mixture of different reactions over several decades, ranging from incredulousness to respect.

A. Responses in 1943–1944

The earliest attempt by the MWA to translate its idea for a new marriage law into a draft bill was in 1939.[95] But it was not until 1943 that the MWA had built up enough momentum to put forward its Bill for equal partnership in marriage. The catalyst for this was the case of *Blackwell v Blackwell*[96] and the campaign that followed it, which is the focus of the next chapter. The appellate stage of this case was funded by the MWA, and the appellant Dorothy Blackwell (who ultimately lost her housekeeping savings to her husband) became the face of a campaign showing how the harsh stipulations of separate property served to deprive married women of the chance for economic independence.

---

[93] Clause 8.
[94] Equal Partnership Bill 1975, above n 46.
[95] Married Persons (Financial Provision) Bill (emanating from the Six Point Group sub-committee), 9 March 1939, 7TBG/2/J/12, TWL.
[96] [1943] 2 All ER 579.

With MWA membership at its peak and exposure of its aims and work in the press and in Parliament,[97] it seemed an ideal time for the Association to push its Bill as an option for reform. The MWA's 1944 Annual Report described how a group of representative members met the Attorney General Donald Somervell and Solicitor General David Fyfe at the Home Office.[98] Both refused to make any undertaking to introduce legislative reform but the MWA representatives still gave them a draft of their Bill for equal partnership in marriage.[99] Though the government had refused to take the MWA's reform proposals forward, the Association reported that they had been given 'a very patient and indeed sympathetic hearing'.[100]

But the government's politeness belied a reaction closer to horror at what the MWA was proposing. This was evident when Edith Summerskill (then MWA President) asked Somervell in the Commons whether he was aware of the *Blackwell* case and prepared to amend the law 'which denies a wife a right to a share of the family income'.[101] Summerskill's proposal was labelled a 'novel and dangerous element in matrimonial relations' by Permanent Secretary to the Lord Chancellor's Office, Claud Schuster.[102] Pressure for change was mounting thanks in part to the MWA campaign, with the records of the Lord Chancellor's Office stating that 'the demand by married women for some pecuniary recognition of their services in the home is strong and is, I suspect, likely to grow'.[103] Writing to Somervell, Schuster said those swayed by the need for reform 'might not realise how many are the legal difficulties which are involved' in what the MWA wanted 'and ... we might find ourselves committed to a course of action which we might subsequently regret'.[104] By the end of 1943, Minister of Labour Ernest Bevin (who previously had been sympathetic to the need for reform), wrote to Somervell telling him: 'The more I think about it, the more I become convinced that we should not attempt to deal with this matter unless we are forced to do so'. If it became impossible to resist pressure, a Bill providing for equal division of savings would be the 'nearest way out of an awkward position'.[105]

This suggests that in 1943, the prospect of more limited reform giving wives a right to half the housekeeping savings was considered as a way to appease those rallied by the MWA campaign. Yet even this much more narrowly constrained reform took a further 21 years to become law.[106]

---

[97] Blackford, 'Ideas, Structures and Practices of Feminism 1939–64', above n 10, 102.

[98] MWA Annual Report 1944, 7TBG/1/32, TWL.

[99] This iteration of the Bill was titled the 'Financial Partnership – Married Person's Bill'.

[100] MWA Annual Report 1944, above n 98.

[101] ibid.

[102] Memo from Claud Schuster, May 1943, LC02/2777, TNA.

[103] Letter from GP Coldstream to ME Reed, 15 July 1943, LC02/2777, TNA.

[104] Letter from Claud Schuster to Donald Somervell, 6 December 1943, LC02/2777, TNA.

[105] Letter from Ernest Bevin to Donald Somervell, 29 December 1943, LC02/2777, TNA.

[106] Pursuant to the Married Women's Property Act 1964.

It is unclear whether the MWA could have achieved this reform of house-keeping savings sooner if it had focused solely on this discrete issue. In the 1940s, the MWA strategy was to push for more extensive reform instead. But as the MWA later learned, it appeared their most comprehensive Bill was to have the poorest chance of success.

B. Responses in 1958

Fifteen years later, the MWA again put forward its Bill for equal partnership in marriage. The Association decided during its 1957 Annual General Meeting that 'the time was not yet ripe' for putting its proposed reform forward because 'public opinion would have to be much more enlightened than it is at present'.[107] Yet in the months that followed, it felt that new factors made it 'imperative' to press on with reform.

First, a system of 'community of surplus' was brought into force in the law of the German Federal Republic in 1958 through what was termed the *Gleichberechtigungs-Gesetz* or 'the law on equal rights of husband and wife in private law'.[108] It is unsurprising that the MWA considered this 'forward looking' and 'great reform' given it was based upon the principle of spousal equality enshrined in the Bonn Basic Law.[109] The reform also shared similarities with the MWA's Bill, as although it was labelled a system of 'community of surplus' Otto Kahn-Freund commented at the time that it was 'not a community at all, as that term is normally understood'.[110] Separate property between husband and wife was maintained, while any surplus property gained during the marriage was equalised on divorce. Unlike the MWA's proposals, it is a method of accounting between spouses, distributing the accumulation of income and property at the end of the marriage and not during it. Even so, the MWA viewed the publicity given to this reform in the UK as creating an opportunity for the Association to present their Bill for equal partnership in marriage and to draw attention to how England and Wales lagged behind.

Although these developments in Germany were important to the MWA, they do not explain why the MWA prepared its Bill with such urgency, especially when members had recently decided against putting it forward. The real reason for this rush was they had learned that a rival group of former MWA members known as the Council of Married Women was preparing a Bill to be sponsored

---

[107] Equal Financial Partnership in Marriage Bill, MWA Newsletter, December 1958, 7TBG/2/J/08, TWL.
[108] O Kahn-Freund, 'Matrimonial Property – Some Recent Developments' (1959) 22 *MLR* 241, 253.
[109] Basic Law for the Federal Republic of Germany of 23 May 1949, art 3, para 2, as cited in ibid, 254.
[110] Kahn-Freund, above n 108.

by an MP. Chapter six explains the activities of this breakaway group in greater detail. The Bill was to advance reform proposals based on the model the MWA had previously discarded – wages for wives. The MWA felt it urgently needed to counteract this with its own response, arguing that the 'most serious danger in the Council of Married Women's proposal' was

> that if by chance it found a sponsor in the House, the whole question of the economic position of the married woman would be debated in Parliament at this rather pitiful level and the wider question of her status in the home and in the national economy would be ignored.[111]

The 1958 draft dealt primarily with the sharing of income during marriage.[112] Spouses could contract out of this by registering at the time of the marriage not to own their income in common, and any other items of property could be designated separate property too. As a result, by distinguishing its Bill from the German reform, arguing it did not go as far as a community system, the MWA was strategically couching its proposals in more conservative terms. The Bill reportedly garnered some interest, with Lord Pethick-Lawrence telling the MWA he hoped to introduce it as a Private Member's Bill in early 1959.[113] But despite the MWA's work, the Bill was never presented to Parliament.

C. A Final Push

By the mid-1970s, the political climate had changed radically and the deadlock between religious conservatives and progressives over divorce reform had finally been broken. The passage of the Divorce Reform Act 1969 had been countered by those who said reform of divorce would not be just to women without reassessing its financial consequences first. As we shall see in chapter eight, this created an opportunity for married women's property rights to be debated in Parliament. This culminated in the Matrimonial Proceedings and Property Act 1970, which explicitly recognised the need to compensate spouses for their unpaid contributions to marriage. Naturally, with the issue of economic equality in marriage finally being considered by Parliament and the executive, in addition to other feminist issues being brought to the surface with the Women's Liberation Movement, the MWA probably felt public opinion was 'enlightened' in a way its members had been waiting for. By this stage, the MWA was considered an 'old style' feminist group,[114] especially in comparison to the feminists of

---

[111] MWA Newsletter, December 1958, above n 107.

[112] ibid. A sub-committee was set up to draft the 1958 Bill, consisting of Roxane Arnold, Teresa Billington-Greig, Hazel Huskins-Hallinan and Juanita Frances.

[113] Letter from Juanita Frances to Teresa Billington-Greig, 17 July 1958, 7TBG/2/J/08, TWL.

[114] Stetson, above n 6, 248.

the 'second wave'. But even though public opinion had changed, getting those in power to take the MWA's proposals forward was another matter.

Over a period of six years, the MWA pressed the Law Commission and Lord Chancellor's office to consider its Bill. Finally, in 1981 MWA members presented Prime Minister Margaret Thatcher with a letter on their work. She passed their letter to the Lord Chancellor to answer. The reply was as follows:

> It is not entirely clear what your Association means by financial equality within marriage but it may be that your suggestion is that the division of the income of a married couple should be regulated by statute and that this should be so even where the marriage has not broken down and the husband and wife are living together. Whilst the hardship for a fair division of the family income must excite sympathy, it is doubtful whether your proposed remedy is sufficiently acceptable to public opinion as a whole; indeed it is likely to provoke strong opposition. To allow suits by a spouse for a share of the family income would be regarded by many as an unjustifiable interference in the family relationship which orders against a recalcitrant husband or wife when the spouses are still living together may well have a disruptive effect on marriage.[115]

The MWA noted that this was 'the official draft reply we have been receiving from the Law Commission and Lord Chancellor for the last six years'.[116]

It seemed the most the MWA could hope for was equal rights in the matrimonial home, as there did not appear to be appetite for reform that would apply also to capital during the marriage. As chapter nine explains further. this was brought before the House of Lords as the Matrimonial Homes (Co-ownership) Bill by Lord Simon, but it failed too, quashed by the backlash of the Campaign for Justice in Divorce that argued the law had gone too far to protect married women.

*

These failed attempts indicate how difficult it was for the MWA to have its Bill taken forward. The Association had what it believed to be the legislative answer to women's economic and financial inequality in marriage, but as Billington-Greig had argued repeatedly, the other side of this reform strategy had to be anticipating and dealing with the opposition to this legislation. As this chapter has shown, the MWA's Bill was not taken seriously by those in power. Yet as this book will show in later chapters, aspects of the Bill re-emerged alongside debates about financial provision for married women. While its proposals might have been radical in the 1940s, by the 1970s they were a viable option, when the question of married women's property rights was brought to the surface alongside reform of divorce.

---

[115] MWA Bulletin, April–May 1981, 5MWA/8/1, TWL.
[116] ibid.

One of the reasons the Bill did not receive the support the MWA had hoped for was that it transgressed the boundaries of the public/private divide; it contained revolutionary provisions that related to the management and ownership of capital during marriage. This was clear in the responses the MWA received from the Lord Chancellor's Office. Politicians such as Jean Mann MP, who supported the idea for wives' right to housekeeping savings considered the MWA proposals as 'impractical' and as inviting unwarranted legal intrusion into private family life, as the Association reported: 'She would not consider any legislation which would encourage more snoopers in homes, nor would she consent to a law which would make a gainfully employed wife the victim of a possibly shiftless and dissolute husband.[117] Whether this perceived threat to autonomy was ultimately why the MWA Bill was never introduced or even officially recognised is unclear. If this is indeed the case, it seems the potential of this Bill has been missed. For it was not a Bill aimed at controlling how spouses manage their assets; it was an attempt to codify the idea that women should know what their husbands earn, have a say in how the income they help generate is spent, and have a legal right in their own family home. This idea eventually *was* considered seriously by the Law Commission in 1988,[118] in a report that the MWA must have supported, though records from this time are sparse. This report did not culminate in reform, but significantly, the Law Commission proposed rules governing property ownership during marriage. That this report was published almost 50 years after the MWA was formed suggests the Association may have been ahead of its time.

D. A Persistent Agenda

The MWA had experienced setbacks and rejection from the beginning, so must have been somewhat accustomed to having its Bill for equal partnership in marriage rejected repeatedly from the late 1930s and early 1940s, through to the 1980s. In 1939, Summerskill already appeared to be familiar with the outrage provoked by the idea a wife could have a legal right to know about and share in her partner's income:

> I remember asking the Prime Minister a question in this House showing that in the household where she is not getting a fair share of the family income, and where she feels that she cannot feed her children properly, the wife should have the right to know what her husband earns in order that she could establish a legal right to a share of the family income. The Prime Minister treated the matter with the utmost flippancy and the House roared with laughter.[119]

---

[117] Deputation to House of Commons, *Wife and Citizen*, February 1949, 7TBG/1/32, TWL.
[118] Law Commission, *Family Law: Matrimonial Property* (Law Com No 175, 1988).
[119] HC Deb 24 October 1939, vol 352, col 1260.

The MWA's persistence in the face of such a reaction must have been exhausting. Four decades later, Summerskill recalled a conversation with Eleanor Rathbone which helps to explain the tenacity she shared with her MWA colleagues:

> I was always impressed by [Rathbone's] capacities to withstand the hostility, the ridicule and indeed the cruelty of certain male Members of the Commons ... In the Women's Room one night I said to her: 'I am very impressed with your struggle. Don't you get downhearted?' She replied: 'No. I have a philosophy. Always remember this. Twenty-five years must elapse between the inception and the fruition of a new idea'. With that philosophy she struggled on.[120]

Here, Summerskill described a sclerotic system prejudiced against women and the issues affecting them, yet her sentiments were still infused with inspiration and hope. Implicit in her words was the notion that pressing for reform was a struggle, but perseverance could work.

From this, it seems the MWA was aware of the *limitations* of legal and political institutions in improving women's position in marriage. For example, the Association somewhat confusingly continued its trade union policy in the early 1940s – which implied the regulation of husband and wife as master and worker – even while it was pushing its Bill for joint ownership in marriage at the same time. Though ostensibly conflicting policies, this trade union concept enabled the MWA to monitor and help wives in their marriages, suggesting the Association's emphasis on pragmatism, not on abstract self-identification. This could also be interpreted as indicating that MWA members knew that legislating for equality would not necessarily achieve it, nor would equal partnership in law mean there would no longer be an imbalance of power between the money earning husband and the non-gainfully employed wife. They were aware that support for married women was necessary regardless of legislative reform, which was not a short-term endeavour.

Meanwhile, the MWA's aims when drafting legislation had to take a different tone from its work as an unofficial trade union. The MWA decided to strike a balance in its Bill that would emphasise equality between husband and wife, in language that avoided treating the wife as subservient to her husband. The concept of joint ownership in marriage could in theory mean that the court, as it did in *re Kendrew*, would not need to further the notion that the 'relationship of husband and wife was not incompatible with that of master and servant'[121] so to provide financial redress to the wife.

Nevertheless, the MWA *was* proposing something radical. Its Bill to reform the economic consequences of marriage was a failed Bill, an obscure piece of legal history, and largely forgotten in histories of family law reform. But this does not mean it was wasted work. Though the Bill never even came before

---

[120] HL Deb 24 January 1973, vol 338, cols 159–60.
[121] *Kendrew*, above n 27.

Parliament, its principles were influential in smaller, subtler but important ways. For instance, as chapter eight reveals, discussions over the MWA's policy of joint ownership of the home influenced MP Edward Bishop before he introduced the Matrimonial Property Bill in 1969. This Bill was important because it played a key role in pushing the government towards agreeing to reform the financial consequences of divorce in 1970.

Questioning why the MWA's Bill failed also makes us probe the recesses of law reform procedures. Repeatedly, the MWA is told its Bill is impractical and paternalistic. The corollary of this, arguably, is that *prudent* reform is perhaps more narrowly constrained in the issues it addresses or shies away from allowing the court to become involved with decision-making in what has been designated the private sphere – inside the family home.

CONCLUSION

Though mindful of law's limitations, MWA members seemingly knew they would face opposition but continued to press on with their Bill regardless. It appears that a factor driving the group's persistence was the belief that its work on the ground assisting financially vulnerable women could only go so far. Instead, structural change was needed to make a difference. Take, for example, this letter written by Teresa Billington-Greig to Juanita Frances in August 1958:

> I am not concerned with past propaganda – the MWA has done as much as it could – for which I admire it – but there are millions of people who have never been touched by it. But they will all be touched by the Bill – at least the great majority of them will.[122]

Her writing evokes a passion and belief that radical change *is* possible if tackled in the right way. And, that legislation would be necessary for real change. A small pressure group like the MWA was in her view best placed to help married women by undermining the structures contributing to their oppression. As she writes in the same letter: 'This Bill is the biggest thing women have asked for since the Vote – it means a domestic revolution'.[123] That she wrote this in a private letter suggests she genuinely believed in the revolutionary potential of this reform to transform women's lives. However, as the next chapter will show, the MWA needed not just a legislative solution, but effective propaganda too. In its efforts to influence law, the Association's most effective form of propaganda stemmed from one case – *Blackwell v Blackwell*.[124]

---

[122] Letter from Teresa Billington-Greig to Juanita Frances, above n 75.
[123] ibid.
[124] [1943] 2 All ER 579.

5

Mrs Blackwell

I get two pounds five from my husband. The other week there was such a to-do because I asked for another 5s. Groceries are 30s, butcher 10s. That leaves me 5s for everything else for the rest of the week. I have always been forced to go out to work to augment the housekeeping allowance, and to buy the children's clothes. Two of my three children are now earning, and I am obliged to take their earnings. My husband has a good job, working seven days a week. The house is in my husband's name. I ask you where is his heart? He goes out every night and has plenty of money to spend on his pleasures.

Anon, Birmingham.[1]

INTRODUCTION

As the law stands today, husband and wife face each other in matters of property like strangers. The fact that they are husband and wife has no effect on their property. Nothing is by law 'theirs', everything, from the kitchen cupboard to the savings bank account, and from the family car to the matrimonial home itself, is, in the absence of an express agreement to the contrary, either 'his' or 'hers'. Sociologists must decide whether this legal rule reflects the mores and ideas of the people. It is strongly suspected that it does not.[2]

WRITING IN 1952, Otto Kahn-Freund identifies an important question for matrimonial property law. To what extent did the doctrine of separate property meet the expectations of married couples? Did spouses at this time strictly divide their own property, or was it more likely that families would intermingle assets and use them jointly? The problem with the law treating spouses as discrete individuals in contrast with the community and dependence of family life was the harsh outcomes this could produce. The case of *Blackwell v Blackwell* is a fitting example of this.[3]

This chapter tells the story of *Blackwell*, which involved a dispute over the ownership of savings made from money left over from household expenses. It is arguably one of the most important yet arcane family property cases of the twentieth century,

---

[1] *Wife and Citizen*, August 1950, 7TBG/1/32, TWL.
[2] O Kahn-Freund, 'Inconsistencies and Injustices in the Law of Husband and Wife' (1952) 15 *MLR* 133, 135.
[3] [1943] 2 All ER 579.

and is often overlooked in historical accounts. Studying this case is an example of feminist legal history in action. It represents, as Stephen Cretney has noted, the 'beginning of the move for further reform of family property law'[4] after the Married Women's Property Act 1882 (MWPA 1882). The Married Women's Association (MWA), which funded the appellate stage of this case and had a watching brief,[5] used it to highlight the shortcomings of the separate property doctrine. *Blackwell* can therefore be seen as firing the starting pistol for revolutionary financial property reform later in the twentieth century – reform that would help ameliorate married women's economic vulnerability and attach value to their unpaid labour.

Dorothy Blackwell's experience became the MWA's most effective propaganda tool in emphasising the injustice suffered by housewives under the law,[6] helping to bring the issue of married women's property rights to a nationwide stage. So, the story of *Blackwell* is much more than a case about one woman's claim to house-keeping savings. It marked the MWA's first and longest large-scale campaign, lasting 20 years. This culminated in the MWA's biggest legislative success: Edith Summerskill's Married Women's Property Act 1964 (MWPA 1964), which gave wives a one-half share in housekeeping savings (and property derived from those savings).[7] Conversely, the campaign brought the divisions in the MWA to a head, and as chapter six will explore, led to the fragmentation of the group.[8] But for this chapter, the focus is on the *Blackwell* case, its effectiveness when used by the MWA to pursue its agenda, and what this reveals about family law reform.

Blackwell is also an apposite example of what is missed when feminist historical and doctrinal legal approaches are *not* combined. As this chapter will show, previous historical analyses of this case did not precisely pinpoint the judicial mistakes as well as the broader legal issues. Similarly, doctrinal analyses of the *Blackwell* issue missed crucial facts about Mrs Blackwell's situation, as so little information can be gleaned from a one-page judgment in the *All England Law Reports*. It is only when both perspectives (feminist historical *and* doctrinal legal approaches) are combined that cases like *Blackwell* can be properly under-stood, looking beyond traditional histories where focus has been on family law doctrine,[9] to glean more information about the meanings of rules like separate property for the housewives the MWA sought to represent.

I. BLACKWELL V BLACKWELL

Not much is known about Dorothy and John Blackwell, or why their marriage broke down, but the facts suggest that Dorothy Blackwell had planned to leave

[4] S Cretney, *Family Law in the Twentieth Century* (Oxford University Press 2003) 115.
[5] A brief held by a barrister to follow a case for a client that is not directly involved in the case.
[6] MWA Annual Report 1944, 7TBG/1/32, TWL.
[7] This Act is considered fully in ch 7.
[8] This is because the aftermath of *Blackwell* highlighted divisions between 'old' and 'new' femi-nists which, as ch 2 explained, had already been simmering as the MWA was formed.
[9] M Minow 'Forming Underneath Everything That Grows: Toward a History of Family Law' (1985) 4 *Wisconsin Law Review* 819, 839.

her husband for some time. As a housewife married in 1925 with a child and no independent income, leaving a marriage was not straightforward. She decided that first she would need some degree of economic independence for herself and her son ('myself and my boy to help him on when he gets older').[10] As chapter two explained, the doctrine of separate property pursuant to the MWPA 1882 made this difficult. Dorothy Blackwell's home belonged to her husband and even though she claimed to have contributed £20 to the purchase of the property,[11] her name was not on the deeds. She had no financial independence. So in 1936, Dorothy Blackwell began taking in lodgers. This brought additional income into the household to help pay the mortgage and other bills. During this time, Dorothy's husband John also gave her money for housekeeping. Some of this money was saved in a bank account she held with the Oxford Cooperative Society (though the parties disagreed over the precise source of this money).

In 1941 Dorothy Blackwell left her husband and wrote to him stating that she did not intend to live with him again.[12] She took the money saved in her Cooperative Society account, which amounted to £103 10s with dividends and interest. Her husband John brought action in the county court to recover this money.

Frank Winstanley, the husband's lawyer, argued on his behalf that the money in Dorothy Blackwell's bank account belonged to the husband. She had left him 'for no reason whatever', Winstanley said, and she had never had any separate property of her own or been out to work. The Blackwell's marital home had always been in the husband's name and he had given his wife £3 3s a week. From this perspective, it was unsurprising that Dorothy Blackwell lost her case at first instance. The MWPA 1882 had achieved so much for married women by eroding coverture and giving wives some legal recognition as being *capable* of independence. But the corollary of this was that the law could not help women like Dorothy Blackwell who wanted to be independent but did not have any means of earning money for themselves.

It is important to note what the judges in this case omitted – that the £103 10s successfully claimed by John Blackwell was Dorothy Blackwell's source of economic independence. She was not legally separated from her husband and was paid no maintenance by him, thus she was left with nothing. *Blackwell* was not reported at first instance, and so this background is gleaned from press reports on the case.[13]

*

The following section presents an analysis of the appeal stage of *Blackwell* in two parts: the facts as stated by the court in the published judgment; and

---

[10] 'Wife to Pay Husband Her Savings', Newspaper clipping (undated), 5MWA/1/3/1, TWL.
[11] ibid.
[12] ibid.
[13] See, eg, Anon, 'Court Of Appeal' *Times* (29 October 1943) 2.

the information gleaned from other accounts, including press reports, archival documents and Hansard. Exposing the gaps left by both the legal and non-legal sources on this case highlights the importance of a combined socio-legal analysis, as the complete story of *Blackwell v Blackwell* – and its importance to reform of family law – is pieced together for the first time.

A. The Judgment in Focus

The facts of *Blackwell* as they are presented in the judgment tell a more straightforward story than the one outlined in the previous section. The husband brought legal action against his wife for housekeeping money. He had provided her with this money during marriage to cover household expenses such as groceries and bills, and once these expenses had been covered, the wife saved the surplus. On separation, the husband claimed this money belonged to him. The case is reported in the *All England Law Reports* at the Court of Appeal stage, where the wife challenged the Court's decision to order her to return the savings to the husband. She lost the appeal.

Much of the detail about Dorothy and John Blackwell from the previous section is noticeably missing. The reported judgment in *Blackwell* is short and includes little information about Dorothy Blackwell's circumstances. There is no information about her financial contributions to the home, or the income she provided through bringing in lodgers. Without this information, it is little wonder the case appears to be so simple. All we are told is that there is '*no justification at all* for the contention that'[14] the £103 10s in the Co-operative account in Dorothy Blackwell's name should belong to her.

Though there is little context about what happened between the parties, the judgment provides some scope for deeper legal analysis as it relates to the broader issue of the transfer of property between spouses. A comprehensive doctrinal account requires understanding the rationale underpinning decades of common law in this area. Looking first to the judgment, the basis for the appellate judges' reasoning is unclear, as not one of the three judges refers to any case law. But their conclusion is unambiguous. Providing the leading judgment, Scott LJ held that because the money in Dorothy Blackwell's account came from a weekly allowance paid by her husband, 'this money was still the property of the husband'.[15]

When analysing this decision in the *Modern Law Review* in 1953, Kahn-Freund had no reason to question the judges' assertion that the money in the bank account was comprised solely of savings from housekeeping money.[16]

---

[14] [1943] 2 All ER 579, above n 3, para B (emphasis added).
[15] ibid.
[16] O Kahn-Freund, 'Inconsistencies and Injustices in the Law of Husband and Wife' (1953) 16 *MLR* 34, 40.

On this basis, the Court of Appeal was simply applying the law as it was – the housekeeping savings represented the husband's separate property under law and the husband was entitled to the contents of Dorothy Blackwell's bank account. However, even if the Court had been correct in its application of the law, this did not mean Kahn-Freund agreed with the principle that was applied. Rather, he asserted that this principle was 'a gross injustice' and that he could 'see no justification whatever for' it.[17] His criticism is important, for as we shall see, it pinpoints why matrimonial property law at this time was inconsistent, defective and in need of reform. Furthermore, as detailed assessment of the law in this area is absent from existing historical accounts of *Blackwell*,[18] it merits some consideration here.

On the face of it, the issue of housekeeping savings is a consequence of the MWPA 1882. The wage-earning husband provides his wife with a weekly allowance to cover household expenses, she saves part of that allowance and – sometimes with, sometimes without her husband's knowledge – lodges it in a savings or bank account in her name. It makes sense that because the MWPA 1882 replaced coverture's unification of property on marriage[19] with the separate property doctrine, wages that represented the husband's separate property would not become the wife's just because he has transferred those wages to her for bills. The money does not act as a gift, and as the Court of Appeal in *Blackwell* made clear, the wife is acting only as her husband's agent.

It might seem that *Blackwell* is a straightforward example of the harsh consequences of the separate property doctrine. However, this assessment is flawed because the principle that the husband would retain ownership of money he transferred to his wife was not created with the introduction of separate property in marriage. Instead, the authority for this rule appears to derive from the 1856 case of *Barrack v M'Culloch*,[20] decades before both the MWPA 1870 and MWPA 1882. Thus, the rule did not in fact stem from the doctrine of separate property – it emerged in the context of coverture.

Despite this, *Barrack* appears to have been applied in the post-coverture world of *Blackwell*. *Barrack* was a case primarily about embezzlement, in which a minor point was raised as to whether money invested by the wife rightfully belonged to her husband. In deciding this point, Page-Wood VC said obiter: 'Any money given to [a wife] by her husband for household purposes, or for dress, or the like, and applied by her in making investments in her own name would belong to her husband'. It is crucial to reiterate, as Kahn-Freund did in his analysis of the issue in 1953, that this statement is *obiter dictum* and no more. Indeed, the point Page-Wood VC was making would have been obvious at the

---

[17] ibid, 35.

[18] The case is mentioned only briefly in other accounts of the MWA, such as C Blackford, 'Ideas, Structures and Practices of Feminism 1939–64' (PhD thesis, University of East London 1996) 93–94.

[19] ie, in the absence of any trust deed or marriage settlement stipulating otherwise.

[20] [1856] 3 K & J 110.

time as in 1856 a married woman's property vested in her husband automatically under common law. This is supported by the even older judgment in *Lady Tyrell's Case* of 1675, where the Court held:

> For if the wife out of her good housewifery to save any thing out of it; he shall reap the benefit of his wife's frugality ... because when the husband agrees to allow his wife a certain sum yearly, the end of this agreement is, that she may be provided with clothes and other necessaries, and whatsoever is saved out of this redounds to the husband.[21]

One would have thought that the introduction of separate property would have rendered this older dictum obsolete and swept away any authority it might once have had. But this did not happen. Instead, as Kahn-Freund vividly described, Page-Wood VC's 1856 dictum rose from its grave with its ghost 'interfering most disturbingly in the drama of the law'.[22] It was not discussed explicitly in the written judgments of *Blackwell* – no cases were – but *Barrack* is listed in the case's headnote.

Blackwell was not the first time that century that the judiciary had applied the 1856 dictum as if it were sound legal principle, even though it had been abrogated by Parliament as a result of the MWPA 1882.[23] But the fact that the Court of Appeal in *Blackwell* did not explain the relevance of *Barrack* does not absolve it of criticism. Luxmoore LJ's statement that it is 'clear law' that housekeeping savings transferred to the wife do not belong to her is patently a nod to *Barrack* and the cases that applied it.[24] Luxmoore LJ does not, however, consider the basis for this 'clear law'.

For Scott LJ, it was significant that the parties did not discuss the legal implications of John Blackwell's transfer of housekeeping money to his wife, because it meant there was no evidence to suggest he had given her rights of ownership over it. But what if the parties *had* reached an agreement that gave Dorothy Blackwell ownership of the money? Goddard LJ said he was 'far from saying that this sort of domestic arrangement can necessarily result in a legal contract'.[25] Here, Goddard LJ appears to be applying *Balfour v Balfour*,[26] which held that mutual promises made between husband and wife were not contractually binding.

Unlike *Balfour*, however, *Blackwell* is about the legal consequences of transfer of property; it is not a matter of contract law.[27] Therefore, it is striking that

---

[21] *Lady Tyrell's Case* (1675), Freeman's Reports 1660–1706, 304, as cited in S Fredman, *Women and the Law* (Oxford University Press 1998) 20.
[22] Kahn-Freund, 'Inconsistencies and Injustices in the Law of Husband and Wife' (1953), above n 16, 38.
[23] As Kahn-Freund notes, ibid, older dictum was also elevated to legal principle in the earlier case of *Birkett v Birkett* (1908) 98 LT 540, ibid, 39.
[24] [1943] 2 All ER 579, above, n 3.
[25] ibid.
[26] [1919] 2 KB 571; [1919] 6 WLUK 33.
[27] Kahn-Freund, 'Inconsistencies and Injustices in the Law of Husband and Wife' (1953), above n 16, 41.

there was no mention in the reported judgment of the equitable presumptions that purposely exist to resolve doubt in the absence of parties' clear intention when property has been transferred. For example, there was no apparent consideration of the presumption of advancement, which presumes that when property is transferred from husband to wife the husband relinquishes both his equitable and legal ownership of that property.[28] In *Blackwell*, had the presumption of advancement been raised, it would have operated in the wife's favour[29] and she would have won her case.

Taking all this into account – the flawed judicial reasoning, the application of contradictory legal principles, the circumstances and legal principle *not* considered – there is much to criticise about the *Blackwell* judgment. Indeed, the issues with this decision are symptomatic of legal problems that are more far-reaching than Dorothy Blackwell's circumstances, and illustrate broader unresolved issues for married women's property law after the MWPA 1882. This context becomes even clearer once non-legal sources are added to the picture.

B. Beyond Legal Sources

Clearly, there are important aspects that the *Blackwell* judgment does not bring to light. Not only is the law report brief and lacking in detail, it also reveals little about the attitude of the judiciary towards Dorothy Blackwell's appeal. This is because the commentator for the *All England Law Reports* only conveyed a snapshot of what was said in court.[30] One example of this is where the judgment noted there was 'some little doubt' that the legal landscape had been 'affected by social change and the various statutes dealing with the property of married women'.[31] But there was no explanation in the judgment as to what was meant by this.

There is also some indication that the judiciary had discretion to determine the property *did* belong to Dorothy Blackwell pursuant to section 17 of the MWPA 1882. Section 17 stipulates that when there is any question between husband and wife as to the title or possession of property, either party can apply to the court and have the judge resolve the issue. In 1947, Lord Denning interpreted this provision as providing the judge with 'a free hand to do what is just'[32] and used it to prevent a husband from turning his wife out of the marital home.[33] And so the discretion alluded to under section 17 could have been used

---

[28] This rebuts the presumption of resulting trust, which presumes the transferee merely holds the property on trust for the transferor.

[29] Unless there are additional unknown facts that would have meant it could have been rebutted.

[30] *Blackwell* was reported by C St J Nicholson, Barrister-at-Law [1943] 2 All ER 579, above n 3.

[31] ibid.

[32] A Denning, *The Due Process of Law* (Butterworths 1980) 208.

[33] *Hutchinson v Hutchinson* [1947] 2 All ER 792; 63 TLR 645. Lord Denning applied this principle in subsequent cases too, such as *Hine v Hine* [1967] 1 WLR 1124, 1127.

to mitigate the harsh effects of the separate property doctrine.[34] But this did not happen in the *Blackwell* case or in other similar cases.[35] By applying cast iron property law principles instead of using this provision to soften these principles' hard edges, the courts were nullifying the beneficial effect section 17 could have had for married women at that time.[36] And frustratingly, the *Blackwell* judgment does not tell us whether there were any circumstances not disclosed in the judgment that could have justified an award in her favour.

Without this additional context, existing criticism of the Court of Appeal's decision in *Blackwell* is mostly speculative. The judgment does not tell us much of what happened before John Blackwell went to court, or how Dorothy Blackwell funded an appeal when her husband had successfully claimed the savings in the Co-op. At the Court of Appeal stage, information is scarce about the basis of Dorothy Blackwell's appeal or what her lawyers argued. We are only told these arguments are irrelevant in the judgment, but we cannot assess this relevance for ourselves. Lastly, the judgment reveals nothing of the consequences for Dorothy Blackwell.

These gaps provide a stark example of the calls from Felice Batlan, Rosemary Auchmuty and others to look beyond legal sources for a better understanding of law, and in particular its social impact.[37] *Blackwell v Blackwell* not only became one of the most important touchstones in MWA history, it also highlighted the need for further reform of married women's property. Before exploring what the case tells us about reform of family law, this section pieces together more about Dorothy Blackwell's circumstances from non-legal sources. The value in using such sources to – as Auchmuty has put it – 'ask the gender question' is that this approach pushes for further explanation for why the Court refused to countenance the arguments made by Dorothy Blackwell's lawyers.[38] Thus, factoring in the broader context of Dorothy Blackwell's story means refusing to accept the law's traditional explanation that her fate in the Court of Appeal was simply down to precedent and statute.

*

In MWA records and contemporaneous press reports, the details on Dorothy Blackwell's appeal reveal much more about why her case reached the Court

---

[34] Kahn-Freund, 'Inconsistencies and Injustices in the Law of Husband and Wife' (1953), above n 16, 38. NB Lord Denning's assertion that the Court's jurisdiction over family assets was 'entirely discretionary', ibid, *Hine* 1127, to make a fair and just order was overruled by *Pettit v Pettitt* [1970] AC 777, when the House of Lords affirmed that s 17 was procedural only.

[35] *Preston v Preston* 1950 SLT 196; *Hoddinott v Hoddinott* [1949] 2 KB 406.

[36] Kahn-Freund, 'Inconsistencies and Injustices in the Law of Husband and Wife' (1953), above n 16, 43.

[37] F Batlan, 'Engendering Legal History' (2005) 30 *Law & Social Inquiry* 823, 847; R Auchmuty, 'Recovering Lost Lives: Researching Women in Legal History (2015) 42 *Journal of Law and Society* 34, 42.

[38] R Auchmuty, 'Legal History' in R Auchmuty (ed), *Great Debates in Gender and Law* (Macmillan 2018) 176.

of Appeal in the first place, even though the judges appear to have treated the issue as an open and shut matter. The MWA funded the appeal, and explained their rationale for taking on the case in their 1944 Annual Report: 'We fought the *Blackwell* case on a point of law, and in order to draw the attention of Parliament and the public to the serf-like position of housewives'.[39] Dorothy Blackwell's solicitor was Carrie Morrison[40] and Constance Colwill (who became a Vice President of the MWA) and Knight Dix were her counsel – notable given there were so few female lawyers in the early 1940s. With Venetia Stephenson holding a watching brief for the MWA in court, alongside MWA board member Ambrose Appelbe appearing as the MWA's solicitor and Edith Summerskill and Juanita Frances, it might have been apparent in the courtroom that the *Blackwell* case was to attract publicity for being part of a feminist cause. As academic Stephen Cretney later observed, this may have come as a surprise for Dorothy Blackwell's husband John, for his case was being used by public figures such as Edith Summerskill to '[exemplify] the law's injustice to married women'.[41]

The *Blackwell* appeal appears to have been based upon three objections to the county court decision.[42] First, building on the momentum of the Beveridge report outlined in chapter two, Dorothy Blackwell's legal team argued for recognition of work done by housewives. The 'keeping of a house was a skilled occupation',[43] counsel argued, and 'even if a wife saved only 2s or 3s a week she used her talent and industry to do it, and was entitled to keep the money'.[44] This argument was dismissed quickly in court, as at that time there was no legal basis for valuing housewives' work in economic terms. Even if there had been a creative way to interpret the law, the appellate judges were not open to it because in their view, this was an ethical question that was no concern of the law.[45]

Second, the money in the account was not just comprised of housekeeping savings; it also represented money Dorothy Blackwell had contributed to the family. The MWA stated in its report: 'as some of Mrs Blackwell's £103 was saved from money paid to her by a lodger, this was in our submission earnings and not housekeeping money'.[46] There was also, according to Dorothy Blackwell's counsel, a 'special agreement'[47] that any profit made from the lodgers would belong

---

[39] MWA Annual Report 1944, above n 6.

[40] Carrie Morrison was the first woman admitted as a solicitor in England and Wales. She shared a law practice with former husband and MWA lawyer Ambrose Appelbe.

[41] Cretney, above n 4, 115.

[42] *Montgomery v Blows* [1916] 1 KB 899 was cited as authority for the County Court decision in *Blackwell* according to the *Times* report on *Blackwell* in the Court of Appeal: above, n 13.

[43] 'Court Of Appeal', *Times*, above, n 13.

[44] Anon, 'Judges Tell Wives Rights of Husbands' *Daily Mirror* (29 October 1943) 5.

[45] ibid.

[46] MWA Annual Report 1944, above n 6.

[47] 'Court Of Appeal', *Times*, above, n 13.

to her solely, though as we have seen, the Court was reluctant to recognise such agreements because of *Balfour v Balfour*.[48]

Finally, there was evidence suggesting that Dorothy Blackwell's claim to the money was legitimate pursuant to section 7 of the MWPA 1882. This stipulates that when money is invested in a married woman's name, there is a presumption that the money is her property. In this case, the onus was on John Blackwell to rebut this presumption, as the money was invested in his wife's name with his express consent.

This additional information is missing from Scott LJ's summation of the question for the Court:

> [W]hether, where money is handed by a husband to his wife for housekeeping purposes and that money is not fully used by her for those purposes, the balance becomes the wife's private property so that she can keep it for herself.[49]

There was no mention of the fact that the money claimed by the husband was comprised of more than housekeeping savings.[50] And as noted above, only oblique reference was made to the 'special agreement', when Goddard LJ says such agreements have no weight. Scott LJ did not mention this agreement at all, having instead focused on the fact that the parties did not specifically discuss ownership of the housekeeping money. This importantly demonstrates an issue not only with the relevant law in *Blackwell*, but with the attitude of the judiciary too.

One of the more revealing comments from *Blackwell* that appeared in press reports but not in the *All England Reports* was from Goddard LJ: if women were permitted to save out of their housekeeping allowance, and then keep the proceeds, he said, 'women would be tempted to give their husbands tinned meat rather than roast meat'.[51] Housewives should be denied rights in property not only because of precedent, but more insidiously, because they cannot be trusted to administer the money for the good of the family. As Summerskill later pointed out, the wife *could* have spent the housekeeping money on herself instead of having the prudence to invest it.[52] She told the press: 'The decision will encourage every housewife in the country to become a spendthrift and a squander bug'.[53] Furthermore, Goddard LJ's comments echoed Victorian views

---

[48] [1919] 2 KB 571; [1919] 6 WLUK 33, above, n 26, whereby a verbal agreement that the husband would pay his wife £30 per week was held not to be binding. See also SH Blake, *The Law of Marriage*, 3rd edn (Barry Rose 1982) 28: 'the mere fact that a husband says that he will give his wife a specific sum each week for house-keeping is very unlikely to be enforced'.

[49] [1943] 2 All ER 579, above n 3.

[50] Though according to the *Times*, 'Court Of Appeal', above n 13, this was considered at first instance (unreported).

[51] 'Judges Tell Wives Rights of Husbands', *Daily Mirror*, above n 44. Goddard LJ's comment was later recalled in the House of Lords when the Married Women's Savings Bill was being debated: HL Deb 5 July 1963, vol 251, col 1153.

[52] E Summerskill, *A Woman's World* (Heinemann 1967) 146.

[53] Anon, 'Housewives Will Fight for the Right to Save' *Daily Mirror* (29 October 1943) 1.

regarding married women's money mismanagement. Ironically, the enactment of the MWPA 1882 was driven in part by families living in poverty because the *husband* was squandering income needed for household expenses or, as Cretney put it, 'the plight of the woman deserted by a drunken labourer and compelled to keep herself' only to find her savings in a Co-operative Society 'seized by the husband in the exercise of his common law rights'.[54] Yet in spite of the MWPA 1882, Dorothy Blackwell's Co-op savings were still being seized by her estranged husband in 1942, albeit for different legal reasons.

The judicial attitudes in *Blackwell* as reported by the press and the MWA also provided further evidence of the intransigence of the law discussed earlier in this chapter, while confirming the courts' reliance on the 1856 case of *Barrack v M'Culloch*.[55] For example, the MWA notes that the appellate judges claimed 'this law has been followed without question since 1856',[56] while the press reported the judges as saying: 'We cannot upset law which has been settled many years'.[57] That the judiciary chose to attach such significant weight to weak obiter dicta authority implies purposive reasoning. Indeed, some of the judges' remarks suggested they did not agree in principle with the argument that a wife could be entitled to share in money set aside for housekeeping. For instance, Goddard LJ thought it was 'a most astonishing proposition that [the wife] can spend as little as she likes and save the rest' and would be utterly unfair to the 'poor husband' who 'has some rights, though not many, I'll allow'.[58] *Blackwell* is therefore not just an example of how the grip of precedent historically operated against women; the injustice of this case is compounded by judicial bias, from judges who could not empathise with the harsh legal consequences faced by women like Dorothy Blackwell.

C. A Common Problem

Blackwell clearly demonstrated how the law had failed married women. Even when Dorothy Blackwell enabled the mortgage on her home to be repaid through her management of household finances and work taking in lodgers, that home could not belong to her unless she was named on the documents of title, and wives rarely were. So, in making these contributions she was acting as her husband's agent and nothing more. The absurdity of strict separation of property in this instance was not lost on her lawyers, with her counsel arguing that the law had left her worse off than a paid housekeeper.[59]

---

[54] Cretney, above n 4, 93.
[55] Which academic Kahn-Freund had suspected: 'Inconsistencies and Injustices in the Law of Husband and Wife' (1953), above n 16, 38.
[56] MWA Journal, November 1943, 7TBG/1/32, TWL.
[57] Specifically Luxmoore LJ, 'Judges Tell Wives Rights of Husbands', *Daily Mirror*, above n 44.
[58] ibid.
[59] PD Cummins, 'Mrs Blackwell and Mrs 1964' *Catholic Citizen* (15 June 1964) 46, 5MWA/1/3/1, TWL.

Perhaps the most shocking aspect of Dorothy Blackwell's case was that the hardship she experienced was by no means exceptional.[60] After *Blackwell*, the MWA claimed to be receiving 40 to 50 letters a day from women in similar situations.[61] As Summerskill observed, 'different versions of the Blackwell case [appeared] in our newspapers every day', whereby women were being left penniless after discovering that the housekeeping money they had saved was in fact legally owned by their husbands.[62]

One noteworthy example of this is the case of *Hoddinott v Hoddinott*,[63] where Atkin LJ found in favour of the husband in a dispute over ownership of the furniture in the family home. The furniture was bought with prize money from a football pool, and the winning teams in this game were selected by the efforts of both wife and husband. However, the original stake money had been paid out of housekeeping savings, which the wife had no legal ownership of. Denning LJ (as he then was) dissented, and his reasoning provides an interesting contrast to Scott LJ's judgment in *Blackwell*. First, Denning LJ argued that the wife's involvement in picking the winning teams entitled her to share in the winnings. He compared the parties' joint efforts in the football pools to writing a book together, stating that 'the stake money in this case was of no more importance than the paper on which such a book was written'.[64] His alternative argument was similar to that put forward by Dorothy Blackwell's counsel. The wife in *Hoddinott* could be entitled to an equitable interest in the housekeeping savings, Denning LJ suggested, since these savings 'were due as much to the wife's good housekeeping as to the husband's earnings'.[65] Furthermore, in his view, the parties evidently intended to have a joint equitable beneficial interest in the furniture when it was purchased, and therefore it should belong to them both instead of to the husband absolutely.[66] However, the majority in this case did not agree, once again underscoring the anomalous and absurd legal position of married women under family property law and the need for it to be reformed.

*

The hardship experienced by Dorothy Blackwell after she lost her case was striking. Separated but not divorced, she was left with no money of her own. Later, Edith Summerskill wrote in her memoirs about what became of her:

> Mrs Blackwell after sixteen years of unremitting toil on behalf of her family was not entitled to a penny for her services. She was a pathetic little figure in her basement

---

[60] See *Preston v Preston* 1950 SLT 196; *Hoddinott v Hoddinott* [1949] 2 KB 406 (where the wife was held to have no legal interest in winnings from a joint investment of husband and wife).
[61] MWA Annual Report 1944, above n 6.
[62] HL Deb 19 November 1952, vol 507, col 1874.
[63] [1949] 2 KB 406.
[64] ibid, paras 406–07.
[65] ibid, para 407.
[66] ibid.

room when I visited her in London ... She was helpless and hopeless, a victim of a legal system which still in the twentieth century treats the wife as a chattel of her husband.[67]

The MWA worked hard to ensure her plight made a mark in the press, and the *Blackwell* case was front-page news.[68] While this had no bearing on the outcome of the case or its chances for further appeal, analysis of press reports indicates that public outrage about her story benefited the MWA's campaigns.[69] This extract from the *Glasgow Herald* is one example of the response at the time:

> The sympathies of nearly all women, and a great many men, are with the lady in whose case the Court of Appeal has ruled that savings by a wife from her house-keeping allowances are the property of the husband. Unfortunately, this is an instance in which sympathy butters no beans; and it is doubly unfortunate that those who have been loudest in their railings against the law have omitted to indicate, even in broad terms, an adequate measure of reform. Nothing can be gained by demands for equality unless there is fairly general agreement on what equality amounts to.[70]

Clearly, the Association needed a strategy for reform. As a result, the MWA not only had to produce a distinct picture of what equality in marriage would look like; it needed those in power to agree to the same vision.

II. WHAT THE MWA DID NEXT

When taking on Dorothy Blackwell's case, the MWA was seeking to challenge the Court's narrow view of wives as mere agents of their husband's money. As Dorothy Blackwell said of her case: 'I claim that the money belongs to me because I had to work hard in the home for it ... He never made me any separate allowance'.[71] Therefore, *Blackwell* was not just a case about housekeeping savings for the MWA; it was about the broader need to value women's work in the home. Since Dorothy Blackwell was not divorced, and was therefore not able to access maintenance, her case provided strong justification for the MWA's equal partnership legislation, which as we saw in the previous chapter, sought to provide married women with property rights during marriage.

When the MWA applied to the House of Lords Appeal Committee to take the *Blackwell* case further, their application was not granted. Thus, having tried unsuccessfully to push for change in the courts, it had become apparent to the

[67] Summerskill, above n 52, 145.
[68] 'Housewives Will Fight for the Right to Save', *Daily Mirror*, above n 53.
[69] See, eg, Anon, 'Wives Start Campaign' *Evening Telegraph* (30 October 1943) 5.
[70] Anon, 'Keeper of the Purse' *Glasgow Herald* (4 November 1943) 4.
[71] 'Wife to Pay Husband Her Savings', above n 10.

MWA members that they could not pursue reform through judicial process alone. In addition to the Court's attachment to dubious precedent like *Barrack*, concerns about what husbands would be served for dinner[72] if wives *did* have a legal right to housekeeping savings suggest that achieving change within the courtroom would have been rather like pushing an elephant up a hill.

Yet out of this failure, the MWA launched the biggest campaign of its history. The MWA Annual Report in 1944 described a swell in numbers:

> We can now claim to be a National Movement spread all over Britain, with an appreciable public support for our work. A large measure of our success is due to the publicity afforded us by the Blackwell case.[73]

This was because the MWA pursued a strategy of channelling public outrage into propaganda and campaigns for reform. The MWA wanted to make it clear that the issue of housekeeping savings was symptomatic of widespread, inbuilt inequality in the law of marriage. And so, an important part of their activism was to make women aware of how the law affected them and to register their indignation over this. They utilised the press effectively,[74] inviting journalists to their meetings and plans for protest, with prominent members like Summerskill declaring that *Blackwell* had 'made a mockery of the marriage vows'.[75] When the MWA appealed for financial contributions, married women reportedly 'hauled in silver and notes', with many admitting 'they were taking it from the housekeeping money'.[76] The campaign also included petitioning Parliament and collecting signatures, as the following letter by Edith Summerskill sent out to members shows:

> The time has arrived when we must take further action if we are to secure justice for the housewife in the post-war world.
>
> Will you, therefore, help me by obtaining as many signatures and addresses as possible (men, women, married or single) on the enclosed Petition which I propose to present to Parliament.
>
> Please enlist the help of friends and sympathisers as this is *urgent and important*. Try to get forms filled in by workers in factories, shops and offices and women's Societies. Call at as many houses as possible; I am quite sure you will find the housewife only too ready to co-operate and, *remember that you will be furthering the cause of women throughout the country*. Ask the Editor of your local paper to write a story and to include your own name and address for further information.[77]

---

[72] 'Housewives Will Fight for the Right to Save', *Daily Mirror*, above n 53.

[73] MWA Annual Report 1944, above n 6.

[74] There was press attendance at MWA conferences from 1943. See, eg, interview with Juanita Frances following Blackwell: 'Wife's Housekeeping Savings Belong To Husband' *Dundee Courier* (4 May 1943) 2.

[75] Anon, 'Savings: Wives New Move' *Daily Mirror* (9 November 1943) 1.

[76] ibid.

[77] Letter from Edith Summerskill to Married Women's Association members, January 1944, 7TBG/1/32, TWL (emphasis in original document).

As well as growing its support on the ground, the MWA brought their protest with Mrs Blackwell's case to policymakers too. By October 1943, Summerskill had collected 10,000 signatures, enough to press for a motion in the House of Commons to secure for married women the legal right to savings from house-keeping allowance.[78] When presenting the petition for debate in the Commons in November 1944, Summerskill said it was from '66,000 working house-wives and others'.[79] Here is another strand of MWA campaigning – exerting maximum pressure on the government to reform the issue. MWA founder Dorothy Evans told the press that the Commons was to become 'full of wives demanding that the law be amended', making the problem impossible for Parliament to ignore.[80] And the MWA publicised their support from men too, in their effort to persuade those in power that equality in marriage was not only a women's issue.[81]

Support for reform seemingly *was* widespread. According to the MWA's Annual Report in 1944, a recent Gallup poll had revealed that 75 per cent of respondents were in favour of housewives having a legal right to housekeeping savings.[82] The MWA interpreted this as a public awakening to the need for legal reform, and that 'something is wrong with the economic status of the 10,000,000 homemakers of Great Britain'.[83]

Next, the MWA organised a deputation to the Home Office.[84] Juanita Frances stated that her own husband 'had cut down her allowance when she saved', and gave examples of husbands providing allowances to wives that would not meet household expenses.[85] In one case, for instance, she told of a wife determined not to have children in view of her being provided with such a

---

[78] Anon, 'Monster Petition For Wives' "Rights"' *Evening Telegraph* (21 February 1944) 4. According to this newspaper report, signatures were collected from all over England, Wales and Scotland.

[79] HC Deb, Housewife's Income (Petition), 2 November 1944, vol 404.

[80] 'Housewives Will Fight for the Right to Save', *Daily Mirror*, above n 53.

[81] The MWA noted in particular: 'Reports of the willingness of men to sign our Petition are being continually received': MWA Annual Report 1944, above n 6. Home Secretary Herbert Morrison also reportedly supported the broader premise that assets should be pooled, according to Edith Summerskill: Anon, 'Understands Wives' Claim' *Dundee Courier* (29 August 1941) 3. However, there were also reports of men protesting against the MWA's deputation to the Commons: 'Monster Petition For Wives' "Rights"', *Evening Telegraph*, above n 78; Anon, 'Housewives Want New Rights' *Hull Daily Mail* (21 February 1944) 4.

[82] MWA Annual Report 1944, above n 6. It has not been possible to locate and verify the survey referred to by the MWA here.

[83] ibid.

[84] MWA members attending the deputation included Edith Summerskill, Dorothy Evans, Ambrose Appelbe, Constance Colwill, Simone Grasse, Juanita Frances, Anne Fraser: Memo on MWA, 17 November 1943, LC02/2777, TNA.

[85] Letter from Donald Somervell to Claud Schuster enc memo on MWA deputation, 23 November 1943, LC02/2777, TNA. Frances' anecdotal evidence pointed to a broader trend, whereby even after the introduction of family allowances in 1945, many women still found it impossible to save any housekeeping money once essential bills had been paid: H McCarthy, *Double Lives: A History of Working Motherhood* (Bloomsbury 2020) 211.

small proportion of her husband's money. However, as we saw in the previous chapter, the Attorney General Donald Somervell refused to undertake to introduce legislative reform.[86] After the deputation Somervell noted that to presume housekeeping money belonged to the wife 'would be wrong and contrary to the intentions of the husband'.[87]

Summerskill also asked questions relating to the *Blackwell* case and the status of housewives in the House of Commons seven times in 1943.[88] While the MWA reported that 'satisfactory replies were not obtained to these questions',[89] their discussions about how to go about achieving reform suggest this was not their primary aim anyway. Instead, repeatedly raising the issue in the Commons was in their view the 'preliminary [step] to having the economic position of the housewife debated in Parliament'.[90] In other words, they were keeping the issue of housewives' economic vulnerability in marriage on the agenda.

The internal files of the Lord Chancellor's Office reveal that the MWA had some success in doing so. In addition to pressure under public indignation whipped up by the MWA, the Lord Chancellor's Office was forced to take notice of the MWA campaign because of its publicised criticism of the National Savings Movement.[91] *Blackwell* was decided in the midst of the Second World War, when the Savings Movement was campaigning to persuade individuals to purchase savings certificates in support of the war effort. The MWA criticised this Movement's advertising as, members claimed, it encouraged housewives to use housekeeping money to buy savings certificates without ever making it clear that 'they are accumulating savings to which they have no legal right'.[92] Thus in raising awareness of the *Blackwell* campaign, the MWA was actively discouraging housewives from investing in savings certificates that would help fund the war effort. As MWA member Anne Fraser wrote to the National Savings Committee: 'many housewives now have a powerful incentive to spend every penny of the housekeeping money if not on household necessities, then on themselves'.[93]

Some letters in the Lord Chancellor's Office files dismissed MWA propaganda, with Permanent Secretary Claud Schuster telling the Lord Chancellor

---

[86] The MWA recalled that the Attorney General and Solicitor General 'gave us a very patient and indeed sympathetic hearing, but would not undertake to introduce legislation to improve the economic status of the housewife': MWA Annual Report 1944, above n 6.

[87] Letter from Donald Somervell to Ernest Bevin, 22 December 1943, LC02/2777, TNA.

[88] eg, she asked the Attorney General whether his attention had been drawn to the *Blackwell* case and whether he would take steps to amend the law which denies a wife a right to a share of the family income. He replied that it was not possible: MWA Annual Report 1944, above n 6.

[89] ibid.

[90] ibid.

[91] Anon, 'Wives Seek War Savings Rule' *Daily Mail* (28 July 1943) 3.

[92] Letter from Anne Fraser to the National Savings Committee, 20 July 1943, LC02/2777, TNA.

[93] ibid.

that 'the feminists are barking up the wrong tree'.[94] A memo to the Lord Chancellor further stated:

> Married women, more than anyone else, realise how inextricably the future of the home depends upon the future of the country ... We cannot believe that housewives will be influenced by the recent decision of the Court of Appeal to withhold the support of their savings from the war effort at this critical moment when husbands and sons are giving their lives to save our homes.[95]

Despite this brusque reaction, it seems unlikely that the Lord Chancellor's Office would have carried out the extensive research it did into married women's property reform had it not felt compelled to take the MWA's campaign seriously.[96] Enquiries were made into community of property in France;[97] dozens of letters set out detailed arguments for reform, and meetings were held to discuss the practicalities of legislation. Notes produced by the Law Officer's Department were at times open-minded to the possibility of reform: 'There may be some force in the contention that she should have some right in moneys which she saves by careful management, by personal economies and by her own work'.[98] Over time, Schuster appeared to move from outright opposition to reform towards a position of ambivalence: 'The more I think about the thing, the more puzzled I am, and the more tangled appears to me to be the path before us'.[99] Thus, in the end the MWA *had* succeeded in forcing the government to pay attention to the economic consequences of marriage for women.[100]

III. *BLACKWELL* AS A CASE STUDY OF FAMILY LAW REFORM

The MWA was unsuccessful in using *Blackwell* to change the law from inside the courtroom. Luxmoore LJ made this abundantly clear in his response to Dorothy Blackwell's counsel: 'You haven't got a leg to stand on ... If you want the law altered you must get Parliament to do it'.[101] In some ways, this response must have been unsurprising. After all, the arguments in *Blackwell* about

---

[94] In the same letter, Schuster said the MWA's proposal to give wives a right to share their husband's wage had 'nothing whatever to do with Blackwell's case': Letter from Claud Schuster to Lord Chancellor 2 November 1943, LC02/2777, TNA.

[95] Memo on Married Women's Savings, undated, LC02/2777, TNA.

[96] Writing to Claud Schuster, Deputy Permanent Secretary to the Lord Chancellor's Office George Coldstream observed: 'If the pressure is as great as the Treasury seem to think ... it may be that the Lord Chancellor will wish to review the subject generally with the Law Officers'. Memo, undated, LC02/2777, TNA.

[97] Letter from GP Coldstream to JG Foster, 20 December 1943, LC02/2777, TNA.

[98] Notes on the Married Women's Deputation, 23 November 1943, LC02/2777, TNA.

[99] Letter from Claud Schuster to Donald Somervell, 6 December 1943, LC02/2777, TNA.

[100] George Coldstream appeared to be convinced reform would happen soon: 'After the war the problem will be raised and no doubt we shall see an alteration in statute'. Letter from GP Coldstream to ME Reed, 15 July 1943, LC02/2777, TNA.

[101] 'Judges Tell Wives Rights of Husbands', *Daily Mirror*, above n 44.

valuing housework were ineffective as housework was not valued in law. But as the MWA's activism and the public's reaction after *Blackwell* made clear, there was a gulf between law and married couples' *perceptions* of the law. Strictly marking out marital property as 'his' and 'hers' was at odds with the expectations of spouses at the time. Furthermore, judges' insistence in adhering to these strict property laws (as well as applying principles that had arguably been rendered obsolete by the MWPA 1882) operated against the person without the property – the housewife.

Outside the courtroom, and on the ground, *Blackwell* had much more significance for family law reform. Dorothy Blackwell's story embodied many of the inequalities between husband and wife that the MWA sought to expose, so could be used to garner sympathy for the economic vulnerability of housewives more generally. It is also important from the perspective of feminist legal history that the MWA helped make visible the experiences of Dorothy Blackwell and other subjugated women: 'Let us go forward determined that the voice of married women will be heard more fully in local, National and International Councils, as well as in the home'.[102] Too often the words of women suffering from the harsh consequences of law were and are not recorded. Yet thanks to the MWA and the press contacts it cultivated, we *do* know what Dorothy Blackwell made of her case, as it was reported in newspapers:

> So I have lost my money, and that is the law so far as wives are concerned ... I have had a hard life, scraping and stinting to save money. I saved it in small amounts. But had I my time over again I would be a spendthrift. I would spend every penny and have a good time. It does not pay a housewife to be thrifty. My advice to housewives is not to save money, but spend it.[103]

Dorothy Blackwell was not alone in her anger. Thus, using her as the relatable face of their reform campaign, the MWA could effectively translate a collective sense of discontentment into support for its policies.

The Association used *Blackwell* to launch a campaign calling for the MWPA 1882 to be amended so that married women could have a legal right in housekeeping savings. This culminated in the MWPA 1964, which as chapter seven will explain, gave wives a legal right to a half-share of housekeeping money. Significantly, this Act was the first time such work could be legally recognised as having economic value. But, as Auchmuty has remarked the feminist activism behind reform such as this, particularly during the first half of the twentieth century, does not feature in contemporary accounts and has instead been 'deliberately erased or reconstructed in safe, non-radical forms with the feminist agency removed'.[104] Such reconstruction is clear in the context of the MWPA 1964. Indeed, the impetus behind the Act is often documented as

[102] MWA Annual Report 1944, above n 6.
[103] 'Housewives Will Fight for the Right to Save', *Daily Mirror*, above n 53.
[104] R Auchmuty, 'Feminists as Stakeholders in the Law School' in F Cownie (ed), *Stakeholders in the Law School* (Hart Publishing 2010) 49.

being fuelled by the Report of the Royal Commission on Marriage and Divorce in 1956[105] with no mention of the MWA; even though it raised consciousness (inside and outside Parliament) about the plight of women such as Dorothy Blackwell and provided evidence crucial to the Royal Commission's report, as the next chapter will explore more fully.

CONCLUSION

Undoubtedly, the *Blackwell* case is important as, for the MWA, it marked the beginning of a 'long and patient struggle' campaigning for reform.[106] Twenty years after *Blackwell*, the prospect of married women's legal right to house-keeping savings – which had once seemed a 'most astonishing proposition'[107] to Goddard LJ – had become law pursuant to the MWPA 1964, thus recognising finally that this money had often been generated through wives' own efforts anyway. Reflecting on reform strategy, this could be seen as highlighting the power of the individual story. While it was important to talk about the scale of a problem, the extent to which gendered inequality was built into the law, or the reasons why a male dominated legal profession was (and still is) detri-mental to justice, nothing could humanise these issues in the way a story like Dorothy Blackwell's could. Reading about her suffering on the front pages of the national press brought matters expressed by the MWA in abstract, statisti-cal, black and white terms into vivid technicolour. It not only boosted MWA membership and support, with 20 new MWA branches set up in 1943 (the year of the *Blackwell* appeal),[108] it contributed to family law reform in the form of the MWPA 1964.

However, as chapter seven explores in greater detail, this reform was inad-equate and only part of a bigger picture. The members of the MWA viewed the Act as being only slight progress towards economic equality in marriage.[109] As they put it in 1944: 'It should be remembered of course that our work is primarily to establish an equal partnership, and that the question of housekeeping savings only serves to emphasise the injustice suffered by housewives'.[110] Put simply, as previous chapters have explained, the MWA's ultimate aim was a new marriage law establishing an equal partnership extending *beyond* ownership of house-keeping money. It must have been deflating for some MWA members when their draft Bill for equal partnership in marriage was submitted for consideration by the Attorney General, only for it to be dismissed immediately as 'impracticable'

---

[105] Law Commission, *Transfer of Money Between Spouses – the Married Women's Property Act 1964* (WP No 90, 1985) para. 4.1.

[106] Summary on context of Married Women's Property Act 1964, 5MWA/1/2/1/1, TWL.

[107] 'Housewives Will Fight for the Right to Save', *Daily Mirror*, above n 53.

[108] Blackford, above n 18, 102.

[109] MWA Annual Report 1944, above n 106.

[110] ibid.

and 'undesirable'.[111] A minor reform regarding housekeeping money would have been little consolation for this.

The MWA's successes and failures to influence policy as a result of the *Blackwell* case tell us a lot about both the power and the shortcomings of the individual story when it comes to law reform. This is familiar terrain for family lawyers in recent years, with the cases of *Steinfeld and Keidan*[112] and *Owens v Owens*[113] providing examples of how the individual story can be used to garner support in the press and public for reform, while at the same time sometimes exposing troubling attitudes among members of the judiciary.[114] The analysis of *Blackwell* in this chapter exemplifies how feminist legal history can be used to confront assumptions that justice is always blind and law is always objective in the courtroom. *Blackwell* is also a reminder of how controversial seemingly discrete issues can be, such as ownership of housekeeping savings. Indeed, it is an understatement to say that finding a solution to this issue was divisive within the MWA. For it was (at least ostensibly) what broke the Association apart.

---

[111] Letter from Donald Somervell to Ernest Bevin, above n 87.

[112] [2018] UKSC 32.

[113] [2018] UKSC 41.

[114] See, eg, Lady Hale's misgivings about the trial judge's approach in *Owens* at [50].

Interlude: A Note About Lord Denning

I N HINDSIGHT, GENDERED inequalities between husbands and wives in the 1940s and 1950s appear obvious. The archetypal housewife smiling out from the pages of women's magazines from this era is more likely to be a symbol of women's oppression than emancipation, thanks in part to the works of Betty Friedan[1] and Ann Oakley[2] in the 1960s and 1970s. But drawing attention to these inequalities at the time was not easy. This is because there was a perception that equality had already been achieved. When this view was held even by those who appeared to advocate for women's elevated status in law, the Married Women's Association's (MWA) urgent calls for reform could be undermined and dismissed rather easily.

As we saw in chapter five, Lord Denning (then Denning LJ) was one of the few members of the judiciary to highlight the injustice of wives' prohibited ownership of housekeeping savings. He also attempted to use section 17 of the Married Women's Property Act 1882 creatively in a way that could benefit deserted wives.[3] His judicial development of the principle of deserted wives' equity[4] paved the way for the Matrimonial Homes Act 1967: important legislation introduced by Edith Summerskill that gave the deserted wife a legal right to stay in the matrimonial home.[5] It is therefore tempting to assume that Lord Denning and the MWA shared similar views about reform of married women's legal status.

But their views were not the same, and a clash of opinion in 1950 makes this clear. In a speech to the National Marriage Guidance Council, Denning publicly stated that equality of the sexes had been accomplished, at *potential cost to society*. The wife, he said, 'is now indeed the spoilt darling of the law', and the husband 'the patient pack-horse'.[6] Denning warned that freedom for women had been 'disastrous' to Roman society, and 'we ought not to ignore the possibility' of it being disastrous for society in modern times. And so, while he was activated by the plight of the deserted wife, and his judicial innovations

---

[1] B Friedan, *The Feminine Mystique* (WW Norton 1963).

[2] A Oakley, *Housewife* (Allen Lane 1974).

[3] *Hutchinson v Hutchinson* [1947] 2 All ER 792; 63 TLR 645; *Hine v Hine* [1967] 1 WLR 1124, 1127: A Denning, *The Due Process of Law* (Butterworths 1980) 208.

[4] *Bendall v McWhirter* [1952] 2 QB 466.

[5] He supported the Bill as it made its way through the House of Lords, ibid, 220.

[6] Anon, 'Cost Of Sex Equality' *Times* (13 May 1950) 3.

could be regarded as progressive and protective of the women the MWA sought to represent, his views could also be regarded as sexist.

MWA Chairman Dora Russell published a letter in the *Times* in response to Denning's speech. Russell argued that the 'average married woman in this country' would 'hardly agree' with his view of women and equality, while reiterating the aims of the MWA:

> It is strange that so many learned persons who concern themselves with marriage and divorce law reform almost always ignore the fundamental problem, from which so many others flow, namely, the equitable distribution of the income of marriage partners within marriage.[7]

But Denning was not alone in the view that wives were in a privileged position, and husbands were the ones unfairly burdened in marriage (even though as Carol Smart has affirmed, 'there is no real evidence to support Denning's claim' and it is 'difficult to understand' how so many lawyers arrived at this conclusion).[8] However, his view provides a clear example of how the rhetoric of equality can disadvantage women. As Rosemary Auchmuty aptly pointed out:

> Simply declaring our equality does not make us equal. In fact, it can remove all justification for protection in situations where protection is, in fact, still needed. If women continue to suffer structural social and economic disadvantage at the hands of men, then the removal of a gendered basis for intervention can place them at a legal disadvantage too.[9]

Denning's assertion of equality undermined the MWA's case for reform. This flawed perception of equality could help explain why the MWA discussed some changes in strategy in the early 1950s; appealing to men seemed to make strategic sense, for 'women's issues' might be taken more seriously if reframed as problems that would affect those in power too (ie, men). As a result, the MWA attempted to highlight the benefits of equal partnership for men as well as women. This is reported in the *Daily Mirror* under the headline: 'Fair deal for wives' society is planning to protect husbands'. In it, Helen Nutting discusses a name change for the MWA: 'we want all the men we can get to come in but they will not join a society with a name like Married Women's Association. I don't blame them – I wouldn't join a bachelors' society'.[10]

The suggested brand change to 'Marriage Partnership Association' never caught on. However, these differing ideas about how to package the MWA's goal of equal partnership in marriage had become divisive, and only a short time later led to an intractable dispute within the organisation.

---

[7] D Russell, 'Equal Partnership In Marriage' *Times* (16 May 1950) 5.

[8] C Smart, The Ties that Bind (Routledge 1984) 29.

[9] R Auchmuty, 'Unfair shares for women: The rhetoric of equality and the reality of inequality' in H Lim and A Bottomley (eds), *Feminist Perspectives on Land Law* (Glass House Press 2007) 180.

[10] Anon, 'Fair Deal For Wives' Society Is Planning To Protect Husbands' *Daily Mirror* (28 April 1950) 5.

6

The Split

The housekeeping allowance is provided to keep house for the entire family; therefore, any money saved from it belongs *jointly* to husband and wife. To say that it belongs to the wife as a reward for good management is ridiculous. The same argument could be used to justify the office boy who delivers his employer's letters by hand and pockets the stamp money.

C Robinson Hertford.[1]

INTRODUCTION

IN JANUARY 1953 Helena Normanton laid a wreath of holly on Gladstone's memorial. It was for the women who fought for the Married Women's Property Act (MWPA) 1882 and, she said, commemorated 70 years since their 'bitter struggle' for legislation that 'has always been regarded as one of the charters of women's freedom'.[2]

Previous chapters have discussed how the MWPA 1882 was highly significant to married women and to the women's movement to end coverture; the idea that husband and wife became one person on marriage, and that that person was namely the husband. Therefore, the MWPA 1882 did not just represent married women's right to own property separately and independently from their husbands. For the women's movement, the Act symbolised recognition in law of married women as people and not legal non-entities, of individuals and not dependants. The problem, as this book has argued so far, was that this did not result in married women's economic independence and, for unpaid housewives with no separate property of their own, it often reinforced their dependence.

But how could the legal inequalities left between husband and wife be addressed without undermining the 'dearly prized rights' of the MWPA 1882?[3] Normanton was concerned that some of the MWA's campaigns for equal partnership would undermine the important gains made by Victorian feminists. And so, only months before Normanton commemorated the MWPA 1882 with

---

[1] *Wife and Citizen*, March 1949, 7TBG/1/32, TWL.
[2] Anon, 'Married Women's Property' *Manchester Guardian* (3 January 1953), 5MWA/2/1, TWL.
[3] Speech of Teresa Billington-Greig, MWA Newsletter, June 1958, 7TBG/2/J/08, TWL.

a wreath, she abruptly and dramatically left the MWA and was followed by several other leading members.[4]

This was, of course, a blow for the MWA. Normanton had been President of the Association at the time of her resignation, and was well known for her activism, having been a suffragette as well as a pioneering barrister. She was a regular contributor to *Good Housekeeping* magazine, explaining the law and in particular women's legal rights in clear and accessible terms. She had decades of experience in legal reform and had been strongly involved in the 1937 divorce reforms.[5] It is therefore unsurprising that the departure of a feminist heavyweight attracted so much public attention. What is less clear, however, is precisely *why* the Association split. Ostensibly, it was because the MWA disagreed over how to address the issue of housekeeping savings, brought to the fore by the case of *Blackwell* as seen in the previous chapter. But the divisions between members went much deeper than this.

Ultimately, the MWA was fractured by the question that continues to divide family lawyers, policymakers and commentators today: how unpaid work in the home should be valued in financial terms. As well as being an important part of MWA history, telling this story is worthwhile when exploring family law reform too. It provides a unique insight into how a group that was united over the aim of economic and legal equality in marriage was also divided over how to achieve it. Moreover, it demonstrates how these divisions could be seen as impeding the potential impact of the MWA's work on law reform.

This chapter explores the MWA's fragmentation by homing in on the incident triggering the resignation of Normanton and others – a fight over the evidence Normanton submitted as MWA President to the Royal Commission on Marriage and Divorce (also known as the Morton Commission[6]), on the Association's behalf. Examining what went wrong for the MWA on this occasion is as revealing – if not more so – than focusing only on the group's achievements. First, the background to the Royal Commission is outlined, as well as the MWA's submissions of evidence and the immediate cause of the split. Then, the second part of this chapter discusses the Royal Commission's report: what it rejected, what it proposed, the MWA reaction to this and what this tells us about reform. This is followed by an exploration of what the MWA and the members who had left the group did next, the group's fragmentation and the different directions

[4] Doreen Gorsky (Chairman); Lady Helen Nutting (Vice Chairman) Evelyn Hamilton (Treasurer), Lady Rhys Williams.
[5] Helena Normanton practised at the English Bar from December 1922 until shortly before her retirement in 1950. She worked in general practice but mainly in matrimonial and criminal matters. She had experience with influencing law reform previously, having worked for the passage into law of the Royal Commission on Marriage and Divorce proposals in 1912. She was also an influential figure behind the Matrimonial Causes Act 1937 (which extended the grounds for divorce), having in 1936 moved the resolution giving support of the National Council of Women to AP Herbert's Bill (which became the 1937 Act).
[6] Because it was chaired by Lord Morton of Henryton. Lord Morton was Judge of Chancery Division, High Court of Justice, 1938–44; Lord Justice of Appeal, 1944–47; and Lord of Appeal in Ordinary, 1947–59.

it branched into. The split undoubtedly diluted the MWA's message and consequently its chances for reform. Studying the split also uncovers how reformists
often need 'difficult' personalities to be successful, yet this can lead to fractious
relationships and can therefore be a hindrance as well as an advantage.

Finally, the chapter will conclude by discussing how the Royal Commission
is often dismissed in the history of family law as a washout. Nothing radical
was proposed, and it was deeply divided over divorce and matrimonial property
law – both of which were in dire need of reform. Yet for legal historians, as
we will see, it provides a valuable window into the strategies of feminist pressure groups, while showing that the Commission's lack of immediate practical
impact is not a reason for its total dismissal. After all, the Commission agreed
wholeheartedly with the MWA's demand for equal partnership in marriage, even
if it rejected most of the MWA's proposals for achieving it.

I. THE MWA SUBMISSIONS TO THE ROYAL COMMISSION
ON MARRIAGE AND DIVORCE

Like other institutional histories of law, accounts of the Royal Commission rarely
acknowledge any role by the MWA and its networks. However, the pressure the
MWA had been exerting on government and policymakers had been relentless,
through the press, questions and debates in the Commons and the Bills it was
drafting and supporting. The *Blackwell* case had given the MWA a mouthpiece,
and they were using it to keep the conversation about legal inequalities in marriage
alive. Now the economic position of the housewife was on the radar of those in
power, and the MWA had a chance to make a difference. The Royal Commission
was MWA members' opportunity to have experts consider their proposals for a
new marriage law. As the Association reported in its magazine *Wife and Citizen*,
it had been advocating for a Royal Commission for 'more than a year'.[7]

A. The Need for a Royal Commission

So far, this book has detailed the need for family law reform because of the
many problems that were affecting married women throughout the middle of
the twentieth century. By 1951, when the Royal Commission was set up,[8] these
problems were becoming increasingly difficult to ignore. Judges were having
to apply either harsh legal principles leaving the deserted wife in dire straits,
or palm tree justice, disregarding such principles to keep her off the streets.[9]

---

[7] Commission on Marriage, *Wife and Citizen*, August 1950, 7TBG/1/32, TWL.
[8] Historically, Royal Commissions have been seen as an 'attractive' way to address building pressure upon Parliament and the Government for reform of family law: D Stetson, *A Woman's Issue:
The Politics of Family Law Reform in England* (Oxford University Press 1982) 161.
[9] See *Rimmer v Rimmer* [1953] 1 QB 63, 71, in which Lord Evershed asserted that the courts were
prepared to apply palm tree justice to achieve a fair outcome.

Meanwhile, groups such as the MWA had been increasing pressure on MPs and policymakers. As chapter two explained, changing economic conditions during and after the Second World War had only served to exacerbate the legal inconsistences between husband and wife. And as seen in the previous chapter, Dorothy Blackwell was left penniless because she was not allowed to keep the money saved in part from housekeeping. The root of the problem was that she had no property of her own; married women's work in the home had no value in law.

During the Second Reading Debate of Eirene White's Matrimonial Causes Bill in 1951, which sought (unsuccessfully)[10] to reform divorce law at that time, there were calls for a Royal Commission to be established.[11] Throughout this parliamentary session, MWA members had been writing to MPs about their views on a Royal Commission.[12] The reality for married women was not reflected in the law, and so as Stephen Cretney pointed out: 'the fact that English law did not recognise the household as a unit for the ownership of property increasingly seemed to be a defect, rather than a virtue'.[13] Clearly, something needed to be done about the issue of married women's property.

Having pressed for a Royal Commission for some time, the MWA believed that any review was better than none. The Association urged Prime Minister Clement Atlee to widen the Commission's scope to include marriage law more broadly as members were concerned that the whole economic and legal basis of marriage was being ignored.[14] Then, a deputation of MWA members told Marcus Lipton MP, who had moved the motion in the Commons requesting for the Royal Commission to be set up, that 'large numbers of separation orders are applied for as this is at present the only means open to a wife and mother of claiming economic rights within marriage'.[15] In other words, the MWA was arguing that if remedies could only be obtained on relationship breakdown, married women in financial difficulty would have little option but to separate in order to have legal recourse. If reform provided married women with economic rights *during* marriage, so the Association argued, couples would be more likely to stay married.

Appealing to the sanctity of marriage was probably a persuasive tactic in the 1950s. Whether or not this convinced the Royal Commission is unclear, but the terms of reference for the Commission *were* ultimately extended, to consider

---

[10] This Private Member's Bill received a significant amount of publicity and the government ultimately made an undertaking that a Royal Commission covering the whole subject of marriage and divorce would be set up in exchange for the Bill not proceeding any further.

[11] HC Deb 9 March 1951, vol 485, col 955.

[12] 'New Year Greetings from Chairman Dora Russell', *Wife and Citizen*, January 1951, 5MWA/8/2, TWL.

[13] S Cretney, *Family Law in the Twentieth Century* (Oxford University Press 2003) 118.

[14] New Chairman's Address, Doreen Gorsky, *Wife and Citizen*, May–June 1951, 7TBG/1/32, TWL.

[15] Commission on Marriage, above n 7.

the property rights of husband and wife both during and at the termination of marriage.[16] By this time, the many problems with matrimonial property law that had been highlighted in case law had demonstrated the need for radical reform. But the Royal Commission took a conservative stance.[17] In its report published in 1956, it *did* recognise a need for reform, that the wife's contribution to the family was not appreciated and that this could lead to hardship, noting: 'There are husbands who look on their income as their own to spend freely on themselves and grudgingly dole out small sums to their wives'. The Commission went on:

> But it is when the marriage breaks down that the wife who has given all her energy to her work in the home may have to face the situation that she has nothing she can call her own; even money she has saved over the years from the housekeeping allowance belongs in law to her husband.[18]

However, the Commission did not consider this problem necessarily justified radical reform. Instead, the Commission believed appropriate reform should consider three things: first, the practical limitations of legislative attempts; second, the 'vital consideration' that law needed to be kept out of the intimate life of the family wherever possible; and third, that husbands could experience 'substantial injustice' as a result of alleviating the hardship of wives.[19] These considerations suggest that the Royal Commission's efforts to address the hardship of married women were belied by a patriarchal system characterised by many of the themes explored in this book. The public/private divide, the intransigence of law, the subordination of women's experiences in relation to men; from a feminist historical perspective, all these issues are brought to the surface when analysing the Royal Commission's approach to family law reform from the 1950s. Moreover, this provides a unique insight into the MWA as reformists, and of law reform more broadly.

The Commission simultaneously represented an opportunity and a barrier to change. In spite of its restraint and reluctance to more radical change, one of the issues the Royal Commission *did* think practicable to reform was the law on housekeeping savings; an issue the MWA had been campaigning on since *Blackwell*. The only problem was that the memorandum of evidence initially submitted on behalf of the MWA by Helena Normanton went against the Association's views on how this area of law should be reformed.

---

[16] The Commission was also charged with reviewing the law of divorce and matrimonial causes in England and Scotland; the powers of magistrates courts affecting husband and wife; and, to suggest any changes in marriage law (specifically, the degree of affinity).

[17] Cretney, above n 13, 124.

[18] *Report of the Royal Commission on Marriage and Divorce* (Cmd 9678, 1956) para 645.

[19] ibid, paras 647–48.

B. Helena Normanton and the MWA's First Submission of Evidence

Chapter four clarified what the MWA chiefly stood for. First, the idea of joint partnership in marriage was key to explaining and justifying the need to value housewives' work in the home in economic terms. Second, in addressing *how* this work should be valued, the Association agreed that instead of pursuing a policy of 'wages for wives', equality in marriage would be achieved better by pooling assets (specifically income and the family home). This was not clear in Normanton's written submission to the Royal Commission.

As their President, Helena Normanton had multiple opportunities to present the MWA message. When it came to diagnosing the problem with law, she believed a 'fundamental cause of disharmony in marriage' was the 'gravely unsatisfactory economic position between the spouses existing at present'.[20] And, she was 'appalled' by the increasing prevalence of divorce.[21] As a retired QC, she was keenly aware of the harsh legal and economic realities of divorce for women in the 1950s.

But she departed from the MWA message when explaining what the solution should be. In her view, husband and wife should 'amicably [agree] part of the family income' to be allocated to her. This agreement should be made privately without outside interference, she said, unless the husband refused to pay his wife any allocation, or if the allocation was derisory. In these cases, she recommended that the agreement between spouses should be subject to arbitration.[22] This was clearly very different from previous MWA proposals that assets should be shared equally. Put simply, she was proposing wages for wives.

Normanton rejected the MWA's policy of joint ownership during marriage, as she believed it would 'lead to the misery and destitution of many wives and children, helpless in the face of the husband's bankruptcy or irresponsible spending'.[23] This suggests Normanton may have associated ideas of joint ownership with the doctrines of coverture and unity, which had served historically to oppress married women and deny them of their individual identity. But as chapter four explained, the MWA's policy of joint ownership was based on a very different premise from coverture, as its policy would entitle the non-earning spouse to property in recognition of their contribution to the marriage.

As well as vetoing the MWA's joint ownership approach in favour of wages for wives, Normanton made a further extraordinary proposal. Speaking as MWA spokesperson (as opposed to expressing her own personal views) in an interview with journalist Ruth Grew, Normanton argued that husbands should

---

[20] Helena Normanton's Submission of Evidence to the Royal Commission on Marriage and Divorce, 7HLN/B/05, TWL.
[21] ibid.
[22] ibid.
[23] ibid.

be compelled to provide their wives with 'personal spending money'.[24] When asked by the interviewer what husbands stood to gain, Normanton replied: 'we ask that wilfully negligent wives shall become *punishable by law*'.[25]

Normanton clarified what she meant by 'punishment' in an interview with the *Daily Mirror*:

> If a wife remained wilfully inefficient at housekeeping after a court gave her every help to improve, her husband should get the legal right to suspend her pocket money. As a very last resort, she might be gaoled. Just a short sentence would do.[26]

Normanton's comments to the press about housewives being punished for their insubordination are rather shocking, and are also baffling considering her life-long dedication to *improving* the position of women in law. Her proposal for a wife's allowance sounds rather like a pay cheque, with the husband as payer able to withhold the cheque, or even to threaten to incarcerate his wife, if she did not perform her wifely duties. The wife would therefore have been in the position of the husband's employee or, possibly worse, domestic servant. And with him as 'boss', it is easy to see how concerns about the master/servant relationship historically characterising the marital union would arguably have been reinforced by Normanton's proposals.

Yet dismissing Normanton's proposals entirely because of these statements is short-sighted. Though the concept of pocket money for wives had limitations, it made sense pragmatically as a way of ensuring housewives would have some property of their own.[27] After all, the grip of property law principles had been made clear in *Blackwell* – the person who directly earned the money owned it, and a wife therefore could not own housekeeping money. But if there was a way she could earn it – if she negotiated a financial return for her work in the home – she would have her own independent income and her hours of housework would have economic value.

Nevertheless, other aspects of Normanton's submission to the Royal Commission are more difficult to explain. As well as stipulating that 'wilfully inefficient housekeeping should become punishable by law', Normanton recommended rules on how wives were to spend their allowance, which included: 'Excessive expenditure upon gambling, smoking or alcoholic indulgence and the like shall not be deemed a proper outlay'.[28] In direct contravention of MWA policy, Normanton's submission also stated that housekeeping money should remain the husband's property, unless the husband had given consent in writing to any other arrangement.

---

[24] Transcript of Ruth Grew interview with Helena Normanton, 3 March 1952, 7HLN/B/05, TWL.

[25] ibid, emphasis added.

[26] Anon, 'They Demand a New Bill of Rights – and Duties, Too – for Wives' *Daily Mirror* (20 February 1952) 1.

[27] See ch 4 for a discussion of the merits of this approach and its relationship to the Wages for Housework campaigns of the 1970s.

[28] Helena Normanton's Submission of Evidence, above n 20.

When evaluating Normanton's submission, it is important to appreciate how these issues were viewed at the time. Normanton believed the MWA's joint ownership approach would be considered preposterous by the Royal Commission. She may have been right, for as we have seen there was a perception in the early 1950s that equality in marriage had been achieved and that the pendulum had swung too far in favour of women's rights. After a career in a male dominated legal profession, and having been involved in reforming law previously,[29] Normanton probably felt her experience qualified her to ascertain a better route for reform. Instead of joint ownership, she saw her own proposal of an 'agreed allocation' as a pragmatic means of extending married women's property rights without threatening men's. As she explained in an interview with the *Daily Mail*:

> We want to fight for the rights of widows and wives on a practical basis. Some of these people [referring to MWA members] are completely anti-man and want to press for legislation which would be unfair to husbands. They demand that a wife should have 50 per cent of her husband's income, but we realise such a division is impossible.[30]

While there is no evidence that MWA members who supported joint ownership were 'anti-man' as Normanton suggests, there were those outside the Association who were unsympathetic towards their calls for reform. As this satirical article on the MWA shows, some individuals used Normanton's dissention with the rest of the group as a reason to criticise the group further:

> The MWA – let the initials take the place of the dreaded words – has now not only fallen out with half of mankind, but it has fallen out with itself. The rolling pins are out and the harsh words of the weaker sex opening fire on femininity crackle like machine-gun fire.[31]

The fight alluded to in this excerpt shows Normanton was not only dealing with an anti-feminist opposition to the MWA; her recommendations to the Royal Commission had not been well received by other MWA members either.

C. The MWA's Reaction to Normanton's Submission

Normanton submitted the memorandum on 15 February 1952, and she was immediately confronted by MWA members for putting forward evidence completely at odds with MWA policy and ideology. Ambrose Appelbe and Alan Nabarro swiftly moved a resolution to withdraw the memorandum of evidence. In response, Normanton resigned. Shortly afterwards, Juanita Frances called an emergency meeting of the MWA.[32] Normanton refused to attend because

---

[29] As noted, above n 5, Normanton played an influential role in the Matrimonial Causes Act 1937.
[30] Daily Mail Reporter, 'Slight Case of Husbands' *Daily Mail* (2 April 1952) 1.
[31] Cassandra, 'Les Girls' *Daily Mirror* (3 April 1952) 6.
[32] 'Slight Case of Husbands', *Daily Mail*, above n 30.

of the 'obvious state of disunion within the organisation'.[33] At this meeting, Chairman Doreen Gorsky read letters of resignation from Normanton, Vice Chairman Helen Nutting, and Treasurer Evelyn Hamilton. She said Normanton would withdraw the evidence. Gorsky then announced her own resignation and declared the meeting closed.[34] The minutes of this meeting describe the 'loud cries of dissent from all parts' that followed,[35] with Legal Committee members Nabarro and Williams pointing out that as the evidence had been submitted on behalf of the MWA, the question of its withdrawal should be left to the MWA too. The meeting continued (minus Gorsky and Hamilton, who left), and members voted by a majority of 46:4 that the submission should be withdrawn and replaced with a new memorandum of evidence.[36]

The MWA was in crisis. It had already been granted two extensions because of Normanton's ill health,[37] so the submission was more than one month past the Royal Commission's deadline. The MWA might not have known whether a resubmission of evidence was possible. Furthermore, members' opposition to the evidence did not just lose them their President. Most of their Executive Committee had walked out, and in the days that followed, Vice President Lady Rhys Williams resigned too.[38] And so the MWA had lost five leading members, and potentially the opportunity to present their case for reform to the Royal Commission.

Privately, there were several members who were outraged by Normanton's actions, with some particularly vocal that this evidence did not represent their views. Ambrose Appelbe felt Normanton's allowance or as he put it, 'pin money' idea was a backward step to the days before the MWPA 1882.[39] Nabarro viewed the evidence as 'platitudinous'.[40] Juanita Frances was adamant that she did not want her name to be associated with the report,[41] and that it was 'illegal' as it defied the MWA's constitution.[42] Dora Russell said she wanted to 'see justice for the poor harassed working woman', and Normanton's evidence 'seemed to be entirely for the leisured woman of property and wealth'.[43] This was because it did

---

[33] ibid.

[34] A resignation letter signed by Nutting, Gorsky and Hamilton stated: 'Continuously irresponsible behaviour by certain members of the Married Women's Association has determined our decision.' 1 April 1952, 5CMW/A/4, TWL.

[35] Report of Special General Meeting of Married Women's Association, 1 April 1952, 5MWA/3/1, TWL.

[36] ibid.

[37] Letter from Doreen Gorsky to MWA members, 16 February 1952, 7TBG/2/J/02, TWL.

[38] Anon, 'Lady Rhys-Williams Resigns' *East Anglian Daily Times* (Ipswich, 4 April 1952), 5MWA/2/1, TWL.

[39] Report of Special General Meeting of Married Women's Association, above n 35.

[40] eg, Nabarro thought Normanton's lengthy discussion of divorce statistics was unnecessary, as the Royal Commission would have already been aware of this, ibid.

[41] Anon, 'Not in Favour' *North Western Evening Mail* (Barrow-in-Furness, 28 February 1952), 5MWA/2/1, TWL.

[42] Report of Special General Meeting of Married Women's Association, above n 35.

[43] ibid.

not purport to give married women rights in housekeeping money and, 'in very many working-class homes there is no surplus left after necessary expenses have been met from which to provide' the allowance Normanton was suggesting.[44]

This anger spilled over into the public domain, and became front-page news.[45] According to the *Daily Mail*, when the MWA meeting ended 'after two hours' denunciation of Mrs Normanton for her "betrayal of equality for wives", those present were astounded to learn that an opposition movement was already in being'.[46] This was the Council of Married Women, a breakaway group of MWA members considered in the last section of this chapter. On behalf of the MWA, Ambrose Appelbe released a statement to the press,[47] claiming Normanton's evidence had been submitted to the Royal Commission 'without previous circulation to executive or members', 'did not implement the principles of the association', and 'disturbed' members of the MWA.[48]

In response, Normanton wrote to Appelbe with what she called 'a kindly warning' to stop making statements in the press, while threatening to refer him to the Law Society for his behaviour.[49] Doreen Gorsky wrote to the MWA, claiming Normanton's memorandum had been circulated on numerous occasions.[50] While several members of the Executive Committee claim not to have seen the evidence,[51] a report in Normanton's papers suggests at least one meeting *had* taken place to discuss the detail of what would be proposed to the Commission.[52] Dora Russell's recollection of this meeting provides a glimpse of Normanton's formidable and authoritative character as MWA President:

> [S]o powerful was Mrs Normanton's hold over her audience that she would not admit of any correction whatever and most of the laymen present were overawed by the letters 'QC' if not by the emphatic banging on the desk by Mrs Normanton when interrupted and her words 'I won't have it altered!'.[53]

Regardless of who had or had not reviewed Normanton's memorandum, the MWA's public rift was caused by dissention over its policy of joint ownership

---

[44] Anon, '"Insult" to Give Wives Pin Money' *Daily Mail* (3 April 1952) 3.

[45] See, eg, 'Slight Case of Husbands', *Daily Mail*, above n 30.

[46] ibid.

[47] ibid.

[48] Anon, 'Wives hope ex-officials will return' *Daily Dispatch* (Manchester, 3 April 1952) 5 MWA/2/1, TWL.

[49] Letter from Helena Normanton to Ambrose Appelbe, 2 April 1952, 7HLN/B/05, TWL.

[50] Letter from Doreen Gorsky to MWA members, above n 37.

[51] See, eg, Dora Russell's account: 'this written evidence should have been in the hands of the Executive Committee before submission to the Royal Commission, instead of which we were told that the hurry was so great that NOBODY saw the written evidence to study it before submission. Certainly there were meetings when notes were read out (not always audible)'. Report of Special General Meeting of Married Women's Association, above, n 35.

[52] Normanton claimed three meetings had taken place with no real opposition. Letter from Helena Normanton to JL Edwards (Secretary to the Royal Commission on Marriage and Divorce) 30 March 1952, 7HLN/B/05, TWL.

[53] Report of Special General Meeting of Married Women's Association, above n 35.

in marriage, and this split may have adversely affected the Association's chances of achieving reform. When Normanton was misleadingly telling journalists that the MWA advocated a system whereby the husband would provide the wife with 'pocket money',[54] the Association's very different message was clouded. It is therefore unsurprising that Juanita Frances publicly dismissed Normanton's evidence: 'Mrs Normanton's report weakened the position of the married woman, for it laid down that the husband should still be regarded as the economic head of the household'.[55] She went on to say it reduced a wife's status to that of a charwoman or domestic help, because instead of valuing housewives' work as equal to men's, Normanton said it would be 'counted as the contribution equivalent to the sum the husband would otherwise have to pay for' domestic services.[56] As chapter four found, the MWA had previously considered and rejected the idea, later summarised by Teresa Billington-Greig:

> [W]e do want women to be paid for their work as other workers are, but we do not want to establish a wage relation between husband and wife. This would give her money but reduce her status.[57]

In a matter of weeks, the MWA had the task of compiling a completely new memorandum of evidence.[58] Their Legal Committee felt it needed to be couched in very simple language.[59]

D. The MWA's New Submission

As the drama in the press over the MWA split began to dissipate, new Chairman Elizabeth Pomeroy conveyed this simplified message to the *Times*:

> Mrs Normanton's document, which reflected certain views held by the association, also contained proposals which seemed to contradict the association's fundamental principle that marriage should be a joint partnership with husband and wife equal in status.[60]

Concerns had been expressed that press coverage of Normanton's views had misrepresented the MWA's true agenda.[61] And so it was important that the

---

[54] She also said she wanted 'the wife to have a little money of her own so that she doesn't have to ask her husband to pay for a wedding present to her sister': Anon, 'Not properly understood: Mrs Normanton defends her report' *Beckenham Advertiser* (13 March 1952) 5MWA/2/1, TWL.

[55] 'Slight Case of Husbands', *Daily Mail*, above n 30.

[56] 'Not properly understood', *Beckenham Advertiser*, above n 54.

[57] Draft of Teresa Billington-Greig speech, 1958, 7TBG/1/31, TWL.

[58] Normanton claimed to own the copyright, thus Appelbe said they needed to be careful not to infringe this and that a completely new submission was necessary. Report of Special General Meeting of Married Women's Association, above n 35.

[59] ibid.

[60] 'Joint Ownership Of Home And Income' *Times* (26 May 1952) 4.

[61] In the meeting where a decision was made to withdraw the evidence prepared by Normanton, Dr Eustace Chesser was noted to have 'thought the results in the press had been terrible and thought

Association's new memorandum made it clear what joint partnership and equal status did and did not mean.

To this end, the MWA's submission to the Royal Commission clearly stated that it was recommending the pooling of respective incomes, sharing of any surplus income and savings and full financial disclosure of all assets during marriage, mirroring the provisions of its Bill for equal partnership in marriage.[62] As chapter four explained, the MWA was keen to distinguish this stance from community of property. Under the MWA's proposal, disposing of income acquired during marriage by mutual agreement would not necessarily mean that everything earned by each spouse would be equally divided. But in property law terms, one does not have outright legal and beneficial ownership of something if they cannot dispose of it in any way they see fit. Therefore, the practical consequences of the MWA's new submission would mean, in effect, giving each spouse some form of proprietary interest in the income of their partner. While this recommendation, if implemented, would not have demolished the doctrine of separate property, it would have chipped away at it. The members who had resigned from the MWA considered this to be 'extremist'.[63]

*

Following the MWA's new written submission, members were invited to give oral evidence before the Royal Commission. Elizabeth Pomeroy and Alan Nabarro spoke, surrounded by a public gallery full of MWA members ('the largest attendance at a sitting of the Commission' the MWA claimed).[64] Pomeroy and Nabarro were emphatic about what the Association did *not* stand for. It could not accept the proposal of a personal allowance allocated by the husband to the wife. In Pomeroy and Nabarro's words:

> While in entire agreement with the view that steps taken to give the wife some degree of financial independence would be a major contribution to the stabilisation of marriage, we could never support measures which would in fact perpetuate her inferior status as a dependant or employee, instead of recognising her position as a full partner for life.[65]

Overall, the MWA summarised its stance in its revised submission as, 'the two spouses should be recognised by law as joint owners of the matrimonial

at all costs no further publicity should be given over the matter to the press'. In response, Ambrose Appelbe said more press coverage of the split *would* be necessary, as 'it will have to be given out that the evidence submitted by Mrs Normanton on our behalf has been withdrawn': Report of Special General Meeting of Married Women's Association, above n 35.
  [62] MWA Oral Evidence to Royal Commission on Marriage and Divorce, Presented by E Pomeroy and A Nabarro, 27 November 1952, 7TBG/2/J/02, TWL.
  [63] Letter from Evelyn Hamilton to Teresa Billington-Greig, 4 April 1952, 7TBG/2/J/02, TWL.
  [64] Married Women's Association Annual Report 1952–1953, 7TBG/1/32, TWL.
  [65] MWA Oral Evidence to Royal Commission on Marriage and Divorce, above, n 62.

home and of the incomes of both'.[66] This should be the case because, they explained, there 'are today many influences at work which are inimical to the stability of marriage and family life' including widespread lack of proper housing and economic precariousness: 'The institution of marriage must be viewed against this changed and changing background. If it is to survive, it must be strengthened and given a status of increased value to both husband and wife'.[67]

Here, another aspect of MWA's strategy as reformists is unveiled. Modern research has shown that when appealing to conservative policymakers and legislators, arguing that change is essential for not only the maintenance, but the *survival* of marriage, is a powerful persuasion tactic.[68] Whether the MWA is deploying this strategy consciously or not, this argument marks a shrewd way of couching radical reform in conservative terms, especially since the government at this time was Conservative, and – as the next section explores – the members of the Royal Commission were reluctant to recommend comprehensive reform.

II. THE ROYAL COMMISSION'S RESPONSE

When the Royal Commission reported in 1956, it said: 'We fully endorse' the view of equal partnership, and: 'the wife's contribution to the joint undertaking, in running the home and looking after the children, is *just as valuable* as that of the husband in providing for the home and supporting the family'.[69] Consequently, the Commission asserted that women were, rightly, no longer prepared to accept the poor treatment that historically their subordinate status had made them suffer.[70] The Commission also saw wives' failed expectations of equal partnership[71] as contributing to escalating divorce rates.[72]

On the face of it, this looks like a victory for the MWA. In its Newsletter reporting on the Royal Commission's findings,[73] it said the Commission's recognition that work inside and outside the home are of equal value was 'nearly

---

[66] MWA Evidence to the Royal Commission on Marriage and Divorce, 5SPG/I/08, TWL.

[67] ibid.

[68] A Gilbert, *British Conservatism and the Legal Regulation of Intimate Relationships* (Hart Publishing 2018) 22.

[69] *Report of the Royal Commission on Marriage and Divorce*, above n 18, para 644 (emphasis added).

[70] ibid, para 45.

[71] While the Royal Commission noted that marriage was under strain because of factors such as housing shortages and the spread of education, it argued that 'the social and economic emancipation of women' was 'probably the most important' factor. ibid.

[72] In 1954 there were 27,471 divorces in England and Wales compared with 4,735 in 1937. RCMD suggested that the new grounds of cruelty and desertion introduced in the Matrimonial Causes Act (1937) together with the more recent provision of legal aid had made divorce more available to people who were previously unable to afford it. *Report of the Royal Commission on Marriage and Divorce*, above n 18, paras 40–41.

[73] 'The Royal Commission on Marriage and Divorce', MWA Newsletter, May 1956, 7TBG/2/J/06, TWL.

word for word what Miss Juanita Frances reported back to the Six Point Group, eighteen years ago when as Chairman of the newly created "Sub-committee of Married Women" she had concluded her preliminary investigation'.[74] However, accepting equal partnership in theory and bringing it to fruition in law are two very different things. Once the Royal Commission acknowledged the need for reform, it saw its task as mitigating the rigour of the separate property doctrine, while preserving the separate property rights of spouses. It had to balance fixed ideas of legal and equitable ownership with giving legal expression to both equal partnership and the factual reality that spouses tended to enjoy their property conjointly. Put simply, the Commission had to develop a framework that fitted the arguably opposing models of the autonomous individual and the interdependent family community. Ultimately, the Royal Commission failed in this endeavour. The remainder of this section will discuss what the Royal Commission rejected, what it proposed, the MWA's reaction to this, and what this tells us about the nature of reform.

A. Rejected Proposals

Even though the Royal Commission had recognised the need for change in general, it could not agree on what specifically needed to be reformed, or on how that reform could be achieved.[75] Of the 17 commissioners, 12 opposed community of property, considering it to be 'a striking departure from the traditional law'.[76] The introduction of community of property, which would trigger joint ownership from the marriage onwards, would in their view require reform that was too radical. And, as noted earlier in this chapter, this was not going to come from a body whose approach to change was conservative, aiming to build upon existing law and with an eye to any potential practical limitations. Community of property did not fit this criteria for reform, as according to the Commission it would not take account of the 'natural and normal desire' to acquire property, would overcomplicate matters such as who makes decisions about the property, and could lead to injustice if one spouse were industrious and the other were not.[77]

The MWA's proposal to give wives a share of their husband's income was rejected unanimously,[78] as were proposals to give each spouse a right to information about their partner's earnings.[79] The Association would not have had any success with the submission of evidence prepared by Helena Normanton

---

[74] ibid. The Newsletter also stated: 'these principles are embodied in both [MWA] Bills'; this had been the MWA's 'main policy' since it came into being in 1938.
[75] Stetson, above n 8, 165.
[76] *Report of the Royal Commission on Marriage and Divorce*, above n 18, para 651.
[77] ibid.
[78] ibid, para 654.
[79] ibid, paras 706–11.

either (which Normanton re-submitted to the Royal Commission independently following her resignation from the Association), as the Commission rejected unanimously the proposition of an agreed allowance to be paid to the wife.[80] The Commission also went against Normanton's assertions that housekeeping money should continue to be the property of the husband. In fact, reform of housekeeping savings was one of the few recommendations it *did* make for reform.

B. Recommendations

The Royal Commission concluded that housekeeping savings should belong to the husband and wife in equal shares.[81] This was not an endorsement of the MWA's broader ethos of joint ownership, but it arguably did demonstrate that the MWA's view was gaining traction. Thanks in part to the MWA's decade of campaigning since *Blackwell*, a spotlight had been shone on the issue of ownership of housekeeping money.

The Commission's other recommendations were carefully ring-fenced so as not to disrupt the doctrine of separate property.[82] This included providing the wife with a right to a pension after divorce and giving the spouse with no ownership rights over the matrimonial home the ability to prevent its sale.[83] If introduced into law, these suggestions could have helped some of the many women the Royal Commission heard about while it gathered evidence – women who had been left homeless and penniless as a result of the state of economic vulnerability marriage had left them in. The financially dependent wife could have received a pension despite divorce, half the housekeeping savings and would have a guaranteed right to occupy the home. Yet, as organisations such as the MWA were arguing at the time, comprehensive reform was needed. The Royal Commission's recommendations did not get to the root of the problem and were instead temporary Band-Aids plastered over serious and deeply embedded inequalities between husband and wife.

C. The MWA's Response

In its Newsletter, the MWA stated that members had responded to the report with 'mixed feelings'.[84] It acknowledged the small successes but was clearly

---

[80] ibid, para 655.

[81] ibid, para 699.

[82] Stetson, above n 8, 166.

[83] This could be achieved by registration of a land charge. The Commission's recommendation for spouses to have a statutory right of occupation of the family home would also be good against successive third parties.

[84] MWA Newsletter, May 1956, above n 73.

disappointed by the Commission's failure to recommend comprehensive reform. The MWA said it was 'good to read that the Commission advises equal shares in all housekeeping savings' but viewed the remainder of the report as consisting mostly of 'small handouts', concluding that it 'is very good indeed when dealing with minor matters of marriage, desertion and divorce but the conclusions on major matters they were set up to deal with are negligible'. Though the Association had made every effort to collate and present the views of the women they represented[85] it said the Royal Commission's recommendations followed 'certain premises' which were 'invalid' for 'thousands of destitute mothers ... and bear little relation to real life'.[86] Here, the MWA is levying two important criticisms against the report of the Royal Commission.

First, it believed the Royal Commission based some of its recommendations on assumptions about married women rather than evidence of their real experiences. Kahn-Freund made similar observations at the time in the *Modern Law Review*, in relation to the Royal Commission's recommendations (or lack thereof) for divorce reform. In particular, he said the report had a 'lack of vision' and an 'absence of well-considered policy based on a real knowledge of the facts'.[87] The Royal Commission's report was of course based on vast amounts of research and evidence, but what Kahn-Freund seems to be saying is that it was not asking the right research questions and it was consequently not gathering the data it needed. Moreover, Kahn-Freund highlighted the normative tendencies of institutional reform processes, and how these can sometimes be based on fiction and prejudice rather than concrete data: 'the law, as we all know, superimposes a complicated set of norms'.[88]

The second charge relates to the Royal Commission's own admission that it would not alleviate hardship for wives if this would lead to injustice for husbands.[89] While the MWA was not suggesting husbands should be put in a position of substantial hardship or injustice – after all, it was advocating for equality – members did see the Commission's concern for the privacy of the deserting husband and father as disproportionate. This is because members saw many examples of destitute women with no maintenance or means of enforcing it because their partner had simply disappeared. The MWA therefore saw 'the desire to protect the interests and rights of defaulting husbands' as being 'the reason for much muddled and reactionary thinking and action in the history of marriage and of the family'.[90] Yet again, the needs of the economically vulnerable wife were not prioritised.

---

[85] Including through submitting written and oral evidence, promoting its reform recommendations in the press, circulating questionnaires to gather data on the most pressing issues for housewives and drawing upon the legal expertise of Alan Nabarro, Roxane Arnold and Ambrose Appelbe.

[86] MWA Newsletter, May 1956, above n 73.

[87] O Kahn-Freund, 'Divorce Law Reform' (1956) 19 *MLR* 573, 600.

[88] ibid, 582.

[89] *Report of the Royal Commission on Marriage and Divorce*, above n 18, para 648.

[90] MWA Newsletter, May 1956, above n 73.

Thus overall the MWA was disappointed with the findings of the Commission. Some members even considered whether their time, effort and sacrifice had all been worth it:

> It is for each one of us to decide whether this Report of the Royal Commission is worth the time and trouble spent by eminent persons during a period of four and a half years ... thereby keeping legislation on issues ... at a standstill during these years.

Reform groups in the meantime 'might have been successful in persuading the Government to bring in some vitally needed legislation'.[91] Maybe, members of the Association thought, it would have been better to keep lobbying and pushing bills in Parliament, as the Commission's report would not lead to meaningful reform any time soon:

> Unfortunately the Government is unlikely to do anything about the Commission's recommendations because they were divided on most of their conclusions; still more unfortunately if anyone should attempt in the future to bring in a Bill so as to ameliorate the most obvious injustices this Report will most likely be produced and that will end the matter.[92]

Therefore, it appears the MWA viewed the Royal Commission's report as a hindrance rather than an opportunity.

D. Insights into Family Law Reform

The Royal Commission's 1956 report might be considered underwhelming given its lack of concrete recommendations. Yet it does invite important insights into processes of family law reform. Its failure to find a compromise between a strictly applied separate property doctrine and the rejected premise of community of property has been something numerous reform commissions have grappled with since.[93] Indeed, the Royal Commission was clearly not prepared to tackle the question of marital property rights systematically, as Germany was to do a year later in 1957.[94] And comprehensive reform of the financial consequences of divorce in England and Wales did not happen until 1970.

As a result, if the Royal Commission was only prepared to reform the property consequences of marriage and divorce in a patchwork manner, the chances of the MWA's more ambitious Bill for equal partnership in marriage being taken forward were poor. As well as failing to propose any significant reform

---

[91] ibid.
[92] ibid.
[93] See, eg, *Family Property Law* (WP No 42, 1971); *First Report on Family Property: A New Approach* (Law Com No 52, 1973); *Second Report on Family Property – Family Provision on Death* (Law Com No 61, 1974); *Third Report on Family Property: The Matrimonial Home* (Law Com No 86, 1978); *Family Law: Matrimonial Property* (Law Com No 175, 1988).
[94] O Kahn-Freund, 'Recent Legislation on Matrimonial Property' (1970) 33 *MLR* 601, 605.

of matrimonial property law, the Royal Commission could not agree on how divorce law should be reformed either. Kahn-Freund called it a 'disappointing document',[95] concluding that

> many readers of this Report will deplore that so little has been done to elucidate the relevant social facts, that so little account has been taken of modern psychological and sociological thought, and that a precious opportunity has been missed of clarifying the policies which underlie the existing law and which should govern its reform.[96]

The Royal Commission's anti-climactic report is an example of the difficulty with pursuing reform by placing pressure on institutions and working within the constraints of legal process. Specifically, the MWA's experience with the Royal Commission raised five problems. The first was that the Commission was divided on many of the issues it discussed, with MP Marcus Lipton even referring to it in the House of Commons after its publication as 'just another example of an unholy deadlock'.[97] A practical but significant obstacle to reform, the deadlock meant that even if the MWA could persuade some members of the need to take on its recommendations, the divisions and controversies between reformers and religious conservatives within the Commission meant there was little consensus on any serious reform.[98]

The four other problems with reform are apparent when the MWA's stumbling blocks with the Royal Commission are assessed through a feminist lens. One problem was the issue of who the Royal Commissioners were. When it was first established, the MWA urged the Commission to include 'the woman's point of view ... by the appointment of both men and women in equal numbers'.[99] However, of the 19 Commission members, only six were female.[100] From the MWA's perspective, predominantly male Commission members would propose reform of the law in a way that suited men, and the Association was not convinced this would address the plight of the women they advocated for. As noted above, the MWA felt the Royal Commission placed disproportionate emphasis on the protection of the deserting husband at the expense of the deserted wife.[101] It therefore makes sense that the MWA wanted the Royal Commission to include gatekeepers who were women and would potentially be more receptive to some of the more insidious and hidden gendered inequalities in marriage that the MWA was trying to highlight.[102] That is, the MWA made clear in its oral evidence to the Commission that it did not just want to address

---

[95] Kahn-Freund, 'Divorce Law Reform', above n 87, 600.
[96] ibid, 573.
[97] HC Deb 26 March 1956, vol 550, col 1747.
[98] See Stetson, above n 8, 166.
[99] Commission on Marriage, above n 7.
[100] *Report of the Royal Commission on Marriage and Divorce*, above n 18, 339.
[101] MWA Newsletter, May 1956, above n 73.
[102] The Commissioners *were* sometimes divided on gender lines. For example, seven commissioners were in favour of some form of community of property: two of the 13 male commissioners (one of

the most extreme forms of suffering experienced by wives; it also wanted to draw attention to the everyday inequalities:

> It is not always major disagreement on financial matters, but minor constant pinpricks which undermine family life. For instance, here is an actual case. A man denied his wife all but the bare minimum for the necessities of life. The daughter of 15, as was natural at her age, was wishful to buy a small box of powder, but found her mother, week after week, unable to spare the 2/- needed. An appeal to the father produced 5/- as a grand benevolent gesture in sharp contrast to the poor mother's apparent meanness.[103]

It is likely that some onlookers would have dismissed this evidence as being petty, given that contemporaneous press reports satirised the MWA as portraying every move a man made as 'absolutely unbearable'.[104] With this in mind, it is likely the MWA wanted members of the Royal Commission to empathise and understand the *humiliation* of these commonplace and easily dismissed instances of power and control. And that with time, these 'constant pinpricks' could do real harm to marriage.

This relates to a third problem with legal reform which the MWA had to grapple with. When putting the spotlight on the more hidden, relational and insidious power imbalances in marriage, the MWA was exposing itself to criticism for placing disproportionate emphasis on the insignificant, when there were possibly more pressing problems to be addressed. Yet when the Association raised those bigger and broader issues, such as the widespread poverty of housewives, it was dismissed for presenting issues that were insurmountable.[105] This is significant for legal historians because it reinforces the importance of assessing legal history from a gendered perspective, and makes us question how women's position was accounted for in family law reform.[106] A gendered analysis also brings to the fore the MWA's fourth problem with reform: the Royal Commission's reluctance to pull back the curtain on the private sphere.

As chapter two discussed, a perennial problem with family law reform is the state's insistence on separating the public and private. Historically, the married woman's problems have been in the world of the private, which judges, policymakers and legislators have sought to avoid. For example, the MWA wanted the Commission to consider how a wife's economic dependence on her husband was exacerbated by her being kept in the dark about the details of his finances. The Commission ultimately rejected the idea that a spouse should be entitled to disclosure of their partner's financial position.[107] But in Olive Stone's

---

whom wished to confine it to the furniture alone) and five of the six female commissioners. *Report of the Royal Commission on Marriage and Divorce*, above n 18, para 650.
[103] MWA Oral Evidence to Royal Commission on Marriage and Divorce, above n 62.
[104] 'Les Girls', *Daily Mirror*, above n 31.
[105] Letter from Donald Somervell to Ernest Bevin, 22 December 1943, LC02/2777, TNA.
[106] See N Lacey, 'Feminist Legal Theory Beyond Neutrality' (1995) 48 *Current Legal Problems* 1.
[107] *Report of the Royal Commission on Marriage and Divorce*, above n 18, paras 706–11.

view at the time, the Commission provided 'doubtful justification' for this conclusion.[108] This is because for the Commission, addressing power imbalances in the home by considering measures to require financial disclosure would mean invading that private sphere.[109] The Commission deemed this unacceptable. It was, it said, 'vital' that 'so far as possible the law should be kept out of the intimate life of the family'.[110] The Commission was made more resolute about this by its desire to protect spouses' (ie, husbands') separate property rights. As Stone pointed out, the Commission had 'an obsession with the sanctity of legal titles to property'.[111] Equality in marriage was therefore a laudable aim, but the overall message of the Royal Commission's report was that it still came secondary to one's right to property. This suggests that by keeping the private sphere 'so long protected in the closet' as Pamela Symes has suggested, the artificial division between public and private has impeded 'real reform in family law for too long'.[112] 'The dichotomy needs to be transcended', Symes said. The 'closet needs to be stormed'.[113]

Fifth and finally, investigating the Royal Commission's report also brings the familiar problem of precedent to light. The power of precedent is a stumbling block well known to feminist legal historians; the notion that law cannot change because this is the way it has always been. As chapter five showed, this problem was common in the courtroom, but here we see it getting in the way of statutory change too. An example of this is the question before the Commission of how to enforce maintenance, which was often unpaid, leaving the housewife in dire financial straits. The MWA and others proposed the introduction of attachment of wages,[114] meaning deductions at source from the husband's wage to ensure payment following a maintenance court order.[115] As the next chapter will investigate, the MWA was eventually successful in achieving reform in this area. But the Royal Commission in 1956 rejected these proposals, considering the practical difficulties too great.[116] The MWA found this unpersuasive as similar

---

[108] OM Stone, 'The Royal Commission on Marriage and Divorce: Family Dependents and Their Maintenance' (1956) 19 *MLR* 601, 609.

[109] *Report of the Royal Commission on Marriage and Divorce*, above n 18, para 710. According to the Commission, at para 711, such invasion would 'not ensure a more secure foundation for marriage'.

[110] ibid, para 647.

[111] Stone, above n 108, 622.

[112] P Symes, 'Property, Power and Dependence: Critical Family Law' (1987) 14 *Journal of Law and Society* 199, 210.

[113] ibid.

[114] As the next chapter will show, MWA members had been campaigning for this for some time and this reform was part of the Women's Disabilities Bill introduced into Parliament by Edith Summerskill in 1952.

[115] The Royal Commission did make some recommendations for reform of maintenance law. For instance, it recommended 'that committal to prison should not cancel the arrears of maintenance in respect of which the imprisonment was imposed': *Report of the Royal Commission on Marriage and Divorce*, above n 18, para 1108.

[116] ibid, para 1107; MWA Newsletter, May 1956, above n 73.

maintenance powers existed in Scotland.[117] When the Commission was faced with this, the MWA reported: 'the Commission blandly says in effect that it is acceptable [in Scotland] because it has long existed,[118] but would not be acceptable in England because it has not existed here for a long time'.[119] This shows once again how, as Rosemary Auchmuty puts it, the doctrine of precedent can be 'used to perpetuate a relationship of male power over women'.[120] The wife was left with little power to enforce her right to maintenance if the husband would not pay it.[121] After the MWA's experience of the judiciary in *Blackwell* and of the Royal Commission in 1956, all corners of the legal system must have seemed steeped in traditions that served to maintain gendered power structures and reinforce the marginalised position of married women. But the MWA did not lose hope when faced with these obstacles. As Stone suggested at the time, there was some reason to be sanguine. While she said '[f]ew will read the Report [of the Royal Commission] without misgivings ... some hopeful tendencies' had emerged. This included, 'rather surprisingly', Stone said, 'fairly wide agreement, on a rather pedestrian level, of what is a reasonable solution, at least for the simpler problems of marriage'.[122]

III. THE AFTERMATH

Symes once argued that the critical family lawyer needs to be alive to the fact that '[r]ocks are not only for hurling but for building'.[123] The recommendations of the Royal Commission were deeply conservative and deserved much of the criticism levied against them. Yet they also opened the way to some radical propositions. After all, the concept of equal partnership in marriage had been, in the Commission's words, 'fully endorsed',[124] the legal inequality of married women had been acknowledged and the Commission had concluded that 'some amendment [was] desirable'.[125] However, the MWA was correct in its Newsletter when it predicted that no immediate legislative reform would come from the report.[126]

---

[117] Scottish courts could deduct wages at source for non-payment of maintenance pursuant to the Arrestment of Wages (Scotland) Act 1871.

[118] Referring to the *Report of the Royal Commission on Marriage and Divorce*, above n 18, para 1103: 'it may be said to be traditional to the country [Scotland] and therefore accepted as a matter of course'.

[119] MWA Newsletter, May 1956, above n 73.

[120] R Auchmuty, 'Legal History' in R Auchmuty (ed), *Great Debates in Gender and Law* (Macmillan 2018) 181.

[121] There was some recourse for husbands to be incarcerated for defaulting on maintenance payments, but this still did not mean the wife got the maintenance she had been granted by the court.

[122] Stone, above n 108, 622.

[123] Symes, above n 112, 210.

[124] *Report of the Royal Commission on Marriage and Divorce*, above n 18, para 644.

[125] ibid, para 647.

[126] MWA Newsletter, May 1956, above n 73.

The government did not take any of the Commission's proposals forward[127] and as Cretney pointed out, it was clear that there 'was no quick fix' in its recommendations about the property rights of husband and wife.[128]

As a result, the MWA's efforts to highlight the need for matrimonial property reform were thwarted. As Dorothy Stetson noted, the issue did not attract 'enough attention to be taken up separately from the other subjects in the report'.[129] The MWA could not get married women's property rights on the public agenda unless or until a decision was made by Parliament on the issue of divorce reform and, Stetson said, 'that would not occur until the deadlock was broken' between religious conservatives (such as the Church of England) and reformers (such as a collective of divorce lawyers). So, the feminist reformers were forced to regroup.

In the aftermath of the Royal Commission's report and the MWA split, the Association returned to its strategy of parliamentary lobbying and prepared a new draft of its Bill for equal partnership in marriage. This time they called it the Married Women (Financial Status) Bill. As we saw in chapter four, the MWA had not intended to put forward another draft Bill for equal partnership in marriage, but new factors had emerged 'which made it imperative to press on'.[130] The Association reported that a 'major factor which made us change our minds about the timing of our Bill'[131] was the Council of Married Women – the group of MWA defectors who had split from the MWA over Helena Normanton's evidence. This section looks more closely at this breakaway group, revealing that while Normanton's memorandum to the Royal Commission might have catalysed the split, disagreement had been building for some time in the MWA over how the law should be reformed. Put simply, examining the views of the MWA rebels reveals more than what caused the split; it demonstrates why the disputes within the MWA were quite so intractable.

A. Council of Married Women

The Council of Married Women (CMW) was established by former leading MWA members Helena Normanton, Doreen Gorsky, Helen Nutting, Evelyn Hamilton and Juliet Rhys-Williams, and was a pressure group that was separate but parallel to the MWA, in that it was also focused solely upon improving the legal status of married women. It is unclear precisely when the group was set

---

[127] Though it later supported the Married Women's Property Act 1964, considered in ch 7.
[128] Cretney, above n 13, 125.
[129] Stetson, above n 8, 167.
[130] 'Equal Financial Partnership in Marriage Bill', MWA Newsletter, December 1958, 7TBG/2/J/08, TWL.
[131] ibid.

up, as in the minutes of the meeting in which Gorsky read out the resignations, there is a postscript:

> On leaving the meeting, members, to their astonishment, were asked by press representatives what they thought of the new organisation which had been formed by Mrs Normanton and Mrs Gorsky. This was their first knowledge of any such action on the part of these officers.[132]

The fact that the CMW was formed so quickly following the split meant the new breakaway group could take advantage of the press attention swirling around these resignations. But it also suggested the creation of the CMW might have been in the air for the MWA rebels for some time. While Normanton had not been an MWA member for long when she took up the presidency of the Association and prepared the first memorandum,[133] Gorsky, Nutting and Hamilton had been long-standing prominent members of the group and were more involved in the politics and tensions within the Association. For this reason, other MWA members were even more shocked when they supported Normanton's memorandum, which so clearly went against the MWA's vision of joint ownership. Juanita Frances, for instance, trusted Gorsky as Chairman to ensure Normanton's evidence was consistent with the aims of the group, saying that she had 'kept her reservations to herself, hoping devoutly that the Chairman ... would intervene with Mrs Normanton, and make her see the points of view of the Association'.[134] With hindsight it is clear that Gorsky failed to do this because she did not agree with the MWA view. Later, when giving her opinion on the MWA proposal for the husband's income to be shared equally with the wife, she said 'It is pure gold digging ... Not only would the men of this country never agree to legislation to effectuate it, but the average wife would never ask it'.[135] Instead, Normanton's agreed allowance idea made much more sense to Gorsky: 'If women of all parties and views would earnestly unite on that one reform, most of the others they desire would be rapidly achieved. The agreed independence allowance is the wife's first step'.[136]

B. The CMW's Ideology

The fault lines within the MWA become more visible when the CMW's feminism is better understood. Their view of spousal equality was in part influenced by the

---

[132] Report of Special General Meeting of Married Women's Association, above n 35.

[133] Indeed, when discussing the withdrawal of Normanton's memorandum with MWA members, Dora Russell said she was 'astonished when a member of only three months standing – Mrs Normanton – was briefed to submit the evidence on this very important occasion': ibid.

[134] ibid.

[135] Press Release, 'New Council of Married Women Formed' (1 April 1952), 5CMW/A/4, TWL.

[136] ibid.

legacy of those Victorian women who had launched the modern women's movement and the view that the MWPA 1882 was sacred and a 'bastion of women's
rights'.[137] This is because it marked husband and wife out as separate and equal
individuals. The concept of separate property did not treat the wife as a dependant or a needy supplicant, but instead as an independent property owner. And
so when it came to the economic position of married women, providing housewives with a wage they negotiated, controlled and earned for their work gave
them an opportunity to earn money as men did, and in their view moved away
from the notion of dependency they saw as handicapping married women. This
interpretation arguably aligns with Normanton's answer to the question 'What
is Feminism?' when previously asked by the MWA:

> A feminist is a man or woman who declines to allow the physical differences between
> the sexes to obscure his view of their essential equivalence. He or she sees that it is
> a plain duty to the race to work for the obliteration of every unjust condition which
> prevents either men or women accomplishing a full task in the world according to
> capacity because of any artificial barriers or obstructions. He or she would work
> positively for the increase of opportunities for the equal exercise of every beneficial
> faculty; and would regard it as a privilege to have suffered to bring about the reign of
> equal justice between the sexes.[138]

This short statement not only foreshadows the turbulence to come within the
group, but provides critical insight into how Normanton and others within the
CMW saw equality being translated into legal terms. For Normanton, equality meant giving men and women the *same* opportunities and rights instead of
being distracted by physical differences. In the context of marriage, wives should
not have an equal right to what Normanton considered to be property belong-
ing to the husband pursuant to the MWPA 1882. Rather, a wage for married
women taking the form of an 'agreed allocation'[139] meant they would be paid
for their work, no more, no less, and the principle of separate property would
not be contaminated. Equality did not mean equal division of all the assets; it
meant economic freedom for wives by giving them tangible property of their
own instead of (as she saw it) a transient right to share. As explained in chapter
two, this view aligned with 'old' equal rights feminism, not the 'new' feminist
ideas of equality in difference, which had been the intellectual inspiration for
the MWA.

The problem with Normanton's model for reform is that it does not account
for the imbalances of power which research shows are endemic in marriage
and intimate relationships.[140] Spouses would have to agree on the amount of

---

[137] Speech of Teresa Billington-Greig, above n 3.

[138] 'What is a Feminist?', *Wife and Citizen*, August 1950, 7TBG/1/32, TWL.

[139] Helena Normanton suggested this phrase was 'the best condensation of our plan': CMW
Bulletin, January 1953, 5CMW/E/07, TWL.

[140] See, eg, S Fredman, *Women and the Law* (Oxford University Press 1998) 40.

allowance, which immediately requires two assumptions to be made about the marital partnership. First, that the spouses have equal bargaining power to agree to terms mutually beneficial to them, which do not undervalue the work being done by the wife. And second, that even if an agreement can be reached, that sum will always be paid by the moneyed spouse. As previous chapters have indicated, law's inability to enforce maintenance orders effectively on relationship breakdown has historically served to oppress women further. There is no evidence to suggest enforcement of an agreed allowance would be any more effective. And spousal inequalities are entrenched even more when law-making is based on assumptions of equal bargaining power over financial matters in the context of marriage. Importantly, however, analysing the CMW's take on family law reform provides fascinating insight into debates about spousal agreements that continue to resonate strongly today, as questions over the weight to be attached to marital property agreements are discussed regularly in Parliament and in the courtroom.

In spite of the difficulties with the allowance for wives model, the other founding members of the CMW were unwavering in their support of it. From this perspective, the split is not all that surprising. Indeed, Joyce Freeguard notes it is 'difficult to understand why differing opinions within the MWA were not expressed before the written evidence was sent' to the Royal Commission.[141] MWA Treasurer Evelyn Hamilton, who resigned alongside Gorsky and Nutting expressed her feelings on the matter in a letter to Teresa Billington-Greig:

> We did our best with the memorandum. I personally wore myself to a standstill getting it … away. I am personally unhappy at the attitude of the 'extremist' group and more so at the giving to the Press of confidential matters discussed at the Executive Committee … [W]hatever we'd put in, some group would have disagreed, perhaps not quite so verbally and publically [sic] and the split within which has been there for many years would have come out anyway![142]

Clearly, she was of the view that the fight over Normanton's memorandum simply catalysed the inevitable split.

C. The CMW's Policy

The CMW was formally established in April 1952 with Normanton as President and Gorsky as Chairman. Helen Nutting later took over the leadership of the Council until it was wound up in 1969.[143] It was clear from the outset that it was

---

[141] J Freeguard, 'It's Time for Women of the 1950s to Stand Up and Be Counted' (PhD thesis, University of Sussex 2004) 147.

[142] Letter from Evelyn Hamilton to Billington-Greig, 15 March 1952, 7TBG/2/J/02, TWL.

[143] Helena Normanton resigned from the CMW in 1954, telling the *Daily Mail*: 'I think the time has come for me to make room for someone else'. Anon, 'QC Resigns' *Daily Mail* (19 March 1954) 5.

to be more conservative than the MWA and its membership was more limited. The Council 'would not admit spinsters or males', would only accept 'women who are or who have been married' and would 'stand for moderate and reasonable reforms, equally fair to both husband and wife and as helpful as possible to children'.[144] In its efforts to achieve justice for wives, mothers and widows, it promoted joint responsibility for the upkeep of the matrimonial home.[145] It also drafted the Married Persons (Allowances) Bill, which mirrored Normanton's memorandum to the Royal Commission and provided that a portion of the employed spouse's income (who at that time was normally the husband) should be paid directly to the non-gainfully employed spouse (normally the wife) in payment for her work in the home.[146]

The CMW aimed to distance itself from what Nutting and other CMW members considered to be the 'ridiculous and impractical' proposals of the MWA.[147] And in differentiating itself from the MWA's proposals for joint ownership, Freeguard has questioned whether the CMW's more moderate stance might have been more palatable to conservative law and policymakers. The notion that neither spouse was entitled to the earnings of the other could have been viewed as pragmatic, as it advocated equality while protecting and endorsing the property rights of the individual.[148] Indeed, when presenting her evidence to the Royal Commission, 'bringing her fist down sharply on the table' to reinforce her point,[149] the CMW reported: 'it was quite obvious all the way through our President's evidence that the whole Commission was listening intently to her recommendations'.[150] This was evidenced by the fact that Normanton was invited to take tea with the members of the Commission in their private room after her evidence; 'an honour', according to the CMW, only to be accorded to one other witness.[151]

If the CMW proposals *were* more agreeable, there was a chance they would be taken forward instead of the MWA's Bill for equal partnership in marriage. This was exactly what the MWA feared when the CMW's Bill emerged in 1958, one year after Normanton's death:

> There are many men to-day who do feel that something should be done to remedy the wife's present position; they might be persuaded, with perhaps a sigh of relief, that to

[144] Freeguard, above n 141, 145; Objects of CMW, 5CMW/A/4, TWL.

[145] Freeguard, above n 141, 146.

[146] In private correspondence, Helen Nutting wrote: 'I realised unless we put forward our proposals first, the MWA would do it sooner or later and this, in my opinion, would put back the question of the financial status of the married woman for many years': Letter from Helen Nutting to Mrs Harries, 11 July 1957, 5CMW/B/03, TWL.

[147] Stetson, above n 8, 172.

[148] Freeguard, above n 141, 146.

[149] Report of Helena Normanton's Oral Evidence to the Royal Commission on Marriage and Divorce, 5CMW/B/01, TWL.

[150] ibid.

[151] ibid.

provide her with pin-money should be enough to keep her quiet and thus the whole matter could be put into cold storage again for another twenty years or so.[152]

For this reason, the MWA 'could not let it go unchallenged' and as we have seen in chapter four, it introduced its own Bill. MWA members could not tolerate the idea of the CMW achieving legislative success that was so 'completely at odds with [their] own views on equal partnership'.[153] According to the Council, however, their Bill did not threaten the MWA's legislative ambitions.[154] In a letter to MWA member Anne Ormrod, Helen Nutting appeared to appeal for cooperation between the two organisations:

> I understood you to say that the MWA would probably feel bound to attack our Bill because of the principles involved. We take the opposite view and think that both Bills should go forward on their own merits as a sincere contribution towards solving the problem of the equal economic status of the married woman. We do not feel that if our Bill were successful it would prevent further action later on and we look upon it as a stepping stone towards the goal we are both aiming at – equality between husbands and wives. It is of course extremely unlikely that either of our Bills will get on to the statute book as they stand now but the best of both might be amalgamated ultimately.[155]

In any case, the MWA need not have worried; MPs were not particularly interested in the Council's Bill and the government did not consider it as the Royal Commission had already rejected Normanton's similar memorandum of evidence. Neither the MWA Bill nor the CMW Bill received a First Reading in Parliament, let alone any official recognition.

CONCLUSION

For feminist groups like the MWA, the Royal Commission on Marriage and Divorce represented an important opportunity to push for change and to get those in power to agree to the idea of equal partnership in marriage. After all, the Commission was the main forum in which married women's legal status was reviewed after the Second World War, and it took five years to report, so it would not have been outlandish for the MWA to expect *some* reform to improve the position of married women. Yet as we have seen, MWA members were ultimately disappointed with the Commission's report.

For legal historians, however, investigating why change did *not* happen can be as important as exploring why it did. The Royal Commission is often

---

[152] 'Equal Financial Partnership in Marriage Bill', above n 130.
[153] ibid.
[154] Although see Helen Nutting's private correspondence, above n 146.
[155] Letter from Helen Nutting to Anne Ormrod, 23 October 1958, 5CMW/A/4, TWL.

dismissed or forgotten because it did not recommend any systematic reform. Even so, it reveals common themes in the process and substance of law reform. As this chapter has explored, the Royal Commission provides hard evidence of how the intransigence of law and the public/private artifice can operate in tandem to prevent reform of family law that could have bolstered married women's economic independence. And how, even when the problem of inequality is acknowledged, the available solutions (particularly when proposed by feminists) are often not palatable to those in power. The frustration this caused the MWA and other feminist pressure groups was captured perfectly by the *Economist*:

> One of the difficulties in getting support for proposals ... is the usual official reaction that marriage is a matter of love and trust, and that the law cannot intervene even where there is neither; some feminists are very angry with the Royal Commission on Marriage and Divorce for taking that line throughout much of its report.[156]

The Royal Commission was important for the history of the MWA not only because it acknowledged the importance of the group's goal of equal partnership in marriage and provided lessons for reform. It also triggered its fragmentation, bringing divisions embedded within the Association to the fore. The different submissions that led to the MWA split expose the divergence of opinion within the group over the practical meaning of equality in marriage. Even more important, however, is the insight this provides beyond the Association's split. As Freeguard has argued:

> How the dispute was caused was less important that the effect it had on the campaign for married women's financial independence. The disagreement undoubtedly weakened the case, gave confused signals to other women's organisations and helped to ensure that the campaign for women's financial independence ... would be left unresolved.[157]

The mixed messages in the press of what the MWA had hoped to achieve may have done irreparable harm to the Association's chances of reform. Helena Normanton's accusations that the MWA was 'anti-man' could have affected its support from members of the public too. And, the pressure applied by the MWA on lawmakers was diluted when the Association was disunited. Yet there was a glimmer of hope in the Royal Commission's report. Though the government had not agreed to take forward any of the Commission's recommendations, its smaller concessions (such as its proposal regarding housekeeping savings to be divided equally) gave the MWA cause for optimism, as the next chapter will show.

---

[156] Anon, 'The Feminists Mop Up' *Economist* (21 April 1956) 243, 5SPG/I/08, TWL.
[157] Freeguard, above n 141.

The story of the MWA, its fragmentation and the Royal Commission is therefore a complex story of reform. It demonstrates perfectly that when reform of family law is examined through a feminist lens, it is, as Rosemary Auchmuty and Erika Rackley have put it 'messy; sometimes conflicted; never simple; unpredictable; usually time – and personality – dependent; and often flawed'.[158] There is no clear blueprint for family law reform.

---

[158] E Rackley and R Auchmuty, 'Standing on the shoulders of giants' *Law Society Gazette*, 14 October 2019, available at: https://www.lawgazette.co.uk/women-in-the-law/standing-on-the-shoulders-of-giants/5101770.article.

Interlude: Reform Movements are Like Builders

T HE MARRIED WOMEN'S Association (MWA) celebrated their '21st birthday' in 1958, and by their own account, there was much talk of the
group's early years throughout these celebrations. By 1958, MWA Vice
President Teresa Billington-Greig was in her eighties, having devoted her life to
feminist campaigns for the vote, the advancement of women in politics[1] and,
of course, the improvement of married women's legal status. Having seen the
MWA split, and the Association's various setbacks thus far, she made a speech
at the birthday celebrations. This is what she said:

> [The MWA] have exposed injustices and absurdities in the legal status of married
> women ... they have given advice and guidance and won sympathy and publicity for
> many victimised wives. All this is recorded in the minutes and publications of the
> Association for the historian to read.

> But ... I want to emphasise another aspect of MWA accomplishment. Reform move-
> ments are like builders; they set out to erect structures in which human beings can
> live better lives but there are few of them which can begin their constructive work
> at once because of the state of the site on which they have to build. This was the
> position which faced the MWA. The ground was littered with obstructions of senti-
> ment, ignorance and prejudice and the little starting group had neither the tools nor
> the training to tackle the job entirely by itself. This obstructing litter was mainly in
> three forms. There was first the inherited disapproval of 'nice women' (reinforced
> by uneasy husbands) for any loud argument about marriage laws and their results.
> Supporting this attitude, or because of it, there was the taboo policy of the older
> women's reform societies – and indeed of the militant suffragists in their early years –
> all of which set out to avoid sex prejudice in their struggle for citizenship and educa-
> tion. This policy had been long and firmly established before the Vote was won and
> it persisted thereafter. There was first the old habit and then a certain attitude of
> opposition as between married and single women as to which remaining disabilities
> were most important. The lone woman on her own saw the married woman as being
> provided for by a life-long protector: the segregated and unpaid wife saw her single
> sister as a free person, an active recognised member of the outside community. This
> co-operation in immediate action was hampered.

> In practical terms this difference worked out in two main lines. The apprehensive
> married woman had her doubts about equal pay; and because of this the resent-
> ful single woman became more resentful. The older section of married women did

---

[1] She was a leading member of both Women for Westminster and the Women's Freedom League.

not question the equal pay principle but were inert in their response to the call for action. They in their turn had another problem of uncertainty: how was the demand for a radical change in the financial status of the married woman going to affect that first great bulwark won in 1882 when the chief Married Women's Property Act was passed? Also, over-riding all else, how was a secure fundamental basis of financial and economic status to be secured for the married woman? It was to face and solve these riddles that the Married Women's Association set itself up; it was for this purpose that the services of a galaxy of skilled legal counsellors was secured.

Now we can claim that the handicaps to be overcome and the plan of action by which to overcome them are clearly understood. Also, we can claim that the difference in viewpoint between married and single women need no longer be a deterrent. The doubts about equal pay have disappeared and the Married Women's Property Acts are seen as an enormously valuable half-way step towards the equal financial status of marriage partnership. The slogans of the movement now at its majority show this development clearly – 'Equal Partnership in Marriage and Equal Pay and Opportunity outside it'. Thus the MWA is seen as clearly pledged to the full emancipation of all women and to the establishment of a really unfettered two-fold humanity with no irrational or unjust restrictions imposed on either sex. Our first successful legislative venture is the beginning of building. Step by step steady progress can be hoped for if we persevere.[2]

Step by step, brick by brick; could the MWA reform family law using an incremental approach?

---

[2] Speech of Teresa Billington-Greig, MWA Newsletter, June 1958, 7TBG/2/J/08, TWL.

7

One Step at a Time

I have been a loyal mother and hardworking wife, having brought three healthy children into the world. I think that, when a woman is a wife and mother in a home such as mine, there should be a law compelling the husband to share some part of his earnings with her. Life would be so different for me if only I had a fraction of the allowance my husband spends on himself. If a woman had an allowance for herself the family would gain by it as she would be able to save for her old age or a rainy day.

It is a crying shame that a man by marrying attains the services and life helpmate for nothing. She must accept clothing and even her medical care as a special favour to be thankful for and not as having any right to them in exchange for her work.

SM, Chelsea.[1]

INTRODUCTION

To ACHIEVE ITS goal of equal partnership in marriage, the Married Women's Association (MWA) was initially determined to target the roots of inequality in marriage instead of lopping a branch or two from the tree. The Association's ambition for comprehensive reform is perhaps clearest in 1949, when members reacted to Jean Mann MP's prospective Bill to give wives a legal right to housekeeping savings and a share of their husbands' wages.[2] Even though the MWA was in the midst of its own campaign on this very issue, it was sceptical of Mann's efforts[3] and was 'so opposed' it sent a deputation to the House of Commons.[4] In its magazine *Wife and Citizen*, it published a segment on the proposed Bill concluding:

On the surface this 'Savings' idea sounds attractive. But let us study just how many women will benefit. First, how many women who are handed housekeeping money are handed sufficient to save? ... Frankly, as woman to woman, do we need a Bill

---

[1] *Wife and Citizen*, February–March 1951, 7TBG/1/32, TWL.

[2] Jean Mann was not successful in the ballot for Private Member's Bills in 1949, and so further details of this proposed Bill are not available.

[3] As well as deciding not to support Jean Mann's proposed Bill, MWA members also did not support Eveline Hills MP's Deserted Wives Bill in 1951. This sought to prevent a husband who had deserted his wife from taking possession of the joint home and requiring her to vacate it. The MWA reported that it had no previous intimation it was to be introduced. The Association consulted its Advisory Council and was told that the Bill was too limited in scope for the full support of the MWA, a view in which the Chairman fully concurred: Annual Report for the Year 1950–1951, *Wife and Citizen*, May–June 1951, 7TBG/1/32, TWL.

[4] Anon, 'Women Want 50-50 Share of Savings' *Aberdeen Journal* (20 January 1949) 1.

which will merely give us the right to own openly those savings which any woman worth her salt (or in this case her savings), could quite easily hide from the rascal who would defy public opinion and drag her to court? We need something more than just a monetary gain; we need equal status and with it equal responsibilities. We want the legal right to discuss how and in what proportion the income shall be spent and on what particular objective. If we gained the right to all savings from housekeeping, how should we ever dare to ask for a half share of surplus, and if not, how can we ever hope to enjoy any savings when one person, the husband, has the right to decide what is housekeeping?[5]

This reaction may have stemmed from the Association's repudiation of the 'wages for wives' idea; that equality within marriage was not possible if a husband paid his wife a wage, as he would be her boss and she his subordinate. This extract is also important because 15 years later, the MWA appeared to have had a remarkable change of heart. In 1964, the MWA celebrated the introduction of a new Married Women's Property Act (MWPA 1964), which gave wives an equal share in housekeeping money. Far from rejecting this Act for being piecemeal, MWA members considered it to be their biggest victory.

Even by the late 1950s, the MWA's strategy was changing. So far, as previous chapters have explored, the Association had been focused on having its Bill for equal partnership in marriage introduced in Parliament. But three events seemed to trigger a change in strategy: the unwillingness of the Royal Commission on Marriage and Divorce to recommend comprehensive reform; rejection of the MWA's Bill in 1958; and the negative reaction in Parliament to Edith Summerskill's Women's Disabilities Bill 1952, the latter of which is explored in this chapter. Teresa Billington-Greig suggested a more pragmatic approach was needed as a result of these setbacks:

> Our legislators are seldom moved by the arguments of principle or logic and they appear to be especially afraid of doing too much for any victimised class at one time. So that slow progress by piecemeal legislation comes to be forced on the reformers. The MWA has discovered and acted on this discovery.[6]

The MWA became increasingly willing to draft legislation that was less ambitious than the Bill for equal partnership in marriage, and therefore – they hoped – less likely to be controversial. This chapter explores this strategy by focusing on two piecemeal reforms in which the MWA played a significant role. First, is the MWA's work to enforce maintenance orders which culminated in the Maintenance Orders Act 1958. As this legislation was ultimately taken forward by the government, the earlier version of this reform, introduced as a Private Member's Bill and sponsored and campaigned for by the MWA, has been forgotten. The second reform considered is the aforementioned MWPA 1964.

---

[5] M Nicholson, 'Deputation to House of Commons', *Wife and Citizen*, February 1949, 7TBG/1/32, TWL.

[6] Draft of Teresa Billington-Greig speech, 1958, 7TBG/1/31, TWL.

I. DEVELOPING A STRATEGY FOR REFORM

As previous chapters have pointed out, a perennial problem with maintenance was its enforcement. The wife could apply to court, and if a husband continued to refuse payment, he faced imprisonment.[7] But this did nothing to remedy the often dire financial situation of the wife. Worse still, until 1958, a husband's imprisonment for non-payment of maintenance under a magisterial warrant of commitment extinguished the debt he owed to his wife, and she could not be compensated for the maintenance arrears she was owed.[8]

Although the MWA was more concerned with reform of property rights during marriage than with maintenance on separation, members could still see the importance of ensuring women received the financial support to which they were entitled by law. The Association viewed the Scottish 'attachment of wages' approach as an apposite solution to the maintenance problem. Here, maintenance claims could be enforced by 'attaching' them to the husband's earnings, such as wages, pensions and other emoluments payable under a contract of service.[9] Edith Summerskill recalled in her memoirs that the Association's initial strategy was to incorporate this idea into the Women's Disabilities Bill; a 'Bill of a comprehensive character' that would 'render the best service to all these unfortunate women'.[10]

A. Women's Disabilities Bill[11]

The Women's Disabilities Bill was what Teresa Billington-Greig referred to as an 'omnibus Bill'[12] because it aimed to reform several issues relating to women's legal and economic status.[13] Summerskill brought it to the House of Commons by Private Member's Bill.[14] The Bill comprised three clauses, which aimed to address issues affecting married women on relationship breakdown and

---

[7] Pursuant to the Debtors Act 1869.

[8] Pursuant to s 74(8) of the Magistrates' Courts Act 1952. This rule was abolished by the Maintenance Orders Act 1958, s 16(1) in line with the recommendations published by the *Royal Commission on Marriage and Divorce* (Cmd 9678, 1956) para 1108.

[9] For further detail on the operation of this provision, see O Kahn-Freund, 'Maintenance Orders Act 1958' (1959) 22 *MLR* 175.

[10] E Summerskill, *A Woman's World* (Heinemann 1967) 145.

[11] Parts of this discussion appear in S Thompson 'Married Women's Property Act 1964' in E Rackley and R Auchmuty (eds), *Women's Legal Landmarks: Celebrating the History of Women and Law in the UK and Ireland* (Hart Publishing 2019).

[12] Draft of Teresa Billington-Greig speech, above n 6.

[13] The 'omnibus Bill' has also been referred to as the 'Christmas tree Bill' because the drafter has 'hung' several policies upon it like baubles on a Christmas tree: House of Commons Select Committee on Political and Constitutional Reform, *Ensuring standards in the quality of legislation* (First Report, 2013) para 11.

[14] HC Deb 5 December 1951, vol 494, col 2391.

unmarried mothers when maintenance orders were not observed. Clause 1 of the Bill stated that if a spouse defaulted in payment of a maintenance order, and was employed, the Court could make an order requiring his employer to make payments to the Court in respect of the money due to the applicant. In other words, it provided for attachment of wages in line with Scottish law. The second clause provided that housekeeping savings could be divided equally between husband and wife, or in any proportion the Court considered just, a matter considered in more detail below. As well as addressing the issue of housekeeping savings, Clause 2 would also have given the wife additional property rights in marriage. It provided that if forced to leave the family home, the wife could have use of household goods and furniture, and in some cases the court could grant tenancy rights to the wife in respect of the family home.[15] Clause 3 of the Bill was more controversial, providing the wife with a right to apply to court to claim a 'reasonable allowance' where her husband refused to provide her with money for the domestic expenses for which she was responsible.[16] Summerskill was prescient in anticipating opposition to her Bill, particularly in relation to Clause 3. It was one thing to provide spouses with additional means of enforcing maintenance provision *on separation*, but to require the husband to pay a sum to his wife *during* marriage was more radical, because it would require the court to step into the private realm of the family, when it was very reluctant to do so.

It would be an understatement to say that the Women's Disabilities Bill did not receive a warm reception when Summerskill moved its second reading in April 1952.[17] Summerskill's perspective on this debate as recounted in her memoirs is particularly interesting. She pointed out that the suspicion in respect of this Bill was not dissimilar to the attitudes of those opposed to the MWPA 1870 and 1882. The battle against coverture might have been fought in a different time, but the prejudice surrounding reform of women's rights 80 years later was much the same.[18] As she incisively stated: 'I have found nothing more calculated to catch a prejudiced man off his guard than a speech advocating the further emancipation of women'.[19] Her Bill was called 'ultra-feminist', 'grossly unpractical' and it was anticipated to 'introduce strife and disharmony into the home'.[20] Indeed, it is farcical that, like those in opposition to the MWPA

---

[15] This foreshadowed the Matrimonial Homes Act that Summerskill later helped to introduce in 1967.

[16] This clause also provided that if an order was made and the husband refused to comply, the 'reasonable allowance' due to the wife could be deducted from the husband's wages.

[17] HC Deb 25 April 1952, vol 499, cols 899–983.

[18] Doreen Gorsky, who had resigned from the MWA and co-founded the Council of Married Women, noted that 'the debate … gave the public a sample of the venom to be found among embittered bachelors and others of a 19th century vintage'. CMW Bulletin, May 1952, 5CMW/E/07, TWL.

[19] Summerskill, above n 10, 148.

[20] HC Deb 25 April 1952, vol 499 col 922 (Ronald Bell). In the Commons, Summerskill later referred to Bell as 'one of my fiercest enemies': HC Deb 1 March 1957, vol 565, col 1584.

1870 and 1882, there appeared to be more concern for the husband's meals than for advancing women's rights, as MPs commented that reform would lead to unpleasant dinners and displeasing breakfasts if the family business was to be 'thrashed out before a bench of magistrates'.[21]

The Bill did not pass its second reading and Summerskill introduced it again.[22] When Dr Horace King led its second reading Debate in May 1953 while Summerskill was on delegation elsewhere,[23] he faced similar opposition, with Charles Doughty MP complaining that the Bill would achieve the *opposite* of removing women's disabilities – it would instead place 'certain women in a highly privileged position not enjoyed by any other class, type or sex in this community' and men would be the victims.[24] Yet even though Summerskill observed that 'the anti-feminists had gathered in force against [her]',[25] she was not without support on this matter. Fifty-four MPs voted in favour of the Bill, and in the public gallery, members of the MWA had filled almost every seat.[26] But Summerskill needed 100 votes to move the Bill. It was a Friday, the whips were off, and only those with a special interest in supporting or opposing the Bill attended. And so, without sufficient support, the Bill became another failed attempt at reform connected to the MWA. Summerskill said she 'felt this setback keenly'.[27]

This does not mean the Bill deserves to be relegated to forgotten corners of family law history, for it helps one understand what the MWA did next. And so, the Bill's failure is best understood as a harbinger of the Association's newly evolving strategy. Previously, MWA members appeared to be exasperated by Jean Mann MP's suggestion that their proposals for comprehensive reform were 'impractical' and 'would help in the disintegration of the Association by combining all its aims in one Bill', with Margery Nicholson delivering the biting response: 'let us be kind to Mrs Mann and dismiss that … statement as facetious'.[28] But after the Women's Disabilities Bill had floundered twice the MWA changed tack. Billington-Greig recognised the difficulty in passing reform that deals with more than one issue: 'The omnibus Bill – which is so dear to our hearts and so much desired on principle and as a common sense method of speedy progress is very generally doomed to fail in this country'.[29] As chapter four explained, the MWA never abandoned its goal of having its Bill for equal partnership in marriage taken forward. Instead, it appeared to adopt a

---

[21] HC Deb 25 April 1952, vol 499, col 975 (Charles Doughty).

[22] HC Deb 19 November 1952, vol 507, col 1874.

[23] Summerskill was on a parliamentary delegation in Strasbourg.

[24] HC Deb 8 May 1953, vol 515, col 831.

[25] Summerskill, above n 10, 150.

[26] ibid, 153.

[27] ibid.

[28] Nicholson, 'Deputation to House of Commons', above n 5.

[29] Draft of Teresa Billington-Greig speech, above n 6.

three-pronged strategy, as Billington-Greig sketched out in her notes: omnibus measures such as the Women's Disabilities Bill, a 'one step at a time stage' to address more specific issues such as enforcement of maintenance, and finally, the Bill for equal partnership in marriage. The focus of this chapter is on the second prong – the piecemeal, one step at a time approach.

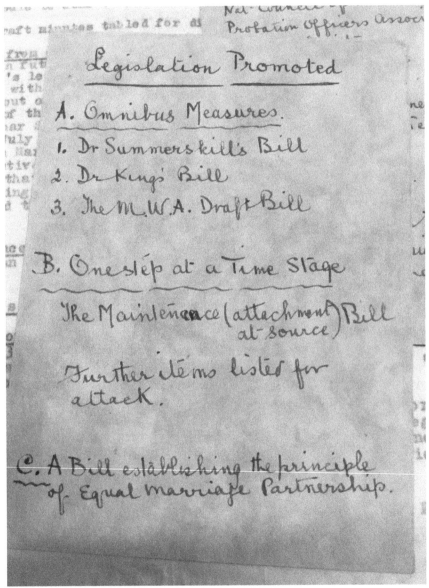

Notes of Teresa Billington-Greig, 7TBG/1/32, TWL

B. Attachment of Wages

The MWA continued to press the issue of maintenance enforcement in line with Scots law and Clause 1 of the Women's Disabilities Bill – that if a husband did not pay maintenance, the debt could instead be 'attached to' or deducted from the husband's wages. As mentioned briefly in chapter six, this proposal was included in the MWA's evidence to the Royal Commission on Marriage and Divorce, and Association members were disappointed when the Commission decided against recommending this reform in 1956. The Commission's reasoning was arguably dubious:

> [I]n our opinion a power to attach wages would not in practice deal effectively with the man who deliberately evades his obligations to his wife and family, the man who will go to prison rather than pay the maintenance ordered by the court. It is this man who constitutes the real problem; the existing law is usually able to deal with the other types of defaulter, such as the man who is merely careless or improvident. But the man who at present will go to prison rather than pay is just the man who would be likely simply to give up his job if his wages were attached.[30]

Otto Kahn-Freund commented at the time that this 'gloomy' prediction was unjustified, especially given that the attachment of wages procedure worked well in Scotland.[31] The MWA did not agree with the Commission's conclusion either, almost immediately launching a campaign for reform.

The Association dedicated its Executive Committee meetings to the issue of maintenance and deserted families.[32] It hosted public meetings at Caxton Hall, inviting speakers from the Howard League, the Haldane Society and the Magistrates Association to speak on the topic of 'Deserting Husbands and the Law'.[33] These activities culminated in the Maintenance Orders (Attachment of Income) Bill drafted by Roxane Arnold,[34] with an explanatory statement drafted by Roger Ormrod (then barrister and later Lord Justice of Appeal).[35] The Bill

---

[30] *Report of the Royal Commission on Marriage and Divorce*, above n 8, para 1107.

[31] Kahn-Freund, 'Maintenance Orders Act 1958', above n 9, 179.

[32] Teresa Billington Greig's handwritten notes, 1955, 7TBG/1/31, TWL.

[33] Leaflet for MWA meeting, undated, 7TBG/1/31, TWL. The Association also held a Caxton Hall meeting on 4 October 1956 on 'Attachment of Earnings'. Juanita Frances did not have a complete list of societies which had spoken in favour of Attachment of Wages but noted a defeated Liberal Party Resolution and that the Women's Institutes Association and the Cooperative Women's Guild were also in favour: Letter from Juanita Frances to Teresa Billington-Greig, 6 November 1956, 7TBG/1/31, TWL.

[34] 'MWA Attachment of Earnings Bill, Caxton Hall meeting, 4 October', MWA Newsletter, November 1956, 7TBG/1/31, TWL.

[35] Letter from Juanita Frances to Teresa Billington-Greig, above n 33. Roger Ormrod also assisted with redrafts of this Bill and helped to draft earlier MWA Bills too, including the Equal Partnership in Marriage Bill. His wife Anne was an MWA member and edited the MWA Newsletter. John Parker MP also assisted and said he would have sponsored the Bill had he been selected in the ballot: MWA Secretary's Report 1956–57, 7TBG/1/31, TWL.

provided that courts could order the defaulting husband's employer to deduct maintenance arrears from his wages and to have it paid into court for the wife.[36] MWA members wrote to MPs asking them to sponsor the Maintenance Bill should they be drawn in the ballot for Private Member's Bills. This strategy had not worked in the past. But this time was different, with Joan Vickers MP coming sixth in the ballot[37] and agreeing to adopt the Bill.[38] This kick-started the MWA's lobbying campaign.[39] The Association published a call to arms on the front page of its Newsletter, asking all its members and readers to give their 'maximum practical help' to gather wide public support,[40] with 'letters in the press and lobbying in the House'[41] thereby increasing the Bill's chances of a second reading.[42]

The Bill passed its Second Reading debate on 1 March 1957, but Vickers still encountered many difficulties in Parliament. The *Evening Standard* reported in October: '"Pay up" Bill is doomed',[43] as Labour and Conservative party members were working to delay the Bill, and proceedings were halted as a quorum had not been reached before Parliament was prorogued.[44] The reform was controversial because it was viewed – particularly by trade unions – as a threat to the principle of the security of the wage packet, and was therefore setting a 'potentially dangerous precedent'.[45] That is, the employee would not be guaranteed payment of his earnings without deductions. The MWA had anticipated this resistance, noting that even though the reform would simply have provided the wife with what she was owed, the issue would likely have 'the effect of engendering fierce emotion, especially in the TUC [Trades Union Congress]'.[46] This tension between protecting the payee's right to maintenance and the payor's right to an inviolable wage appeared to be what ultimately stalled and killed this iteration of the Bill.

---

[36] Pursuant to clause 9 (1a and b), the Bill included earnings from all types of employment with the exception of the self-employed, who would instead receive a custodial sentence. Before making payments, the employer would have been allowed to deduct 6d on each one of the payments to cover his expenses: HC Deb 1 March 1957, vol 565, col 1540.

[37] Normally the first seven MPs to be drawn in the ballot could take the Bill forward.

[38] As reported in MWA Minutes of Executive Committee meeting, 4 December 1956, 7TBG/1/31, TWL.

[39] Juanita Frances wrote to Billington-Greig seeking her experience on this, and asking for advice on the procedure for a lobby campaign to get a Second Reading for the Bill: Letter from Juanita Frances to Teresa Billington-Greig, 27 November 1956, 7TBG/1/31, TWL.

[40] According to Teresa Billington-Greig's handwritten notes, January/February 1957, this included issuing leaflets and copies of the Bill, arrangements to address local branches of the National Council of Women and contacting MPs to secure their agreement to attend the debate on the Bill if tabled: 7TBG/1/31, TWL.

[41] 'MWA Attachment of Earnings Bill, Caxton Hall meeting, 4 October', above n 34.

[42] 'Attachment of Income Bill', MWA Newsletter, January 1957, 7TBG/1/31, TWL. These efforts were reported in the press: Political Correspondent, 'Help Sought for Deserted Wives – Women Lobby MPs' *Daily Telegraph* (26 February 1957) 5MWA/1/2/1/2, TWL.

[43] Anon, 'Pay up Bill is doomed' *Evening Standard* (31 October 1957) 7TBG/1/31, TWL.

[44] Anon, 'No Quorum' *Manchester Guardian*, undated (clipping) 5MWA/1/2/1/2, TWL.

[45] JC Wood, 'Attachment of Wages' (1963) 26 MLR 51, 51.

[46] 'Attachment of Earnings Bill', MWA Newsletter, November 1956, 7TBG/1/31, TWL.

But hope for reform was not lost. After Joan Vickers' failed attempts with the MWA Bill, Fergus Morton – Chairman of the Royal Commission – authorised the Home Secretary to say that in his view the advantages of attachment outweigh the disadvantages. And so, the government decided to take this reform forward and the Home Secretary introduced the Maintenance Orders Bill in late 1957. It became law in 1958 and came into effect in 1959.

As the Maintenance Orders Bill underwent its Second Reading debate,[47] the MWA commented that it was 'cheering to note' the many tributes made to Joan Vickers' earlier efforts.[48] For example, Lena Jeger MP remarked: 'I am sure the Bill we are considering is all the better for the time and thought that was given to the earlier Measure which was introduced as a Private Member's Bill'.[49] Jocelyn Simon, then Joint Under-Secretary of State for the Home Department (and later Solicitor General and President of the Family Division) also acknowledged that the Vickers Bill had had a 'very big effect upon public opinion'.[50] Simon pointed out the remarkable influence of this earlier Bill upon Lord Morton, who 'came out so clearly in support of the principle' of attachment of earnings when his Royal Commission had so recently rejected it.[51] Finally, Simon acknowledged the earlier failed efforts of Summerskill to reform the issue in 1952: 'One ought not to forget, in passing such encomiums, the right hon Lady the Member for Warrington ... who blazed the trail in this field'.[52] He had, in Summerskill's words, given her 'the most powerful support' in these earlier efforts.[53]

Simon's recognition of the broader context of the Maintenance Orders Act 1958 and the knockbacks faced by Summerskill and Vickers sits in stark contrast to accounts of the reform in academic journals such as the *Modern Law Review*.[54] In these accounts, the failed attempts of Summerskill and Vickers are omitted. And explicit acknowledgement of the MWA's role is nowhere to be found. This shows that accounts of how legal reform happened can be skewed, helping us understand how the MWA's story has been virtually obliterated from histories of family law.

*

The immediate effect of the Maintenance Orders Act 1958 was that far fewer individuals were imprisoned for non-payment of maintenance.[55] Longer term,

---

[47] HC Deb 12 December 1957, vol 579, cols 1540–1610.
[48] MWA Memo, undated, 5MWA/1/2/1/2, TWL.
[49] HC Deb 12 December 1957, vol 579, col 1591.
[50] ibid, col 1603.
[51] ibid.
[52] ibid.
[53] Summerskill, above n 10, 153.
[54] See, eg, Kahn-Freund, 'Maintenance Orders Act 1958', above n 9; and Wood, above n 45.
[55] HC Oral Answers To Questions, 18 June 1959, vol 607, Question 19 (David Renton): 'the Maintenance Orders Act which came into force in February this year has had an immediate and striking effect, because the prison population of persons committed in respect of maintenance orders has dropped from about 900 at the beginning of this year to 345 on 2nd June'.

the Act provided more discretion to the court to enforce maintenance orders, and attachment of earnings is still possible today, having been reformed by the Attachment of Earnings Act 1971[56] and the Maintenance Enforcement Act 1991.

The MWA marked the introduction of the 1958 Act as important progress, noting that 'the first assault on the sanctity of the pay packet has been made and the first step towards equal partnership has been taken'.[57] But this reform did not just indicate MWA members' willingness to pursue piecemeal reform (and their relative success in doing so). It also showed that the Association was concerned with the position of married women's property rights *after marriage* as well as when the relationship subsisted. This suggests that the MWA did not draw a neat dividing line between married women's rights during the relationship and after it had broken down, as modern family law has tended to do.

The following section focuses on the MWA's next legislative triumph, which achieved reform in a more controversial category of reform: property ownership during marriage.

II. HOUSEKEEPING SAVINGS

The issue of housekeeping savings became the MWA's first major campaign in the early 1940s, when it funded Dorothy Blackwell's unsuccessful appeal. As chapters five and six explored, the MWA used this case to raise awareness of the need for reform of housekeeping savings. This section sets out how the campaign triggered by the *Blackwell* case – which in many ways is the centrepiece of the MWA's story – culminated in the MWA's most significant reform, the MWPA 1964. Connecting this Act with the MWA's campaign contradicts institutional accounts of the MWPA 1964, such as the Law Commission, which stated that 'the origins of this Act lie in the Report of the Royal Commission on Marriage and Divorce'.[58] This claim is arguably misleading, because it disregards numerous attempts by Summerskill and the MWA to reform this very issue. As well as correcting historical narratives of the MWPA 1964's origin, exploring the aftermath of this reform also provides valuable insight into both the merits and demerits of piecemeal legislation, especially from the perspective of feminist reformers.

*

Although the Women's Disabilities Bill did not pass, it did provide a precursor to the Report of the Royal Commission four years later. As explained in

---

[56] This reform meant that the husband could not change jobs to avoid his maintenance obligations. Instead, the obligation would attach to the new employer.

[57] 'Attachment of Wages and Salaries Act', MWA Newsletter, December 1959, 7TBG/1/33, TWL.

[58] Law Commission, *Transfer of Money Between Spouses – the Married Women's Property Act 1964* (WP No 90, 1985) para 4.1.

the previous chapter, the Commission proposed that 'savings made from money contributed by either the husband or the wife or by both for the purpose of meeting housekeeping expenses'[59] should belong to each spouse in equal shares. The Royal Commission's report undoubtedly led to more widespread public consciousness of the plight of married women like Dorothy Blackwell. But by the early 1960s, this had still not translated into legislative reform. And so Summerskill, by now a life peer, made another attempt to reform the issue, this time in the Lords, not the Commons.

She drafted one of the shortest bills in history titled the Married Women's Savings Bill.[60] It consisted of 25 words: 'If a wife makes savings out of what her husband gives her for housekeeping, half of any money so saved shall belong to her absolutely'. The change in temperature in the House of Lords towards this Bill was plain, and 11 years after the Women's Disabilities Bill, the Married Women's Savings Bill passed its Second Reading in the House of Lords.[61]

Yet even with additional support, dissenters of Summerskill's reform efforts adopted a familiar refrain during this debate – husband's stomachs. In 1943, Goddard LJ expressed concern that wives permitted to save housekeeping allowance would cook poor quality meals;[62] in 1952 Charles Doughty suggested the Women's Disabilities Bill would ruin family meals,[63] and now Lord Boothby was echoing these sentiments. He argued that although the husband might not be 'starved', he would be 'badly fed' if the housewife were 'encouraged to save out of housekeeping in order to have that little bit extra in pocket'.[64] He almost comically explained:

> If this were confined to herrings, I should not mind, but the temptation to feed the husband on lentils or chips or some ghastly concoctions which can be obtained for 6d in a tin and turned out – no trouble at all – and not to go to the market and buy good, fresh, solid meat, and then to 'collar' half of what is left over, will, in my view, be very great.[65]

In her abrupt style, Summerskill's retort was to remind Boothby that his obsession with food was perhaps ill advised given his doctors had told him not to eat so much.[66]

The Married Women's Savings Bill could not progress further because the parliamentary session had run out of time, but before reintroducing the

[59] *Report of the Royal Commission on Marriage and Divorce*, above n 8, para 701.

[60] If the wording of this particular Bill had been introduced it would have been the shortest English statute in history. This is currently the Parliament (Qualification of Women) Act 1918, which consists of 27 words.

[61] Summerskill, above n 10, 156.

[62] As reported in Anon, 'Judges Tell Wives Rights of Husbands' *Daily Mirror* (29 October 1943) 5; and HL Deb 5 July 1963, vol 251, col 1153.

[63] HC Deb 25 April 1952, vol 499, col 975.

[64] HL Deb 5 July 1963, vol 251, col 1157.

[65] ibid.

[66] ibid, col 1161.

Bill in the new session of Parliament, Summerskill had it redrafted as the Married Women's Property Bill 1964 to incorporate the language of the Royal Commission's report, so that the housekeeping money would belong to the husband and wife in equal shares instead of granting the wife a one-half share absolutely. However, the wording in the Bill differed from the report as it was not gender neutral, only granting the wife an equal share in housekeeping money derived from the husband, and not vice versa.

This time, with government support, the Bill passed successfully through the House of Lords and was moved by Douglas Houghton in the House of Commons. Procedurally, Private Member's Bills only require one Member of the House in order to obstruct them. The first time the Married Women's Property Bill was called it was defeated by a single, anonymous objector. And so the following week, Summerskill described bracing herself 'waiting for the fatal word [object] like some poor unfortunate creature waiting for the executioner's axe, with an iron determination not to wince when the blow fell'.[67] But no one objected and the Bill was passed.[68] Summerskill was successful in introducing reform that would enable married women to save in their own right. This was seen by some as important at the time because it would ensure

> that the status of wives is not a hollow mockery as it was in the days of the unfortunate Mrs Blackwell who, for all her 'status', proved to be far worse off than if she had been a paid housekeeper.[69]

*

Though MWA members did not view the MWPA 1964 as a panacea for married women's equality, they still considered the Act a 'major triumph'[70] and 'felt the work and aims of the Association had reached a milestone'. As they saw it: 'The door leading to the economic rights of a wife during marriage has been opened'.[71] Decades after the *Blackwell* case, married women had a legal right to a half share of housekeeping money, in recognition of the fact that this money had usually been generated through wives' own efforts anyway. For the MWA, it was especially significant, as unlike the Maintenance Orders Act, the MWPA 1964 reformed property ownership during marriage and members saw this as a culmination of their efforts:

> For more than 25 years we have addressed meetings and passed resolutions, sent letters continuously to Ministers of the Crown, Members of Parliament and to the

[67] Summerskill, above n 10, 158.
[68] MWA members attended the Bill's Royal Assent in the House of Lords on 14 April 1964: 5MWA/1/2/1/1, TWL.
[69] PD Cummins, 'Mrs Blackwell and Mrs 1964' *Catholic Citizen* (15 June 1964) 46, 5MWA/1/3/1, TWL.
[70] Anon, '"Only slight progress" in the fight for equality' *Hampstead Highgate Express* (11 December 1964) 5MWA/9/3, TWL.
[71] MWA Annual General Report, 10 June 1964, 5MWA/3/1, TWL.

House of Lords. We have 'begged and beseeched' to draw attention to, to urge and to demand a change in the marriage property law and this year we witness the first amendment to ancient law on the economic rights of a wife during marriage.[72]

But the members of the Association were clear that the Act represented only slight progress within the broader context of their aims.[73] As legal academic and MWA adviser Olive Stone put it in 1964, the amount of money wives could acquire under the Act would likely have been very little.[74] Nevertheless, Stone recognised that the Act was important because it had established a principle based on equality. As a result, it would be short-sighted to criticise the MWPA 1964 for not doing enough to address the financial position of married women. The strategy for reform adopted by the MWA was *necessarily* incremental, as the prospects of broader legislation at that time were unrealistic.[75] Summerskill's attempts to achieve broader reform for women in the Women's Disabilities Bill had been met with considerable resistance, but this resistance decreased substantially when she drafted the Married Women's Property Bill, because it was short, pragmatic and sought to erode only one cause of women's economic inequality in marriage.[76] However, the MWPA 1964's relatively smooth passage did not mean it was without criticism.

A. Criticism of the MWPA 1964

One of the major criticisms of the MWPA in 1964 was that it discriminated against men, as it only applied to housekeeping money received by the wife, and therefore differed from the recommendations of the Royal Commission in 1956.[77] But an arguably powerful aspect of the MWPA 1964 was that it was *not* gender neutral, because the issue it addressed was an issue that affected married women in a way that *did not* affect married men. It was almost exclusively women who were responsible for the unpaid work in the home, and who were financially vulnerable as a result of this. Thus, the Act's discriminatory focus was arguably *crucial* in highlighting the sexual division of labour and the limitations of separate property.[78] Though the Act did not protect housewives who did not receive any allowance from their husbands,[79] the spirit of the

---

[72] ibid.

[73] '"Only slight progress" in the fight for equality', *Hampstead Highgate Express*, above n 70.

[74] O Stone, 'Married Women's Property Act 1964' (1964) 27 MLR 576, 580. MWA members also noted that 'very few housekeeping allowances have a margin for saving', 5MWA/6/1, TWL.

[75] Law Commission, *Transfer of Money Between Spouses*, above n 58, para 4.4.

[76] Indeed, the Royal Commission's 1956 recommendation on housekeeping savings was the furthest extent it would go to improve economic equality in marriage: C Smart, *The Ties That Bind* (Routledge 1984) 38.

[77] J Dewar, *Law and the Family* (Butterworths 1989) 119.

[78] However, this explicitly discriminatory provision has been removed by the Equality Act 2010 s 199, which has yet to be introduced.

[79] O Kahn-Freund, 'Matrimonial Property – Some Recent Developments' (1959) 22 MLR 241, 249.

legislation – that *both* spouses are entitled to the financial fruits of the marital partnership – paved the way for the most significant divorce reform for generations; the Matrimonial Causes Act 1973. Yet the Law Commission argued persuasively in 1985 that most people would not expect the law to be explicitly discriminatory, and reform should not create more difficulties by establishing apparently arbitrary new rules.[80]

Even if the essence of the legislation could be justified, however, the Act was peppered with technical difficulties, which become apparent on closer inspection of the Act's wording. It provided that money

> derived from any allowance made by the husband for the expenses of the matrimonial home or for similar purposes, or to any property acquired out of such money, the money or property shall, in the absence of any agreement between them to the contrary, be treated as belonging to the husband and the wife in equal shares.[81]

The meaning of this provision could arguably be interpreted in numerous different ways. One point of contention is what is included within the term 'expenses of the matrimonial home' or 'similar purposes'. In *Tymoszczuk v Tymoszczuk*,[82] the Court held these expenses did not include money given to the wife by the husband to make mortgage repayments.[83] The Law Commission also later suggested the phrasing 'derived from' was problematic, as it was not clear whether this referred to the allowance itself, or only to money saved from the allowance.[84] Though this distinction seems semantic, it could be important in practice. A wife might use her housekeeping allowance to purchase a car in weekly instalments, or she might save part of her allowance each week and then purchase the car once she has saved enough. In the second example, the car has been purchased with 'money derived from' the allowance. But in the first scenario, the Law Commission said this would not necessarily be the case and could arguably have been purchased using the allowance – not money derived from it – which is not technically covered by the wording of the MWPA 1964.[85]

Of course, from the MWA's point of view, the Act would only be effective if it could be used to protect the women they sought to help and represent. Their involvement with the unreported case of *Ince v Ince* shows not simply the

---

[80] Law Commission, *Transfer of Money Between Spouses*, above n 58, para 3.2. Most respondents to this Law Commission Working Paper agreed with the Commission's suggestion that the Act should be made to apply equally to husband and wife (para 2.7).

[81] s 1 (the only substantive section of the Act).

[82] (1964) 108 SJ 676.

[83] Similarly, in *Re John's Assignment Trusts* [1970] 1 WLR 955, 960, Goff J stated: 'I must not be taken as accepting the view that where section 1 [MWPA 1964] does apply, moneys paid to discharge a mortgage on the marital home are not expenses of the matrimonial home or expenses for similar purposes within the section'.

[84] John Dewar also notes it is unclear whether the phrase 'derived from' refers to the allowance itself, or only to money saved from the allowance: above n 77, 119.

[85] Law Commission, *Transfer of Money Between Spouses*, above n 58, para 4.7.

flaws of the MWPA 1964, but the shortcomings of law itself, in helping women without access to legal advice, or the opportunity to tell their side of the story.

B. Mrs Ince

Soon after the MWPA 1964 came into effect, the MWA became aware of Lily Ince's imprisonment. She had been in prison for six months for failing to give her husband a share of the housekeeping savings, but she contended this money was *her* money, not money derived from an allowance. As Blackpool County Court held that Mrs Ince was withholding money from her husband, she was found to be in contempt of court. Pursuant to the MWPA 1964, he still had a right to half of all money derived from the housekeeping allowance. At this time there was no fixed period for Lily Ince's imprisonment,[86] and she could remain there indefinitely. The MWA Executive Committee decided to mobilise its resources to assist her. Summerskill raised the issue in the House of Lords,[87] emphasising Mrs Ince's diabetes and poor health. As there was no published judgment, the MWA obtained copies of newspapers reporting the case, copies of the court documents relating to the case, and details of Mrs Ince's account through interviews with her in prison and her family in Ashton-under-Lyne.[88]

According to the MWA accounts, Lily Ince was an 'ordinary housewife' who married shortly before the Depression in the 1920s and had five children. Mr Tom Ince was a miner, though was often unemployed or absent without pay as a result of sickness. He belonged to clubs, gambled and 'spent all the money that came into his hands'.[89] Mrs Ince told the MWA that she never saw her husband's pay cheque, except for when his earnings were low in the 1920s. And so, she saved all she could. She walked where she might have taken a bus, shopped in the market instead of the local shops and earned money from light domestic work and selling her crocheted items. Mrs Ince's children also gave her a proportion of their earnings. She saved this money over the course of 20 years, beginning to put some of it into National Savings Certificates in 1940.

By 1963, Mr Ince had retired.[90] Mrs Ince had almost £2,000 in a building society, a quantity of National Savings Certificates, and had been able to purchase a house from savings in the joint names of herself and her husband. Then, *even though he was still living with his wife*, Mr Ince took court proceedings against

---

[86] This was amended by the Contempt of Court Act 1981 s 14, which required a period of imprisonment for contempt to last for a fixed term (not exceeding two years for a superior court and one month for an inferior court).

[87] Lords Chamber, 7 April 1965, vol 265, The Case Of Mrs Lily Ince.

[88] Interviews were undertaken by MWA legal advisor and solicitor Dennis Walker, and MWA member Elizabeth Ambridge respectively. MWA Executive Committee Minutes, March 1965, 5MWA/3/1, TWL.

[89] MWA Bulletin, May–June 1965, 5MWA/1/3/2, TWL.

[90] Tom Ince had retired in 1959 through ill health on a pension.

her. He claimed one half of the money in the building society and one half of the National Savings Certificates as his, on the ground that they were savings from housekeeping money. Mrs Ince did not attend the hearing of the case. She was a diabetic and said she did not feel fit to do so. And notably, in the words of an MWA report, 'she felt convinced that no Court would take away from her the money she had so laboriously and industriously saved and give it to her husband who would gamble and spend it'.[91]

It therefore came as a shock when Lily Ince was taken from her home and put in prison after refusing to comply with the court's order to give her husband £939 from the building society account and 1,800 (all that she then had left) of the National Savings Certificates. She went to prison saying 'I shall die first' before revealing where the savings were hidden, the *Daily Telegraph* reported.[92]

*

The Association faced two major problems in pursuing Lily Ince's appeal. First, the time for an appeal against the original decision of the court had passed; and second, the judge would not listen to the counsel briefed for Mrs Ince unless she first deposited the National Savings Certificates. By the MWA's account, assurances were made by Judge Bell at Blackpool County Court that Mrs Ince would be released, and her appeal would be heard if she deposited her 1,800 National Savings Certificates with the court registrar. Having paid for an application for an extension and having persuaded Mrs Ince to disclose the location of the certificates and transfer them to the court, Mrs Ince was released, and the Association prepared to sponsor her appeal.[93] However, despite the MWA apparently resolving the issues impeding the appeal, when the case came before the county court judge who had made assurances about extending Mrs Ince's time for an appeal, he denied having done so, and the appeal failed. To the MWA this decision seemed 'grossly unfair,' and the Association's legal advisers suggested they appeal the decision.[94] Counsel had been briefed, the MWA lawyers were prepared and an appeal was argued before the Court of Appeal for three hours. To the MWA's palpable dismay, the Court decided against Mrs Ince.[95] The 1,800 National Savings Certificates and the £939 10s became the legal property of her husband.

[91] MWA Bulletin, May–June 1965, above n 89.
[92] Daily Telegraph Reporter, 'Savings Hoard Revealed' *Daily Telegraph* (15 April 1965) 5MWA/1/3/2, TWL.
[93] The savings were at a local vicarage in Blackpool. Lily Ince had given a sealed envelope containing the savings to the Reverend Joseph Handley Vaughan, who claimed to have been unaware of its contents. Above n 92.
[94] ibid.
[95] The MWA reported that 'regrettably', the Court 'made a number of critical comments' about Mrs Ince in their judgments, 'some of which were wholly unjustified': ibid. The detail of these comments was not included in MWA archival materials.

In its subsequent Newsletter, MWA members expressed their sentiments about the case:

> The worst feature of the whole case is that, despite the fact that Mrs Ince spent six months in prison as a result of adhering to her principles, her side of the story had never been heard by the Court, and her claim that almost the whole of her savings came from her own earnings and what she saved from money given to her by her children has never been given any consideration.[96]

The MWA was not blind to the law's impotence even after legislative reform had been achieved. Instead of providing Lily Ince with protection, the MWPA 1964 was used against her by her husband, and without legal representation, or even an understanding of the serious consequences of her case, she had limited chance to defend herself. The MWA was convinced that it could have prevented her incarceration, and potentially her loss of savings too, had Mrs Ince sought their help earlier, but members had intervened when it was, as they put it, 'five minutes after midnight'.[97]

Lily Ince's misfortune did not end with her failed appeal. MWA member Elizabeth Ambridge visited her in October 1965 at home with her husband.[98] Mr Ince had been giving his wife half of his sick benefit, while Mrs Ince said she would bequeath her money to strangers who had helped in her time of need. The matter seemed settled. Yet only a month later, it was reported that Mrs Ince had written to the MWA seeking assistance.[99] Her husband had left her, and she was concerned he would sell the matrimonial home. By April 1966, though the MWA had been helping her pursue proceedings to assert her legal right in her home,[100] Mrs Ince reportedly was 'giving up and letting Mr Ince have it'.[101] After approximately 40 years of marriage, five children and years of careful saving, Mrs Ince had served time in prison, lost her savings, been deserted by her husband and finally, lost her home.

Telling Lily Ince's story is important when exploring the MWA's relationship with law. As well as the MWPA 1964's failure to assist Mrs Ince, there were other factors at play, including her access to legal advice at the crucial time, knowledge of her legal rights and numerous other relational and contextual factors. In this case, the Association's demand recalled at the beginning of this chapter seemed especially astute: 'We need something *more* than just a monetary gain;

---

[96] ibid.

[97] ibid.

[98] MWA Executive Committee Minutes, October 1965, 5MWA/3/1, TWL.

[99] MWA Executive Committee Minutes, November 1965, 5MWA/3/1, TWL.

[100] MWA solicitor Dennis Walker wrote to Elizabeth Ambridge saying that although Mrs Ince had agreed to proceedings under the Married Women's Property Act with regard to her house in Gordon Street, she had failed to sign the affidavit. Walker is most likely referring to the MWPA 1882, s 17 which provides the court with discretion to determine property interests where there is a dispute between a husband and wife on this matter. MWA Executive Committee Minutes, April 1966, 5MWA/3/1, TWL.

[101] ibid.

we need equal status and with it equal responsibilities'.[102] By the end of Lily Ince's case, it was all the more evident this was not something that could be achieved through piecemeal reform alone.

III. PIECEMEAL REFORM: AN EFFECTIVE STRATEGY?

It is not difficult to see why piecemeal reform is generally criticised when juxtaposed with comprehensive change, as this tends to involve comparing short-term fixes to long-term solutions. Indeed, the reforms considered in this chapter did not get to the root of the problems with which the MWA was most concerned. And as Kahn-Freund argued: 'Surely, the Married Women's Property Act 1964 – which is a hopeless enactment – cannot remain the last word in this matter?'[103] There is nothing to suggest the MWA intended it to be so. On the contrary, it was a strand within the Association's broader strategy as Billington-Greig had sketched out in her notes: to pursue reform one step at a time.[104]

Viewed in the context of the time and circumstances the MWA was working in, their piecemeal achievements were arguably the best they could have hoped for and were extraordinary given the size and available resources of the Association.[105] As Dorothy Stetson pointed out: 'Lack of publicity for women's rights issues plagued activities of feminists during the 1950s and 1960s. A generation of women grew up believing that feminism was as dead as the suffragettes'.[106] This apparent lack of public consciousness, compounded by the split in 1952, meant that support for the MWA was not what it had been at the time of the *Blackwell* campaign in the 1940s. In the MWA's own words, they were left with 'too few women [and men] having to cope with too much work'.[107]

According to the MWA themselves, the period in which these reforms were achieved was understandably a time of 'excitement and success', and 'a very great achievement for a comparatively small association' proving as they saw it 'what can be accomplished by justice of cause, sincerity of purpose and persistent hard work'.[108] But this positive spin belies what it must really have been like for an organisation like the MWA at that time. The hidden stories behind

---

[102] Nicholson, 'Deputation to House of Commons', above n 5 (emphasis added).

[103] O Kahn-Freund, 'Law Commission: Published Working Paper No 42: Family Property Law 1971' (1972) 35 *MLR* 403, 406.

[104] Notes of Teresa Billington-Greig, 7TBG/1/32, TWL.

[105] Speaking about the MWPA 1964 in Parliament, Summerskill stated: '[The Act] means little, but that was all I could get Parliament to accept at that time because that was all that was recommended by the Royal Commission on Marriage and Divorce which sat to discuss these matters': HL Deb 4 November 1971, vol 325, col 167.

[106] D Stetson, *A Woman's Issue: The Politics of Family Law Reform in England* (Oxford University Press, 1982) 166.

[107] MWA Secretary's Report 1956–57, 7TBG/1/31, TWL.

[108] ibid.

the legislation in this chapter show why the MWA took so long to achieve its more modest aims, and why – in legislative terms at least – it achieved so little. Their strategies, effective or not, help debunk what Erika Rackley and Rosemary Auchmuty refer to as the usual 'straightforward narrative of success ... with never a hint of disappointment or setback'.[109]

But by working within the system and doing what was possible for a small feminist pressure group at that time, the MWA's experience also supports Mavis Maclean and Jacek Kurczewski's claim that the 'process of law making is an ongoing struggle and it is therefore quite rational to value short-term effects as well as long-term ones'.[110] In doing so, the importance of smaller legislative successes can be better appreciated. For instance, the MWPA 1964 was considered by some to be a 'definite step forward on a particularly thorny path' because it gave the 'partnership of marriage a practical connotation'.[111] And while there is little evidence of its effectiveness in practice, it did appear to align with public views. A 1972 study by Jean Todd and Leslie Jones found that the Act's principles matched public expectations, with respondents equally split between those who thought all housekeeping savings should belong to the wife and those who thought they should belong equally to both spouses.[112]

The MWPA 1964 also arguably led to more radical discussions of automatic equal division of property between husband and wife. In 1985, the Law Commission produced a working paper centred on dramatically extending the principle of equal division in the 1964 Act, by proposing a rule whereby any money transferred by either spouse would immediately belong jointly to husband and wife.[113] Although this rule was never implemented, the paper triggered a broader conversation around financial equality between spouses at this time, and this was *directly* facilitated by the MWPA 1964. These developments all form an important, albeit unrecognised part, of the historical context surrounding current principles of financial provision on divorce. Today, substantive equality underpins the courts' approach to asset redistribution, and while the MWPA 1964 is not directly responsible for this model, it was notably the *first* legislative reform that recognised the need for economic equality in marriage.[114]

The Maintenance Orders Act 1958 could also be seen as attacking the public/private divide that had helped reinforce and protect the sanctity of the male pay

---

[109] E Rackley and R Auchmuty, 'The Case for Feminist Legal History' (2020) 40 *Oxford Journal of Legal Studies* 878, 898.

[110] M Maclean and J Kurczewski, *Making Family Law* (Hart Publishing 2011) 110.

[111] Cummins, above n 69.

[112] JE Todd and LM Jones, *Matrimonial Property* (HMSO 1972) 31–32.

[113] Law Commission, *Transfer of Money Between Spouses*, above n 58. This was subsequently recommended by the Commission in 1988: *Family Law: Matrimonial Property* (Law Com No 175, 1988).

[114] The MWPA 1964 was repealed in Scotland by the Family Law (Scotland) Act 1985. The Act remains in force in England and Wales. The Family Law (Property and Maintenance) Bill 2005 sought to extend the Act's provisions to civil partners but was not passed. The Act was never introduced in Northern Ireland.

packet. It is remarkable that a majority of commissioners opposed attachment of wages in 1956 and only a year later Chief Commissioner Lord Morton had changed his mind. That the MWA helped turn the tide on this matter, even in the face of staunch opposition from trade unions, is no small feat. More than a decade later, MWA members Roxane Arnold and Juanita Frances reported that a former member of the Royal Commission had told them he regretted not supporting attachment of earnings at the time.[115] This open acceptance of a principle once strongly opposed is another reminder of how controversies today can become orthodoxies tomorrow.[116]

It is notable that the MWA's one step at a time strategy relied heavily on the Private Member's Bill procedure, the Association viewing it as their best way of getting their draft bills before Parliament. Rebecca Probert has pointed out that 'one of the most startling aspects of family law reform in the 20th century' is just how many reforms were instigated by this procedure.[117] It *is* startling, because the procedure depends 'quite literally, on the luck of the draw'.[118] Once the MWA had been fortunate enough to have an MP agree to sponsor their draft Bill *and* be successful in the Private Member's Bill ballot, it was very easy for a dissenter to block it. All that is needed procedurally is for one MP to shout 'object' and as the MWA put it, a 'single member of Parliament holds up a progressive measure'.[119] This also helps explain why the MWA faced much more disappointment and setback than success in its efforts to have reform brought forward; piecemeal, or otherwise.[120] But as Summerskill explained, Private Member's Bills were MWA members' only option when their campaigns were ignored in government:

> Successive Governments, fearful of jeopardising the male vote, lack the moral courage to tackle legal disabilities which stem from custom and prejudice. Consequently these are dealt with in a piecemeal fashion by Private Members' legislation ... The noble and learned Lord [Diplock] ... complained at this being piecemeal legislation. I invite him to examine over the last few years the legislation which seeks to remedy injustices suffered by women, and he will find that it has been done in precisely the same way, by Private Members' legislation.[121]

---

[115] Report on a visit to Lambeth Palace to the Secretary of the Archbishop of Canterbury dated '1966 or 1967', 5MWA/5/1, TWL.

[116] R Probert, 'The History of 20th-Century Family Law' (2005) 25 *Oxford Journal of Legal Studies* 169, 179.

[117] ibid.

[118] ibid.

[119] MWA Bulletin, April 1965, 5MWA/1/3/2, TWL.

[120] Interestingly, the parliamentary session in which the MWPA 1964 was passed had the most successful Private Member's Bills on record by a large margin: House of Commons Information Office, *The Success of Private Members' Bills*, FS no L3, June 2010, available at: https://www.parliament.uk/globalassets/documents/commons-information-office/l03.pdf.

[121] HL Deb 20 April 1971, vol 317, col 550.

If the MWA had waited for comprehensive and perfect reform of the law, they would likely find it would not happen.[122]

CONCLUSION

The MWA's successful campaigns on attachment of wages and housekeeping savings proved members were willing to adapt the group's strategy and no longer reject piecemeal reform, in the hope that this could build an easier path to their more radical ambitions. The Association saw the 'milestone'[123] MWPA 1964 not as a reason to relax its efforts, but to increase them and to push for further reform:

> The next step must be a share of all income and earnings after the upkeep of the household has been met. We hope that this will take place in a much shorter time for we have created by propaganda and agitation a public opinion that marriage is a partnership.[124]

As the MWA's broader and more radical reform had been knocked back, the MWA sought to mitigate the rigour of the doctrine of separate property through a series of patchwork reforms. Evaluating the merits and demerits of a piecemeal approach to reform in this chapter is important. It is tempting in legal history to focus only on the successes. But when we do this, our view is skewed, the myth of linear progress is reinforced, and the MWA becomes a group associated *only* with piecemeal reform. Such blinkered focus also means that failed attempts, such as the Women's Disabilities Bill, are forgotten. When widening the frame to look to their unsuccessful reform too, it becomes clear that while MWA members began appreciating the pragmatic need to sometimes support reform dealing with narrowly confined issues, they also considered both the Maintenance Orders Act 1958 and the MWPA 1964 to be stepping stones to realising bigger goals. This shows the Association's relationship with law cannot be described using simplistic narratives of progress, as it was an ongoing struggle of compromise and negotiation, without much, if any, credit for their work when gains were made.

Perhaps the most important consequence of the piecemeal reforms discussed in this chapter is how their shortcomings powerfully highlighted the need for further reform. Indeed, Kahn-Freund aptly summarised the problem with the MWPA 1964 (and similar piecemeal reform) when he said: 'However important and beneficial, all this legislation is patchwork, a series of responses to the needs of the moment. The problem of matrimonial property has never been

---

[122] As noted by Eirene White MP when agreeing with Summerskill: ibid, col 553.
[123] MWA Annual General Report, 10 June 1964, above n 71.
[124] ibid.

tackled systematically'.[125] This is the point the MWA had been making all along. Realistically, one short statute was never going to fix the broader problem of married women's financial inequality in marriage. For both the MWPA 1964 and the Maintenance Orders Act 1958 were barely 'Band-Aids', let alone antidotes to the problems the MWA sought to address. Just ask Lily Ince.

---

[125] O Kahn-Freund, 'Recent Legislation on Matrimonial Property' (1970) 33 *MLR* 601, 604–05.

8

Resistance as a Reform Strategy

I am a terrified elderly lady of 67 years. My husband (now 70) left me some years ago for someone younger. On several occasions he has returned to me but has gone back to 'the other woman' when she has called him ... He is of course now retired on pension ... He has no other means, nor capital. To provide for 'the other woman' he now wishes to divorce me under the [Divorce Reform] Act [1969] so that the widow's pension will go to her – his admitted sole reason for seeking a divorce ... I make ends meet by working in a full-time job – not well paid because I am untrained and started late when I was left alone. It has no pension. In due time, because of my age, my employers will put me out to grass. When that time comes the widow's pension will pay my ever-rising local rates, and provide warmth and necessities. Without it I must give up my home and I am terri-fied at the prospect of being without a roof when I shall need it most ... To have this linchpin abruptly removed, as it will be by the [Divorce Reform Act] is surely against all justice for the elderly wife. We are now too old to make alternative plans and, without these pensions, sufficient means to keep our homes will vanish.

Anon, Surrey.[1]

INTRODUCTION

I N AUGUST 1968 Sir Jocelyn Simon,[2] at that time President of what is now known as the Family Division of the High Court,[3] wrote a remarkable let-ter to Edith Summerskill. Other letters he had sent her were typed on A4 paper, signed 'JES Simon'. But this one was different. Handwritten on small note paper, it read:

A rumour has reached me that an attempt is being made to re-introduce the Divorce Reform Bill ... If there is any truth in this, it is not too soon to start mobilising the women's organisations. Married women are in grave danger; and after all the disrepu-table agitation in favour of the Bill, the promoters are likely to be held in restraint only if it is seen that the passage of the Bill is likely to be highly unpopular ...

Yours very sincerely,

Jack Simon[4]

---

[1] Letter from [undisclosed] to Edith Summerskill, 27 June 1969, SUMMERSKILL/1/102, TWL.
[2] Who later became Lord Simon of Glaisdale.
[3] It was then known as the Probate, Divorce and Admiralty Division of the High Court. This became the Family Division in 1970.
[4] Letter from Jocelyn Simon to Edith Summerskill, 5 August 1968, SUMMERSKILL/1/102, TWL.

Simon is referring to what became the Divorce Reform Act 1969, eventually introduced in 1971 and generally considered to be a landmark of family law history.
It is noteworthy that the President of the Family Division warned of the Bill's
'grave danger' for married women. Simon had previously attacked the common
law rules about matrimonial property,[5] and this private correspondence suggests
that when it came to opposing divorce reform, he was Summerskill's ally.

Reading Simon's letters to Summerskill provides a glimpse behind the scenes
of reform. How connections between those in politics and law have played an
important, yet underappreciated role. How the tactics of those who wish to
promote or resist change often influence developments, sometimes in an unfore-
seen way.[6] And, that there are interesting insights to be gleaned about the process
of law reform by not always looking just to the proponents of reform, but to
those who have resisted it too.

If these observations are aligned with feminist legal history, two things are
clear. First, legal historians do not pay much attention to the resisters of reform
if that reform is ultimately successful. And second, in the history of women's
interaction with law, and feminist efforts to enhance women's legal rights, resistance is a key strategy if the law being proposed will affect women detrimentally.

With this in mind, this chapter argues that Edith Summerskill (with the
Married Women's Association's (MWA) backing) was among the most important and formidable rivals of the Divorce Reform Act 1969. Her intervention was
arguably crucial in having the 1969 Act delayed so that comprehensive financial
provision reform could finally be introduced. The idea of resistance as a reform
strategy is examined by focusing on Summerskill and the MWA's involvement in
reform of divorce and its financial consequences at the end of the 1960s into the
1970s. Perhaps the least known, yet most important part of this story was their
role in the 1969 Matrimonial Property Bill, which as well as slowing the passage
of divorce reform, was the closest the law in England and Wales had come to
accepting joint ownership of property during marriage.

As the MWA engaged in these high-profile struggles, it was experiencing
lower membership numbers and dwindling funds.[7] Yet members continued to
use their connections to law and policy to influence the direction of reform.
While it is impossible to measure the precise impact these interventions had,
this snapshot beneath the surface of reform processes again demonstrates the
complexity of family law history. The competing forces, relational influences
and backroom deals can imperceptibly, yet importantly influence law as we
know it.

[5] J Simon, 'With all my Worldly Goods ...', Presidential Address (Holdsworth Club, University of
Birmingham, 1 January 1964). Olive Stone described this address as 'a long, cool look at the law of
matrimonial property' and a 'witty attack' on the common law: OM Stone, '"With all my Worldly
Goods ..."' (1965) 14 *International & Comparative Law Quarterly* 707, 707.
[6] S Cretney, *Family Law in the Twentieth Century* (Oxford University Press 2003) vii.
[7] 5MWA/3/1, TWL.

I. THE CONTEXT OF DIVORCE REFORM IN THE 1960S

By the late 1960s, the MWA still did not have its new marriage law. The piece-meal statutes explored in the previous chapter relating to housekeeping savings and maintenance made a difference, but did not resolve the fundamental prob-lem of women's economic vulnerability in marriage. The Matrimonial Homes Act 1967 – spearheaded by Edith Summerskill[8] – was invaluable in that it gave deserted spouses a legal right of occupation in the matrimonial home.[9] Still, it did not provide a wife with a proprietary interest in her home. The Royal Commission on Marriage and Divorce had not recommended comprehensive reform, nor did it manage to break the deadlock overhanging the question of divorce reform; the issue which had triggered the establishment of the Royal Commission in the first place. But it had endorsed the principle that husband and wife should be regarded as equal partners in law.

Meanwhile, momentum was gathering in support of change to divorce. The need for modernisation was becoming more urgent because the current system had not undergone comprehensive reform since 1937[10] and clearly was not work-ing. This was because divorce was based entirely on the fault of *only one* of the parties and required proof of a matrimonial offence by the party petitioning for divorce. Therefore, if the husband petitioned for divorce on the ground of his wife's desertion (a matrimonial offence under the law) he would be barred from divorce if he had committed adultery (another matrimonial offence), even if this had only happened on one occasion. This meant that in marriages where both parties were at fault, or indeed where neither party was at fault, divorce was not possible. By the 1960s, it was clear that this position had become untenable as there was widespread consensus that it was not in the public interest to legally keep a marriage in existence when it had in actuality broken down.[11]

*

When the Royal Commission reported in 1956, one of the main stumbling blocks preventing comprehensive reform recommendations being made was the impasse between religious conservatives and proponents of a more liberal divorce law. As a result, the Established Church's dramatic decision to play a major role in liberalising divorce laws in the 1960s was, as Stephen Cretney put it, something 'nobody could have predicted'.[12] In 1966, the Anglican Church (under the direc-tion of a group formed by the Archbishop of Canterbury) published *Putting*

---

[8] Notably with the support of Lord Denning: A Denning, *The Due Process of Law* (Butterworths 1980) 220.

[9] Provided she had registered a charge in the Land Register. The MWA launched an initiative to help raise awareness that married women needed to do this in order to be protected.

[10] Pursuant to the Matrimonial Causes Act 1937.

[11] Parts of this discussion appear in S Thompson, 'Against Divorce? Revisiting the charge of the Casanova's Charter' (2021) 33(3) *Child and Family Law Quarterly* 193.

[12] Cretney, *Family Law in the Twentieth Century*, above n 6, 354.

Asunder, recommending divorce on the sole ground of irretrievable breakdown of marriage.[13] The newly established Law Commission published a report responding to *Putting Asunder* in the same year, which mirrored many of its recommendations, including the need to replace the matrimonial offence with the ground of irretrievable breakdown.[14] The policy behind both reports was that many marriages were 'empty shells'[15] that could not legally end, and that this had become a widespread social problem. The Law Commission described the existing divorce law as failing to 'aid the stability of marriage, but tends rather to discourage attempts at reconciliation. It does not enable all dead marriages to be buried, and those that it buries are not always interred with the minimum of distress and humiliation'.[16] In other words, the many marriages that had already broken down without any possibility of reconciliation should be able to legally dissolve, allowing the parties to move on. On this basis, the Law Commission stated that the objectives of divorce reform should be:

(i)   To buttress, rather than to undermine, the stability of marriage; and

(ii) When, regrettably, a marriage has irretrievably broken down, to enable the empty legal shell to be destroyed with the maximum fairness and the minimum bitterness, distress and humiliation.[17]

In 1967, Labour MP William Wilson introduced the Divorce Reform Bill to enact the Law Commission's proposal for a new divorce law based on irretrievable breakdown, and when it did not progress through Parliament before the parliamentary session was prorogued, it was reintroduced in the Commons by Alec Jones MP and moved in the Lords by Lord Stow Hill.[18] This Private Member's Bill is probably what triggered Simon's warning to Summerskill at the start of this chapter. Under the Bill, establishing irretrievable breakdown would require one of five facts: adultery; behaviour that would make it unreasonable to be expected to live with the respondent; desertion; two years' separation with consent; or five years' separation without consent.[19] While this Bill marked a radical shift away from previous divorce law, it had widespread support. Politicians such as Labour MP Leo Abse kept the issue of divorce reform in the public eye throughout the 1960s using (in Abse's own words) 'histrionics, panache and style'.[20] Even Conservative MPs, for whom the sanctity of marriage was core

---

[13] Church of England, Archbishop of Canterbury's Group on the Divorce Law; and M Ramsey, *Putting Asunder: A Divorce Law for Contemporary Society* (SPCK 1966).

[14] Law Commission, *Reform of the Grounds of Divorce: The Field of Choice* (Cmnd 3123, 1966).

[15] ibid, para 15.

[16] ibid, para 28.

[17] ibid, para 15.

[18] Also known as Sir Frank Soskice.

[19] Later enshrined in s 1(2) of the Matrimonial Causes Act 1973.

[20] L Abse, *Private Member* (Macdonald London 1973) 169. Data based on contemporary polls reproduced in BH Lee, *Divorce Law Reform in England* (Peter Owen 1974) 96–97 indicated public support for divorce based on separation rather than fault.

to their conservative ideology,[21] were not expected by their party to oppose the Divorce Reform Bill.[22] From this perspective, it seemed almost inevitable that the Divorce Bill would get Royal Assent. After all, the reform seemed both urgent and justifiable given what June Carbone has referred to as the 'hypocrisy and deceit inherent in a system that made divorce available only if one party were at fault'.[23] But there was one stumbling block in particular that almost prevented the Bill from becoming law – the financial consequences of divorce for women.

A. New Fight, Old Problem

President of the Family Division, Jocelyn Simon, had warned of the 'grave danger' of divorce reform. The problem was that for many married women, divorce meant financial disaster. The main concern – and a major threat to the passage of the Divorce Reform Bill – was the clause providing that a woman could be divorced by her husband without her consent after a period of five years' separation.[24] With this new era of divorce on a no-fault basis, including divorce without consent, traditional notions of marriage as a lifelong commitment were challenged like never before. Although this would be potentially liberating for women stuck in unhappy marriages, it had as much potential to oppress women, given equal economic status in marriage was still far from being a reality.

There was no single unified feminist response to this provision, but the resistance to divorce without the other spouse's consent was not new. More than a decade earlier, when the Royal Commission on Marriage and Divorce was considering divorce after seven years' separation without the other spouse's consent, Helena Normanton warned it would draw 'most serious attention to the grave economic disadvantages which would be inflicted upon the wife if such a retrograde measure should ever become law'.[25] Normanton was not against divorce reform per se. She prided herself on having played an important role in AP Herbert's Matrimonial Causes Act 1937[26] which extended the grounds for divorce.[27] But like Simon, Summerskill and her former peers in the MWA, she had concerns about the notion of divorce without consent.

---

[21] See, eg, A Gilbert, *British Conservatism and the Regulation of Intimate Relationships* (Hart Publishing 2018).

[22] Cretney, *Family Law in the Twentieth Century*, above n 6, 354.

[23] J Carbone, 'A Feminist Perspective on Divorce' (1994) 4(1) *Future of Children* 183, 187.

[24] Which was one of the routes to establishing irretrievable breakdown pursuant to the Divorce Reform Act 1969 and s 1(2)(e) of the consolidating Matrimonial Causes Act 1973.

[25] Helena Normanton's Submission of Evidence to the Royal Commission on Marriage and Divorce, 7HLN/B/05, TWL.

[26] ibid.

[27] The Act extended the grounds for divorce to include desertion for over three years, cruelty and incurable insanity.

The letter that prefaces this chapter sent by a 'terrified' 67-year-old woman to Summerskill encapsulates the fears middle-aged and older married women had about desertion and economic destitution. Divorce reform had brought the persistent problems of separate property to the fore. Married men and women tended not to own property on equal terms, were not paid equally when both worked outside the home, and were not even taxed in the same way.[28] As Edward Bishop MP argued in Parliament in 1969, many women were now gainfully employed outside the home, but would still be in an economically vulnerable position:

> It is difficult to prove, where a wife does not work outside the home but works in the house caring for the family and doing the many jobs which a wife and mother must do, what contribution she has made and what repayment she can get when the marriage goes on the rocks. Many wives earn money outside to contribute towards holidays, clothing and school affairs. This is not easy to prove.[29]

'So', Bishop concluded, 'the wife, whether she works in the home or outside, is at a great disadvantage'.[30] While this had been a growing problem throughout the history of the MWA, now the prospect of wives being deserted under a new divorce law with insufficient protection made reforming the issue of married women's property rights even more imperative.

Though the MWA had successfully been part of the introduction of new maintenance legislation, it was clear maintenance was not enough. This is because the social and economic background of marriage had transformed dramatically, which in turn changed the nature of family assets. Maintenance arguably made sense when the family income was spent on immediate needs: clothes, food and shelter.[31] But patterns of family consumption had changed, and a significant proportion of the family income was instead spent on 'durable assets' like the marital home and its contents. The efforts of the family were directed towards acquiring property, and the law's failure to recognise this, and to provide the wife with a corresponding proprietary interest in recognition of her efforts created what Otto Kahn-Freund referred to as a 'new time lag between social and legal developments'.[32] As he argued in 1970:

> The link between the law of matrimonial property and the law of matrimonial maintenance is as close today as ever it was, but how can one seriously assert that the supply by the husband of the means to cover these elementary needs can be an equivalent to the wife's economic contribution (in whatever form) where a large part of the contribution is destined for the acquisition of durable goods, and especially of a home for the family?[33]

[28] See chs 2 and 5.
[29] HC Deb 24 January 1969, vol 776, col 803.
[30] ibid, col 804.
[31] O Kahn-Freund, 'Recent Legislation on Matrimonial Property' (1970) 33 *MLR* 601, 606.
[32] ibid, 605.
[33] ibid, 606.

The judiciary failed to deliver satisfactory solutions to this problem in *Pettitt v Pettitt*[34] and *Gissing v Gissing*,[35] as trusts law only allowed the court to recognise a spouse's direct financial contribution to the purchase price of property. And section 17 of the Married Women's Property Act 1882 was not much use either. As seen in chapter five, this provision appeared to provide the court with some discretion to distribute family assets, yet it had seemingly lost its potency to provide sufficient redress.[36]

Against this backdrop of changes to property acquisition and distribution within marriage, the Maintenance Orders Act 1958 and the Married Women's Property Act 1964 (considered in the previous chapter) were important measures for mitigating the rigours of the separate property doctrine. But they were clearly inadequate. With divorce reform on the horizon, reform of financial provision law could not come soon enough.

*

Importantly, those pushing for reform were not apathetic about the financial consequences of divorce for the non-moneyed spouse.[37] This is evident both in the arguments for divorce reform, and in the provisions that were eventually introduced. Proponents of the Divorce Bill argued that the hardship of the existing law for wives made reform of divorce *more* urgent, with the Law Commission and Archbishop of Canterbury's group both emphasising the harsh consequences of the law for the more economically vulnerable spouse. This concern was reflected in the drafting of the Divorce Reform Act, whereby section 4 could prevent divorce without consent in the event of 'grave financial or other hardship to the respondent and that it would in all the circumstances be wrong to dissolve the marriage' and section 6, facilitating postponement of the decree absolute (the legal end of the marriage) so that financial provision for the non-moneyed spouse could be arranged.[38]

Moreover, the Divorce Reform Act 1969 was not brought into effect until 1971 so that the Law Commission could investigate fully the financial consequences of divorce. The recommendations in the Law Commission's report sought to ameliorate the concerns of those opposed to divorce because of the potential consequences for married women.[39] These were enshrined in the Matrimonial Proceedings and Property Act 1970, now consolidated in the Matrimonial Causes Act 1973 and still in force today. The effect of the 1970 Act was transformative

---

[34] [1970] AC 777.
[35] [1970] UKHL 3.
[36] Kahn-Freund, above n 31, 607.
[37] C Smart, *The Ties That Bind* (Routledge 1984) 70.
[38] ss 4 and 6 of the Divorce Reform Act 1969 became ss 5 and 10 of the consolidating Matrimonial Causes Act 1973.
[39] Law Commission, *Financial Provision in Matrimonial Proceedings* (Law Com No 25, 1969).

in that where the court previously made maintenance and lump sum orders on a discretionary basis – which operated to penalise the spouse 'at fault'[40] – the new legislation gave the court wide-ranging discretionary powers to make financial orders regardless of fault, which included the power to redistribute property. This redistributive power was a turning point in family law, as it marked a shift in emphasis away from making the wife dependent on maintenance towards helping her become economically independent by providing her with property and therefore 'purchasing power'.[41]

While Summerskill's concern for deserted wives is sometimes acknowledged in accounts of divorce and financial provision reform such as these, it is not properly examined and understood. Conventional top-down accounts of the Divorce Reform Act focus primarily on the role of the Law Commission and the established Church,[42] both of which had encouraged reform, and – like many accounts of legal reform – tend to underplay the significance of those who *resisted* reform, such as Summerskill and the MWA. Similarly, mainstream accounts of divorce reform tend not to explore what the views and experiences of deserted wives *actually were* – they simply register that opponents of reform were anxious about how these women would be affected by it. Thus, by exploring opposition to the Divorce Reform Act further in the next section an alternative history of divorce reform is produced.

II. RESISTING DIVORCE, STRATEGISING REFORM

So far in this chapter, focus has been mainly on the institutional story of divorce reform. Proponents of the Divorce Reform Act 1969 had not forgotten about the plight of the deserted wife and so the government delayed reform so that the Matrimonial Proceedings and Property Act 1970 could be introduced. Yet even in the retelling of this story, the gaps are glaring. Is it accurate, for instance, to attribute the abrupt curtailing of the Divorce Bill at the eleventh hour solely to those in government? Or were there other forces at work? To make sense of this story, focus must instead turn to the MWA, its networks and in particular to Edith Summerskill, who continued to work closely with the Association.

First, it is important to debunk the notion that passage of the Divorce Reform Act was inevitable. It is clear this is not the case when looking at contemporary press reports. In May 1969, for example, only months before the Act was passed, the *Sunday Times* published the headline 'Divorce reform faces death on a

---

[40] There was no rationale for such orders and there was a clear lack of consistency in case law, see: G Douglas, *Obligation and Commitment in Family Law* (Hart Publishing 2018) 118.

[41] As noted in Douglas, ibid, 118 and in *Trippas v Trippas* [1973] Fam 134, CA; *O'D v O'D* [1976] Fam 83, CA.

[42] See R Auchmuty, 'Legal History' in R Auchmuty (ed), *Great Debates in Gender and Law* (Macmillan 2018).

Friday'.[43] Leo Abse MP, a leading advocate of the Act, wrote in his memoirs that it was a 'real wonder ... that the Divorce Bill ever reached the statute book'[44] at all because of the grievances levied against it by Edith Summerskill. Abse's frustration in his memoirs is palpable: 'No one was more successful in delaying its passage, and in arousing hostility to its objectives, than ... Summerskill', he said.[45]

By this time, Abse had been clashing with the MWA and Summerskill for just over a decade. He is best known for his pioneering work in drafting, tabling and sponsoring what became the Sexual Offences Act 1967, which decriminalised private homosexual acts in England and Wales.[46] Yet although he was an important social reformer, he did not agree with the MWA's views on improving married women's legal status. His conflicts with the MWA came to a head over reform of divorce and financial provision; first in the 1960s, when he sought to introduce divorce reform and then in the 1980s when he was a leading figure in the Campaign for Justice in Divorce. This campaign sought to curtail maintenance provision and the MWA's efforts to challenge it are examined in chapter nine.

The MWA was apprehensive about the Divorce Reform Act because of its potential economic impact on economically vulnerable married women. As noted in section I, members' concerns especially related to section 2(e) of the Divorce Reform Act 1969,[47] which enabled a spouse to establish irretrievable breakdown of the marriage without the consent of their partner after a period of five years' separation. In the members' view, this provision disadvantaged deserted wives, whose husbands would be empowered to leave their wives, marry younger women, and financially support their new family instead of their old one.

The MWA's opposition on this basis was not new. They had a record of speaking against such reform throughout the 1960s. Summerskill had opposed the earlier Matrimonial Causes and Reconciliation Bill 1963, introduced by Leo Abse. By then a life peer in the House of Lords, she condemned it for being a 'husband's Bill, drafted by a man who doubtless means well but has failed to recognise that marriage has different values for men and women'.[48] At its Executive Committee meeting, the MWA passed a resolution of appreciation to Summerskill and submitted statements opposing the Bill to MPs, the press, the Archbishop of Canterbury and the Archbishop of York, and to the Mother's Union.[49]

---

[43] E Jacobs, 'Divorce reform faces death on a Friday' *Sunday Times* (4 May 1969), SUMMERSKILL/1/99, TWL.

[44] Abse, above n 20, 180.

[45] However, see also Lee, above n 20, 117, who argued that K Bruce Campbell QC was the 'toughest opponent' of the Bill.

[46] Pursuant to s 1, for individuals over the age of 21.

[47] s 1(2)(e) of the consolidating Matrimonial Causes Act 1973.

[48] HL Deb 22 May 1963, vol 286, col 401.

[49] MWA Executive Committee Minutes, 24 April 1963, 5MWA/3/1, TWL.

Examination of internal Law Commission files reveals the extent of Summerskill's influence upon this reform. At the end of 1967, Leo Abse met Law Commission Chairman Leslie Scarman, Lord Chancellor Gerald Gardiner, Permanent Secretary to the Lord Chancellor Denis Dobson and MP William Wilson, stating he could not commit to a Bill 'without something to meet the Lady Summerskill lobby'.[50] Summerskill's opposition had become so dangerous to the future success of divorce reform that the divorce reformers felt the need to strategise accordingly, with Scarman having been advised by a colleague: 'it is so important that she [Summerskill] should understand what we are doing and why we are doing it'.[51] During this meeting Dobson suggested what would become section 4 of the Divorce Reform Act.[52] The 'best answer would be a refusal of a [divorce] decree', he said, where satisfactory financial arrangements could not be made.[53] Abse and Wilson 'agreed this was a practicable solution' and advised that the presentation of this clause 'should include a certain amount of "window dressing"'.[54] In the Lords, when it became clear this provision would only apply if one of the parties could prove grave hardship to the court,[55] Summerskill tore this 'window dressing' down, saying it provided insufficient protection to women and comprehensive reform was required.[56] By the late 1960s, Summerskill had refined her critique and became known for designating the 1969 Act a 'Casanova's Charter' for permitting divorce without the consent of both spouses.[57] Summerskill appears to have used the phrase 'Casanova's Charter' for the first time in a speech to the MWA.[58] Described by Cretney as a crude but effective caricature,[59] the soundbite became an effective tool in raising awareness about the potential repercussions of the Act without extending married women's property rights.

The debate started by Summerskill's 'Casanova's Charter' charge was clearly a formidable force in pressurising the government to change course. Legislation on financial provision was introduced alongside legislation on divorce as the economic consequences for deserted wives was recognised as being a genuine problem in need of reform. Moreover, the phrase helped ensure the Divorce Bill was seen as 'highly unpopular', as Simon had suggested in his letter at the start of this chapter. Yet Summerskill's view of divorce reform is understood

---

[50] BC3/378, TNR.

[51] Letter from JM Cartwright-Sharp to Leslie Scarman 2 October 1967, BC3/402, TNA.

[52] s 5 of the consolidating Matrimonial Causes Act 1973.

[53] Above, n 50.

[54] ibid.

[55] For further discussion of Summerskill's criticism of this provision, see Thompson, 'Against Divorce?', above n 11.

[56] HL Deb 10 July 1969, vol 303, col 1295.

[57] HL Deb 8 November 1967, vol 286, col 428.

[58] M Summerskill, Unpublished Biography of Edith Summerskill, SUMMERSKILL/7, TWL.

[59] Cretney, *Family Law in the Twentieth Century*, above n 6, 373.

historically as being anti-divorce per se. Her promotion of marriage has been criticised by academics such as Carol Smart, who argued that Summerskill and her supporters were of the view that 'the best a middle-aged wife could hope for was to hang onto her husband'.[60] Summerskill's opposition has also been considered 'illogical',[61] with her feminism challenged for being 'contradictory'[62] given that other feminists were in support of an easier divorce process that would allow women to be liberated from unhappy marriages.[63] However, disproportionate focus on the efforts of Summerskill and the MWA to resist divorce reform risks misunderstanding their core philosophies. When it came to divorce, Summerskill summarised the MWA position as follows:

> Apart from moral considerations, the Married Women's Association objected to the [Divorce Reform] Bill on economic grounds. They declared that the second wife would be regarded by the husband as the first call on his income, and consequently the strict observance of a maintenance order would be in jeopardy. And the pension provisions of the Welfare State would be enjoyed by the second wife irrespective of the fact that the first wife might have lived with the deceased man for a far longer period than his new partner.[64]

Clearly, the MWA shared Summerskill's view that proper provision could not be made for deserted wives under the present system. Meanwhile, Summerskill had been working hard to mobilise women's organisations as the Divorce Bill moved through Parliament. This included writing to organisations such as the Council of Married Women (the MWA breakaway group)[65] and the Committee of Civil Rights for Women and Children of Broken Families.[66] The National Council of Women held a conference in Caxton Hall where several women's groups congregated.[67] Summerskill's influence as a political heavyweight seemed to make a difference, as Helen Nutting (who had previously chaired the MWA and now led the Council of Married Women) appeared to have less success. She told Summerskill: 'I have worked behind the scenes trying to get unity among all the women's organisations' but neither the National Council of Women nor the Salvation Army would sign a petition she was organising. This, she said, 'was disappointing as their large memberships could have carried weight'.[68]

[60] Smart, above n 37, 71.

[61] Abse, above n 20, 180.

[62] Smart, above n 37.

[63] D Stetson, *A Woman's World: The Politics of Family Law Reform in England* (Oxford University Press 1982).

[64] E Summerskill, *A Woman's World* (Heinemann 1967) 240.

[65] Helen Nutting wrote: 'My Council is very disturbed that the above Bill may slip through Parliament without adequate provision being made for the divorced wife – or perhaps I should say the discarded wife': Letter from Helen Nutting to Edith Summerskill, undated, SUMMERSKILL/1/102, TWL.

[66] Letter from Committee of Civil Rights for Women and Children of Broken Families to Edith Summerskill, 7 December 1967, SUMMERSKILL/1/99, TWL.

[67] Leaflet for conference on divorce reform, 1 February 1968, SUMMERSKILL/1/99, TWL.

[68] Above, n 65.

As well as mobilising the weight of these women's organisations, Summerskill continued to work closely with the MWA. The Association published her speeches in Parliament about divorce reform in several issues of its Newsletter and it was a central focus of MWA activity at that time.[69]

Once the women's groups were assembled, Summerskill's next move was to make the unpopularity of the divorce reform clear in the press, and to rally support in the wider population. She had a strong presence in the media, and her 'Casanova's Charter' soundbite featured in numerous headlines and press reports, where she was recognised as a 'leading opponent' of the reform.[70] Her stance was especially supported by middle-aged and older women, as evinced by the hundreds of letters from deserted wives in Summerskill's files.[71]

*

Summerskill's resistance was undoubtably made effective by her catchy critique of the 'Casanova's Charter'. But equally important was Summerskill's ability to explain constructively what needed to be done before divorce reform could be acceptable. Take, for example, this passage, where Summerskill uses the phrase 'Casanova's Charter' for the first time in Parliament:

> There is a tendency in many quarters to disregard the fact that men can earn their income and accumulate capital only by virtue of the division of labour between themselves and their wives ... Sir Jocelyn Simon, President of the Divorce Court ... [has] said: 'The cock bird can feather his nest precisely because he is not required to spend time sitting on it'. This being so, a separation of goods between married people cannot be said to do justice to the wife
>
> ...
>
> My purpose to-day is simply to try to persuade the Government, before they embark – or before a Private Member embarks – on legislation calculated to undermine the institution of marriage as we understand it in Britain, to change the policy. However, if they find that a Private Member is persuaded to draft a Casanova's Charter, then they must incorporate ... a matrimonial property law which includes community of goods, in order to protect the discarded wife.[72]

Here, Summerskill was demanding a new matrimonial property law. She wanted women's unpaid labour to be recognised in economic terms, and for spouses to share the financial fruits of the marriage when it dissolved. This argument sits at

[69] Correspondence with Juanita Frances discusses how meetings with the Lord Chancellor (Gerald Gardiner) could be used to influence reform, with Frances asking Summerskill what she wanted her to do next: Letter from Juanita Frances to Edith Summerskill 12 December 1967, SUMMERSKILL/1/99, TWL.

[70] Anon, 'Pension Share Sought for First Wives', newspaper clipping, SUMMERSKILL/1/99, TWL.

[71] For analysis of these letters, see S Thompson, 'Edith Summerskill: Letters from Deserted Wives' (2022) *Women's History Review* (forthcoming).

[72] HL Deb 8 November 1967, vol 286, cols 427–28.

the heart of Summerskill's opposition to divorce reform and reflects the letters she had been receiving from deserted wives. In these letters, women described a range of personal and individual experiences, but the fundamental problem in each of them was financial. As one letter objecting to divorce reform put it: 'The money question is SERIOUS – for a woman with children to bring up alone … this Bill will create a new poor in our welfare state'.[73] For this reason, the significance of the delay of the Divorce Reform Act 1969 to facilitate sweeping reform of financial remedies pursuant to the Matrimonial Proceedings and Property Act 1970 should not be underestimated.

There are a number of interesting points revealed in this extract from one of Summerskill's many speeches on the subject. She utilised the 'Casanova's Charter' soundbite in the same breath as calling for financial reform. Yet her specific demands for economic spousal equality are rarely associated with this soundbite. Summerskill's rationale for financial provision mirrors the modern rationale underpinning the redistribution of assets on divorce, which is not just about protection, but is also about entitlement generated by financial *and* non-financial contributions. Simon's cock bird metaphor[74] perfectly encapsulated Summerskill's own assertion that it is the 'fundamental division of labour between husband and wife which frees the husband for the acquisition of goods'.[75]

The gendered division of labour in the marriage meant that the wife, as Summerskill put it, 'must be able to count on her share of the goods accumulated through the marriage'.[76] She went on to explain that the wife has earned this share by bearing and rearing the children and in tending the home. This language of entitlement is important as it denotes a broader context in which MWA members had been fighting for property rights for married women since the early 1940s. Summerskill's son Michael Summerskill discovered when interviewing Lord Denning that when Summerskill was pushing for wives' right not to be evicted under the Matrimonial Homes Act 1967, it was a real struggle to achieve reform where 'the wives' interest would be a fetter on property'.[77] She must have known that arguing for financial relief far beyond maintenance and lump sum orders was controversial, but as former Conservative politician and editor of the *Daily Telegraph* Bill Deeds noted: 'I don't think she was a lady who was very easily pushed off her point of view. She stuck to it'.[78] So, instead of framing wives' property rights in terms of need, in the context of divorce

---

[73] SUMMERSKILL/1/101, TWL.
[74] Summerskill is quoting Sir Jocelyn Simon from a speech he delivered to the Law Society at the Holdsworth Club in 1964: above n 5.
[75] HL Deb 8 November 1967, col 427.
[76] ibid, col 426.
[77] Lord Wilberforce and Lord Upjohn were very worried about this according to Lord Denning: Interview by Michael Summerskill with Lord Denning, SUMMERSKILL/1/46, TWL.
[78] Interview by Michael Summerskill with Bill Deeds, SUMMERSKILL/1/46, TWL.

reform Summerskill argued instead for recognition of wives' entitlement. Those familiar with the House of Lords case of *White v White*[79] in 2000 will recognise this terminology, and it is interesting to see Summerskill framing financial provision in a similar way more than 30 years previously.

For Summerskill at this time, the most radical and straightforward way to reflect the equal importance of financial and non-financial roles in marriage was 'community of goods' or community of property; a matrimonial property regime explored in chapter four. Both the Royal Commission on Marriage and Divorce in 1956 and the Law Commission in 1988 considered introducing community of property, deciding against it as it would be too complex. Edward Bishop's 1969 Private Member's Bill arguably came closer to realising this aim. But in hindsight, it is unlikely this Bill would have been a successful or effective way of achieving equality in marriage. As Cretney wrote at the time, it would have been 'very easy for any lawyer to excoriate the bill, and make a mordant analysis of its numerous gross errors of principle and drafting'.[80] Though Summerskill did support this Bill, as the next section explores, other MWA members' views were less straightforward.

III. MATRIMONIAL PROPERTY BILL 1969

Edward Bishop's Matrimonial Property Bill sought to introduce an element of community of property into English law by requiring 'equitable division of jointly owned matrimonial property' by the court.[81] The Bill appeared to have widespread support[82] and Bishop admitted to having introduced the Bill to slow down the progress the Divorce Bill was making at the time.[83]

A lesser-known aspect of the Bill is that it originated from discussions with the MWA over joint ownership of the matrimonial home.[84] The MWA had drafted its *own* Matrimonial Property Bill. It aimed to extend the right won by Summerskill for married women to occupy the home under the Matrimonial Homes Act 1967, by providing women with a *proprietary* interest in the home equal to that of their husbands, even when the property was in his sole name.[85]

---

[79] [2000] UKHL 54.
[80] S Cretney, 'The Community of Property' (1969) 113(7) *Solicitors Journal* 116.
[81] HC Deb 24 January 1969, vol 776, col 811. Cretney, ibid, 117: The Bill provided that the court 'on the application at any time of either spouse may, and whenever a petition for nullity of marriage, divorce or separation is presented, shall make an equal division of matrimonial property between the spouses'.
[82] Cretney, 'The Community of Property', above n 80.
[83] Cretney, *Family Law in the Twentieth Century*, above n 6, 134.
[84] Stetson, above n 63, 193.
[85] The Association invited other women's organisations 'to participate with us in trying to obtain a sponsor for the Matrimonial Property Bill' and found 'the response was poor' (with the exception of the Women's Cooperative Guild, the Business and Professional Women's Clubs and the Divorce Law Reform Union): MWA Bulletin, September–October 1968, 5SPG/I/08, TWL.

When Bishop came third in the Private Member's ballot, he agreed to sponsor their Bill.[86] The MWA reported the news in its October 1968 Bulletin, asking MWA members to write at once to their MP.[87] However, the Bill had been redrafted when it came up for debate in the Commons and went further than the original terms of the Bill. Instead, it provided for equal division of all property acquired during the marriage, excluding property owned at the time of the marriage or obtained through gift or inheritance.[88]

Closer inspection of the Bishop Bill suggests that while the arguments in favour of community of property merit consideration, the Bill could have had disastrous consequences if introduced. Cretney noted that lawyers severely criticised it: 'to any progressively minded lawyer the saddening thing about the treatment of the bill is the paean of exultation in the press that the bill was passed in spite of opposition from lawyers'.[89] It appears this opposition was warranted based upon Cretney's analysis; the Bill had 'manifold defects', he said,[90] was limited in scope[91] and the narrow range of problems to which it applied could already be addressed under the existing framework of marriage breakdown law. Abse's condemnation of the Bill appeared to be based more on his perception that the concerns of Summerskill and others were 'overblown',[92] and, with apparent reference to Dr Olive Stone – who helped prepare the Bill – described it as 'hideously drafted by some supporting shameless academics'.[93]

Abse's biting remarks aside, the issues with the Bill were not confined to its drafting. Cretney also noted that the Act could have the unintended consequence of leaving a wife worse off under the Act that she would be otherwise.[94] This is because it only applied to matrimonial property, that is, property acquired during the marriage.[95] As a result, if the matrimonial home had been purchased with the husband's money earned before the marriage, the wife would not receive half of the value of the house. She would be entitled only to half of the increase in value of the home during the marriage. The Bill could therefore

---

[86] Bishop asked legal academic Olive Stone for assistance in drafting a Bill. He acknowledged Stone's assistance in the House of Commons: HC Deb 24 January 1969, vol 776, col 809.

[87] Above n 85.

[88] Stetson, above n 63, 193–94.

[89] Cretney, 'The Community of Property', above n 80, 117.

[90] ibid. According to Cretney, the defects included: 'the provision that spouses can contract out of the Act, but then providing that this can be disregarded; the failure to consider the effect on third parties, or in relation to estate duty, capital gains tax or bankruptcy; the absence of a power to set aside dispositions in fraud of the bill'.

[91] The Bill related only to property, not capital and if the marriage had not broken down, a spouse would be required to go to court to seek redress, which Cretney argued would not assist the 'wife who is sufficiently loyal not to take' her husband to court: ibid.

[92] Stetson, above n 63, 196.

[93] Abse, above n 20, 190. As well as Stone, lecturer in law Joseph Harper was also credited by Bishop (above, n 86).

[94] ibid.

[95] Also known as deferred community of property.

have *entrenched* spousal inequality instead of promoting its goal of furnishing married women with rights beyond maintenance.[96]

Behind the scenes, the Law Commission and Lord Chancellor's Office were alarmed by the prospect of the Bishop Bill becoming law, as in their view it was so poorly drafted it was 'incurably bad'.[97] So alarmed, in fact, that the Law Commission – a non-political, independent body – joined forces with Lord Chancellor Gerald Gardiner to quash the Bill. 'I am taking the unusual course of writing to you about this myself' Law Commission Chairman Leslie Scarman wrote to Gardiner in 1968, because 'I believe that this Bill should not receive a Second Reading'.[98] 'If it does', Gardiner later replied, we 'will have to consider urgently what should be done'.[99] Scarman's notes indicate he was concerned there was a strong chance the Bill could pass:

> Superficially, the Bill is attractive, and the fact that its passage would remove a great deal of opposition from the women's lobby to the Divorce Reform Bill may tempt supporters of the latter Bill to support the former. But on careful consideration the Bill is clearly unsound and ill-thought out in many basic respects.[100]

Thus, Scarman was worried that supporters of the Divorce Reform Bill would view the Bishop Bill as way of putting an end to the 'Casanova's Charter' charge levied so effectively by Summerskill and her supporters to hinder the progress of divorce reform.

Attempts by the government to kill the Bill were later described by Law Commissioner LCB Gower as 'ham fisted'.[101] A three-line whip issued to ministers backfired when MPs became 'very upset'.[102] When the whip was overturned, the Bishop Bill was able to have its Second Reading debate. The strategy agreed by the Law Commission and the government was not to offer any drafting assistance to Bishop, to *appear* sympathetic to the underlying purpose of the Bill and 'not to allow any Minister to say or imply that the Law Commission want the Bill killed'.[103] Following this, the Commission informed the Lord Chancellor's Office that it would work on alternative reform that could 'achieve what appear to be the basic objectives of' the Bishop Bill, but on very different terms.[104]

The tactics of the Commission and the government worked. Ultimately, Bishop withdrew his Bill and it never became law. After it successfully passed its

---

[96] This departed from the purpose of the original MWA Matrimonial Property Bill, which provided for spouses to have equal rights in the matrimonial home: Matrimonial Property Bill, 5SPG/I/08, TWL.

[97] Letter from Leslie Scarman to Gerald Gardiner, 20 December 1968, BC3/406, TNA.

[98] ibid.

[99] Letter from Gerald Gardiner to Leslie Scarman, 24 January 1969, BC3/914, TNA.

[100] Leslie Scarman's notes for discussion with Leo Abse on the Matrimonial Property Bill, BC3/914, TNA.

[101] Letter from LCB Gower to Allan Leal, 12 February 1969, BC3/914, TNA.

[102] Letter from Gerald Gardiner to Leslie Scarman, 24 January 1969, BC3/914, TNA.

[103] Letter from LCB Gower to JW Bourne, 9 January 1969, BC3/406, TNA.

[104] Law Commission memo to Lord Chancellor, 11 February 1969, BC3/914, TNA.

second reading in the House of Commons (despite criticism from every lawyer who spoke in the debate) Bishop made a deal with the government agreeing that if the Law Commission could draft a better Bill, the government would give it time and it would pass.[105] This paved the way for the Matrimonial Proceedings and Property Act 1970. As a result, while the Bishop Bill was clearly flawed, it proved to be a suitable delaying tactic to ensure divorce reform was not passed without reforming divorce's financial consequences. The Commission 'had great hopes' of proposing reform of financial provision in a future session of Parliament,[106] but without the deal for the Bishop Bill to be withdrawn, Scarman later admitted to Abse in private that he was 'certain' the reform culminating in the 1970 Act 'would not have been ready in time'.[107]

Textbook histories of divorce fail to acknowledge this crucial role played by the Bishop Bill in reforming financial remedies. It is easy to dismiss a Bill that is riddled with defects, with Gower calling it 'the most hopeless piece of drafting that I have ever seen'[108] and Scarman concluding it would have proven to be 'an embarrassing addition to our statute law'.[109] But this hidden history shows that poorly drafted, unsuccessful reform can be significant, for it can impel the government and/or the Law Commission to act.

Correspondence between Bishop and Summerskill shows their collaboration in these reform efforts, and of Bishop's feelings about his strategic compromise with the government:

> In the proceedings in the House discussion was curtailed voluntarily in order to get the Bill through, and also to make it possible for other Bills to be discussed and passed in the same Sitting. Hence, much of what could and should have been said was left unsaid ... We had no alternative but to co-operate to get the Bill through, and we should have been very worried had it not done so. However, it is certain there will have to be amendments to it in the near future and we shall have to consider the form they should take.

> I think we can claim that had we not exerted the pressure we did, this Bill would not have been introduced and passed in this Parliament. There is hardly need for me to say how much I have appreciated the immense amount of work which you and a few others have given, and I hope we can keep in touch to stimulate changes to the Act in the near future.

> Yours, Ted Bishop[110]

[105] Stetson, above n 63, 199. Leo Abse revealed in his memoirs that it had been his plan to feign support for the Bishop Bill and to ask the government to intervene at the proper time: 'I laid on the scheme with the connivance of those in authority': Abse, above n 20, 199.

[106] Letter from Leslie Scarman to Gerald Gardiner, 20 December 1968, above n 97.

[107] Letter from Leslie Scarman to Leo Abse, 17 September 1969, BC3/410, TNA.

[108] Letter from LCB Gower to JW Bourne, 9 January 1969, above n 103.

[109] Letter from Leslie Scarman to Gerald Gardiner, 20 December 1968, above n 97.

[110] Letter from Edward Bishop to Edith Summerskill, 28 May 1970, SUMMERSKILL/1/101, TWL.

Though the extent of Summerskill's involvement with the Bishop Bill is unclear, her connection to it was widely publicised. In the *Times*, she was reported as saying that if the Bishop Bill were passed, she would drop her opposition to the Divorce Reform Bill as the first wife would have some financial protection.[111]

The Matrimonial Proceedings and Property Act 1970 was radical when compared with the lack of family law reform achieved in previous decades, and undoubtedly deserves its status as a landmark moment. Yet this account of the backstage deals and trade-offs indicates how close England and Wales came to something *much more radical* – a new law of family property. The Bishop Bill is the closest England and Wales have ever come to accepting community of property. Though it did not pass, it has an important place within the history of the 1970 reforms, because as Dorothy Stetson has pointed out, it forced elites to include additional safeguards for married women's protection, and without it, the implementation of property reform on divorce would have been much more difficult.[112]

In the press, the MWA was reported as backing the Bishop Bill.[113] After all, it was the Association's Matrimonial Property Bill to begin with, and a new marriage law is something the MWA had always sought.[114] However, MWA members' views on the Bill were more complicated than the newspapers suggested. In its report of Summerskill's House of Lords speech on divorce reform, the MWA noted that while the Association supported Summerskill's general opposition to divorce reform, it did not agree with her calls for community of property.[115] Throughout its history, Summerskill and the MWA seemed to speak as one voice, but by the time the 1970 Act was introduced, their opinion on this precise issue was divided. The MWA argued that 'community of property fails as a means to create equity in marriage',[116] and instead viewed the reform that had been introduced as preferable:

> The Matrimonial Proceedings and Property Act 1970 has wide discretionary powers. It clearly states that up to one half of the joint estate could be settled on a deserted spouse and, in assessing maintenance, consideration is to be given to a wife's contribution during the marriage. In the opinion of the Married Women's Association this Act takes the place of and is superior to a system of Community of Property.[117]

The MWA concluded by arguing that too much emphasis on community of property could distract from the central purpose of reform: improving the economic position of married women.

---

[111] Legal Correspondent, 'Financial protection for wives in new Bill' *Times* (3 January 1969) 3.

[112] Stetson, above n 63, 209.

[113] 'Financial protection for wives in new Bill', *Times*, above n 111. See also, J Innes, 'Battling Betty starts her new fight today' *Daily Mail* (17 April 1969) 10.

[114] Stetson, above n 63, 193.

[115] MWA Bulletin, November–January 1968, SUMMERSKILL/1/99, TWL.

[116] MWA notes on Law Commission Working Paper No 42, 5SPG/I/09, TWL.

[117] ibid.

The Matrimonial Proceedings and Property Act 1970 was therefore viewed by the MWA as a step in the right direction because it appeared to endorse the value of work typically carried out by women. That is, the Act's discretionary guidance required the court to consider the 'contributions made by each of the parties to the welfare of the family, *including any contribution made by looking after the home or caring for the family*'.[118] The MWA's own Bill for equal partnership in marriage had provided for similar discretionary distribution of assets in the event of divorce. Yet this did not rule out the need for further reform; the 1970 Act had changed the property consequences of divorce, not the property consequences of marriage.

Perhaps the Law Commission summarised what the MWA wanted best:

> In effect what women are saying, and with considerable male support, is: 'We are no longer content with a system whereby a wife's rights in family assets depend on the whim of her husband or on the discretion of a judge. We demand definite property rights, not possible discretionary benefits'.[119]

Possible discretionary benefits were what the 1970 Act provided.[120] It did not deliver *definite* property rights.

CONCLUSION

Before the Matrimonial Proceedings and Property Act 1970 was introduced, the Divorce Reform Act 1969 posed a threat to the economic stability and security of many married women. In the late 1960s, the work of Edith Summerskill in particular made the struggle and frequent destitution of these women visible in Parliament. As Leo Abse (somewhat resentfully) recalled, 'it is to Summerskill's credit, or discredit, that she succeeded in delaying' the 1969 Act.[121] MWA members' resistance to divorce reform also reveals an important strategy. By blocking the passage of government backed reform, or by opposing a decision Parliament was in the middle of making, it was possible for the Association to persuade the legislature to redefine family law proposals in feminist terms.[122]

---

[118] s 5(1)(f) Matrimonial Proceedings and Property Act 1970; s 25(2)(f) of the consolidating Matrimonial Causes Act 1973 (emphasis added).

[119] Law Commission, *Family Property Law* (WP No 42, 1971) para 0.22.

[120] The consequences of discretionary benefits are summarised by J Eekelaar, *Family Law and Personal Life* (Oxford University Press 2007) 144: 'There was an uncomfortable air of paternalism about a male-dominated judiciary deciding how wives should, or should not, be rewarded at the termination of their marriages, particularly as the courts maintained their view that a married person should not be allocated any part of the business assets of their partner if they had not worked in the business or contributed directly to it'. This did not change until *White* in 2000 (above n 79).

[121] Abse, above n 20, 180.

[122] Stetson, above n 63, 229.

As this chapter has shown, the 1970 reforms may not have been introduced until a later date were it not for the pressure of the Matrimonial Property Bill. Yet because divorce reform ultimately passed, the significance of this feminist resistance is not acknowledged in mainstream accounts. Moreover, the Matrimonial Property Bill is known as the 'Bishop Bill', and its origins from within the MWA are hidden.

However, as we shall see in the next chapter, resistance as a reform strategy also had pitfalls. When MWA members attempted to resist the backlash against the 1970 reforms, they were forced into a defensive position and had to abandon their hopes of reform.

Interlude: Poor Reggie

THE FOLLOWING EXCHANGE appeared in the MWA's November–January 1978–79 Bulletin:[1]

WHY I THINK MEN GET A ROTTEN DEAL OVER DIVORCE BY REGGIE

Daily Mirror, 27 November 1978

Twice-married Reginald Bosanquet, newscaster of ITN is fighting for Men's Lib and has become a patron of the Campaign for Justice in Divorce, a pressure group which aims to stop ex-husbands being treated as 'meal tickets for life'. The policy of the organisation is spelled out as follows: Maintenance harms all who are involved in divorce and its aftermath. The present divorce law undermines marriage, family life and trust between the sexes. After divorce, both parties should again become responsible for themselves, as they were before marriage. Neither should expect to be maintained, giving nothing in return. Courts should not discriminate in favour of either partner without regard for the right needs and feelings of the other. For a deserted partner to have to support the deserter is to add injustice to injury. Second wives should be accepted as true spouses. Society should not seek to transfer to former partners its own responsibility for those unable to support themselves. State aid should be available to them as it is to other unemployed persons. Children are the responsibility of both parents and their contact with both is as important as financial provision.

MWA Reply to Daily Mirror

Poor Reggie: One cannot help feeling sorry for him. We suggest he takes a more intelligent view of his situation. In the sharing institution of marriage, wives too are part of the economic system of a country. Even if poor Reggie had a private arrangement that wife No 2 was only required to be the domestic and social factotum to poor Reggie, a luxury few couples could afford, but most likely she was also one of the 8 million married women who are also employed.

---

[1] MWA Bulletin, November–January 1978–79, 5MWA/8/1, TWL.

But either way, poor Reggie obviously belongs to a high income bracket. The £16,000 settlement presumably was a redundancy payment to Wife No 2. Also, we must remember that our Social Security pay annually more than 300 million to mothers and children for whom a man somewhere is responsible. Before we take sides on this important matter, could we be informed if poor Reggie shared his income with wife No 2 week by week as it arose all through the marriage?

Signed, MWA

9

Two Steps Forward, One Step Back

My husband's weekly take-home pay, with overtime, is about £50. Yet he only gives me £13 to keep the two of us. After paying the rent I only have £6.50 left for food. I manage by taking the odd 50 pence and 10 pence out of his pockets while he's asleep.

Mrs S, Canning Town, London

I have never had a square deal from my husband in 20 years of marriage. He gives me £14, and out of that I have to pay the rent, TV rental, food and everything else. Yet my husband spends at least £12 a week in the pub.

Mrs D, West Midlands.

My husband's take home pay is £37.50, but he only gives me £10 to feed and clothe me and our three children. I wouldn't mind managing on so little if my husband was in the same position. But he's not. Once he paid the rent, TV rental, and petrol for his car, he still ends up with £17 in his pocket. I know he earns it, but I reckon I earn a bit as well.

Mrs P, Banbury, Oxon

My husband is a bit of a meanie. He gives me £7 a week housekeeping. I also earn £7 from a part-time job, but I can't spend this money on myself because I need it to subsidise my housekeeping. I'm 47 and would like to have a few weeks off for a rest, but my husband said he wouldn't give me any more money if I did.

Mrs C, Essex

In our home, my husband is the one who has not had a rise recently. He has a small amount of spending money each week, and to make it stretch further, gave up smoking. Right from the start of our marriage we have always shared out money. I feel sorry for all the wives whose selfish husbands keep a large chunk of their wages for themselves.

Mrs S Harper, Warrington, Lancs[1]

INTRODUCTION

IT WAS LATE September 1970 – only months before the Divorce Reform Act 1969 and the Matrimonial Proceedings and Property Act 1970 became law on 1 January 1971 – and a seminar that would inform the direction of the Law Commission's further work on family law was taking place in Manchester.[2]

---

[1] Letterbox, *The Sun*, 25 March 1975, reproduced in MWA Bulletin May–June 1974, 5SPG/I/09, TWL.
[2] These Acts were later consolidated in the Matrimonial Causes Act 1973.

As we saw in the previous chapter, the 1969 and 1970 Acts were landmark family law reforms, introducing changes to divorce alongside a new framework of financial remedies. Property adjustment could be made in favour of the homemaking spouse on divorce. More generally, the value of non-financial contributions such as caring for the family was finally anchored in statute. This was thanks in part to resistance from Edith Summerskill, the Married Women's Association (MWA) and supporters of the Bishop Bill,[3] who supercharged the Law Commission and government into addressing the complex question of financial remedies on divorce. One might understandably assume that following such momentous reform, further revision of property rights in the matrimonial context would slip to the bottom of the reform agenda, at least for a while. Yet seated around a room in Langdale Hall at the University of Manchester, academic lawyers, sociologists, politicians, judges, legal practitioners and law commissioners gathered to discuss the Law Commission's confidential preliminary draft working paper titled 'Family Property Law'. Instead of quashing the need for family law reform, the Manchester seminar was proof that the 1970 Act had sparked the start of a fresh inquiry into matrimonial property law. The MWA had not been invited to attend.

Meanwhile, keen to capitalise on the recent interest into married women's rights, the MWA kept pushing for property rights to be extended to during marriage too.[4] This chapter begins by examining how this next step might have seemed within reach to MWA members; following the Manchester seminar the Law Commission examined the possibility of joint ownership of the home during marriage and a Bill on the issue was subsequently put forward by Lord Simon. Yet there were others who believed reform had shifted *too far* in wives' favour and now discriminated against husbands who – so the argument went – were unfairly required by law to provide their ex-wives with a 'meal ticket for life'. This culminated in the Campaign for Justice in Divorce; a high-profile movement led by Leo Abse MP and backed by the *Times*, which successfully shifted public sympathy from married women to married men. The latter half of this chapter explores the MWA's confrontation with this movement in the late 1970s and early 1980s, when Association members struggled under a backlash against improvements to married women's legal status, and saw their hopes for equal partnership quashed.

I. THE NEED FOR FURTHER REFORM

Although Edith Summerskill helped delay divorce reform, which in turn facilitated the 1970 reforms, this did not mean she saw cause for celebration.

---

[3] Also known as the Matrimonial Property Bill 1969.

[4] The MWA also argued that the 1970 reforms had not adequately addressed the issue of pension provision for wives, an issue that was not dealt with comprehensively until the introduction of the Welfare Reform and Pensions Act 1999.

In Parliament, Summerskill made her feelings about the Matrimonial Proceedings and Property Act clear. It was 'a confidence trick against the women of this country',[5] she said, because it was pitched as the solution to women's economic vulnerability by facilitating property adjustment between spouses on divorce, yet did nothing to address women's lack of property rights while the marriage subsisted. In one of her personal letters, Summerskill wrote that she was 'losing faith' in the Law Commission.[6]

It could be argued that questions of property ownership only become important when the relationship breaks down and that Summerskill was misguided. But as chapter four found, there were important reasons for Summerskill's discontent. The strict demarcation of ownership under the doctrine of separate property meant that the law did not match spousal expectations. Indeed, research published by Jean Todd and Leslie Jones in 1972 found that 91 per cent of husbands and 94 per cent of wives agreed that the matrimonial home and its contents should be jointly owned.[7] And, while the moneyed spouse might be unconcerned about joint ownership, the consequences of the separate property doctrine during marriage might be very important to spouses with no separate income or property.[8] In more pragmatic terms, the clarification of property ownership during marriage could have significance in crises other than divorce, such as bankruptcy and death.

The Law Commission had also failed to propose comprehensive solutions to what it referred to as 'the pension problem', that is, wives' loss of pension expectations on divorce, that they otherwise would have benefited from as widows under the Occupational Pension Schemes. The Commission had previously noted the MWA's opposition to divorce reform unless such losses could be compensated,[9] but subsequently concluded in its 1969 report that: 'we believe [the issue] to be incapable of direct and complete solution'.[10] Instead, the Commission argued that the 'increased and more flexible powers' enabling the court to make lump sum payments and property adjustment would 'alleviate the problem' by reducing the extent of any hardship which the wife would suffer through being deprived of the pension expectations she would have enjoyed as her husband's widow, had she stayed married.[11]

---

[5] HL Deb 6 November 1970, vol 305, col 500.

[6] SUMMERSKILL/1/99, TWL.

[7] JE Todd and LM Jones, *Matrimonial Property* (HMSO 1972) 31–32.

[8] This was noted in Law Commission, *Family Law: Matrimonial Property* (Law Com No 175, 1988) para 1.4.

[9] Memo by JM Cartwright-Sharp, who attended a 'teach in' organised by the Federation of Clubs for Divorced and Separated Persons. At the meeting, Sharp reported: 'The organiser of the meeting announced that the Married Women's Association proposes to campaign against the proposed availability of divorce where the respondent objects until respondent women can be compensated for the loss of expectation of widows' pensions. 27 September 1967, BC3/401, TNA.

[10] Law Commission, *Report on Financial Provision in Matrimonial Proceedings* (Law Com No 25, 1969) para 112.

[11] ibid, para 114.

The MWA leadership therefore agreed with Summerskill that further change was needed, and members contacted the Law Commission to demand more comprehensive reform of family property in line with the Association's Bill for equal partnership in marriage.[12] Before the Bishop Bill, there is evidence that the Law Commission may have been prepared to only pay lip service to these demands. Their internal files recorded discussions in 1967 leading up to the publication of the Commission's Working Paper on financial relief,[13] stating that their aim for reform was 'to achieve liberalisation of the grounds of divorce on the basis of the Commission's recommendations relating to financial orders on divorce *without* the need to wait for the overhaul of family property'.[14] As Stephen Cretney observed, had Summerskill been aware of this, she would have likely been even more convinced that she, the MWA and other advocates of family property reform had been duped.[15]

Even so, MWA members appeared optimistic about future change following the 1970 reforms. Conservative MP Jill Knight wrote to Law Commission Chairman Leslie Scarman, asking whether he would consider giving a hearing to a delegation of MWA members, whose 'close knowledge of the problems [with marriage] may be of value and interest' to the Commission's work.[16] But writing separately to family law professor Peter Bromley, Law Commissioner LCB Gower noted that Scarman felt 'the confrontation should be postponed' until their working paper was published.[17] Further inspection of the Commission's private correspondence about the MWA appears to convey a desire to maintain distance from the Association. Unbeknownst to the MWA, Law Commission Secretary JM Cartwright-Sharp had also suggested privately that delaying publication of this working paper would help mollify what it considered to be the 'extremists' of the 'married women's lobby'[18] and the 'pater familias' trade unionist lobby so that 'the voices of sweet reason can be heard'.[19] Thus, the MWA was excluded from directly influencing the Commission during this period. They were reformers pushed to the periphery of law-making processes.

This did not necessarily mean the views of reformers on the margins were inconsequential to the Law Commission's work. An indication to the contrary was evident at the Manchester University seminar on matrimonial property,

---

[12] 5MWA/3/1, TWL.

[13] Law Commission, *Matrimonial and Related Proceedings – Financial Relief* (WP No 9, 1967).

[14] 24 February 1967, BC3/400, TNA (emphasis added).

[15] S Cretney, *Family Law in the Twentieth Century* (Oxford University Press 2003) 136.

[16] Letter from Jill Knight to Leslie Scarman, 5 May 1970, BC3/600, TNA.

[17] Letter from LCB Gower to Peter Bromley, 6 May 1970, BC3/600, TNA. However, Jill Knight was subsequently invited to the aforementioned Manchester seminar.

[18] As noted previously, this did not consist only of the MWA. There were several other noteworthy organisations forming this lobby, which Edith Summerskill had helped to mobilise (see ch 8).

[19] M Cartwright Sharp notes: 'Family Property: Working Paper and Seminar', 22 August 1969, BC3/600, TNA.

where the Commission reported that it was concerned primarily with the question of

> whether, and to what extent, the present system of individual ownership of family property should be replaced by some form of 'community' between husband and wife and the consequential changes that this would entail in the law relating to house ownership, succession, family provision and the like.[20]

Though the efforts of Edith Summerskill and Edward Bishop had been unsuccessful in achieving their objective of community of property in 1969, they attracted significant support for their cause in the process of opposing the Divorce Reform Act. This seemed to exert a subtle, lingering influence upon Law Commission strategy. Not only was community of property a focus of the Manchester seminar and subsequent working paper; when the Commission ultimately decided it would not recommend the principle be introduced, Scarman privately expressed a desire for the Commission to give the impression it had been properly considered:

> I do not expect the reform of the Law Commission to introduce the principle of community of property between spouses ... Nevertheless, I think it necessary that we face fairly and fully the question of community and various forms that it can take in our working paper. We owe it to those who supported Mr Bishop's Bill to give community a reasonable run with the public. Even that extremely masculine body, the House of Commons would have to take notice if, for instance, an influential section of the Press should espouse the community principle. We must see that a genuine opportunity is given for public debate.[21]

*

The MWA leadership continued to contend that their Bill for equal partnership in marriage, which fell short of community of property, was preferable to the provisions of the Bishop Bill. In 1971, the Association launched the 'Equal Partnership Campaign to the Law Commission' to pressurise the Commission into considering these proposals.[22] The impetus for this campaign was the Law Commission's publication of its Working Paper on Family Property Law in 1971,[23] which following the Manchester seminar recommended co-ownership of the matrimonial home between spouses and for surviving spouses to receive a half share of their deceased partner's estate. Though the MWA noted these recommendations would 'do a great deal to recognise a wife's contribution to the marriage' if introduced, they also pointed out 'fundamental

---

[20] Press Notice issued by the Lord Chancellor's Office, 1 October 1970, BC3/600, TNA.

[21] Memo on seminar, 30 September 1970, BC3/600, TNA.

[22] MWA Annual General Meeting, 11 May 1972, Secretary's Report for year ended 30 April 1972, 5MWA/3/1, TWL.

[23] Law Commission, *First Report on Family Property: A New Approach* (WP No 42, 1973).

omissions'.[24] The MWA wanted the Law Commission to include two further recommendations in its final report:

1.   After the upkeep of the home and family from the joint income the remainder should be equally shared, and if invested the name of both spouses should be documented.
2.   A spouse should have the legal right to know the income of the other on application to an employer or to a government department, where necessary.[25]

Both proposals were taken from the MWA's decades-long equal partnership campaign outlined in chapter four, but by the 1970s they were not alone in making these assertions. Otto Kahn-Freund's view echoed the MWA's first point. He was especially critical of the Law Commission for doing nothing about the law applicable to liquid assets accumulated for household purposes, such as a savings bank account.[26] Like the MWA, he was suggesting that transformative reform of property ownership during marriage would focus not only on real property, but on personal property.

The MWA's second point related to another root cause of power imbalance as they saw it – that a wife could be completely excluded from information about her husband's finances, giving him greater economic power in the marriage. This was not a new cause taken on by the MWA, as it had long been part of their draft bills.

*

The MWA reported that the year following the introduction of the Matrimonial Proceedings and Property Act 1970 was 'exceptionally busy'.[27] In 1971, the MWA's Executive Committee and Sub-Committee on Policy increased meetings from monthly to weekly because of 'pressing demands'. The Association held meetings on the Law Commission's working paper and sought further drafting advice on its Equal Partnership Bill[28] from Gerald Gardiner, who had resigned as Lord Chancellor the previous year following Labour's 1970 election defeat.

As well as seeking the help of lawyers and politicians,[29] the Association launched 'a very extensive press campaign … to all newspapers throughout the country'. MWA Chairman Juanita Frances was credited for her 'most extensive correspondence', not only with public figures and the press, but with MWA

---

[24] MWA opinion on Law Commission Working Paper No 42, 5SPG/I/09, TWL.
[25] ibid.
[26] O Kahn-Freund, 'Law Commission: Published Working Paper No 42: Family Property Law 1971' (1972) 35 *MLR* 403, 408.
[27] MWA Annual General Meeting, 11 May 1972, above n 22.
[28] eg, it was sent to legal adviser Dennis Walker, ibid.
[29] The Association sent details of its aims and proposals to 'all MPs, all Legal Departments, and all the University Social Science and Law Faculties, ibid.

members and the general public. As the report from the MWA's 1972 Annual General Meeting noted: 'Articles are written, and addresses made. Constant interviews take place with the Press, BBC and ITV'.[30]

Work with Summerskill continued too. 'Many members' of the MWA came to the House of Lords to hear her plea to Parliament for the 'emancipation of the housewife'[31] and months earlier, Summerskill facilitated a meeting for the Association at the Houses of Parliament; one of three that year which the MWA used as opportunities to recruit MPs to their cause and spread their message. With MWA Secretary Joyce Nottage's admission that the 'healthy membership of the 50s and 60s was dwindling',[32] the MWA strategy instead appeared to be focused on participation in legal and political processes. Members attended conferences on family property reform and Executive Committee members joined Edward Bishop's All Parliamentary Equal Rights Group, which involved attending regular meetings in the House of Commons.

Another important MWA contact at this time was legal academic Dr Olive Stone.[33] She advised the Association on family property reform, drafted MWA bills and wrote letters on the group's behalf to the Law Commission and MPs. She operated as a valuable intermediary between the Association and policy-makers because she provided guidance that highlighted the significance of the MWA's equal partnership proposals and translated legal documents into accessible language for MWA members with no legal training. Perhaps most importantly, Stone shared similar ambitions to the MWA for reform of property ownership during marriage. In a letter to Helen Nutting – then Chairman of the Council of Married Women – she expressed her disappointment that provisions for joint ownership in the Bishop Bill (which she had helped draft) had not been incorporated into the 1970 reform:

> My own impression is that we shall delude ourselves if we think that the [Bishop] Bill had done its job. It has raised a real and substantial point and the judges have shown since that they largely agree with its aims. *But property is the holy of holies.* If women want it they will have to go in and get it. Nobody will offer it to them on a plate, but all sorts of smokescreens about bad drafting and the like will be raised to head them off. I hope they will keep on target.[34]

Stone therefore seemed well aware of the difficulties facing the MWA, having experienced defeat in her own legislative efforts. She was also an important

[30] ibid.

[31] HL Deb 4 November 1971, vol 325, col 170. Summerskill was specifically referring to the Law Commission Working Paper No 42 (above n 23) that had been published 10 days previously, and asking her peers to recognise the importance of the proposals within it.

[32] R Gorb, 'Wives' Unequal Battle' *Hampstead and Highgate Express* (11 July 1986).

[33] See R Auchmuty and J Temkin, 'The Road to Olive Stone' in U Schultz, G Shaw, M Thornton and R Auchmuty (eds), *Gender and Careers in the Legal Academy* (Hart Publishing 2021).

[34] 5CMW/B/22, TWL (emphasis added), cited in D Stetson, *A Woman's Issue: The Politics of Family Law Reform in England* (Oxford University Press 1982) 203.

contact as she was influential in the world of law reform. As well as publishing in the leading British academic law journal the *Modern Law Review*, she played an important role at the Law Commission's University of Manchester seminar, providing the report on legal rights of inheritance and general advice on the problems affecting family property law. As Cretney noted, this seminar 'seems to have very much set the agenda for subsequent Law Commission work on the subject',[35] and many of the conclusions reached at Manchester University clearly fed into the Commission's *First Report on Family Property*.[36]

II. EQUAL RIGHTS IN THE HOME

When the Law Commission published its report on family property in 1973 it revealed that a 'great majority' of respondents to the working paper favoured the introduction of a 'new principle upon which the property rights of husband and wife would be determined in accordance with fixed principles' and that there was more support for co-ownership of the matrimonial home than community of property.[37] Most significantly, the Commission maintained that the 'difference between the rules applied to married couples and those applied on divorce *can no longer be regarded as acceptable*'.[38] This must have seemed like a huge victory for MWA members at the time. It also must have been equally disappointing when these Law Commission recommendations were never implemented. But for a while, it seemed possible.

The next task undertaken by the Law Commission was draft legislation implementing co-ownership of the matrimonial home. The MWA saw this as a further opportunity to push a new draft of its Equal Partnership Bill in 1975 with the help of Olive Stone, because it too provided for equal rights in the home. But again, this was to no avail.[39] The Commission decided that other aspects of the MWA Bill, such as a share of the family income, would 'provoke strong opposition' and would be regarded 'as an unjustifiable interference'.[40] Indeed, reform focused on the comparatively narrowly circumscribed issue of home ownership during marriage was a complex enough task for the Law Commission; it did not submit its draft Bill until 1978 – five years after its report – and even then, the Bill was a 'densely reasoned document', spanning more than one hundred pages.[41]

---

[35] Cretney, above n 15, 136.

[36] Law Commission, *First Report on Family Property*, above, n 23.

[37] ibid, 137–38.

[38] Law Commission, *First Report on Family Property: A New Approach* (Law Com No 52, 1973) para 138 (emphasis added).

[39] The Association also drafted a separate Married Persons Income Disclosure Bill in 1975, which provided spouses with information about their partner's income. It was never brought before Parliament, as none of the MPs or peers in the Lords who had been successful in the Private Member's ballot agreed to sponsor it: 5MWA/1/2/2/2, TWL.

[40] MWA Bulletin, April–May 1981, 5MWA/8/1, TWL.

[41] Cretney, above n 15, 139.

Thus it is perhaps unsurprising that the MWA's more ambitious proposal did not appear to have been considered seriously by the Law Commission.

After the government indicated that it would not be proceeding with the Law Commission's Matrimonial Homes (Co-ownership) Bill, it was eventually brought before the House of Lords by Summerskill's old ally Jocelyn Simon (by then Lord Simon of Glaisdale) in 1980, the year Summerskill died. This was closely followed and supported by the MWA. At an MWA meeting in May 1980, Nora Bodley relayed Lord Simon's speech about the Bill from a Status of Women event and said 'a powerful lobby' would be needed, and that 'all members should write to their MPs'.[42]

That same year, the House of Lords handed down a landmark judgment.[43] It held that a married woman could have an overriding equitable proprietary interest in a house owned legally by her husband.[44] In practice, this transformed conveyancing procedure so that the names of both spouses would appear on the title documents of the home. According to Rosemary Auchmuty, the case 'spelt the death-knell of the custom of putting the matrimonial home in the husband's sole name'.[45] Yet this did not necessarily render the Matrimonial Homes (Co-ownership) Bill obsolete.[46] Even if the majority of homes were jointly owned by husband and wife, embedding this principle in statute would turn it into a normal and legally recognised feature of marriage.[47] Thus, the Bill was withdrawn to be redrafted in line with the House of Lords decision, and Lord Simon wrote to Juanita Frances to seek support: 'I think I shall have to rely on you to do the requisite lobbying' when it is reintroduced.[48]

Less than a year later, MWA news on the Matrimonial Homes (Co-ownership) Bill was much less optimistic. The minutes from the April 1981 Executive Committee meeting note: 'It seems certain that Lord Simon's Bill to be presented next session will be opposed by Leo Abse'.[49] This is exactly what happened. The Matrimonial Homes (Co-ownership) Bill was blocked because the Lord

---

[42] MWA Executive Committee Minutes, 28 May 1980, 5MWA/3/1, TWL. See also the Association's statement: 'We believe that the Government's policy on this most important question affecting the rights of married women could be influenced in no small degree by the reception given to Lord Simon's Bill when it comes before the House'. MWA Bulletin, January–February 1980, 5MWA/8/1, TWL.

[43] *Williams & Glyn's Bank Ltd v Boland* [1980] UKHL 4.

[44] ibid.

[45] R Auchmuty, 'Williams & Glyn's Bank v Boland (1980)' in E Rackley and R Auchmuty (eds), *Women's Legal Landmarks: Celebrating the History of Women and Law in the UK and Ireland* (Hart Publishing 2019) 362.

[46] The Law Commission's response to this decision is summarised in *Property Law: The Implications of Williams & Glyn's Bank Ltd v Boland* (Law Com No 115, 1982). The Commission concluded that a scheme of equal co-ownership of the matrimonial home should be introduced in line with this Bill to 'establish the existence and extent of co-ownership interests more effectively' (para 121).

[47] MWA Bulletin, November–December 1979, 5MWA/8/1, TWL.

[48] Letter from Lord Simon to Juanita Frances, MWA Bulletin, November–December 1981, 5MWA/8/1, TWL.

[49] MWA Executive Committee Meeting, 22 April 1981, 5MWA/3/1, TWL.

Chancellor had been 'pelted with opposition' from MPs.[50] The momentum behind the Bill was extinguished by Leo Abse's new charge – that far from *extending* rights to married women, reform had gone too far, and it was now the husbands who were the victims.[51] Thus that flickering chance for reform of family property, supported by feminists such as the MWA, had been snuffed out by what Leslie Scarman had once referred to as 'that extremely masculine body, the House of Commons'.[52]

III. THE 'MEAL TICKET FOR LIFE' BACKLASH

By the late 1970s, public discourse about family law reform had shifted away from women's rights towards serious concern for men's rights instead. This was caused by a perception that maintenance law was out of step with the recent reforms that had aimed to make it easier to divorce and enable 'empty shell' marriages to be destroyed.[53] Fuelling this contention was section 5(1) of the Matrimonial Proceedings and Property Act 1970, which had been consolidated in section 25 of the Matrimonial Causes Act 1973. It required the courts to

> place the parties, so far as it is practicable and, having regard to their conduct, just to do so, in the financial position in which they would have been if the marriage had not broken down and each had properly discharged his or her financial obligations and responsibilities towards the other.

This objective, known as the 'minimal loss principle',[54] placed the onus on the moneyed spouse (usually the husband) to continue to provide for his former spouse financially, unless she remarried. It was considered to be problematic as it seemed to guarantee ex-wives to a right to lifelong maintenance, though this right was never absolute.[55] Gillian Douglas has described the minimal loss principle as the Law Commission's 'solution to the plight of the innocent wife divorced against her will',[56] aiming to reassure those (such as Summerskill) who were concerned that the Divorce Reform Act 1969 was a 'Casanova's Charter'. In theory, the principle appeared to acknowledge that an economically vulnerable spouse rendered dependent by marriage could not easily move on from divorce in the same way the economically self-sufficient breadwinner could. As Douglas

---

[50] MWA Bulletin, April–May 1981, above n 40.

[51] L Abse, *Private Member* (Macdonald London 1973) 180.

[52] Memo on seminar, 30 September 1970, above, n 21.

[53] Law Commission, *Reform of the Grounds of Divorce: The Field of Choice* (Cmnd 3123, 1966) para 42.

[54] Gillian Douglas notes that John Eekelaar coined this term in G Douglas, *Obligation and Commitment in Family Law* (Hart Publishing 2018) 117, citing J Eekelaar, *Family Law and Social Policy*, 2nd edn (Weidenfeld and Nicolson 1984) 109.

[55] C Smart, *The Ties That Bind* (Routledge 1984) 166.

[56] Douglas, above n 54, 116.

noted, it stemmed from the concept of financial provision as 'repudiation of the marriage tie' whereby the first husband must 'pay for his freedom'.[57] In practice, however, the principle was swallowed in a furious backlash, catapulting discussions surrounding the abolition of maintenance into the mainstream, while making calls for further reform to address married women's property issues seem out of the question. Indeed, for first husbands and their new partners, the idea of lifelong maintenance was considered to be a grave injustice – a view that attracted increasingly popular support by the end of the 1970s.[58]

A. The Campaign for Justice in Divorce

These sentiments were concentrated into the Campaign for Justice in Divorce, which sought to extinguish the minimal loss principle and to reform maintenance law to improve the rights of divorced husbands and their new partners. The pressure group had high-profile leadership, and with Leo Abse leading the charge with the backing of the *Times* newspaper in autumn 1979, the Campaign for Justice in Divorce dominated headlines and 'burdened MPs postbags'.[59] Their accusation was that the current system of financial provision was unfair for men. This was ostensibly persuasive – why should a husband have to maintain two households, when the first marriage had been dissolved? It was arguably harsh for the husband, did not enable the parties to properly move on, and suggested that the wife was necessarily a needy supplicant.

The Campaign caught the public imagination using the slogan 'meal ticket for life' as a description of wives' lifelong maintenance support from former husbands. Juanita Frances was clearly concerned about the consequences of this slogan and the Campaign's extensive media coverage:

> The controversy has vilified women and branded them with a 'meal ticket for life' syndrome. Accusations in the press have made them out as 'alimony drones', and the public has responded with concern that there could not be smoke without fire. Both men and women have jumped into the fray, showing bias and prejudice against the true state of the economically depressed position of women and children in divorce.[60]

Frances incisively captures the harm caused by stereotypes about women on divorce.[61] The media's portrayal of wives as unfairly leeching from their ex-husbands in the 1980s[62] influenced public opinion and undermined the spirit

---

[57] ibid, 117.

[58] Smart, above n 55, 167.

[59] Cretney, above n 15, 139.

[60] Letter from Juanita Frances to MPs, 25 January 1983, 5MWA/8/1, TWL.

[61] S Thompson, 'A Millstone Around the Neck? Stereotypes About Wives and Myths About Divorce' (2019) 70 *Northern Ireland Legal Quarterly* 181, 181.

[62] See A Gilbert, *British Conservatism and the Legal Regulation of Intimate Relationships* (Hart Publishing 2018) ch 3.

of the Matrimonial Proceedings and Property Act 1970, that is, recognition of the property entitlements of spouses as a result of their unpaid work in the home.

The reality was that even with more women in the workforce, the traditional division of labour in marriage persisted, with the wife undertaking most of the housework and childcare. Women's average earnings in the early 1980s were approximately 74 per cent of men's.[63] So, while women's dependence in marriage was not what it had been in the MWA's early days, the Law Commission acknowledged that most married women were not the economic equals of their husbands.[64] As Juanita Frances, who was MWA President by the 1980s, told the press: 'Yes, things are better for us here in London perhaps, but throughout the country the status of married women, the women who are the housekeepers and who do very important work, has not changed enough'.[65] This was why Lord Simon's Matrimonial Homes (Co-ownership) Bill was so significant to the MWA cause. In 1980, the Association included in its Bulletin a letter Olive Stone had sent to the *Times* on the Bill, but which was never published. Stone asserted the Bill was important for two reasons that mirrored the MWA view:

1. Previous legislation has sought to regulate matrimonial property rights on relationship breakdown. This Bill is of 'far greater and more general significance'[66] because it would grant equal rights and responsibilities by law to wives and husbands during the *continuance* of their marriage.
2. The law would make a decided shift from treating the married woman in the family home as her husband's dependant, to recognising her as his equal co-owner, 'with the status, responsibilities and rights that only ownership can bestow'.[67]

Especially frustrating for the MWA at this time was the fact that support for the Matrimonial Homes (Co-ownership) Bill was being eclipsed by the Campaign for Justice in Divorce and its supporters. Stone's letter was not published in the *Times*, but an article by Ruth Deech was, titled 'Why Maintenance is a Bad Bargain for all Concerned'.[68] Like Stone, Deech was a legal academic in the early 1980s.[69] Yet as her article title suggests, her view was (and still is) very different from Stone's.[70] For Deech, advances in women's status compared with previous decades needed to be recognised in the courts, by either abolishing maintenance

---

[63] Law Commission, *Transfer of Money Between Spouses – the Married Women's Property Act 1964* (WP No 90, 1985) para 4.12, referring to OPCS, *Social Trends* 14 (1984) 74.

[64] ibid, para 4.12.

[65] Gorb, above n 32.

[66] MWA Bulletin, January–February 1980, 5MWA/8/1, TWL.

[67] ibid.

[68] R Deech, 'The Divorce Debate "80"' *Times* (14 February 1980) 8.

[69] She was a fellow and tutor of law at St Anne's College, Oxford.

[70] Now a peer in the House of Lords, Baroness Deech continues to recommend reform of maintenance after divorce.

or reducing it drastically.[71] The MWA rightly saw Deech's article on mainte-nance reform as giving legitimacy to the Campaign for Justice in Divorce, and described it as follows:

> It was a diatribe against division of assets at divorce. No sympathy nor advice was given for mothers having to provide sustenance to child or children bereft of house-keeping allowance. Presumably she must salvage what she can from the divorce and subsist on social security and supplementary benefits, such is the lowly status of women with children. How blind can some people become?[72]

Deech believed housework was a choice, dependency was reinforced by main-tenance and the only way women could achieve full citizenship was to be emancipated from the home. Deech's view was shared by other feminist groups at the time such as the Women's Liberation Campaign for Legal and Financial Independence, which criticised maintenance for reinforcing women's depend-ence upon men.[73] The views of MWA members were different; instead of arguing women should be released from housework and childcare, they contended that this work should be recognised in economic terms. The women in employment writing to the MWA were mainly employed in low-paid or part-time work but also undertook all the domestic labour. For the MWA, therefore, the route out of dependence for married women was not the abolition of maintenance; it was its obsolescence through equal partnership during marriage. Before this could be achieved, cutting financial support on divorce as Deech was advocating would only reinforce dependence in their view, by making women more economically vulnerable.

As a result, the MWA's experience in the 1980s was still not of liberated, economically independent wives. As MWA Secretary Joyce Nottage saw it, the problems of the older generation were more prominent than for younger couples:

> Of course, younger marriages are more equal, but people think everything has been put right by the women's movement, which just isn't true; the status of a wife is still not properly established. The women we get joining us now are divorced women looking for help.[74]

Contemporary research findings suggested that the amount of mainte-nance transferred to former wives was significantly lower than media reports suggested.[75] Far from husbands being the victims of alimony droning former wives, the effectiveness of the minimal loss principle in protecting the lesser-earning spouse was more dubious in practice. Summerskill had been ambivalent about the minimal loss principle at the time it was being introduced because

[71] R Deech, 'The Principles of Maintenance' [1977] *Family Law* 229.
[72] MWA Bulletin, January–February 1980, above, n 66.
[73] Stetson, above n 34, 250.
[74] Gorb, above n 32.
[75] J Eekelaar and M Maclean, *Maintenance after Divorce* (Clarendon Press 1986) 102.

her view was that husbands could not financially support two households, even if there was legislative principle saying they should. An unenforceable law is a 'bad law', she said.[76] In many ways, Summerskill was right. The minimal loss principle arguably *was* 'bad law' as most husbands could not support two households according to members of the judiciary,[77] and research published in 1977 indicated that the principle had been virtually abandoned.[78] According to John Eekelaar, very small numbers of ex-wives were being 'kept' by their former husbands. Where maintenance payments were made (usually when the woman was caring for a child of the marriage), these were not 'meal tickets', as they were normally too small to support the former wife without her also needing to rely on social security or low-paid work. Therefore, as Eekelaar put it, the Campaign for Justice in Divorce had 'concentrated on a largely illusory problem'.[79] The danger, then, was not the incidence of 'meal tickets for life' but the fear of them.

Yet denying this reality is a long-standing and effective political tactic, which research shows continues to skew perceptions on the law of financial remedies today.[80] Instead of ameliorating this by extending married women's property rights further, the protests surrounding the minimal loss principle were instead dominated by a *repudiation* of economic support and ongoing maintenance on relationship breakdown. This was what the MWA had to contend with in the final decade of its campaigns.[81]

B. Counteracting the Campaign

As the Campaign for Justice in Divorce was catching fire, the MWA appeared to be winding down. On 6 December 1981, an entry is made by Nora Bodley in the MWA's Rough Minute Book stating there would be no further meetings 'owing to the ill health of some of our members together with family commitments'.[82] Yet MWA bulletins after this date showed the group was preoccupied with one last push – to counteract the messages promulgated by Justice in Divorce.[83]

---

[76] HL Deb 8 November 1967, vol 286, col 427.
[77] See *Wachtel v Wachtel* [1973] Fam 72, 77 (Ormrod J). Lady Hale referred to the minimal loss principle as the 'equal misery' principle: Lady Hale, *Spider Woman: A Life* (Penguin 2021) 106.
[78] W Barrington Baker, *The Matrimonial Jurisdiction of Registrars* (SSRC Centre for Socio-Legal Studies, Wolfson College, Oxford 1977) cited in Douglas, above n 54, 118.
[79] J Eekelaar, *Family Law and Personal Life* (Oxford University Press 2007) 143.
[80] J Miles and E Hitchings, 'Financial remedy outcomes on divorce in England and Wales: Not a "meal ticket for life"' (2018) 31(2) *Australian Journal of Family Law* 43; Thompson, above n 61.
[81] NB: it is unclear when the MWA dissolved. Archival records stop in 1989 but the Association is mentioned in Hansard in 1996: see HL Deb 29 February 1996, vol 569, col 1625 (MWA President Baroness Gardner, in relation to the need for reform of pension sharing on divorce).
[82] MWA Rough Minute Book, 5MWA/3/3, TWL.
[83] eg, in the April–May 1981 MWA Bulletin (above n 40) the Association appealed: 'We urgently need more support from the public than we get – can anyone help?'.

MWA members were reportedly 'vociferous' in their condemnation of Leo Abse's 'meal ticket for life' debate. 'Saying a woman is not entitled to financial security after divorce', the MWA asserted, was 'making her redundant without redundancy money'.[84] The Association organised a joint lobby with other women's organisations,[85] and even attempted to 'think up a slogan to combat the meal ticket slogan'.[86] The best they appeared to come up with was that men had built for themselves their own kinds of meal ticket for life by creating structures favouring men's interests, such as 'golden handshakes and bonuses and other privileges'.[87] Though the Campaign for Justice in Divorce was supported by some feminist groups aligned with the Women's Liberation Movement,[88] the MWA saw it as being 'anti-feminist' and 'anti-women' and said it was a 'media campaign to benefit men and to displace women in divorce'.[89]

It is important to note that when countering the Campaign for Justice in Divorce, the MWA was *not* arguing that the minimal loss principle should be retained. In the Association's 1981 Bulletin it considered that the principle should be repealed, but that section 25 of the Matrimonial Causes Act 1973 should otherwise be left intact, so that when making financial awards on divorce, the court would simply be directed to consider all the circumstances of the case.[90] This would get rid of the principle's 'elusive objective' of placing the parties in the financial position in which they would have been if the marriage had not broken down and allow 'fresh principles' to be developed by the courts.[91]

As a result, the MWA's problem with Abse's campaign was not its objection to the minimal loss principle, but its calls to abolish maintenance entirely. Furthermore, the MWA was objecting to the argument underpinning the Campaign for Justice in Divorce – that women had now achieved equality with men. Writing at the time, Carol Smart observed: 'where law is concerned there is even sometimes a presumption that women receive *more favourable* treatment than men'.[92] This 'climate of opinion' pointed out by Smart, which appeared 'to exist independently of any real empirical evidence',[93] seemed to contribute to the notion that financial remedies law disproportionately favoured women at 'disgruntled husbands''[94] expense. As Douglas noted, the Law Commission was

---

[84] Gorb, above n 32.
[85] MWA Executive Committee Minutes, 25 March 1980, 5MWA/3/1, TWL.
[86] ibid.
[87] 'The Unspoken Deal', MWA Bulletin, January–February 1982, 5MWA/8/1, TWL.
[88] Stetson, above n 34, 250.
[89] MWA Bulletin, October–December 1982, 5MWA/8/1, TWL.
[90] This view was expressed in response to: Law Commission, *The Financial Consequences of Divorce: The Basic Policy, A Discussion Paper* (Law Com No 103, 1980).
[91] MWA Bulletin, January–March 1981, 5MWA/8/1, TWL.
[92] Smart, above n 55, 167 (emphasis added).
[93] ibid.
[94] Douglas, above n 54, 121.

persuaded to focus on husband's alleged hardship[95] and in 1980 recommended that the minimal loss principle should be repealed.[96]

This culminated in the Matrimonial and Family Proceedings Act 1984 which was supported by the Law Commission, Lord Chancellor Lord Hailsham, the Law Society and the Campaign for Justice in Divorce. It inserted section 25A into the Matrimonial Causes Act 1973, encouraging courts to make 'clean break' orders which would eliminate, or at least greatly reduce, the length of time for which husbands would be required to support financially their former wives after divorce. The consequences of the Act for women are perhaps summarised best by Smart, who argued it introduced: 'a firm principle into family law, namely that women must bear the full adverse consequences of their economic dependence on men – even though it is men who continue to accrue the benefits of that dependence'.[97] Indeed, at the time it was implemented a clean break was not a realistic option for spouses unable to become financially independent on divorce, and ever since the introduction of the clean break principle, research has consistently indicated that women take longer to recover financially from divorce than men do.[98] This is because, as Pamela Symes pointed out, a year after the Act's introduction, a coherent, clean break divorce would be unlikely unless the marital relationship had become 'a partnership of two economically independent individuals through the abolition of marital dependency and when the corresponding changes in the social infrastructure' were brought about.[99] And so, as the MWA had argued over the course of five decades, the goal of equal partnership *in* marriage needed to be attained if there was to be any hope of equality *after* divorce. In their view, the 1984 Act represented 'the first step to put back the clock on women's rights'.[100] Regrettably, the 'meal ticket for life' phenomenon continues to obscure this reality as debates about financial remedies on divorce continue today.[101]

CONCLUSION

In June 1977, the MWA's Bulletin led with the headline A SPECIAL ANNOUNCEMENT: PARTNERSHIP AT LAST?

> We take the opportunity to inform our MWA members and friends that two women Members of Parliament, one Conservative and one Labour, intend to present our

---

[95] ibid.

[96] Law Commission, *The Financial Consequences of Divorce: The Basic Policy, A Discussion Paper*, above n 90; Law Commission, *The Financial Consequences of Divorce* (Law Com No 112, 1981).

[97] Smart, above n 55, 242. For a contemporary summary of the impact of the clean break principle's introduction in 1984, see P Symes, 'Indissolubility and the clean break' (1985) 48 *MLR* 44.

[98] See, eg, H Fisher and H Low, 'Recovery from divorce: comparing high and low income couples' (2016) 30 *International Journal of Law, Policy and the Family* 338.

[99] Symes, above n 97, 60.

[100] MWA Bulletin, January–March 1983, 5MWA/8/1, TWL.

[101] See Thompson, above n 61.

Equal Partnership Bill at the next Parliament. Their names will be announced when we receive confirmation of their intention.[102]

This must have been an exciting time for the Association. Finally, regulation of property during marriage was a possibility, and the Law Commission was considering it too. Yet only three years later, the chances of such reform seemed remote. Instead, the MWA was having to defend the 'modicum of equality' so far achieved.[103]

Counteracting the Campaign for Justice in Divorce quashed the momentum it had been building for more progressive reform. The Association was placed in a position whereby members had to compromise their ambitions, instead following what Smart has described as 'a specific reformist framework' imposed by those in power, 'which simply does not allow for feminist alternatives'.[104] On this occasion, this meant either championing or denouncing the principle of maintenance: parameters which had been fixed by the more powerful Campaign for Justice in Divorce. While the MWA saw the pragmatic need for maintenance, it was not part of its plan for equal partnership in marriage. MWA members were clear that they wanted to shift the perception of married women in law from that of a dependant to a co-owner.[105] And in their view, equal partnership in marriage 'would eliminate the need for maintenance' anyway.[106] However, such nuance was not possible when opposing the Campaign for Justice in Divorce. The Association was compelled instead to put its own campaigns to one side in order to defend maintenance and challenge the notion that equality had already been achieved – something the MWA knew all too well was not the case.

[102] MWA Bulletin, June–July 1977, 5SPG/I/09, TWL.
[103] Frances, Letter from Juanita Frances to MPs, 25 January 1983, above n 60.
[104] Smart, above n 55, 223.
[105] MWA Bulletin, March–April 1980, 5MWA/8/1, TWL.
[106] MWA Executive Committee Minutes, 25 March 1980, above n 85.

10

A Subterranean Influence

I have not heard from [the MWA] for a long time, being swallowed up by earning a living, and it is time I thanked you again for the moral support you gave me in the past … I only wish more women would have the courage *to believe* in the possibility of changes in the future, but many are so shattered and afraid after things happen to them and their families. But no doubt your wisdom and experience is potently working behind the scenes and giving heart and courage to many.

MB Seaford, East Sussex, 1979[1]

Our daughters and grand-daughters may sit in this same room in the future, planning campaigns to bring about entirely new reforms and looking back upon our own efforts with a certain amount of amusement, because they will feel that the objectives we are so eager to achieve were so manifestly just that they should have been taken for granted.

Edith Summerskill's Retiring Address from the Married Women's Association, 1951[2]

Much of history is a story of elusive, intangible shifts in mores, in changes in public habits and opinions and attitudes which defy analysis … It may be that the successful campaign is successful only when it coincides with the imperceptible tide. But are the imperceptible processes of themselves ever successful in the practical course of progress? Can they ever manage without the campaign? I think not.

Lena Jeger, 1968[3]

INTRODUCTION

PARADOXICALLY, MARRIED WOMEN'S Association (MWA) members were characterised in the press as both 'fragile', 'little' women[4] and threatening man haters. In a 1969 *Daily Mail* article about the MWA, reporter Judy Innes suggests 'the name of the association is misleadingly innocuous. It conveys an image of tea parties, chat and good works'.[5] If Innes was correct, and the name 'Married Women's Association' meant the group was sometimes

---

[1] MWA Bulletin, October–December 1979, 5MWA/8/1, TWL.

[2] *Wife and Citizen*, May–June 1951, 7TBG/1/32, TWL.

[3] L Jeger, 'Power in Our Hands' in H Huskins-Hallinan (ed), *In Her Own Right* (Harrap 1968) 148.

[4] P Bewsher, 'Romance With C.O.D.' *Daily Mail* (10 September 1938) 7.

[5] J Innes, 'Battling Betty starts her new fight today' *Daily Mail* (17 April 1969) 10.

perceived as a social forum for married women to eat cake and donate to charity, the MWA's almost total absence from histories of family law is perhaps less surprising.

Yet in 1952, rather than being dismissed as innocuous, the MWA was looked upon in some newspaper reports as anti-man instead:

> 'The Married Women's Association!' How it rolls off the tongue like a peal of distant thunder! The sound of it is deep and ominous. Even the sight of the four words in type looks like the iron-maw of a fifteen inch gun – menacing, resolute, implacable. It conjures up the spectacle of a composite woman. A fierce now-no-nonsense-from-you-my-man character who has something of the mental acerbity of Lady Astor combined with the verbal muscularity of Mrs Braddock.[6]

Thus, when depicted as feminists during the 1950s the Association is described in absurd, hyperbolic, highly emotive terms. But when juxtaposed against the emerging Women's Liberation Movement a decade and a half later, the Association is portrayed as bland and ineffective. This book has demonstrated that the MWA was neither. As a non-party group, emphasising the language of equality and welcoming men into its fold,[7] the MWA was clearly attempting to *avoid* the men-versus-women-narrative, stating it was 'most definitely a MAN *and* WOMAN group and as such was an outstanding example of full partnership'.[8] Members also understood that successful legislative reform would hinge upon support from those in power, who were nearly all male. The issue of equality in marriage therefore needed to be seen as an issue of justice for *everyone*. And so, the challenge for the MWA was not to stop individual controlling and abusive behaviour in marriage; it was to find a way of reforming structures through legislation, so that the law could limit the damage these individuals could do. This suggests the Association was not inefficient. It was pragmatic.

Legislation was needed as the law had failed married women. The Married Women's Property Act (MWPA) 1882 was a crucial marker of equality, because by introducing the doctrine of separate property, married women could retain control over their own property instead of losing everything to their husbands. But despite the rhetoric of equality underpinning it, this Act was not a panacea. In the context of family life, treating men and women as equal in a way that assumed they were *the same* disadvantaged women. Strict application of the separate property doctrine served to disregard the work in the home that men typically did not do, while upholding protection of property that women typically did not have. This was not the equal partnership in marriage the MWA sought.

---

[6] Cassandra, 'Les Girls' *Daily Mirror* (3 April 1952) 6.

[7] This becomes clear when studying minutes of MWA meetings. For example, it is noted at one meeting in 1980 that Mr Wilson is the only gentleman in attendance but is 'of course a regular attender with his wife': MWA Annual General Meeting Minutes, 30 April 1980, 5MWA/3/1, TWL.

[8] MWA Newsletter, April 1954, 7TBG/1/32, TWL.

This book has focused on how the MWA sought to address these problems through reform of marriage law. In this final chapter, the questions asked at the beginning are revisited: How did the MWA influence family law? And, what can be learned from the MWA's strategies as family law reformers?

I. THE MWA'S INFLUENCE UPON FAMILY LAW

Conceptually, the MWA broke new ground in its demands for marriage reform. It used 'new feminist' ideas propounded by Eleanor Rathbone to call attention to structural inequalities in marriage. In demanding a 'new marriage law' – which would provide spouses with rights in their partners' property during marriage – it was politicising the family sphere and breaking down the barriers between public and private. By achieving legal and economic equality inside the home, so the argument went, women would be better equipped to pursue equality also in the public sphere. And, by representing housewives in a legal setting, the MWA was mounting the first significant challenge against the legal status of married women since the MWPA 1882. As MWA founder Juanita Frances put it: 'I'm not asking for protection [for married women], I'm asking for legal rights in hard cash'.[9] In the context of family law, this was radical and had huge significance.

This made strategic sense given the broader socio-political context, whereby the deeply entrenched roles of housewife and breadwinner represented the archetypal marriage of the 1940s and 1950s. By strengthening the domestic position of married women as different but of equal value to the breadwinning husband, the MWA could couch radical property reform in relatively conservative terms that did not threaten the conventional marriage contract of the day. As Dorothy Stetson has pointed out, feminists have been most effective in reforming family law in the twentieth century when they have adopted this approach, arguing for role equity and not for role change.[10] However, in valuing housewives' work and seeking to fortify the marital partnership, the Association also sometimes failed to recognise that the institution of marriage was responsible for married women's economic vulnerability and marginalisation from public life. Unlike the feminists of the Women's Liberation Movement from the 1960s and beyond, they did not seek to tear down the sex-segregated spheres of housewife and breadwinner.

In spite of this, the MWA's housewife-centred approach drew out central tensions of family law. Rather than dealing with how married women can move away from gendered roles like childcare to do the same work as men, the MWA placed focus on the fact that in the 1940s and 1950s, *this was the work*

[9] From a leaflet by the Humanist lobby, as quoted in BH Lee, *Divorce Law Reform in England* (Peter Owen 1974) 201.
[10] D Stetson, *A Woman's Issue: The Politics of Family Law Reform in England* (Oxford University Press 1982) 230.

married women were doing. And so, without properly valuing care, housewives' economic vulnerability would be intensified. As the MWA saw it, married women's work was not valued. When the Association formed, married women had no rights over their husband's separate property, little opportunity to earn money outside the home, and depended on their spouse for housekeeping allowance. As we saw in chapter two, while the Beveridge report and the beginnings of the welfare state alongside policy-based assertions of housewives' crucial contribution to society were welcome, they also bolstered the notion that the married woman's place was in the home, not in the political arena. But MWA members were often personally ambivalent about the notion of a marriage as a career,[11] and it is particularly notable that several of the leaders were high-status professional women.[12] Members emphasised the value of housewives' labour in pursuit of marriage as an equal partnership, often while campaigning within other women's organisations for equal pay and better rights *outside* the home too.[13] These MWA efforts, though relatively arcane within family law history, were vital for their time, and add important context to current debates too. Even today, the question of how to value unpaid care and domestic work in the family home remains at the forefront of family law reform.[14] Unpaid caregiving continues to be both ubiquitous and invisible.[15]

A. Small Yet Powerful

> Results have not been commensurate with effort and argument. But, as a pressure group, we must remind ourselves that far-reaching reforms have invariably had their beginnings in the ardent beliefs of a dedicated progressive few.[16]

The MWA was distinctive from other women's organisations of the mid-twentieth century as it took reform of family property law as its chief focus. When the MWA was at its largest in the 1940s, it had only 2,000 members; tiny in comparison with other contemporary women's organisations such as the Women's Cooperative Guild, which had nearly 60,000 members in the early 1950s.[17] With gaps in membership records, it is not possible to know

[11] See, eg, MWA members' opinions as expressed in O Campbell, *The Feminine Point of View* (Williams & Norgate Ltd 1952).
[12] As ch 3 outlined, several leading MWA members were also involved in campaigns for equal pay and the women's peace movement.
[13] Several MWA members were also involved in organisations such as Women for Westminster and Equal Rights International.
[14] See, eg, G Douglas, *Obligation and Commitment in Family Law* (Hart Publishing 2018); J Miles and E Hitchings, 'Financial remedy outcomes on divorce in England and Wales: Not a "meal ticket for life"' (2018) 31(2) *Australian Journal of Family Law* 43.
[15] J Conaghan, 'Introduction' (2007) 58 *Northern Ireland Legal Quarterly* 245, 245.
[16] MWA Annual General Report, May 1963, 5MWA/3/1, TWL.
[17] C Beaumont, 'What *Do* Women Want? Housewives' Associations, Activism and Changing Representations of Women in the 1950s' (2017) 26 *Women's History Review* 147, 150.

how far MWA membership extended beyond its core leadership in later years. Frequent complaints about numbers and resources suggest members wanted the Association to be bigger and richer; however, its membership boasted some powerful women. Considering its size it is extraordinary how much the Association achieved, and this was also observed by MWA members themselves.[18] As we saw in chapter seven, the Maintenance Orders Act 1958, which enabled maintenance to be deducted from the defaulting spouse's pay packet, was prompted by an MWA campaign and Bill drafted by MWA members. Then, the Married Women's Property Act (MWPA) 1964, which gave wives a one-half share in housekeeping savings, represented the first and only statute that allocates rights in property *during* marriage. As the default in English law is still separate property ownership during marriage today, this 1964 Act continues to be an anomaly. It was a stepping stone towards the MWA's ultimate ambition of equal sharing during marriage; a destination that was never reached.

It is easy to overlook these legislative developments when they are described as 'piecemeal'. This is because they address only a tiny aspect of married women's grievances, and in hindsight, appear neither radical nor controversial. Yet as Rebecca Probert has aptly put it, the history of family law shows us that 'today's controversies are tomorrow's orthodoxies'.[19] On the one hand, the MWA's campaign to reform the enforcement of maintenance payments did not secure any additional property rights for married women – it was simply reform facilitating access to funds to which they were already entitled. On the other hand, *any* reform threatening to interfere with private property rights is arguably controversial. To reiterate Olive Stone's observation recounted in chapter nine, 'property is the holy of holies'.[20] And in this case, reform attaching maintenance obligations to wages faced staunch opposition from trade unionists, for it threatened the sanctity of the pay cheque.

Analysing the overall impact of the MWA is more complex. As suggested throughout this book, this analysis requires an understanding of how law changes, and how the MWA understood it to change. The law does not operate 'in linear or progressive ways', as Russell Sandberg has pointed out; instead, the 'ebb and flow of legal ideas' need to be explored.[21] This can be seen throughout the history of the MWA. During most of the time the MWA was active, there were few major legislative reforms, but there had been a major shift in *perspective* about women's legal status in marriage. As the MWA observed in 1964, the language of partnership had slipped into the vocabulary, which they saw

---

[18] See, eg, MWA Secretary's Report 1956–57, 7TBG/1/31, TWL, where the MWA regarded its achievements as 'very great' for a 'comparatively small association'.

[19] R Probert, 'The History of 20th-Century Family Law' (2005) 25 *Oxford Journal of Legal Studies* 169, 179.

[20] 5CMW/B/22, TWL.

[21] R Sandberg, *Subversive Legal History* (Routledge 2021) 133.

themselves as having contributed to: 'we have created by propaganda and agitation a public opinion that marriage is a partnership'.[22]

To appreciate the importance of the MWA, therefore, we need to change
our understanding of what success in the context of law reform looks like. For
failures can be precursors to successes. Orthodox accounts of law reform record
the bills that have passed, and the cases that have been won, but the MWA
viewed their own success in different terms. In one Executive Committee report,
they described their work as being more notable for its 'ricochets' than its
'bulls'-eyes'.[23] The 'bulls'-eyes' are marked clearly by a new statute or precedent.
The ricochets are the ostensible failures, that did in fact leave their mark. The
MWA did not have many of the former to point to, noting instead: 'Experience
has taught us not to expect the bulls'-eyes, but to view with satisfaction such
ricochets as have furthered our cause'.[24] This perspective is vital when understanding feminist impact upon law reform. As MWA Chairman Dora Russell
argued, 'you can't just look at women's progress in terms of laws and Acts'.
Instead, 'you have to look at the area of relationships where women have been
influential, and there you will see that there have been enormous changes'.[25] The
MWA's Bill for equal partnership in marriage is a clear example of this.

B. A Bill for Equal Partnership in Marriage

The MWA's Bill, in its various drafts, sought to implement what the Law
Commission referred to more broadly as a 'genuine law of family property'.[26]
This was a framework of property ownership that applied *during* marriage,
rather than on separation. As chapter four explained, this Bill was repeatedly
redrafted and renamed throughout the 1940s, 1950s, 1960s and 1970s, and was
never sponsored in Parliament. But its influence can be traced in a few important
developments.

The first is Edward Bishop's Matrimonial Property Bill in 1969, a Private
Member's Bill that was explored more fully in chapter eight. It was the closest
England and Wales came to introducing some form of community of property.
As Stephen Cretney stated, it was a 'significant historical landmark' as the last
Bill on this issue 'ever to be fully debated in either House of Parliament'.[27] To
be clear, the MWA did not seek a community of property regime, and its Bill for
equal partnership in marriage would instead have facilitated pooling of certain

---

[22] MWA Annual General Report, 10 June 1964, 5MWA/3/1, TWL.

[23] Quoting VS Pritchett 'the long drawn out campaign for emancipation of women has been
more noticeable for its ricochets than its bulls' eyes': MWA Annual General Meeting, 11 May 1972,
Secretary's Report for year ended 30 April 1972, 5MWA/3/1, TWL.

[24] ibid.

[25] D Spender, *There's Always Been a Women's Movement This Century* (Harper Collins 1983) 104.

[26] Law Commission, *Family Property Law* (WP No 42, 1971) para 0.2.

[27] S Cretney, *Family Law in the Twentieth Century* (Oxford University Press 2003) 136.

assets such as income. But an MWA draft Bill titled the Matrimonial Property Bill inspired the Bishop Bill of the same name,[28] which subsequently leveraged a deal made between Bishop and the government. In return for the Bishop Bill's withdrawal, the government agreed to support a Bill drafted by the Law Commission reforming the financial consequences of divorce, and by extension, married women's property rights. As a result, the Bishop Bill is an overlooked, yet significant part of family law history. It helped delay the Divorce Reform Act 1969 so that economic inequalities between husband and wife on relationship breakdown could be addressed. And it brought the debate about how to value women's work in the home to the House of Commons. This debate in the Commons appears to have been taken into account by the Law Commission when preparing what became the Matrimonial Proceedings and Property Act 1970.[29] As we have seen, this reform provided for property redistribution on divorce that could account for the contributions made by spouses through looking after the home or caring for the family, and continues to underpin the law of financial remedies in England and Wales today.[30] The influence of the Bill is especially significant given that the Law Commission had originally planned to save its recommendations with respect to property division for a later report.[31] It is possible, therefore, to draw a connection between the pressure exerted by those seeking reform of married women's property rights, the MWA's draft Bill, the Bishop Bill and the radical reform of financial remedies in the 1970s.

The MWA's calls for equal partnership through joint ownership during marriage also helped ignite conversations about reform during the 1970s and 1980s. As we have seen in chapter nine, the MWA worked with Lord Simon and supported his 1980 Matrimonial Homes (Co-ownership) Bill, which was quashed in Parliament almost entirely by a lobby of MPs concerned about men's rights.[32] The spirit of the MWPA 1964 also provided a launchpad for further debate. For example, in the Law Commission's investigation into repealing the 1964 Act, broader questions were raised about a more holistic approach to family property.[33] While it would be a blatant oversimplification to attribute the work of the Law Commission to the campaigns of the MWA, failing to recognise MWA influence entirely – as many accounts of family law history have – would be equally wrong. Rather, the MWA undeniably played a significant part.

---

[28] As detailed further in ch 8. The MWA draft Bill sought to implement some, not all, of the provisions within the Association's more ambitious Bill for Equal Partnership.

[29] BC3/401, TNA; Stetson, above n 10, 202. Stetson also notes the influence of the concept of family assets developing in the courts in the late 1960s.

[30] s 5(1)(f) Matrimonial Proceedings and Property Act 1970 and s 25(2)(f) of the consolidating Matrimonial Causes Act 1973 1973.

[31] Stetson, above n 10, 202.

[32] MWA Bulletin, April–May 1981, 5MWA/8/1, TWL.

[33] Law Commission, *Transfer of Money Between Spouses – the Married Women's Property Act 1964* (WP No 90, 1985); Law Commission, *Family Law: Matrimonial Property* (Law Com No 175, 1988).

The MWA's chronicle as family law reformers *is* perhaps best described in their own words as a series of 'ricochets', the impact of which can be seen by taking a feminist legal historical approach. Looking more closely at these ricochets and failed attempts at reform uncovers further evidence in support of the claims made in chapter one – specifically that law is not a neutral arbiter, progress does not happen naturally and institutions are not solely responsible for change. And this has implications for family law reform today, as will be shown in the remainder of this chapter.

II. LESSONS FROM FAMILY LAW REFORMERS

Clear-cut success stories of reform might not be the most helpful for those seeking to reform law now. As numerous commentators have argued, the Bill that passes often depends upon multiple factors lining up perfectly, many of which are completely outside both the reformers' and legislators' control.[34] Fluctuations in public interest, the political zeitgeist and judicial reasoning are all important. It might, therefore, seem pointless to consider what can be learned about family law reform tactics, given that these external factors can influence the success or failure of any given campaign. Nevertheless, the experiences of the MWA suggest that some strategies are more effective than others in swaying public, political and judicial opinion. Identifying these strategies – both effective and ineffective – produces a better understanding of the MWA's struggle and of the broader ambivalence feminists throughout history have experienced when using law as a tool to further women's emancipation. While turning to the law to advance their goal of equal partnership in marriage, the MWA could also see that the law itself is deeply implicated in furthering the inequalities the Association struggled against.[35] This section first looks to the benefits and pitfalls with feminist engagement with law reform, followed by exploration of whether the MWA's quest to value women's work in the home is still relevant today.

A. Five Findings

i. *The Iconic Case*

At the MWA's Annual General Meeting following Edith Summerskill's death in 1980, Juanita Frances – then President of the MWA – retold the story of

---

[34] M Maclean and J Kurczewski, *Making Family Law* (Hart Publishing 2011) 108.
[35] Indeed, Carol Smart and Rosemary Auchmuty have both argued in favour of *non*-legal methods when bringing about women's emancipation in the marriage context: C Smart, *Feminism and the Power of Law* (Routledge 1989); R Auchmuty, 'Law and the power of feminism: How marriage lost its power to oppress women' (2012) 20 *Feminist Legal Studies* 71.

Dorothy Blackwell.[36] Of all the cases the MWA had funded or held watching briefs for, the 1943 case of *Blackwell v Blackwell*[37] was the one the members returned to most often. But as we saw in chapter five, this case did not have a successful outcome for Dorothy Blackwell, who had her £103 savings confiscated because the court held they were derived from housekeeping savings. In 1943, housekeeping savings belonged entirely to the husband.

So, what does Dorothy Blackwell's unsuccessful appeal, which was funded by the MWA, have to do with reform? It showed the MWA that individual stories have power. Before the *Blackwell* case, the MWA had been trying to raise awareness about the need for reform with limited success. But the press attention given to Dorothy Blackwell brought the injustice of the law home to the public in a way that MWA members' speeches could not. Her loss highlighted the law's failure to protect women when marriage went wrong.

Many married women did not know that they had no legal rights to the housekeeping money they used to run the family home. They wrote to the MWA,[38] evidently appalled to learn of the poverty Dorothy Blackwell had been thrust into after years of taking in lodgers, which in turn helped pay off the mortgage on the family home – a home she had no rights in. This helped create public pressure for reform. It was the MWA's most effective propaganda, Vice President Teresa Billington-Greig said.[39]

However, one of the pitfalls of the iconic case is that it can sometimes obscure the campaigners' demands for reform. The MWA was clear that the significance of *Blackwell* extended far beyond the specific issue of housekeeping savings. As the Blackwells were not legally separated or divorced, Dorothy Blackwell was paid no maintenance by her husband John. This highlighted the need to reform married women's property rights *during* marriage. But a campaign to give wives a right to housekeeping savings *without* this broader reform is simpler and less controversial. So, the iconic case eventually helped Edith Summerskill reform housekeeping savings by getting the MWPA 1964 through Parliament (20 years after *Blackwell*), but it did not persuade Parliament to go any further.

This helps demonstrate why historically, feminists might be frustrated, despairing or even ambivalent about the common law.[40] Change is slow, change is incremental and change often depends upon parliamentary intervention. But the iconic case also shows how these frustrations can be used constructively. *Blackwell* reinforced the conviction that something needed to be done as it exposed the law's failure to deal with changing economic conditions and the inequality this created in marriage. And case law has shaped modern family law in similar ways. The press attention given to Tini Owens, the wife who was

---

[36] MWA Annual General Meeting Minutes, 30 April 1980, 5MWA/3/1, TWL.
[37] [1943] 2 All ER 579.
[38] MWA Annual Report, March 1944, 7TBG/1/32, TWL.
[39] Draft of Teresa Billington-Greig speech, 1958, 7TBG/1/31, TWL.
[40] J Conaghan, *Law and Gender* (Oxford University Press 2013) 5.

denied a divorce from her husband in the 2018 Supreme Court case of *Owens v Owens*,[41] undoubtedly helped the case for no fault divorce pursuant to the Divorce, Dissolution and Separation Act 2020. *Steinfeld and Keidan*, the different sex couple who argued in the Supreme Court for the right to formalise their relationship by civil partnership instead of marriage,[42] were influential in the amendment of the Civil Partnership Act in 2019, enabling equal civil partnerships.

However, iconic cases often have a sell-by date, and when it comes to noteworthy family law judgments, Dorothy Blackwell may share more in common with Valerie Burns than others. She was the plaintiff in *Burns v Burns*, the famous 1984 case that family law students still study as an example of the need to reform the law applicable to unmarried cohabitants.[43] Fewer women are represented today by Valerie Burns, the unmarried 'wife' of 19 years left penniless and denied a share in the family home because of the law's lack of protection for cohabitants on relationship breakdown.[44] Similarly, when the MWA was still recounting *Blackwell v Blackwell* in the 1980s, it was no longer possible to argue that the majority of women were *just like* Dorothy Blackwell in the 1940s, as many more married women worked and fewer were completely economically dependent on their husbands. Circumstances and lifestyles change, which can turn an individual story from decades earlier into an anachronism.

This is the problem with iconic cases. Sometimes, they can help the case for reform. But the power of the iconic case may diminish over time, even if the need for reform might still be present.

ii. The Omnibus Bill

The MWA's ultimate objective was a new marriage law that would reform married women's legal status comprehensively. Strategically, members thought it was important for their Bill to reform several aspects at once, from rights in the home and income as well as rights to know their spouses' finances and to share in housekeeping savings. The reason for this was summarised by MWA member Margery Nicholson in 1949: 'Any Bill on Marriage will probably be the last for many years, so that all interested people are naturally anxious that it should be the best and most comprehensive of its kind'.[45] In other words, reform of women's legal status is so unusual, that when the opportunity arises it should be used to achieve the best reform possible.

---

[41] [2018] UKSC 41.

[42] *R (on the application of Steinfeld and Keidan) v Secretary of State for the International Development (in substitution for the Home Secretary and the Education Secretary)* [2018] UKSC 32.

[43] [1984] Ch 317.

[44] See, eg, J Mee, 'Burns v Burns: The Villain of the Piece?' in R Probert, J Herring and S Gilmore (eds), *Landmark Cases In Family Law* (Hart Publishing 2011).

[45] M Nicholson, 'Deputation to House of Commons', *Wife and Citizen*, February 1949, 7TBG/1/32, TWL.

One of the reasons this was so difficult was, as Edith Summerskill once noted rather drily, that neither women nor women's organisations were represented in Parliament in great numbers.[46] The Royal Commission in the 1950s, the Law Commission in 1960s and the courts at this time were almost entirely male too.[47] Therefore, drawing attention to issues affecting women was challenging. This was not helped by the fact that according to historian Martin Pugh, even female MPs often neglected to press a distinctive women's agenda in Parliament for fear of being side-lined in other debates.[48] So, once the MWA had the attention of policymakers and politicians, why not propose reform that was ambitious or even revolutionary, when it could be the Association's only chance to be heard?

The 'omnibus Bill', as we saw in chapter seven, was an example of such ambitious reform covering several issues. Teresa Billington-Greig considered the omnibus Bill to be 'a common sense method of speedy progress'.[49] Yet as the MWA was to learn, this strategy – for them – was 'doomed to fail'.[50] The Women's Disabilities Bill, a Private Member's Bill summarised in chapter seven, was criticised heavily when it was brought to Parliament in 1951 and 1952. It provided for reform of maintenance, housekeeping savings, rights to a reasonable income during marriage, and rights in the family home on separation, at a time when Lord Denning was saying publicly that equality between spouses had been achieved and the wife was the 'spoilt darling of the law'.[51] In the Commons, several MPs were outraged about the privileged position in which these reforms would purportedly place married women, to the disadvantage of men.

This experience underscored the obstacles for feminists when negotiating law reform. Streamlined, comprehensive reform required ambitious change, but as chapters six and seven argued, this was easily dismissed by politicians and policymakers as impractical, as 'going too far', or as seeking to address problems that were insurmountable. This raises the question of whether family law reform – especially when it claims to advance the status of women – must be cloaked in conservative terms of bolstering the institution of marriage.

Is the omnibus Bill always doomed to fail? The experiences of the MWA suggest that piecemeal reform is easier to achieve, and that although reform through the Private Member's Bill procedure is unpredictable, dependent on the vagaries of Parliament and easily defeated, it *is* possible for this procedure to succeed when the issues being addressed are narrowly circumscribed. Yet by the late 1970s, MWA members did not see this working for its more transformative and ambitious equal partnership reform. In a private letter to

---

[46] HL Deb 10 July 1969, vol 303, col 1295.

[47] Brenda Hale became first female Law Commissioner in 1984, and Elizabeth Lane, the first female judge, was appointed to the County Court in 1962.

[48] M Pugh, *Women and the Women's Movement in Britain since 1914*, 3rd edn (Palgrave 2015) 93 and 162.

[49] Draft of Teresa Billington-Greig speech, 1958, above n 39.

[50] ibid.

[51] Anon, 'Cost Of Sex Equality' *Times* (13 May 1950) 3.

her daughter, May Carroll confided 'I doubt if it will ever be possible to get our Equal Partnership Bill passed'.[52] This is not to say revolutionary reform is impossible for family law. The Children Act 1989 is a notable, yet rare example of this. As the Lord Chancellor put it at the time, the Children Act was 'the most comprehensive and far-reaching reform of child law which has come before Parliament in *living memory*'.[53] From this perspective, it is arguably unsurprising that the MWA never got its radical 'new marriage law'.

iii. Resisting Reform

Once MWA members succeeded in extending legal protection for married women, resistance and retaliation was to be expected. It is well documented by feminist historians that when reform threatens existing power structures, there will be push back from those in power. But could resistance also be a reform strategy for women's organisations? As we saw in chapters eight and nine, this again has benefits and pitfalls. The MWA was one of several women's organisations that opposed the Divorce Reform Act 1969 on the grounds that the financial consequences had not yet been reformed. The benefits of this were that the plight of the women the MWA represented was made more visible in Parliament, especially as a result of Summerskill's staunch opposition to divorce reform in the House of Lords. This resistance also made it possible for family law reform to be redefined in feminist terms. Built into the 1970 reforms was explicit acknowledgement of the contributions made to the welfare of the family by looking after the home or caring for the family.[54] This was an important step forward for the MWA, even if the property consequences of marriage had not been reformed.

Resistance as a reform strategy can be empowering if it challenges and questions popular opinion in a way that opens up a forum for debate. But it can also mean that campaigners are forced to shift their own arguments to contribute to current debates. In the context of the Divorce Reform Act 1969, the MWA had to argue for the need to change the financial consequences of divorce, taking focus away from its ultimate goal of marriage reform. Thus, while this strategy can be effective it can also force feminists to reframe their demands to fit with the government's agenda.

iv. The Problem with Maintenance

As chapter nine explored, the MWA in the 1980s was swept into a position where members felt they had to defend the merits of maintenance. This was because the reactionary Campaign for Justice in Divorce sought to abolish maintenance,

---

[52] Letter from family's private collection, 13 November 1978.
[53] HL Deb 6 December 1988, vol 502, col 488 (emphasis added).
[54] s 5(1)(f) Matrimonial Proceedings and Property Act 1970; s 25(2)(f) of the consolidating Matrimonial Causes Act 1973.

capturing the attention and support of the press and public with its slogan that married women got a 'meal ticket for life'. Instead of the MWA pursuing its own agenda, it was forced into a defensive stance against the Justice in Divorce's claim that the property consequences of divorce were unfair to men, not women.

The problem with defending maintenance, however, was that it was viewed by many MWA members as a necessary evil rather than a laudable aim. This is because rather like the 'wages for wives' debate outlined in chapters four and six, the MWA was keen for joint ownership of property to make married women financially independent in marriage. Payment of a wage for housework during marriage, or payment of maintenance after divorce, were expedient means of valuing work in the home when there was no pooling of income or other resources. But it made women dependent upon men. And so, the MWA sought for the *need* for maintenance to be abolished by introducing its demands for equal partnership.

This need had not and has not been abolished. But having to assert repeatedly the importance of maintenance arguably did a disservice to the MWA's message of equal partnership in marriage. As Carol Smart put it, the question of whether individual husbands should support their ex-wives after divorce 'does not allow for a feminist answer'[55] within the existing legal framework. The MWA was forced to argue in favour of wives' economic dependence through – in Juanita Frances' words – 'damned maintenance',[56] because in many marriages, it was the only way to ensure their financial protection.

Although in many ways the tenor of feminist debates over financial provision on relationship breakdown has changed, there are still problems when it comes to maintenance. Baroness Deech, who supported the Campaign for Justice in Divorce in the 1980s, is now claiming that periodical payments for maintenance should be limited to a period of no longer than five years.[57] Yet research shows women's recovery rates on divorce are not equal to men's, and cuts to these payments would harm women disproportionately.[58] Unless an alternative means of ameliorating these inequalities can be found, arguing against Deech's proposed reform could once again force feminists into the position of defending maintenance instead of pursuing new feminist policy alternatives.

v. Repetition

One of Edith Summerskill's most quoted observations is from a speech she gave to the MWA in 1960: 'Nagging is the repetition of unpalatable truths'.[59] For the

[55] C Smart, *The Ties That Bind* (Routledge 1984) 223.

[56] Lee, above n 9.

[57] Divorce (Financial Provision) Bill 2021–22.

[58] H Fisher and H Low, 'Recovery from divorce: comparing high and low income couples' (2016) 30 *International Journal of Law, Policy and the Family* 338.

[59] Speech to the Married Women's Association, House of Commons, 14 July 1960. *Oxford Essential Quotations* 4th edn, available at: https://www.oxfordreference.com/view/10.1093/acref/9780191826719.001.0001/q-oro-ed4-00010531.

MWA, it was repetition of the truth of women's domestic and caregiving labour in the home having value – unpalatable, perhaps, to husbands with property to protect. As Summerskill put it in the House of Lords:

> Although it is not she who has brought in the wages, she has in fact enabled her husband to earn wages or a salary. It is she who has cooked, worked and brought up the children, having borne them in the first place; but after fifteen or twenty years of marriage she has no nest egg.[60]

MWA members were prepared to repeat this message decade after decade on deputations to policymakers, Attorneys General and Lord Chancellors. Their energy in doing so might have been spurred on by the letters the Association was receiving. Again and again, married women wrote to the MWA about their financial destitution: deserted by their husbands and left with no savings and no home. And little, if any, recourse to law.[61]

The MWA's strategy of persistence and repetition was familiar to some members of the Association who had been involved with multiple organisations within the women's movement. Repetition could be effective, but it could also wear campaigners out. MWA President Vera Brittain, for example, admitted that the 'fight for acknowledgment' ultimately bored rather than enthralled her. She continued to agitate, she said, 'only because she desires to abolish the need for agitation'.[62]

Not only is repetition wearing; it is difficult to produce clear evidence that it was an effective strategy for the MWA. They argued it was. By the late 1960s, the MWA claimed issues they had discussed *ad nauseam*[63] were beginning to catch fire. However, the complexity of law reform makes it difficult to show a direct link between the MWA's repetition and the shift towards family law explicitly valuing domestic contributions to marriage.

This strategy arguably only becomes visible when law reform is viewed through the lens of feminist legal history. By focusing on the role of feminist campaigners in law, it becomes clear that the law has been sclerotic when it comes to improving women's legal status. This book has shown the MWPA 1964 to be an example of this. After 20 years of campaigning, the substantive part of the Act reforming ownership of housekeeping savings was only 72 words long. And this Act was not the end of the story. MWA member Hazel Holt wrote to the *Financial Times* in 1977[64] stating that the MWA 'is constantly brought into contact with cases of the most incredible hardship caused by the failure

---

[60] HL Deb 13 October 1969, vol 304, col 1271.

[61] Particularly before the Matrimonial Homes Act 1967, as before this Act married women had no right to stay in the home.

[62] V Brittain, 'Why Feminism Lives' in P Barry and A Bishop (eds), *Testaments of a Generation: The Journalism of Brittain and Winifried Holtby* (Virago Press Ltd 1985) cited in C Blackford, 'Ideas, Structures and Practices of Feminism 1939–64 (PhD thesis, University of East London 1996) 43.

[63] As Summerskill put it, above n 60.

[64] MWA Bulletin, June–July 1977, 5SPG/I/09, TWL.

of some husbands to provide their wives and families with sufficient [house-keeping] money'.[65] This shows that reform giving married women a share in housekeeping savings did not mean much if husbands did not allocate sufficient money for this purpose. Again, the pitfalls with legislative reform are evident; often it cannot be used to correct inequality in marriage, even when feminists are successful in influencing change.

When legal change is inexorably slow, there is also a risk the campaign becomes redundant over time, especially when it relates to a specific issue such as housekeeping savings.[66] As more married women entered paid employment, the phenomenon of housekeeping money died out. Indeed, many students of family law today have never heard the term 'housekeeping money'. Then again, the MWA's repetition of its broader goal of equal partnership in marriage continues to resonate today, albeit in a different context, as we shall see in the following section.

III. THE RELEVANCE OF THE MWA'S CAMPAIGNS TODAY

The MWA's attempts to translate equality into a distinctive legal framework give us interesting insights into marriage law reform both then and now. By focusing on the idea of equality in difference and by refusing to use men as yard-sticks, the MWA was emphasising questions over how to value unpaid care and domestic labour in the home. These questions mattered to the wife who had no separate income. But what about now – when the 1950s housewife is no longer representative?

For many reasons, the position of the spouse doing most of the unpaid work in the home is very different today. Indeed, in *Child and Family Law Quarterly*'s twenty-fifth anniversary issue in 2014, Carol Smart compared revisiting family law reform in the 1970s and 1980s to travelling through time to a past that was akin to a foreign country, as perspectives about women and their role within marriage have changed so much.[67] Yet the broader problems of inequality still exist today, albeit in a different social context. There is *still* a gulf in financial outcomes for spouses on divorce which is divided along gender lines.[68] The issue of pension provision *still* creates and reinforces significant financial inequalities

---

[65] ibid.

[66] The Law Commission discussed whether the relatively specific issue addressed by the MWPA 1964 no longer existed 'to any extent sufficient to justify amending legislation' as the position of women had changed. The Commission concluded it had been justified in principle as many married women were not in employment in the 1960s and of those who were, employment was part-time and women's average earnings were 74% of mens: Law Commission, *Transfer of Money Between Spouses*, above n 33, para 4.12.

[67] C Smart, 'Law and Family Life: Insights from 25 Years of Empirical Research' (2014) 26(1) *Child and Family Law Quarterly* 14, 15, quoting LP Hartley, *The Go Between* (Hamish Hamilton 1963), the first line of which is: 'The past is a foreign country; they do things differently there'.

[68] See, eg, Fisher and Low, above n 58.

between spouses.[69] Statistics show that women are *still* left significantly poorer than men when their marriage has broken down.[70] Mothers are *still* more likely to make career sacrifices than fathers. Dismissing these statistics as simply reflecting women's 'choice' becomes difficult when the price of childcare continues to rise to the extent that employment often reaps no financial gain.[71] This is a stark reminder that the 'vast army of the great unpaid'[72] is not a relic confined to the era of the MWA. Modern marriage still has echoes of the past; the message that women work for free inside the home endures.

There are other inequalities that did not arise when the MWA was active. For example, home-working has taken on new meaning since 2020. The boundaries between public and private are drawn in new ways. And the definition of women's work in the home is no longer limited to housework. Indeed, recent data suggests inequalities have worsened during the Covid-19 pandemic and have taken a tremendous toll on women with families – married *and* unmarried.[73]

Taking all this into account, while it is no longer seen as outlandish to demand equality between husband and wife as it was when advocated by the MWA in the 1940s and 1950s, it is quite another thing to achieve substantively. The story of the MWA is one way to understand why this is the case. Exploring how the Association furthered the idea of equal partnership helps show why addressing pervasive gendered inequalities within marriage continues to be so difficult. The story of the MWA is not just an addition to historical record; it is a guidebook for the problems affecting financial provision on divorce today.[74] The Association's campaigns have informed debates that have been repeated throughout the twentieth century and into the twenty-first; wages for housework, equal division of property on divorce and women's pension rights. Thus, by examining the detail of MWA campaigns for equal partnership in marriage it is possible to see both how equal the law of marriage is now and the inequalities that persist.

*

Equal partnership is now, at least in principle, a guiding light for the courts on divorce.[75] But there is still no legal regulation of property ownership between

[69] See, eg, J Buckley and D Price, 'Pensions on divorce: where now, what next?' (2021) 33(1) *Child and Family Law Quarterly* 5.
[70] Fisher and Low, above n 58.
[71] See, eg, M Jourdainde-Muizon, 'Why do married women work less in the UK than in France?' (2018) 51 *Labour Economics* 86.
[72] HC Deb 24 October 1939, vol 352, col 1254.
[73] L Mitchell and M Weldon-Johns, 'Law's Invisible Women: The Unintended Consequences of the Covid-19 Lockdown' (2022) 3 *Amicus Curiae* 188.
[74] A characteristic of feminist legal history identified by E Rackley and R Auchmuty, 'The case for feminist legal history' (2020) 40 *Oxford Journal of Legal Studies* 878, 903.
[75] *White v White* [2000] UKHL 54; *Miller v Miller; McFarlane v McFarlane* [2006] UKHL 24.

spouses, and many will argue there does not need to be. The home – which is one of the most significant family assets aside from pension entitlements – is often jointly owned.[76] The wide discretion for the court to redistribute assets on divorce, which was not an option for most of the MWA's active years, arguably means the ownership of property during marriage does not matter.[77] And, as families and lifestyles are increasingly diverse, it is arguably not possible to find a consistent way to regulate property ownership across a vast constellation of different contexts.

Despite this, the Law Commission recognised in 1988 that there *could* be occasions during the marriage, such as bankruptcy and death, when knowledge of who owns what could be important. Furthermore, if inequalities still continue to exist within marriage then why should questions of property ownership only matter when the marriage has broken down? As the Commission put it:

> It is a false dichotomy to split marriages into the happy and the unhappy, and to say that while the couple are happy, property ownership does not matter and that, if they are not, they will get divorced and that the court will reallocate the property. Most marriages do not end in divorce.[78]

This underscores the prescience of the MWA, which had been making this argument decades earlier. In 1988, the Law Commission proposed a Matrimonial Property Bill which was never introduced. It was an 'Act to make new provision with respect to the beneficial ownership of matrimonial property', clarifying and extending the spirit of the MWPA 1964. It set out rules for determining beneficial ownership of property when property was transferred between spouses or used for the benefit of both spouses. These rules would not apply to separating spouses, but could clarify ownership interests and streamline the distribution of property on divorce.

In the context of England, Wales and Northern Ireland today, these proposals could still have merit, not only for couples who are married, but for unmarried couples too, for whom reform is long overdue. Determining beneficial ownership in unmarried cohabiting relationships still requires navigating complex and often harsh trust law principles as there is no bespoke legal framework that can accommodate how such couples manage property and finances. This often leads to injustice and vulnerability in cases of death and relationship breakdown. As a result, improving marriage for the next generation of married women should not leave behind unmarried women, who often face similar inequalities.[79]

*

[76] R Auchmuty 'The limits of marriage protection in property allocation when a relationship ends' (2016) 28 *Child and Family Law Quarterly* 303.
[77] Law Commission, *Family Law: Matrimonial Property*, above n 33.
[78] ibid, para 1.4.
[79] Smart, *The Ties That Bind*, above n 55, 223.

While none of these debates are settled easily, what they do show is that the MWA's attempts to reform law should not be relegated to an obscure corner of family law history. Far from it – many of the debates the Association started are still very relevant today. Yet MWA members did not appear to seek a historical legacy. Speaking about his grandmother Edith Summerskill, Ben Summerskill surmised that 'she would have just taken the view of, "We get what we want, whose fingerprints are on it doesn't really matter"'.[80] And similarly, Juanita Frances said in 1975:

> Looking at the past I feel it's boring. People who want to go back [and say] 'oh look we've achieved this!' – to me it's insignificant and any person or organisation are just cogs in a wheel. We do what we can but it doesn't rest on us if we go under and somebody else will come along.[81]

This is not to say that Frances and Summerskill failed to recognise the importance of their work. But they knew their feminist history, and so they probably knew that women's influence upon law quietly from behind the scenes, even when significant, often leaves a little visible imprint. Thus, just because the MWA never got its 'new marriage law' giving spouses property rights in their partner's assets during marriage does not mean its story should not be told. We have the MWA to thank (as least in part) for principles such as the instituting of equality within marriage. Yet reflecting upon why the MWA *did not* succeed with its 'new law' of family property also provides a unique insight into both family law reform and the use of law by feminists as a tool to improve women's everyday lives.

---

[80] Author interview with Ben Summerskill, 20 June 2018.
[81] Brian Harrison interview with Juanita Frances, 14 November 1974, 8SUF/B/022, TWL.

Afterword

WHEN I WRITE of the Married Women's Association (MWA), I am reminded of Joyce's remark 'in the particular is contained the universal'.[1] That is, when studying any *particular* corner of history, researchers so often end up revealing aspects of human history as a whole. In this way, the MWA's story is a microcosm of feminist legal activism. Like so many others before and after them, members dedicated their lives to improving the lot of women, working long and hard, decade after decade, only to be met with derision, ridicule, wilful ignorance and reactionary backlash. And, after all that, credit for any small breakthroughs was taken away from them and given by a patriarchal narrative to established legislative bodies, or simply credited to the 'inevitability of progress'. Such is the treatment of the dispossessed in law throughout the ages. In this book I have tried to right this wrong, not because the MWA themselves were desperate for the attention (they made it clear they were not bothered by said fate), but because feminists and family law reformers today deserve to know their story, and can know what to expect when engaging with the law themselves. After all, these challenges still exist today.

---

[1] Quoted in A Power, *From the Old Waterford House* (Mellifont 1944) 65.

Acknowledgements

THOUGH THIS BOOK is the product of several years of archival and empirical research, almost all of it was written during my year of academic study leave from Cardiff University from 2020 to 2021. I spent most of that year in Eglinton in the company of my loving friend Monty. He was my constant – but at times disruptive – companion, whose demands for walks, play and pets could prompt moments of inspiration and amusement in equal measure. Aside from Monty, the support and patience of my mother Marion and husband Chris have been fundamental to the completion of this book. Chris read an entire draft, and I owe many alterations to his alert eye. Above all, I want to thank him for his unwavering love and encouragement. He will never know how grateful I am.

Despite his own pressing work commitments, my colleague and friend Russell Sandberg also read multiple drafts of this book. He has helped me immeasurably with *Quiet Revolutionaries* by suggesting improvements and discussing ideas. It is impossible not to feel enthusiastic about legal history after reading Russell's work or hearing him talk about it.

Thanks also to Amanda Mitchison for her immense help with several chapters of this book. Amanda is a remarkably talented writer; I can never thank her enough for changing my relationship with writing and for giving me the confidence to enjoy it.

I am indebted to the staff at The Women's Library and The National Archives, where I spent many hours, especially Anna Towlson and Gillian Murphy. I am also incredibly thankful to Maryly Lafollette, Ben Summerskill, Felix Appelbe, Joey Freeman, John Butler, Stephen Holden, John Carroll, Geoff Tan and Kate Steane for sharing their recollections of MWA members. Thanks to historians Judith Bourne, Caitríona Beaumont and Elizabeth Cruickshank for discussing the MWA with me, and to Inns of Court archivists Ben Taylor, Meghan Dunmall and Andrew Mussell for the information they provided on female barristers in the MWA. I am also grateful for the support of the Socio-Legal Studies Association, which funded the empirical and archival work on which this book is based.

To my colleagues past and present at Cardiff University – thanks for being wonderful friends and for making my job fun: Dan Newman, Phil Fennell, Kathy Griffiths, Jess Mant, Gillian Douglas, Lydia Hayes, Nicky Priaulx, Anna Heenan, Bernie Rainey, Ludivine Petetin, Ambreena Manji, Steve Smith, Antoinette Samuel, Julie Doughty, Amie Jordan-John, Eleanor Rowan, Elen Stokes, Rachel Cahill-O'Callaghan, Rachael Blakey, Lucy Series, Katie Richards, Leanne Smith, Pauline Roberts and Annette Morris. Within the wider academic community, I am grateful for support and guidance from Mavis Maclean, Carole Pateman, Rebecca Probert, Andy Hayward, Anne Barlow and Jo Miles (whose aunt Lena Jeger was affiliated to the MWA and is quoted several times in this book). Thanks also to Rosemarie Mearns, Anne Bevan and the team at Hart Publishing for their help throughout the writing and editing process.

Finally, I owe much to Rosemary Auchmuty and Erika Rackley, as I would not have written *Quiet Revolutionaries* without their collection *Women's Legal Landmarks*.[1] In 2014, when they suggested I contribute a chapter on the Married Women's Property Act 1964, I had no idea that behind this statute lay the rich history of the MWA. I am grateful to Rosemary and Erika for opening my eyes to feminist legal history, and for encouraging me to investigate the history of family law through a different lens.

---

[1] E Rackley and R Auchmuty (eds), *Women's Legal Landmarks: Celebrating the History of Women and Law in the UK and Ireland* (Hart Publishing 2019).

Archive References

THE WOMEN'S LIBRARY (TWL), LONDON[1]

Oral Evidence on the Suffragette and Suffragist Movements (8SUF)

Records of Edith Summerskill (SUMMERSKILL)

Records of Helena Normanton (7HLN)

Records of Teresa Billington-Greig (7TBG)

Records of the Council of Married Women (5CMW)

Records of the Equal Rights International Group (5ERI)

Records of Lady Helen Nutting (7LHN)

Records of the Married Women's Association (5MWA)

Records of the Six Point Group (5SPG)

THE NATIONAL ARCHIVES (TNA), LONDON[2]

Records of the Lord Chancellor's Office (LCO2)

Records of the Law Commission (BC3)

[1] References available at: https://digital.library.lse.ac.uk/collections/thewomenslibrary.
[2] References available at: https://www.nationalarchives.gov.uk/.

Bibliography

BOOKS

Abse, L, *Private Member* (Macdonald London 1973)

Atkins, S and Hale, B, *Women and the Law* (Institute of Advanced Legal Studies 2018)

Barrington Baker, W, *The Matrimonial Jurisdiction of Registrars* (SSRC Centre for Socio-Legal Studies, Wolfson College, Oxford 1977)

Bartley, P, *Labour Women in Power: Cabinet Ministers in the Twentieth Century* (Palgrave 2019)

Beaumont, C, *Housewives and Citizens: Domesticity and the Women's Movement in England 1928–64* (Manchester University Press 2015)

Blackstone, W, *Commentaries on the Laws of England*, 21st edn (Sweet, Maxwell, Stevens and Norton 1844) book 1.

Blake, SH, *The Law of Marriage*, 3rd edn (Barry Rose 1982)

Bostridge, M and Berry, P, *Vera Brittain: A Life* (Virago 2016)

Bostridge, M, *Vera Brittain and the First World War: The Story of Testament of Youth* (Bloomsbury 2015)

Bourne, J, *Helena Normanton and the Opening of the Bar to Women* (Waterside Press 2016)

Bracton, H, *On the Laws and Customs of England* (Belknap Press of Harvard University 1968–77) book 4

Brittain, V, *Testament of Youth* (Victor Gollancz 1933)

Bromley, P, *Family Law* (Butterworths 1957)

Brown, A, *What is the Family of Law? The Influence of the Nuclear Family* (Hart Publishing 2019)

Caine, B, *English Feminism 1780–1980* (Oxford University Press 1997)

—— *Biography and History* (Palgrave Macmillan 2010)

Campbell, O, *The Feminine Point of View* (Williams & Norgate Ltd 1952)

Carr, EH, *What is History?* (Kompf 1962)

Cole, GDH, *Chartist Portraits* (Macmillan 1941)

Conaghan, J, *Law and Gender* (Oxford University Press 2013)

Cooke, E, Barlow, A and Callus, T, *Community of Property: A Regime for England and Wales?* (Nuffield Foundation 2006)

Cott, N, *Public Vows: A History Of Marriage And The Nation* (Harvard University Press 2002)

Cretney, S, *Family Law in the Twentieth Century* (Oxford University Press 2003)

Degler, C, *At Odds: Women and the Family in America from the Revolution to the Present* (Oxford University Press 1980)

Denning, A, *The Due Process of Law* (Butterworths 1980)

Dewar, J, *Law and the Family* (Butterworths 1989)

Diduck, A and O'Donovan, K, *Feminist Perspectives on Family Law* (Routledge-Cavendish 2007)

Douglas, G, *Obligation and Commitment in Family Law* (Hart Publishing 2018)

Downs, L, *Writing Gender History* (Bloomsbury 2010)

Eekelaar, J, *Family Law and Social Policy*, 2nd edn (Weidenfeld and Nicolson 1984)

—— *Family Law and Personal Life* (Oxford University Press 2007).

Eekelaar, J and Maclean, M, *Maintenance after Divorce* (Clarendon Press 1986)

Fredman, S, *Women and the Law* (Oxford University Press 1998)

Friedan, B, *The Feminine Mystique* (WW Norton 1963)

Gilbert, A, *British Conservatism and the Legal Regulation of Intimate Relationships* (Hart Publishing 2018)

Glew, H, Gender, *Rhetoric and Regulation: Women's Work in the Civil Service and the London County Council, 1900–55* (Manchester University Press 2016)

Hale, B, *Spider Woman: A Life* (Penguin 2021)

Harrison, B, *Prudent Revolutionaries: Portraits of British Feminists Between the Wars* (Oxford University Press 1987)

Hartley, LP, *The Go Between* (Hamish Hamilton, 1963)

Holcombe, L, *Wives and Property* (University of Toronto Press 1983)

Lee, BH, *Divorce Law Reform in England* (Peter Owen 1974)

Liddington, J, *The Road to Greenham Common: Feminism and Anti-militarism in Britain Since 1820* (Syracuse University Press 1991)

Maclean, M and Kurczewski, J, *Making Family Law* (Hart Publishing 2011)

McCarthy, H, *Double Lives: A History of Working Motherhood* (Bloomsbury 2020)

Oakley, A, *Housewife* (Allen Lane 1974)

Okin, SM, *Justice, Gender, and the Family* (Basic Books 1989)

Pateman, C, *The Sexual Contract* (Polity 1988)

Phillips, M, *The Divided House: Women at Westminster* (Sidgwick & Jackson 1980)

Power, A, *From the Old Waterford House* (Mellifont 1944)

Pugh, M, *Women and the Women's Movement in Britain since 1914*, 3rd edn (Palgrave 2015)

Ramsey, M, *Putting Asunder: A Divorce Law for Contemporary Society* (SPCK 1966)

Rathbone, E, *The Disinherited Family* (Falling Wall Press 1924)

Rowbotham, S, *Hidden from History* (Pluto Press 1973)

—— *Woman's Consciousness, Man's World* (Pelican 1973)

Rubin, G, *The Traffic in Women* (Duke University Press 2011)

Russell, D, *The Tamarisk Tree* (Virago 1977)

Sandberg, R, *Subversive Legal History* (Routledge 2021)

Seabourne, G, *Women in the Medieval Common Law* (Routledge 2021)

Smart, C, *The Ties That Bind* (Routledge 1984)

—— *Feminism and the Power of Law* (Routledge 1989)

Somerville, J, *Feminism and the Family: Politics and Society in the UK and USA* (Palgrave Macmillan 2000)

Spender, D, *There's Always Been a Women's Movement This Century* (Harper Collins 1983)

Stetson, D, *A Woman's Issue: The Politics of Family Law Reform in England* (Oxford University Press 1982)

Strachey, R, *The Cause: A Short History of the Women's Movement in Great Britain* (Bell 1928)

Summerskill, E, *A Woman's World* (Heinemann 1967)

Todd, JE and Jones, LM, *Matrimonial Property* (HMSO 1972)

Wallbank, J, Choudhry, S and Herring, J (eds), *Rights, Gender and Family Law* (Routledge 2010)

Wilson, E, *Only Halfway to Paradise: Women in Postwar Britain 1945–1968* (Tavistock 1980)

Woolf, V, *Three Guineas* (Hogarth Press 1938)

CHAPTERS IN EDITED VOLUMES

Appleton, S, 'How feminism remade American family law (and how it did not)' in R West and C Bowman, *Research Handbook on Feminist Jurisprudence* (Elgar 2019) 426

Auchmuty, R, 'Unfair Shares for Women: The Rhetoric of Equality and the Reality of Inequality' in A Bottomley and H Lim (eds), *Feminist Perspectives on Land Law* (Glass House Press 2007) 174

—— 'Feminists as Stakeholders in the Law School' in F Cownie (ed), *Stakeholders in the Law School* (Hart Publishing 2010) 35

—— 'Legal History' in R Auchmuty (ed), *Great Debates in Gender and Law* (Macmillan 2018) 173

—— 'Married Women (Restraint Upon Anticipation) Act 1949' in E Rackley and R Auchmuty (eds), *Women's Legal Landmarks: Celebrating the History of Women and Law in the UK and Ireland* (Hart Publishing 2019) 241

—— 'Williams & Glyn's Bank v Boland (1980)' in E Rackley and R Auchmuty (eds), *Women's Legal Landmarks: Celebrating the History of Women and Law in the UK and Ireland* (Hart Publishing 2019) 357

Auchmuty, R and Temkin, J, 'The Road to Olive Stone' in U Schultz, G Shaw, M Thornton and R Auchmuty (eds), *Gender and Careers in the Legal Academy* (Hart Publishing 2021) 441

Baker, AP, 'Russell, Dora Winifred [née Black] (1894–1986)' in *Oxford Dictionary of National Biography* (Oxford University Press 2004).

Beaumont, C, 'The Women's Movement, Politics and Citizenship 1918–1950s' in I Zweiniger-Bargielowska, *Women in Twentieth-Century Britain* (Routledge 2001) 262

Blackford, C, 'Wives and Citizens and Watchdogs of Equality: Post-War British Feminists' in J Fyrth (ed), *Labour's Promised Land: Culture and Society in Labour Britain 1945–51* (Lawrence & Wishart 1995) 59

—— 'Dorothy Evans (1888–1944)' in *Oxford Dictionary of National Biography* (Oxford University Press 2004)

—— 'Juanita Frances (1901–1992)' in *Oxford Dictionary of National Biography* (Oxford University Press 2004)

Brittain, V, 'Why Feminism Lives' in P Barry and A Bishop (eds), *Testaments of a Generation: The Journalism of Brittain and Winifried Holtby* (Virago Press Ltd 1985) 99

Butler, S, 'Discourse on the Nature of Coverture in the Later Medieval Courtroom' in T Stretton and K Kesselrin, *Married Women and the Law: Coverture in England and the Common Law World* (McGill-Queen's University Press 2013) 24

Corfield, P, Purvis, J and Weatherill, A, 'History and the Challenge of Gender History' in S Morgan (ed), *The Feminist History Reader* 116

Cowman, K, 'Collective Biography' in S Gunn and L Faire, *Research Methods for History*, 2nd edn (Edinburgh University Press 2016) 85

Delmar, R, 'What is Feminism?' in J Mitchell and A Oakley (eds), *What is Feminism?* (Blackwell 1986) 9

Hayward, A, 'Married Women's Property Act 1882' in E Rackley and R Auchmuty (eds), *Women's Legal Landmarks: Celebrating the History of Women and Law in the UK and Ireland* (Hart Publishing 2019) 71

Huskins-Hallinan, H, 'A Revolution Unfinished' in H Huskins-Hallinan (ed), *In Her Own Right* (Harrap 1968) 9

Jeger, L, 'Power in Our Hands' in H Huskins-Hallinan (ed), *In Her Own Right* (Harrap 1968) 147

Mayall M, '"No surrender!": the militancy of Mary Leigh, a working-class suffragette' in J Purvis and M Joannou, *The Women's Suffrage Movement: New Feminist Perspectives* (Manchester University Press 1998) 173

Mee, J, 'Burns v Burns: The Villain of the Piece?' in R Probert, J Herring and S Gilmore (eds), *Landmark Cases In Family Law* (Hart Publishing 2011) ch 10

Pateman, C, 'Feminist Critiques of the Public/Private Dichotomy' in S Benn and G Gaus (eds), *Private and Public in Social Life* (Croon Helm 1983) 281

Probert, R, 'Family Law Reform and the Women's Movement in England and Wales' in S Meder and C Mecke (eds), *Family Law in Early Women's Rights Debates: Western Europe and the United States in the Nineteenth and Early Twentieth Centuries* (Bohlau Verlag 2013) 170

Purvis, J, 'Doing Feminist Women's History: Researching the Lives of Women in the Suffragette Movement in Edwardian England' in M Maynard and J Purvis (eds), *Researching Women's Lives From A Feminist Perspective* (Routledge 1994) 166

Rathbone, E, 'The Old Feminism and the New', Presidential Address at the Annual Meeting of NUSEC (11 March 1925) in E Rathbone (ed), *Milestones* (Liverpool 1929) 29

Samuels, H, 'Education Act 1944' in E Rackley and R Auchmuty (eds), *Women's Legal Landmarks: Celebrating the History of Women and Law in the UK and Ireland* (Hart Publishing 2019) 219

Stephanson, A, 'The Lessons of *What is History?*' in M Cox (ed), *EH Carr: A Critical Appraisal* (Palgrave Macmillan 2000)

Thompson, S, 'Married Women's Property Act 1964' in E Rackley and R Auchmuty (eds), *Women's Legal Landmarks: Celebrating the History of Women and Law in the UK and Ireland* (Hart Publishing 2019) 263

Vickers, L, 'Family Allowances Act 1945' in E Rackley and R Auchmuty (eds), *Women's Legal Landmarks: Celebrating the History of Women and Law in the UK and Ireland* (Hart Publishing 2019) 227

Whately, M, 'Dorothy Evans: The Story of a Militant' in C Madden (ed), *Dorothy Evans and the Six Point Group* (Published by Claire Madden for the Six Point Group 1945) 47

Workman, J, 'Normanton, Helena Florence (1882–1957)' in *Oxford Dictionary of National Biography* (Oxford University Press 2004)

JOURNAL ARTICLES

Adkins, L and Dever, M, 'Housework, Wages and Money' (2014) 29 *Australian Feminist Studies* 50

Auchmuty, R, 'Law and the power of feminism: How marriage lost its power to oppress women' (2012) 20 *Feminist Legal Studies* 71

—— 'Recovering Lost Lives: Researching Women in Legal History (2015) 42 *Journal of Law and Society* 34

—— 'The limits of marriage protection in property allocation when a relationship ends' (2016) 28(4) *Child and Family Law Quarterly* 303

Auchmuty, R and Rackley, E, 'Feminist Legal Biography: A Model for All Legal Life Stories' (2020) 41 *Journal of Legal History* 186

Baldwin, M, 'Subject to Empire: Married Women and the British Nationality and Status of Aliens Act' (2001) 40 *Journal of British Studies* 522

Barlow, A, 'Configuration(s) of Unpaid Caregiving within Current Legal Discourse In and Around the Family' (2007) 58 *Northern Ireland Legal Quarterly* 251

Bartie, S, 'Studying women legal scholars: the challenges' (2018) 25 *International Journal of the Legal Profession* 279

Batlan, F, 'Engendering Legal History' (2005) 30 *Law & Social Inquiry* 823

Beaumont, C, 'Citizens not feminists: The boundary negotiated between citizenship and feminism by mainstream women's organisations in England, 1928–39' (2000) 9 *Women's History Review* 411

—— 'What Do Women Want? Housewives' Associations, Activism and Changing Representations of Women in the 1950s' (2017) 26 *Women's History Review* 147

Benjamin, D and Kochin, L, 'Searching for an Explanation of Unemployment in Interwar Britain' (1979) 87 *Journal of Political Economy* 441

Birmingham Feminist History Group, 'Feminism as femininity in the nineteen-fifties?' (1979) 3(1) *Feminist Review* 48

Buckley, J and Price, D, 'Pensions on divorce: where now, what next?' (2021) 33(1) *Child and Family Law Quarterly* 5

Caine, B, 'Feminist biography and feminist history' (1994) 3 *Women's History Review* 247

Carbone, J, 'A Feminist Perspective on Divorce' (1994) 4(1) *Future of Children* 183

Conaghan, J, 'Introduction' (2007) 58 *Northern Ireland Legal Quarterly* 245

Cretney, S, 'The Community of Property' (1969) 113(7) *Solicitor's Journal* 116

Cross, R, 'The Family Allowances Act, 1945' (1946) 9 *MLR* 284

Deech, R, 'The Principles of Maintenance' [1977] *Family Law* 229

Finer, M, 'The Personal Injuries (Civilians) Scheme 1941' (1942) 5 *MLR* 224

Fisher, H and Low, H, 'Recovery from divorce: comparing high and low income couples' (2016) 30 *International Journal of Law, Policy and the Family* 338.

Glendon, M, 'Is There a Future for Separate Property?' (1974) 8 *Family Law Quarterly* 315

Hirschmann, NJ, 'The Sexual Division of Labor and the Split Paycheck' (2016) 31 *Hypatia* 651

Irwin, M, 'What Women Want On Television: Doreen Stephens and BBC Television Programmes For Women, 1953–64' (2011) 8(3) *Westminster Papers in Communication & Culture* 99, 99.

Jourdainde-Muizon, M, 'Why do married women work less in the UK than in France?' (2018) 51 *Labour Economics* 86

Kahn-Freund, O, 'Inconsistencies and Injustices in the Law of Husband and Wife' (1952) 15 *MLR* 133

—— 'Inconsistencies and Injustices in the Law of Husband and Wife' (1953) 16 *MLR* 34

—— 'Divorce Law Reform' (1956) 19 *MLR* 573

—— 'Maintenance Orders Act 1958' (1959) 22 *MLR* 175

—— 'Matrimonial Property – Some Recent Developments' (1959) 22 *MLR* 241.

—— 'Recent Legislation on Matrimonial Property' (1970) 33 *MLR* 601

—— 'Law Commission: Published Working Paper No 42: Family Property Law 1971' (1972) 35 *MLR* 403

Lacey, N, 'Feminist Legal Theory Beyond Neutrality' (1995) 48 *Current Legal Problems* 1

Land, H, 'The Family Wage' (1980) 6(1) *Feminist Review* 55

Miles, J and Hitchings, E, 'Financial remedy outcomes on divorce in England and Wales: Not a "meal ticket for life"' (2018) 31(2) *Australian Journal of Family Law* 43

Minow, M, 'Forming Underneath Everything That Grows: Toward a History of Family Law' (1985) 4 *Wisconsin Law Review* 819

Mitchell, L and Weldon-Johns, M, 'Law's Invisible Women: The Unintended Consequences of the Covid-19 Lockdown' (2022) 3 *Amicus Curiae* 188

Polden, P, 'Portia's progress: Women at the Bar in England, 1919–1939' (2005) 12 *International Journal of the Legal Profession* 293

Probert, R, 'The History of 20th-Century Family Law' (2005) 25 *Oxford Journal of Legal Studies* 169

Rackley, E and Auchmuty, R, 'The case for feminist legal history' (2020) 40 *Oxford Journal of Legal Studies* 878

Smart, C, 'Law and Family Life: Insights from 25 Years of Empirical Research' (2014) 26(1) *Child and Family Law Quarterly* 14

Smith, C, 'The Disruptive Power of Legal Biography: The Life of Lord Phillimore – Churchman and Judge' (2020) 41 *Journal of Legal History* 164

Sonrab, J, 'Women and Social Security' (1994) 1 *Journal of Social Welfare & Family Law* 5

Stone, OM, 'The Royal Commission on Marriage and Divorce: Family Dependents and Their Maintenance' (1956) 19 *MLR* 601

—— 'Married Women's Property Act 1964' (1964) 27 *MLR* 576

—— '"With all my Worldly Goods …"' (1965) 14 *International and Comparative Law Quarterly* 707

Symes, P, 'Indissolubility and the clean break' (1985) 48 *MLR* 44

—— 'Property, Power and Dependence: Critical Family Law' (1987) 14 *Journal of Law and Society* 199

Thompson, S, 'A Millstone Around the Neck? Stereotypes About Wives and Myths About Divorce' (2019) 70 *Northern Ireland Legal Quarterly* 181

—— 'Against Divorce? Revisiting the charge of the Casanova's Charter' (2021) 33(3) *Child and Family Law Quarterly* 193

—— 'Edith Summerskill: Letters from Deserted Wives' (2022) *Women's History Review* (forthcoming)

Williams, G, 'The Legal Unity of Husband and Wife' (1947) 10 *MLR* 16

Williamson, L, 'Women's History and Biography' (1999) 11 *Gender & History* 379

Wood, JC, 'Attachment of Wages' (1963) 26 *MLR* 51

Xanthaki, H, 'Gender inclusive legislative drafting in English: A drafter's response to Emily Grabham' (2020) 10(2) Feminists@Law

REPORTS

Beveridge, W, et al, *Social Insurance and Allied Services* (The Beveridge Report) (Cmd 6404, 1942)

House of Commons Select Committee on Political and Constitutional Reform, *Ensuring standards in the quality of legislation* (First Report, 2013)

Law Commission, *Reform of the Grounds of Divorce: The Field of Choice* (Cmnd 3123, 1966)

—— *Matrimonial and Related Proceedings – Financial Relief* (WP No 9, 1967)

—— *Financial Provision in Matrimonial Proceedings* (Law Com No 25, 1969)

—— *Family Property Law* (WP No 42, 1971)

—— *First Report on Family Property: A New Approach* (Law Com No 52, 1973)

—— *Second Report on Family Property – Family Provision on Death* (Law Com No 61, 1974)

—— *Third Report on Family Property: The Matrimonial Home* (Law Com No 86, 1978)

—— *The Financial Consequences of Divorce: The Basic Policy, A Discussion Paper* (Law Com No 103, 1980)

—— *The Financial Consequences of Divorce* (Law Com No 112, 1981)

—— *Property Law: The Implications of Williams & Glyn's Bank Ltd v Boland* (Law Com No 115, 1982)

—— *Transfer of Money Between Spouses – the Married Women's Property Act 1964* (WP No 90, 1985)

—— *Family Law: Matrimonial Property* (Law Com No 175, 1988)

Ministry of Labour, *Report on the Operation of the Anomalies Regulations, 3rd October 1931 to 29th April 1933* (Cmd 4346, 1933)

Morton, F, et al, *Report of the Royal Commission on Marriage and Divorce* (Cmd 9678, 1956)

OTHER

Blackford, C, 'Ideas, Structures and Practices of Feminism 1939–64' (PhD thesis, University of East London 1996)

Blakey, R, 'The Conceptualisation of Family Mediation: Access to Justice after LASPO' (PhD thesis, Cardiff University 2021)

Freeguard, J, 'It's Time for Women of the 1950s to Stand Up and Be Counted' (PhD thesis, University of Sussex 2004)

Gotby, A, 'They Call It Love: Wages For Housework And Emotional Reproduction' (PhD thesis, University of West London 2019)

Index

Lightning Source UK Ltd.
Milton Keynes UK
UKHW022230130922
408814UK00003B/208